Writing to Read, Reading to Write

Alison Kuehner

Ohlone College

Writing to Read, Reading to Write

Alison Kuehner

Ohlone College

WRITING TO READ, READING TO WRITE

Published by McGraw-Hill Education, 2 Penn Plaza, New York, NY 10121. Copyright © 2020 by McGraw-Hill Education. All rights reserved. Printed in the United States of America. No part of this publication may be reproduced or distributed in any form or by any means, or stored in a database or retrieval system, without the prior written consent of McGraw-Hill Education, including, but not limited to, in any network or other electronic storage or transmission, or broadcast for distance learning.

Some ancillaries, including electronic and print components, may not be available to customers outside the United States.

This book is printed on acid-free paper.

1 2 3 4 5 6 7 8 9 LCR 21 20 19

ISBN 978-1-259-28448-9 (bound edition)
MHID 1-259-28448-4 (bound edition)

ISBN 978-1-259-27892-1 (instructor edition)
MHID 1-259-27892-1 (instructor edition)

ISBN 978-1-260-56537-9 (loose-leaf edition)
MHID 1-260-56537-8 (loose-leaf edition)

Portfolio Manager: *Erin Cosyn*
Product Developer: *Beth Tripmacher*
Marketing Manager: *Byron Kanoti*
Content Project Manager: *Lisa Bruflodt*
Buyer: *Sandy Ludovissy*

Design: *Jessica Cuevas*
Content Licensing Specialist: *Jacob Sullivan*
Cover Image: *©McGraw-Hill Education*
Compositor: *Lumina Datamatics, Inc.*

All credits appearing on page or at the end of the book are considered to be an extension of the copyright page.

Library of Congress Cataloging-in-Publication Data

Names: Kuehner, Alison, author.
Title: Writing to Read, Reading to Write / Alison Kuehner, Ohlone College.
Description: New York, NY : McGraw-Hill Education, [2020]
Identifiers: LCCN 2018029875| ISBN 9781259284489 (hardcover : alk. paper) |
   ISBN 1259284484 (bound edition : acid-free paper) | ISBN 9781260565379
   (loose-leaf edition : acid-free paper) | ISBN 1260565378 (loose-leaf
   edition : acid-free paper)
Subjects: LCSH: College readers. | English language—Rhetoric—Problems,
   exercises, etc.
Classification: LCC PE1417 .K84 2020 | DDC 808/.0427—dc23
LC record available at https://lccn.loc.gov/2018029875

The Internet addresses listed in the text were accurate at the time of publication. The inclusion of a website does not indicate an endorsement by the authors or McGraw-Hill Education, and McGraw-Hill Education does not guarantee the accuracy of the information presented at these sites.

mheducation.com/highered

About the Author

ALISON KUEHNER

Alison Kuehner loves teaching students. She was fortunate to discover her passion for teaching during her senior year of college working as a peer tutor, where she enjoyed the challenge of helping fellow students effectively express their ideas in writing. After earning an undergraduate degree in English literature from the University of California, Berkeley, and a master's degree in literature from the University of Chicago, she became a teacher, earning an English credential through the Graduate School of Education at the University of California, Berkeley, and a master's in reading instruction at Cal State East Bay.

©Alison Kuehner

Although she enjoyed her time teaching middle school and high school students, Professor Kuehner is most inspired and energized by the diversity and potential of community college students. She has taught a range of courses at Ohlone College in Fremont, California, for thirty years, including literature and composition courses; developmental reading and writing classes; and online, hybrid, and traditional classes. Over the years, she has honed her skills as a teacher, thanks to her students' feedback and advice, and her colleagues' willingness to share and collaborate.

When Professor Kuehner is not teaching, she enjoys reading, spending time with her family and friends, and riding her bike, swimming, and playing soccer. She is married to a physicist; they have two children. They live in the San Francisco Bay area with two overweight cats.

Brief Contents

Contents

CHAPTER 5
Reading and Writing Essays 118

Theme: Why Is Sleep So Important?

CHAPTER 6
Writing about Reading 148
Theme: What Is the Value of a College Education?

PART 3

Reading and Writing about Texts 193

CHAPTER 7
Responding to Texts 194
Theme: What Makes People Happy?

CHAPTER 8

Reading and Writing Arguments 220

Theme: Should the Minimum Wage Be Raised?

CHAPTER 9

Planning a Research Paper 252

Theme: Researching Antibiotic Resistance: How Can We Stay Healthy Using Antibiotics?

CHAPTER 10

Writing a Research Paper 276

Theme: Writing about Antibiotic Resistance: How Can We Stay Healthy Using Antibiotics?

PART 4

Anthology of Theme-Based Readings 319

THEME

Do Social Media Connect Us—or Isolate Us? 320

THEME

What Makes Us Healthy? 337

THEME
Can Head Injuries Be Prevented in Sports? 353

Preface

In California, where I teach, education in the community college and state college systems has experienced profound shifts in the past years—changes for the better—with a move toward integrating reading and writing, rather than teaching them as isolated skills. Recently, legislation mandated that students who place below college level must have a path to complete a transfer-level composition course within one year, which supports acceleration and co-requisite models of instruction.

Well before this legislative mandate, my colleagues and I redesigned the English curriculum at our college in light of compelling research and evidence that integrating reading and writing worked and that students, regardless of their educational backgrounds, had a considerable capacity to achieve. We realized that if we set high standards while providing appropriate academic and motivational support, students typically labeled as "developmental" could succeed in rigorous classes. Drawing on our many years of experience teaching students at all levels, we considered how to scaffold lessons and activities to support students so they can accomplish college-level composition learning outcomes. We recognized the intellectual capacity of students by selecting engaging readings while being cognizant of students' interests and motivational needs. The time, effort, and thought that went into developing a new curriculum at my college is reflected in this new, brief rhetoric that may be used to support the diversity of students in college-level composition as well as the co-requisites that will support them.

Why an Integrated Approach to College-Level Composition?

Reading and writing are complementary processes that experienced readers and writers engage in recursively. Unfortunately, community colleges today are filled with developing readers and writers who require more guided practice and explicit strategies instruction to be successful in first-year composition. Reading provides students with concrete exemplars of how good writing is structured; idea generation when they lack background knowledge; and aids in generating complex and thoughtful text. That's why *Writing to Read, Reading to Write* presents reading, writing, and critical thinking as engaging and complementary endeavors. This focus on reading also gives students who are underprepared for the first-year composition course, or in the co-requisite support sections, a chance to practice those skills and re-apply them as they develop college-level work.

Designed for the broad mix of students who enter today's first-year composition course—and for the instructors who support them—*Writing to Read, Reading to Write* offers a process-oriented, recursive approach that supports student learning. Each chapter is based on a thought-provoking question to provide opportunities for critical thinking, and includes essay prompts for students to focus their reading and plan their writing.

The structure of *Writing to Read, Reading to Write* allows for flexibility in different approaches to teaching first-year composition:

- **Part 1, Welcome to College Reading, Writing, and Thinking** introduces students to the right mindset for college success, foundational reading strategies, and the steps of the writing process.

- **Part 2, Essential Elements of College Reading and Writing** presents paragraph and essay structure, and the elements of writing about reading.

- **Part 3, Reading and Writing About Texts** leads students through an Argument assignment. Students plan and write a research paper, and learn how to locate and evaluate sources.

- **Part 4, Anthology of Theme-Based Readings** is a brief collection of nine additional readings with essay prompts.

- The **Grammar and Style Handbook** presents grammar in context by modeling the use of effective words, sentences, and punctuation through examples of professional or student writing. This approach encourages students to read as writers and to emulate strong writing.

- The **Documentation Resource Guide** includes explanations and examples of how to correctly format a paper, use in-text citations, and create a list of sources in MLA and in APA style. It also demonstrates how to create attribution, use appositives, and acknowledge sources in sentences so students can strengthen their writing by giving proper credit and by citing the credentials of sources.

Writing to Read, Reading to Write has been developed so that it's easy for instructors who opt to use McGraw-Hill Connect courseware (see chart on page xxiv) to create accompanying assignments that utilize the research-based pedagogy of Power of Process and LearnSmart Achieve. For instance, reading strategies, such as previewing or predicting before reading, annotating or responding during reading, summarizing main ideas or evaluating evidence after reading can be completed in Power of Process. Learn-Smart Achieve provides extra practice and support for the major reading and writing strategies presented in each chapter, such as understanding the writing process, mastering the art of quoting from texts, and evaluating arguments.

Text Features of *Writing to Read, Reading to Write*

Writing to Read, Reading to Write is designed to be a brief, flexible text as a starting point for more in-depth practice and exploration of topics. The following features support the text's approach.

- The **graphic that opens every chapter** reminds students they are at the center of their learning and must actively participate to be successful as they read, write, think, and engage with the chapter theme. The graphic also reminds instructors that reading, writing, thinking, and motivating students is critical to an effective learning process. The icons, indicating reading [📖], writing [📝], thinking [💭], and engaging [👤], appear throughout the chapter to identify the primary skills needed for students to complete each Read to Write activity.

After reading this chapter, you will be able to

- Identify your use of strategies for college success.
- Recognize key factors in succeeding in college.
- Read and write about fixed and growth mindsets.
- Define key terms.
- Read and write about an infographic.
- Develop a critical-thinking mindset.

Look for these icons throughout the chapter. They signal key strategies to use in Read to Write Activities.

- **Read to Write activities** guide students through selecting a topic, prewriting, drafting, revising, editing, and proofreading to develop a complete piece of writing using the readings, visuals, and other information in that chapter. The first Read to Write activity in each chapter asks students to evaluate and choose a writing prompt, so students can develop their thinking as they move through the readings and activities.

Here's an example of a Read to Write activity from Chapter 6, which starts with this question: "What is the value of a college education?"

Read to Write Activity 6.1

Evaluate Topics and Choose a Writing Prompt about College Student Debt

Read and evaluate the following topics on a scale of 1 to 3, with 1 being an interesting topic, 2 being a topic you feel neutral about, and 3 being a topic you are not interested in. Using complete sentences, briefly explain your level of interest in each topic. Then select the topic you plan to use for an essay you will write. Explain why this topic appeals to you.

- **"Before Reading," "During Reading,"** and **"After Reading"** exercises support each reading, providing students with strategic reading skills that enable deep comprehension of the selections, which is necessary for students to produce thoughtful prose. These assignments, which can be completed in Power of Process in the Connect Master Course, prompt students to be active readers as they preview, annotate, and reflect on the reading.

Before Reading: Recognize Prior Knowledge

Write answers to the following questions using complete sentences.

1. Do you view higher education as a good investment? Why or why not?

2. The article's title claims that a large majority of college students believe higher education is a "good investment." How do you think those students might define "good investment"? What are they getting for their money? Why might other students (14%) feel that college is *not* a good investment?

- **"Engage with the Reading"** questions follow each reading and prompt students to think critically about the reading. For instance, students may reread to explain complex passages or respond to the author's arguments with their own ideas or analysis; they may consider the way a writer begins or ends a piece and how those writing strategies could apply to their own essays.

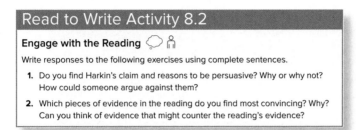

Read to Write Activity 8.2

Engage with the Reading

Write responses to the following exercises using complete sentences.

1. Do you find Harkin's claim and reasons to be persuasive? Why or why not? How could someone argue against them?

2. Which pieces of evidence in the reading do you find most convincing? Why? Can you think of evidence that might counter the reading's evidence?

- A **Spotlight on Student Writing activity** at the end of each part profiles college students and showcases their essays. This feature gives students an opportunity to practice the skills they gained in the previous chapters in a more holistic fashion and by using actual student work. Students can read and annotate a variety of student papers to analyze the writing, practice peer review, and apply annotation and evaluation strategies to improve their own writing.

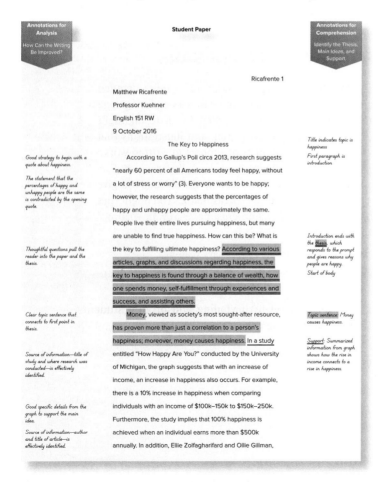

Annotations for Analysis

How Can the Writing Be Improved?

Student Paper

Annotations for Comprehension

Identify the Thesis, Main Ideas, and Support.

Ricafrente 1

Matthew Ricafrente

Professor Kuehner

English 151 RW

9 October 2016

The Key to Happiness

According to Gallup's Poll circa 2013, research suggests "nearly 60 percent of all Americans today feel happy, without a lot of stress or worry" (3). Everyone wants to be happy; however, the research suggests that the percentages of happy and unhappy people are approximately the same. People live their entire lives pursuing happiness, but many are unable to find true happiness. How can this be? What is the key to fulfilling ultimate happiness? According to various articles, graphs, and discussions regarding happiness, the key to happiness is found through a balance of wealth, how one spends money, self-fulfillment through experiences and success, and assisting others.

Money, viewed as society's most sought-after resource, has proven more than just a correlation to a person's happiness; moreover, money causes happiness. In a study entitled "How Happy Are You?" conducted by the University of Michigan, the graph suggests that with an increase of income, an increase in happiness also occurs. For example, there is a 10% increase in happiness when comparing individuals with an income of $100k–150k to $150k–250k. Furthermore, the study implies that 100% happiness is achieved when an individual earns more than $500k annually. In addition, Ellie Zolfagharifard and Ollie Gillman,

Good strategy to begin with a quote about happiness.

The statement that the percentages of happy and unhappy people are the same is contradicted by the opening quote.

Thoughtful questions pull the reader into the paper and the thesis.

Clear topic sentence that connects to first point in thesis.

Source of information—title of study and where research was conducted—is effectively identified.

Good specific details from the graph to support the main idea.

Source of information—author and title of article—is effectively identified.

Title indicates topic is happiness

First paragraph is introduction

Introduction ends with the thesis, which responds to the prompt and gives reasons why people are happy. Start of body

Topic sentence: Money causes happiness.

Support: Summarized information from graph shows how the rise in income connects to a rise in happiness.

- Important **Vocabulary Strategies**, such as defining words in context, using word analysis, and using dictionary skills, are introduced in each chapter so that students can apply a vocabulary strategy to understanding key words from the reading.

Vocabulary Strategy: Defining Words in Context in the Reading

Sometimes writers define a word by including a definition—set off by parentheses, commas, or dashes—in the sentence in which the word appears. Other times, writers give strong clues to the meaning of a word by providing examples. For their part, readers can make an educated guess about a word's meaning by considering the *context* of the writing—that is, by thinking about the meaning of the sentence in the work as a whole. When trying to understand an unfamiliar word, always look for clues to its meaning in the sentence in which the word appears—and also think about the larger context.

- **Content-specific visuals, such as graphs,** in each chapter give students non-text sources for study. Students learn to read visuals and to glean information from these for their writing.

READING AND WRITING ABOUT SIDEBARS

A *sidebar* presents information in a box that appears alongside a more detailed discussion of a particular topic. Sidebars are common in textbooks and magazine articles. Their purpose is to provide information to supplement or to highlight aspects of the main reading, including examples, research, and illustrations that can aid understanding. Sidebars can be useful sources of support in written work.

The sidebar shown in Figure 4.3 is from the textbook *Peak Performance: Success in College and Beyond* by Sharon Ferrett (2015). Reading the sidebar will give you a concrete sense of what characteristics define a procrastinator. You might find information in the sidebar with which to describe a procrastinator in your writing.

To read a sidebar, do the following:

- First consider how the information relates to the primary reading.

- Read the sidebar as you would any other text: from top to bottom and from left to right.

- Consider the relationship between the sidebar text and any featured illustrations, such as graphs, diagrams, and photographs.

THEME-BASED CHAPTERS

Writing to Read, Reading to Write walks students through each theme-based chapter with thought-provoking questions and opportunities for critical thinking. Personally appealing and academically appropriate, the chapter themes include student-relevant topics such as these:

> *How can you develop a successful college mindset?*

> *What is the effect of multitasking on your work or learning?*

Through reading related articles and thinking about visuals, students have an opportunity to understand a topic in depth, and the text provides students with more material with which to draft their resulting work. Readings and visuals come from a variety of sources—newspaper, magazine, and journal articles; Web sites and government sources; essays, reports, and textbooks—and reflect the types of readings that are most likely to be assigned in college classes or encountered by students in their personal or professional lives.

For example, Chapter 7 focuses on the question, "What Makes People Happy?" As they work through the chapter, students

- Read an article summarizing research that links economic wealth to life satisfaction in various countries.

- Read an interview with a psychologist explaining research on the link between money and personal happiness.

- Study a bar graph with data from a research study correlating personal income to happiness.

- Develop their own answer to the chapter question and support their thesis using information from the readings and visuals in the chapter.

Support for Instructors

Annotated Instructor's Edition

Alison Kuehner created the annotations in the *Writing to Read, Reading to Write* to share her course-proven in-class activities and teaching tips. Marginal notes also alert instructors to handouts and resources, as well as Power of Process and LearnSmart Achieve assignments in the pre-built Connect course.

Instructor's Manual

Today's first-year composition course, and the co-requisite support course, require new ways of teaching. The Instructor's Manual for *Writing to Read, Reading to Write* includes three parts:

1. **Using *Writing to Read, Reading to Write* in first-year composition.** Includes areas of integration, sequencing, additional essay prompts, and sample syllabi.

2. **Using *Writing to Read, Reading to Write* in co-requisite courses.** Includes a general framework for teaching first-year composition with a co-requisite support course, as developed by a board of instructors teaching co-requisites around the country.

3. **Co-Requisite Board of Advisor recommendations.** McGraw-Hill Education partnered with a team of 13 instructors at the forefront of co-requisite education today to develop a list of recommendations for instructors and institutions launching their own co-requisite programs.

Writing to Read, Reading to Write Pre-Built Connect Composition Course

In this pre-built Connect Composition course, which can be copied to your own Connect account and adapted as you wish, you will find pre-built assignments aligned with every chapter of *Writing to Read, Reading to Write*. Connect seamlessly integrates with every learning management system, which means that students have single sign-on access and instructors have assignment results that sync to their LMS's gradebook.

Feature	Description	Instructional Value
Power of Process	Assignments for Before, During, and After Reading are created for: • each reading selection in every chapter. • student papers in the Spotlight chapters • Anthology reading selections	Guides students through performance-based assessment activities using the pedagogy of strategies instruction. Students use strategies to read and respond to the text, and instructors can assess students' depth of engagement with the text.
Writing Assignments	Writing prompts are aligned to Read to Write Activities in every chapter. Students can engage in peer review through the writing tool. Instructors can create rubrics and assess student writing around specific learning outcomes.	Students can draft responses to writing prompts and receive feedback from instructors. An available rubric provides assessment transparency to students, and allows them to see why they got their grade and how to improve.
LearnSmart Achieve	A module is aligned to each chapter Additional grammar-focused modules are aligned to each section in the Grammar and Style Handbook.	Provides students with adaptive practice and additional learning resources for important topics, either before or after class or in a support course.

Additional Resources

These additional teaching resources are downloadable from the Online Learning Center. Please contact your local McGraw-Hill representative for the username and password to access these resources.

- **Handouts.** These printable pages, useful for in-class, hands-on practice, make preparing for class easier.

- **Topical *PowerPoint* Presentations.** The topical organization allows for maximum flexibility across traditional composition sections and support courses. All *PowerPoint* presentations are fully accessible.

- **Pre-formatted readings for Power of Process.** Each reading in *Writing to Read, Reading to Write* is available to be uploaded to accompany a Power of Process assignment.

Acknowledgments

Writing may seem like a solitary act, but it is not. So many people have helped me along the way to creating this book. My initial thanks goes to Team JAM: Jennifer Hurley and Meghan Swanson-Groupa, the J and M in our triad, who ventured forth with me to revise the English curriculum. I am forever indebted to Katie Hern, Summer Serpas, and the many amazing folks involved in the California Acceleration Project, especially Guillermo Colls, Andrew Kranzman, and Julia Raybould-Rodgers, my fellow honey badgers in crime, who inspired me to be a better teacher. My long-time colleague Bruce Bennet, who read early drafts, and faithful friend, Thea Johnson, never stopped believing that a textbook could come from my class handouts.

Many folks at McGraw-Hill provided support, encouragement, and much-needed professional expertise. A huge thank you to Kelly Villella for realizing that my approach to teaching developmental students could become a textbook and for seeing me through a multiyear process. I am indebted to a team of thoughtful editors who read carefully and truly understood the book: Sylvia Mallory, Katharine Glynn, and Linda Stern. It has been a humbling and enriching experience to have you as cowriters. Penina Braffman and especially Beth Tripmacher guided me with grace and skill through the publishing process. It was great fun and my pleasure to work with Ashley Sandoval to teach an online professional development class.

My thanks to the many reviewers who provided insightful comments and excellent suggestions on drafts of the book: Leigh Adams, *Missouri State University*; Joe Antinarella, *Tidewater Community College*; Seth Batiste, *Lone Star College System–North Harris*; Gail Bauer, *Richland Community College*; Carl Becker, *Delaware Tech Community College-Wilmington*; Joanna Bolick, *Asheville-Buncombe Technical Community College*; Sarah Bruton, *Fayetteville Technical Community College*; Jeremy Burris, *Isothermal Community College*; Grisel Cano, *Houston Community College*; Neeta Chandra, *Cuyahoga Community College–Metro*; Glenn Dayley, *Brigham Young University–Idaho*; Kim Davis, *Oakland Community College–Southfield*; Shari De Licco, *Navarro College–Waxahachie*; Brian Dickson, *Community College of Denver*; Romaldo Dominguez, *South Texas College–Pecan*; Kelly Edmondson, *Cincinnati State Technical and Community College*; Jason Ellis, *Cincinnati State Technical and Community College*; Jennifer Ferguson, *Cazenovia College*; Debra Gibes, *Mott Community College*; Christopher Gibson, *Skyline College*; Debbie Hall, *Lindsey Wilson College*; Umber Hanief, *Gwinnett Technical College*; Marie Hannan-Mandel, *Corning Community College*; Stacey Higdon, *Houston Community College–Central*; Michael Hill, *Henry Ford College–Dearborn*; Andrew Howard, *University of the District of Columbia Community College*; Karen Jensen, *University of Texas–San Antonio*; Alyssa Johnson, *Horry Georgetown Technical College*; Beth Laurence, *McMurry University*; Desmond Lewis, *Houston Community College*; Kenneth McNamara, *Georgia Perimeter College*; Terence McNulty, *Middlesex*

Community College; Maureen Maas-Feary, *Finger Lakes Community College*; Anna Maheshwari, *Schoolcraft College*; Stacey Miller, *Los Medanos College*; Cherise Millsaps, *Surry Community College*; Kerry Moley, *Cape Fear Community College*; Emily Moore, *Wake Technical Community College*; Amanda Mosley, *York Technical College*; Lisa Mott, *Santa Rosa Junior College*; Camille Mustachio, *Germanna Community College–Fredericksburg*; Karen Nelson, *Craven Community College–New Bern Campus*; Karen O'Donnell, *Finger Lakes Community College–Geneva*; Robin Ouzts, *Thomas University*; Jessica Palumbo, *East Georgia State College–Swainsboro*; Terry Peterman, *Navarro College–Corsicana*; Sue Rauch, *Germanna Community College–Locust Grove*; Karen Redding, *University of North Georgia*; David Reinheimer, *Missouri Valley College*; Erin Renfroe, *Holmes Community College*; Nancy Risch, *Caldwell Community College and Technical Institute–Caldwell*; Linda Robinett, *Oklahoma City Community College*; Jamie Sadler, *Richmond Community College*; Esther Sapell Rachelson, *DeVry University*; Ashley Simpson, *Hinds Community College*; Ann Spurlock, *Mississippi State University*; Matilda Stadt, *Palo Alto College*; Kevin Still, *Blinn College*; Gina Thompson, *East Mississippi Community College–GT Campus*; Jacqueline Tiermini, *Finger Lakes Community College–Canandaigua*; Kellyanne Ure, *Snow College*; Dawna Upshaw, *Northwest Vista College*; Tondalaya VanLear, *Dabney S. Lancaster Community College*; Shari Waldrop, *Navarro College*; Joy Walsh, *Butler County Community College*; Charles Warnberg, *Dallas County Community College District–Brookhaven*; Stephanie Webster, *Ivy Tech Community College*; Tammy White, *Forsyth Technical Community College*; Nikki Williams, *El Camino College Compton Center*; Michelle Williamson, *Davidson County Community College*; Jessica Woodruff, *Ivy Tech Community College*; and Marilyn Yamin, *Pellissippi State Community College*.

My students have been some of my best teachers, helping me understand how to be clear, compassionate, and creative in the classroom, so as to inspire us all to read deeply, write well, and be our best selves. Special thanks to my embedded tutors who taught alongside me: Dima Gorodetsky, Alejandra Jimenez, and Thanh Loi Nguyen. You are amazing. Much appreciation to Veronica Alvarez, Raven Capras, Jingting Chen, Alejandra Jimenez, Brittney Kiel, Gabrielle Reyez, Matthew Ricafrente, and Miguel Tolentino for generously allowing me to use their writing in this book to inspire their fellow students with their essays and ideas. You are wonderful.

Finally, having unconditional love and support from my family has been invaluable. Thank you, Mom and Dad, Gillian and Norman, Aunt Ann, Steve and Carrie, for asking about this book and anticipating its arrival. David, Eleanor, and Andrew—after putting up with too many early-morning risings, I'm looking forward to spending more quality time with you!

Alison Kuehner

PART ONE

Welcome to College Reading, Writing, and Thinking

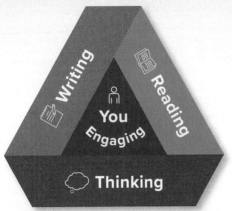

After reading this chapter, you will be able to

- Identify your use of strategies for college success.
- Recognize key factors in succeeding in college.
- Read and write about fixed and growth mindsets.
- Define key terms.
- Read and write about an infographic.
- Develop a critical-thinking mindset.

Look for these icons throughout the chapter. They signal key strategies to use in Read to Write Activities.

Theme: How Can You Develop a Successful College Mindset?

Having the right mindset is crucial to college success. Successful students also have strategies for approaching their reading and writing assignments. They are motivated and interested in studying and actively engage in learning. This chapter considers the kinds of reading and writing expected in college and identifies strategies and attitudes to help you succeed.

IDENTIFYING YOUR USE OF STRATEGIES FOR SUCCESS

The illustration shown in Figure 1.1 represents what it takes to be successful. In the image, the iceberg represents success itself. Above the waterline is what people see, such as a successful person. Below the waterline is what people don't see, such as the characteristics that make people successful. Before reading further, stop and think:

- How does each characteristic below the waterline help create success?
- Why is the illustration titled "The Iceberg Illusion"?

In this chapter, you will read about what it takes to be successful in college. For instance, persisting when reading, working hard when writing, and being dedicated to your college education are hallmarks of successful college students. College students develop good study habits. Moreover, successful college students are not daunted by failure or disappointment; they are willing to make sacrifices to prioritize their learning. As you read through the chapter, think about how the images in this illustration reveal the "hidden" characteristics of success.

FIGURE 1.1 The Illusion Iceberg

Source: Sylvia Duckworth; *Sketchnotes for Educators;* EdTechTeam, 2016.

Read to Write Activity 1.1

Teaching Tip

Ask students to think about the classes they are taking and how they need to read, write, and study for those classes.

Handout

The survey is a reproducible handout in the Instructor's Resources.

Complete the College Reading, Writing, and Learning Survey

The survey shown in Figure 1.2 identifies strategies you may already be using—or could be using—for reading, writing, and learning. Taking this assessment will help you pinpoint areas of strength and areas for improvement.

Identify how frequently you use the reading, writing, and learning strategies listed in Figure 1.2 by circling the number that best represents how often you engage in each activity. Respond honestly: there are no right or wrong answers. Then complete the activities that follow the survey.

FIGURE 1.2 College Reading, Writing, and Learning Survey

College Reading: How Often Do You Do the Following When You Read?					
	Never	**Rarely**	**Sometimes**	**Often**	**Always**
1. Preview the reading by looking at the title and introductory material.	1	2	3	4	5
2. Understand why I am reading the assigned material.	1	2	3	4	5
3. Read and reread the material.	1	2	3	4	5
4. Realize when I understand what I have read and when I do not.	1	2	3	4	5
5. Make notes in the margins or highlight the text when I read.	1	2	3	4	5
6. Ask questions before, during, and after reading.	1	2	3	4	5
7. Pause periodically to summarize or to restate in my own words what I've just read.	1	2	3	4	5
8. Identify the main ideas and examples in the reading.	1	2	3	4	5
9. Look up unfamiliar words and understand how they are used in the reading.	1	2	3	4	5
10. Discuss the reading with other students or the instructor.	1	2	3	4	5

continued

College Writing: How Often Do You Do the Following When You Write?

	Never	Rarely	Sometimes	Often	Always
11. Understand the purpose of a writing assignment.	1	2	3	4	5
12. Brainstorm or prewrite to get ideas before writing.	1	2	3	4	5
13. Write with my audience in mind.	1	2	3	4	5
14. Write several drafts of a paper.	1	2	3	4	5
15. Reread my writing to check that it has a clear thesis and is logically organized.	1	2	3	4	5
16. Reread my writing to check that sentences are clearly and correctly written.	1	2	3	4	5
17. Ask the instructor or a tutor to read my draft and give me feedback.	1	2	3	4	5
18. Start working on my writing as soon as I get an assignment.	1	2	3	4	5

College Learning: How Often Do You Do the Following When You Learn?

	Never	Rarely	Sometimes	Often	Always
19. Keep trying to learn even if I have a setback or failure.	1	2	3	4	5
20. Work as long and as hard as I need to do well.	1	2	3	4	5
21. Accept challenging assignments.	1	2	3	4	5
22. Work with classmates to understand the assigned material.	1	2	3	4	5
23. Get help from others when I need it.	1	2	3	4	5
24. Reflect on what I am learning and how it applies to me or my life.	1	2	3	4	5

College Reading, Writing, and Learning Survey Scores

1. Add up the numbers you circled in each category in Figure 1.2—reading, writing, and learning. Write down the total for each. Then, using the score for each category, check the following assessments to determine where your strengths lie and where you can improve.

Answer

1. Answers will vary. Stress to students the need to create separate scores for each category.

continued

College Reading Scores Assessment

50–40   You use many strategies that can benefit your reading. Reading is an area of strength for you.

39–30   You sometimes use effective reading strategies but could learn more strategies and apply them more often. Reading is an area of some strengths and some room for improvement.

29–10   You would benefit from learning more reading strategies and using them regularly. Reading is clearly an area to improve.

College Writing Scores Assessment

40–32   You use many strategies that can benefit your writing. Writing is an area of strength for you.

31–24   You sometimes use effective writing strategies but could learn more strategies and apply them more often. Writing is an area of some strengths and some room for improvement.

23–8   You would benefit from learning more writing strategies and using them regularly. Writing is clearly an area to improve.

College Learning Scores Assessment

30–24   You have an effective attitude toward learning. This is an area of strength.

23–18   You sometimes have an effective attitude toward learning but could learn more about effective ways to learn. This is an area of some strengths and some room for improvement.

17–6   You would benefit from changing your attitude toward learning. This is clearly an area to improve.

Answers

2. Answers will vary. Suggest that students list categories from weak to strong.

3. Answers will vary. This activity encourages active reading; also answers can be used in the Apply What You Learned exercises.

2. Using your answers to question 1, identify the areas you most need to improve in reading, writing, and learning for college.

3. Review the places in the survey where you circled 1 or 2. Write down the strategy associated with that score. As you read through this textbook, take notes on what that strategy involves and why, how, and when you should use it. If you did not circle 1 or 2, consider looking at places you marked as 3.

RECOGNIZING KEY FACTORS FOR SUCCEEDING IN COLLEGE

Why are some students more successful in college than others? It would be nice if we could simply say, if you just study every day for 10 hours or if you consume energy drinks while you read, you will succeed. Unfortunately—or maybe fortunately—life is more complicated than that. Many factors contribute to college success, including your

- Approach to college reading.
- Approach to college writing.
- Motivation and interest (short- and long-term goals).
- Beliefs about learning.

College Reading: Sinking In

Look at Figure 1.3 and consider: *What do you like to read, and why?* You may read for a variety of reasons: personal, emotional, intellectual, and practical. Reading is a way of discovering new ideas, sharing information, and getting in touch with others. Reading can be a source of knowledge and of personal pleasure.

Class Activity

Use the question "What do you like to read, and why?" as a brainstorming or freewriting activity.

FIGURE 1.3 Reading and Writing—Content and Purpose

What We Read and Write: Content	Why We Read and Write: Purpose
• E-mails, blogs, text messages, *Facebook* or other social media postings	• Interact socially with friends, family, or interest groups.
• Magazines, school newspaper, local newspaper, informational Internet sites	• Learn about community, neighborhood, school, or the wider world.
• Novels, graphic novels, manga, poems, songs	• Understand human feelings, experience different times and places, escape reality, or let imagination soar.
• Bible, Koran, Torah, religious texts	• Think deeply about values and morality.
• Books about hobbies, manuals, lists	• Gain practical advice or help.

Much of what students learn in school is communicated through reading—through textbooks, articles, and scholarly publications. Reading, along with writing, is the means by which educated people interact, share concepts and knowledge, communicate ideas and information, and test theories and evidence.

Your college courses will involve reading various kinds of **texts**—printed or written documents such as textbooks and other books, articles, essays, and Web sites that you will read and study. There is no *one* way to read these different texts; however, knowing which reading approaches work well for the assigned reading, the course expectations, and your own abilities can help you get the most from your reading. Successful college students read to understand rather than to memorize information. They do not just run their eyes over the page and cram for the test. Instead, they work hard to understand what they read by checking their comprehension as they go along.

In one study of students in an introductory accounting course, the academically successful students had a reading approach the researchers termed **sinking in**. That is, these students took time to *sink into* the material, which means they

- Read slowly and concentrated on the text.
- Took notes while reading.

- Highlighted important topics and main ideas.
- Reread difficult passages.
- Reviewed previous chapters or their class notes while reading.
- Persisted in their reading even when the material was difficult.
- Asked for help when they needed it.

In contrast, the students who did not do well in the class read quickly and superficially, or **skimmed**, just to get the reading done. They were more likely to skip over difficult information or tell themselves that they would come back to the reading later and review it more carefully. They rarely did. In contrast, the successful students did not wait to clear up their confusion; they dealt with it right away.

To sum up: Successful college students read with the intent to learn. They persist if the reading is difficult and immediately try various strategies for resolving confusion.

College Writing: Giving It Time and Effort

Class Activity

Use the question "What do you like to write, and why?" as a brainstorming or freewriting activity.

Look at Figure 1.3 again and consider: *What do you write, and why?* Just as you read for a variety of purposes, you may write for many reasons: personal, emotional, intellectual, and practical. Like reading, writing is a way of sharing information, getting in touch with others, and discovering new ideas.

In college, students write often. They may take notes during class or as they read. Students might be required to compose papers, respond to short-answer test questions, or write essay exams. Just as it is important to be an effective reader, it is important to be a skillful writer. So, what makes for good writing in college?

College professors value the complexity of ideas and intellectual risk taking. That means your professors will expect more than grammatically correct sentences: they will expect you to read carefully, apply **critical thinking** by actively questioning arguments and assessing evidence, and express your thoughts clearly. In addition, to produce an academic paper, you may need to do the following:

- Conduct research on a topic.
- Use information from class readings and lectures.
- **Analyze** (break down into parts to understand the whole).
- **Evaluate** (determine the value or significance).
- **Synthesize** (combine different ideas into a new whole).

The advice "Don't wait until the night before it is due to write your paper" certainly applies in college. Why? Good writing takes time and effort. As a strategic student and writer, you will want to go through the stages of the writing process. You will need to

- Spend time before you write to read and reread class materials.
- Take notes on your reading.
- **Brainstorm** (discuss informally with others) or **freewrite** (write continuously without regard to grammar and spelling errors) to generate a lot of ideas quickly.
- Make an **outline**, or a writing plan, to prepare to write.

- Compose a first **draft** (an initial version of your paper).
- Revise your first draft, often several times.
- Ask someone else to read your drafts or reread your paper yourself.
- Check over your work before turning it in.

One college professor advises freshmen students to think of writing as a skill that they are learning—like painting a picture, driving a car, or playing baseball. As a student, you must practice that skill to improve. The more you practice your writing, the better your writing will get. Figure 1.4 summarizes the key strategies for successful college reading and writing.

FIGURE 1.4 Strategies for College Readers and Writers

For both reading and writing, practice and persistence are the keys to success.

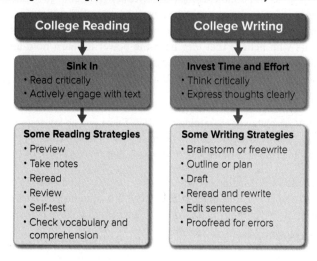

Motivation and Interest

Students' motivation to learn and interest in learning are fundamental to success. Consider the experience of Andrew Paine, who dropped out of college after two years of partying with his soccer and fraternity buddies and getting poor grades. Looking back, he observes, "I didn't know what direction I was going in. There wasn't really a light at the end of the tunnel" (qtd. in Shea). (Note: Throughout the text you will see information in parentheses—usually, the author's last name and sometimes additional information, as in the preceding sentence. This information indicates the source of the quotation used in the sentence. Turn to the list of works cited at the end of the chapter for more information on the source.)

If people don't know why they are in college (if they lack concrete short- and long-term academic goals) or if they are going to school to please their parents or because all their friends are going, they may not be genuinely interested in attending class or studying. Under any of these circumstances, they may not do well in college.

Successful students are typically those who have a goal: they know what they want to study, or they have a career path in mind. Other successful students are motivated simply by their desire to learn or by their enjoyment of intellectual

Class Activity

Use the question "Why are you in college?" as a brainstorming or freewriting activity.

pursuits. Prospective students need to ask themselves whether they truly want to be in college. They should be able to give clear and heartfelt reasons for their choice. People who find that they don't really want to be in college might think about what other productive activity they would prefer to do instead for a while, at least until they feel ready to take on college work.

Andrew Paine, for instance, spent time away from college, until he discovered that he was interested in environmental science. When he was ready, he returned to college, explaining that his time away from studying helped him sort out his priorities. "Now, I'm getting the most out of college academically," says Paine. "It really worked out" (qtd. in Shea).

Beliefs about Learning

Finally, students' ideas about learning can influence their college success. Students who believe that luck, chance, a bad instructor, or a difficult assignment determines whether they will succeed do not have control over their learning. In contrast, students who believe that *they* have the power to learn hold an advantage over students who believe they have little or no such control.

Consider the example of Roy, a student in a difficult introductory psychology course. Roy believes that

> effort is the absolute key to learning a subject. Talent and ability go to waste without effort. . . . [E]ffort means reading to learn, striving to retain, applying material to life situations, and redoing, reading, and studying as often as necessary. (qtd. in Beyeler 309)

Roy's attitude toward learning is that *he* has to *work hard* to do well in college. This is most likely one factor that made him a successful student and earned him a B+ in his challenging psychology class. In short, successful college students

- Understand that they must be independent, active learners.
- Know what is expected of them by their professors and in their classes.
- Know why they are reading and have strategies for comprehension.
- Understand that good writing requires time, effort, and practice.
- Are motivated to learn and interested in learning.
- Believe they are in control of their learning.

READING AND WRITING ABOUT FIXED AND GROWTH MINDSETS

So far, you have seen that taking an active role in your learning is a prerequisite for college success. Let's review what being active entails. First, as a reader, remember to employ well-established reading strategies and practice persistence to ensure that you genuinely understand what you read. That is, before reading, think about the topic and what you will read. Then during and after your reading, use writing not only to enhance your reading comprehension but also to develop your writing competence. Second, as a writer, be sure to prewrite, draft, reread, and revise your work to improve its quality. Third, have a positive attitude toward your education and take the ultimate responsibility for it.

Having a positive mindset is so basic that some researchers judge a student's attitude to be one of the biggest predictors of success. In "Brainology," the reading selection that follows, you will review research showing that what students believe about their learning and how they respond to challenges make a big difference in their academic success.

READING SELECTION

"BRAINOLOGY: TRANSFORMING STUDENTS' MOTIVATION TO LEARN"

In this reading the author uses American Psychological Association (APA) style to indicate source information. Notice that some sentences include parentheses, inside of which are a name and date: (Dweck, 2006). These are parenthetical *citations,* or references to research. The name is the researcher's last name, and the date indicates when the research was published. A list, headed "References," arranged by the researchers' last names, and including full publication information, appears at the end of the reading. As pointed out earlier, in the text portions of this book, citations are also given for quoted or referenced material, but in a different style (called Modern Language Association, or MLA, style), which uses the author's last name and source page number in parenthesis.

Complete the "Before Reading" assignment. Then read the selection while you complete the "During Reading" activities. Finally, complete the "After Reading" assignments.

 ### Before Reading: Predict; Recognize Prior Knowledge

Look over "Brainology: Transforming Students' Motivation to Learn" before you answer these questions. For instance, read the comments that immediately precede the reading—and then examine the title and the headings in the reading. Write answers to these questions using complete sentences.

1. What do you think the reading will be about? For example, what could *brainology* mean? How might brainology relate to a student's motivation to learn?

2. What do you already know about human intelligence? Is intelligence fixed, or can it change?

Connect

You will find a coordinated Power of Process assignment for this reading in your Connect course.

Teaching Tip

Assign students to read "Simple Sentences" in "Grammar and Style Handbook" for a review of complete sentences.

Answers

1. "Brainology" could mean the study of the brain. Demonstrate how to break apart the word— brain + ology— to guess the meaning.

2. Answers will vary. Encourage students to provide examples of what they have observed to support their answers.

During Reading: Annotate

Write responses to the following exercises using complete sentences.

3. Try reading the selection in "chunks." That is, use the boldface headings to divide the reading into sections, or chunks, and then read one section at a time. After reading a section, stop to reflect on the important ideas, using the headings as a guide. Write down the main ideas in your own words.

4. As you read, mark any lines you find interesting or thought-provoking or that you particularly agree with.

5. As you read, mark any lines that confuse you or that you disagree with.

Brainology: Transforming Students' Motivation to Learn

By Carol S. Dweck

The National Association of Independent Schools, Winter 2008

Carol Dweck, professor of psychology at Stanford University, spent many years trying to understand how people deal with failure and what that means for their future success. Her ideas about fixed and growth mindset came out of this research. In this article, she argues that students' beliefs about their brains and about learning powerfully impact their achievement.

This is an exciting time for our brains. More and more research is showing that our brains change constantly with learning and experience and that this takes place throughout our lives. 1

Does this have implications for students' motivation and learning? It certainly does. In my research in collaboration with my graduate students, we have shown that what students believe about their brains—whether they see their intelligence as something that's fixed or something that can grow and change—has profound effects on their motivation, learning, and school achievement (Dweck, 2006). These different beliefs, or mindsets, create different psychological worlds: one in which students are afraid of challenges and devastated by setbacks, and one in which students relish challenges and are resilient in the face of setbacks. 2

How do these mindsets work? How are the mindsets communicated to students? And, most important, can they be changed? As we answer these questions, you will understand why so many students do not achieve to their potential, why so many bright students stop working when school becomes challenging, and why stereotypes have such profound effects on students' achievement. You will also learn how praise can have a negative effect on students' mindsets, harming their motivation to learn. 3

Mindsets and Achievement

Many students believe that intelligence is fixed, that each person has a certain amount and that's that. We call this a *fixed mindset*, and, as you will see, students 4 with this mindset worry about how much of this fixed intelligence they possess. A fixed mindset makes challenges threatening for students (because they believe that their fixed ability may not be up to the task), and it makes mistakes and failures demoralizing (because they believe that such setbacks reflect badly on their level of fixed intelligence).

Other students believe that intelligence is something that can be cultivated through effort and education. They don't necessarily believe that everyone has the same abilities or that anyone can be as smart as Einstein, but they do believe that everyone can improve their abilities. And they understand that even Einstein wasn't Einstein until he put in years of focused hard work. In short, students with this *growth mindset* believe that intelligence is a potential that can be realized through learning. As a result, confronting challenges, profiting from mistakes, and persevering in the face of setbacks become ways of getting smarter.   5

To understand the different worlds these mindsets create, we followed several hundred students across a difficult school transition—the transition to seventh grade. This is when the academic work often gets much harder, the grading gets stricter, and the school environment gets less personalized with students moving from class to class. As the students entered seventh grade, we measured their mindsets (along with a number of other things) and then we monitored their grades over the next two years.   6

The first thing we found was that students with different mindsets cared about different things in school. Those with a growth mindset were much more interested in learning than in just looking smart in school. This was not the case for students with a fixed mindset. In fact, in many of our studies with students from preschool age to college age, we find that students with a fixed mindset care so much about how smart they will appear that they often reject learning opportunities—even ones that are critical to their success (Cimpian, Arce, Markman, & Dweck, 2007; Hong, Chiu, Dweck, Lin, & Wan, 1999; Mangels, Butterfield, Lamb, Good, & Dweck, 2006; Nussbaum & Dweck, 2008).   7

Next, we found that students with the two mindsets had radically different beliefs about effort. Those with a growth mindset had a very straightforward (and correct) idea of effort—the idea that the harder you work, the more your ability will grow and that even geniuses have had to work hard for their accomplishments. In contrast, the students with the fixed mindset believed that if you worked hard it meant that you didn't have ability, and that things would just come naturally to you if you did. This means that every time something is hard for them and requires effort, it's both a threat and a bind. If they work hard at it, that means that they aren't good at it, but if they don't work hard, they won't do well. Clearly, since just about every worthwhile pursuit involves effort over a long period of time, this is a potentially crippling belief, not only in school but also in life.   8

Students with different mindsets also had very different reactions to setbacks. Those with growth mindsets reported that, after a setback in school, they would simply study more or study differently the next time. But those with fixed mindsets were more likely to say that they would feel dumb, study less the next time, and seriously consider cheating. If you feel dumb—permanently dumb—in an academic area, there is no good way to bounce back and be successful in the future. In a growth mindset, however, you can make a plan of positive action that   9 can remedy a deficiency (Heyman et al., 1992; Hong et al., 1999; Nussbaum & Dweck, 2008).

Finally, when we looked at the math grades they went on to earn, we found that the students with a growth mindset had pulled ahead. Although both groups had started seventh grade with equivalent achievement test scores, a growth mindset quickly propelled students ahead of their fixed-mindset peers, and this gap only increased over the two years of the study. **10**

In short, the belief that intelligence is fixed dampened students' motivation to learn, made them afraid of effort, and made them want to quit after a setback. This is why so many bright students stop working when school becomes hard. Many bright students find grade school easy and coast to success early on. But later on, when they are challenged, they struggle. They don't want to make mistakes and feel dumb—and, most of all, they don't want to work hard and feel dumb. So they simply retire. **11**

It is the belief that intelligence can be developed that opens students to a love of learning, a belief in the power of effort and constructive, determined reactions to setbacks. **12**

How Do Students Learn These Mindsets? **13**
In the 1990s, parents and schools decided that the most important thing for kids to have was self-esteem. If children felt good about themselves, people believed, they would be set for life. In some quarters, self-esteem in math seemed to become more important than knowing math, and self-esteem in English seemed to become more important than reading and writing. But the biggest mistake was the belief that you could simply hand children self-esteem by telling them how smart and talented they are. Even though this is such an intuitively appealing idea, and even though it was exceedingly well-intentioned, I believe it has had disastrous effects.

In the 1990s, we took a poll among parents and found that almost 85 percent endorsed the notion that it was *necessary* to praise their children's abilities to give them confidence and help them achieve. Their children are now in the workforce, and we are told that young workers cannot last through the day without being propped up by praise, rewards, and recognition. Coaches are asking me where all the coachable athletes have gone. Parents ask me why their children won't work hard in school. **14**

Could all of this come from well-meant praise? Well, we were suspicious of the praise movement at the time. We had already seen in our research that it was the most vulnerable children who were already obsessed with their intelligence and chronically worried about how smart they were. What if praising intelligence made all children concerned about their intelligence? This kind of praise might tell them that having high intelligence and talent is the most important thing and is what makes you valuable. It might tell them that intelligence is just something you have and not something you develop. It might deny the role of effort and dedication in achievement. In short, it might promote a fixed mindset with all of its vulnerabilities. **15**

The wonderful thing about research is that you can put questions like this to the test—and we did (Kamins & Dweck, 1999; Mueller & Dweck, 1998). We gave two groups of children problems from an IQ test, and we praised them. We praised the children in one group for their intelligence, telling them, "Wow, that's a really good score. You must be smart at this." We praised the children in the other group for their **16** effort: "Wow, that's a really good score. You must have worked really hard." That's all we did, but the results were dramatic. We did studies like this with children of different ages and ethnicities from around the country, and the results were the same.

Here is what happened with fifth graders. The children praised for their intelligence did not want to learn. When we offered them a challenging task that they could learn from, the majority opted for an easier one, one on which they could avoid making mistakes. The children praised for their effort wanted the task they could learn from. 17

The children praised for their intelligence lost their confidence as soon as the problems got more difficult. Now, as a group, they thought they weren't smart. They also lost their enjoyment, and, as a result, their performance plummeted. On the other hand, those praised for effort maintained their confidence, their motivation, and their performance. Actually, their performance improved over time such that, by the end, they were performing substantially better than the intelligence-praised children on this IQ test. 18

Finally, the children who were praised for their intelligence lied about their scores more often than the children who were praised for their effort. We asked children to write something (anonymously) about their experience to a child in another school, and we left a little space for them to report their scores. Almost 40 percent of the intelligence-praised children elevated their scores, whereas only 12 or 13 percent of children in the other group did so. To me this suggests that, after students are praised for their intelligence, it's too humiliating for them to admit mistakes. 19

The results were so striking that we repeated the study five times just to be sure, and each time roughly the same things happened. Intelligence praise, compared to effort (or "process") praise, put children into a fixed mindset. Instead of giving them confidence, it made them fragile, so much so that a brush with difficulty erased their confidence, their enjoyment, and their good performance, and made them ashamed of their work. This can hardly be the self-esteem that parents and educators have been aiming for. 20

Often, when children stop working in school, parents deal with this by reassuring their children how smart they are. We can now see that this simply fans the flames. It confirms the fixed mindset and makes kids all the more certain that they don't want to try something difficult—something that could lose them their parents' high regard. How *should* we praise our students? How *should* we reassure them? By focusing them on the process they engaged in—their effort, their strategies, their concentration, their perseverance, or their improvement. 21

"You really stuck to that until you got it. That's wonderful!" 22

"It was a hard project, but you did it one step at a time and it turned out great!" 23

"I like how you chose the tough problems to solve. You're really going to stretch yourself and learn new things." 24

"I know that school used to be a snap for you. What a waste that was. Now you really have an opportunity to develop your abilities." 25

Brainology 26

Can a growth mindset be taught directly to kids? If it can be taught, will it enhance their motivation and grades? We set out to answer this question by creating a growth mindset workshop (Blackwell, Trzesniewski, & Dweck, 2007). We took seventh graders and divided them into two groups. Both groups got an eight-session workshop full of great study skills, but the "growth mindset group" also got lessons in the growth mindset—what it was and how to apply it to their schoolwork. Those lessons began with an article called "You Can Grow Your Intelligence: New Research Shows the Brain Can Be Developed Like a Muscle." Students were mesmerized by this article and its message. They loved the idea that the growth of their brains was in their hands.

This article and the lessons that followed changed the terms of engagement for students. Many students had seen school as a place where they performed and were judged, but now they understood that they had an active role to play in the development of their minds. They got to work, and by the end of the semester the growth-mindset group showed a significant increase in their math grades. The control group—the group that had gotten eight sessions of study skills—showed no improvement and continued to decline. Even though they had learned many useful study skills, they did not have the motivation to put them into practice.   27

The teachers, who didn't even know there were two different groups, singled out students in the growth-mindset group as showing clear changes in their motivation. They reported that these students were now far more engaged with their schoolwork and were putting considerably more effort into their classroom learning, homework, and studying.   28

Joshua Aronson, Catherine Good, and their colleagues had similar findings (Aronson, Fried, & Good, 2002; Good, Aronson, & Inzlicht, 2003). Their studies and ours also found that negatively stereotyped students (such as girls in math, or African-American and Hispanic students in math and verbal areas) showed substantial benefits from being in a growth mindset workshop. Stereotypes are typically fixed-mindset labels. They imply that the trait or ability in question is fixed and that some groups have it and others don't. Much of the harm that stereotypes do comes from the fixed-mindset message they send. The growth mindset, while not denying that performance differences might exist, portrays abilities as acquirable and sends a particularly encouraging message to students who have been negatively stereotyped—one that they respond to with renewed motivation and engagement.   29

Inspired by these positive findings, we started to think about how we could make a growth mindset workshop more widely available. To do this, we have begun to develop a computer-based program called "Brainology." In six computer modules, students learn about the brain and how to make it work better. They follow two hip teens through their school day, learn how to confront and solve schoolwork problems, and create study plans. They visit a state-of-the-art virtual brain lab, do brain experiments, and find out such things as how the brain changes with learning—how it grows new connections every time students learn something new. They also learn how to use this idea in their schoolwork by putting their study skills to work to make themselves smarter.   30

We pilot-tested Brainology in 20 New York City schools. Virtually all of the students loved it and reported (anonymously) the ways in which they changed their ideas about learning and changed their learning and study habits. Here are some things they said in response to the question, "Did you change your mind about anything?"   31

I did change my mind about how the brain works . . . I will try harder because I know that the more you try, the more your brain works.

Yes . . . I imagine neurons making connections in my brain and I feel like I am learning something.

My favorite thing from Brainology is the neurons part where when you learn something, there are connections and they keep growing. I always picture them when I'm in school.

Teachers also reported changes in their students, saying that they had become more active and eager learners: "They offer to practice, study, take notes, or pay attention to ensure that connections will be made." 32

What Do We Value? 33

In our society, we seem to worship talent—and we often portray it as a gift. Now we can see that this is not motivating to our students. Those who think they have this gift expect to sit there with it and be successful. When they aren't successful, they get defensive and demoralized, and often opt out. Those who don't think they have the gift also become defensive and demoralized, and often opt out as well. 34

We need to correct the harmful idea that people simply have gifts that transport them to success, and to teach our students that no matter how smart or talented someone is—be it Einstein, Mozart, or Michael Jordan—no one succeeds in a big way without enormous amounts of dedication and effort. It is through effort that people build their abilities and realize their potential. More and more research is showing there is one thing that sets the great successes apart from their equally talented peers—how hard they've worked (Ericsson, Charness, Feltovich, & Hoffman, 2006). 35

Next time you're tempted to praise your students' intelligence or talent, restrain yourself. Instead, teach them how much fun a challenging task is, how interesting and informative errors are, and how great it is to struggle with something and make progress. Most of all, teach them that by taking on challenges, making mistakes, and putting forth effort, they are making themselves smarter. 36

References

Aronson, J., Fried, C., & Good, C. (2002). Reducing the effects of stereotype threat on African American college students by shaping theories of intelligence. *Journal of Experimental Social Psychology, 38*, 113–125.

Binet, A. (1909/1973). *Les idées modernes sur les enfants* [Modern ideas on children]. Paris: Flamarion.

Blackwell, L., Trzesniewski, K., & Dweck, C. S. (2007). Implicit theories of intelligence predict achievement across an adolescent transition: A longitudinal study and an intervention. *Child Development, 78*, 246–263.

Cimpian, A., Arce, H., Markman, E. M., & Dweck, C. S. (2007). Subtle linguistic cues impact children's motivation. *Psychological Science, 18*, 314–316.

Dweck, C. S. (2006). *Mindset*. New York, NY: Random House.

Ericsson, K. A., Charness, N., Feltovich, P. J., & Hoffman, R. R. (Eds.). (2006). *The Cambridge handbook of expertise and expert performance*. New York, NY: Cambridge University Press.

Good, C., Aronson, J., & Inzlicht, M. (2003). Improving adolescents' standardized test performance: An intervention to reduce the effects of stereotype threat. *Journal of Applied Developmental Psychology, 24*, 645–662.

Hong, Y. Y., Chiu, C., Dweck, C. S., Lin, D., & Wan, W. (1999). Implicit theories, attributions, and coping: A meaning system approach. *Journal of Personality and Social Psychology, 77*, 588–599.

Kamins, M., & Dweck, C. S. (1999). Person vs. process praise and criticism: Implications for contingent self-worth and coping. *Developmental Psychology, 35,* 835–847.

Mangels, J. A., Butterfield, B., Lamb, J., Good, C. D., & Dweck, C. S. (2006). Why do beliefs about intelligence influence learning success? A social-cognitive-neuroscience model. *Social, Cognitive, and Affective Neuroscience, 1,* 75–86.

Mueller, C. M., & Dweck, C. S. (1998). Intelligence praise can undermine motivation and performance. *Journal of Personality and Social Psychology, 75,* 33–52.

Nussbaum, A. D., & Dweck, C. S. (2008). Defensiveness vs. remediation: Self-theories and modes of self-esteem maintenance. *Personality and Social Psychology Bulletin, 34(5),* 599–612.

After Reading: Reflect on the Text

Write responses to the following exercises using complete sentences.

6. Review your annotations and recall the lines from the reading you marked as interesting or thought-provoking or that you particularly agree with. Write down these lines. Put quotation marks around the words you copied from the text to indicate these are the author's words. After the last quotation mark, write the author's last name, Dweck, and the text page number in parentheses. Then explain why you agree with the lines or find them interesting or stimulating.

7. Review your annotations and recall the lines from the reading that confused you or that you disagree with. Write down these lines. Put quotation marks around the words you copied from the text to indicate these are the author's words. After the last quotation mark, write the author's last name, Dweck, and the text page number in parentheses. Then explain why you find the lines confusing or disagree with them.

Answers

6. Answers will vary. Encourage students to give detailed explanations or specific examples to support their answers.

7. Answers will vary. Encourage students to give detailed explanations or specific examples to support their answers.

Connect

Activity 1.2 can be found as a writing assignment in Connect.

Answers

1. Main ideas include developing a growth mindset and praising children for effort to improve success.

2. Main ideas also include not being afraid to fail and embracing challenges to lead to success.

3. Dweck claims people value talent, but they should prize effort instead. Students may agree or disagree with Dweck.

Read to Write Activity 1.2

Engage with the Reading

Write responses to the following exercises using complete sentences.

1. In writing, explain the main ideas from "Brainology: Transforming Students' Motivation to Learn" and give specific examples of how these ideas relate to your learning, your attitude toward college, or your success as a student.

2. In writing, give specific examples of how the main ideas from "Brainology: Transforming Students' Motivation to Learn" relate to your life *outside school*—your relationships, your hobbies, your job, and anything else.

3. The last section of the reading has the heading "What Do We Value?" According to the author, what do people in our society value? What *should* they value? Do you agree with the author about what people do value or should value? Write a few sentences that address these questions.

Vocabulary Strategy: Defining Key Terms in the Reading

Authors may use particular words and phrases to represent important ideas. Examples of these *key terms* are the words in bold print in this book. Key terms are defined in the writing itself, right before or after the term, and at the end of the chapter.

Vocabulary Practice

Each item below contains a quotation from the reading selection "Brainology: Transforming Students' Motivation to Learn." Write a definition for each underlined word using the information in the sentences. The example below demonstrates how to define the first key term.

Example: "These different beliefs, or <u>mindsets</u>, create different psychological worlds. . . ."

Answer: Mindsets are beliefs.

1. "Many students believe that intelligence is fixed, that each person has a certain amount and that's that. We call this a <u>fixed mindset</u>, and, as you will see, students with this mindset worry about how much of this fixed intelligence they possess."

2. "Other students believe that intelligence is something that can be cultivated through effort and education. . . . In short, students with this <u>growth mindset</u> believe that intelligence is a potential that can be realized through learning."

3. "To do this, we have begun to develop a computer-based program called 'Brainology.' In six computer modules, students learn about the brain and how to make it work better."

Answers

1. A fixed mindset is the belief that everyone is born with a set amount of intelligence.

2. A growth mindset is the belief that everyone can develop his or her intelligence.

3. Brainology is a computer program that teaches students about how the brain works.

READING AND WRITING ABOUT INFOGRAPHICS

An *infographic* is a visual presentation combining text and pictures. Infographics add interest to the explanation of a technical topic and make the subject easy to understand. Infographics use visual elements, such as lines, arrows, photographs, diagrams, and graphs, as well as words, phrases, and sentences.

For a writer, studying an infographic from a reliable source can provide information that is useful to include (with proper citations) in written work. For a reader, an infographic embedded in a text can aid comprehension, as it may condense, focus, and thus clarify the main ideas. For example, the infographic in Figure 1.5 summarizes some important differences between a fixed and a growth mindset.

To read an infographic

- Read the title for insight on what the infographic represents.

- Look for clues as to what path to take when reading. Some infographics are best read from top to bottom; others, from left to right.

- Consider the relationship between the graphic and the text: typically the graphic visually represents a concept discussed in the text.

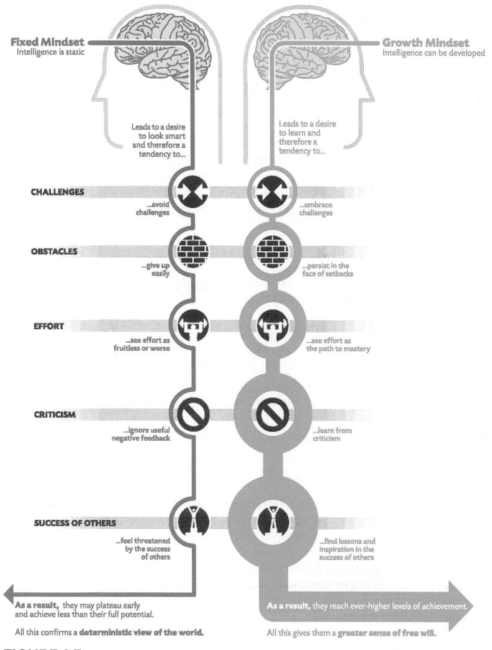

FIGURE 1.5 Two Mindsets

©Carol Dweck. Used with permission.

Study the infographic shown in Figure 1.5, and answer these questions:

1. What is the infographic's title? What is the infographic explaining?

2. Look at the images, text, colors, lines, and arrows. What is the best order in which to read the information? How do the different parts of the infographic relate to one another?

3. After studying the infographic, explain *in your own words* the main differences between a fixed mindset and a growth mindset.

DEVELOPING A CRITICAL-THINKING MINDSET

When faculty from universities, state colleges, and community colleges were surveyed to determine what reading, writing, and thinking skills they felt were important for student success in college, more than 75% identified the following four "intellectual habits of mind" as most crucial:

Exhibit curiosity . . .

Experiment with new ideas . . .

See other points of view . . .

Challenge their own beliefs. . . . (*Academic Literacy 13*)

These habits of mind—to be open to new ideas and to test one's thinking—are part of developing a critical-thinking mindset. When you exercise **critical thinking**, you do not simply accept what you read or what you are told. Rather, you question, check, and assess that information (see "Strategies for Critical Thinking"). For instance, after reading Carol Dweck's ideas about fixed and growth mindsets, you might be *curious* to find out more about how Dweck developed her theories. You could *experiment* by applying Dweck's ideas of fixed and growth mindsets to people you know to determine whether these mindsets explain people's actions and

Strategies for Critical Thinking

- Question what you see, hear, or read by asking whether the ideas seem valid and are supported by logical reasons and convincing evidence.

- Evaluate the quality of the support for ideas, looking for convincing and sufficient evidence that an idea is acceptable.

- Consider the source of the information, including the qualifications or expertise of the person or organization providing the ideas and support.

- Seek out other points of view that challenge or question what you have read and compare them to each other.

- Have an open mind and be willing to change your own thinking if you read or hear ideas that are more compelling or convincing than what you originally thought.

Answers

1. The title is "Two Mindsets." The graphic explains Dweck's theories about fixed and growth mindsets.

2. The graphic should be read from top to bottom. The left and right images contrast these mindsets.

3. A fixed-mindset person believes intelligence doesn't change and avoids stress and hard work, but a growth-mindset person believes intelligence can improve and perseveres even when challenged.

Class Activity

Before reading this section, ask students what reading, writing, and thinking skills they think college professors expect of their students. You can find the ICAS report online and generate a survey based on faculty responses that students can rank.

Handout

"Strategies for Critical Thinking" is a reproducible handout in the Instructor's Resources.

behaviors. You might investigate *other points of view*, such as whether other researchers support—or disagree—with Dweck's theories. You might observe whether your *own beliefs* fit neatly into the categories of fixed and growth mindsets. "Strategies for Critical Thinking", will help you get started on developing critical thinking skills.

The next reading is designed to start you down the critical-thinking path. You will read further research by Dweck and others that suggests students' mindsets are determined not only by internal factors, such as beliefs about learning, but also by external factors, such as income.

Connect

You will find a coordinated Power of Process assignment for this reading in your Connect course.

READING SELECTION

Answers

1. The title indicates the reading will be about how poverty affects students. It's not clear what the impact of poverty is, but a good guess is that it can have detrimental effects on students' mindsets.

2. *Deficit* means small or lacking and *ideology* is a belief system, so a *deficit ideology* could be the idea that poor students lack knowledge or that they have a fixed mindset.

Answers

3. In the introduction, the author explains that low-income students are more likely to have fixed mindsets, but if they have growth mindsets, they can achieve academically as well as their high-income peers. In the section "Growth Mindset in Students—Deficit Ideology?" some people question whether mindsets place the blame on students for not achieving when poor schools could be the problem. In "How It Works in the Classroom," teachers need professional development to foster growth mindsets in their students. They should not just praise students for effort but provide strategies for success.

"IMPACT OF POVERTY ON STUDENTS: ALL IN THEIR MINDS?"

Complete the "Before Reading" and "During Reading" exercises. Then read the selection. Finally, complete the "After Reading" exercises.

 Before Reading: Preview; Predict

Look at the reading selection title and read the information that immediately precedes the reading. Then write responses to the following using complete sentences.

1. Look at the title of the reading selection. What do you think the reading will be about? For instance, what impact could poverty have on a student's mindset?

2. The first subheading in the reading selection includes the phrase *Deficit Ideology*. What do you think this means? How could a deficit ideology relate to a fixed or growth mindset?

 During Reading: Annotate

Write responses to the following exercises using complete sentences.

3. Try reading the selection in "chunks." That is, use the boldface headings to divide the reading into sections, or chunks, and then read one section at a time. After reading a section, stop to reflect on the important ideas, using the headings as a guide. Write down the main ideas in your own words.

4. As you read, mark any lines you find interesting or thought-provoking or that you particularly agree with.

5. As you read, mark any lines that confuse you or that you disagree with.

4. Answers will vary. Encourage students to explain and give examples to support their agreement.

5. Answers will vary. Encourage students to explain why they are confused and give examples to support why they disagree.

Impact of Poverty on Students: All in Their Minds?

By Mary Ellen Flannery

NEA Today, 29 September 2016

Carol Dweck's ideas about fixed and growth mindsets have become popular with educators since the publication of her book Mindset: The New Psychology of Success *in 2006. Some people, however, question whether mindsets alone can account for student success or failure, or whether it is fair to focus on students' beliefs about their learning when other issues may be more powerful predictors of academic success. In this article, published by the National Education Association, the author describes Dweck's further research on the links between poverty, mindsets, and achievement.*

1 Students from low-income families who believe that they can develop skills and do better in school if they work hard and practice—a "growth mindset," in other words—may be buffered from the effects of poverty on student achievement, a Stanford University study has found.

2 But students who live in poverty are less likely to have growth mindsets. Instead, they have what researchers call a "fixed mindset," or the idea that intelligence and skills are more like foot size or eye color: an unchangeable trait.

3 The topic of growth vs. fixed mindsets, and their effects on student achievement, has been a popular—and controversial—one since Stanford's Carol Dweck published her book, *Mindset: The New Psychology of Success* in 2006. But the recent Stanford study, which involved 168,000 10th-grade students across all of Chile, is the most expansive, and goes the furthest to explore how family income interacts with mindset.

4 Typically, students from low-income families score worse on standardized tests than their wealthier peers. But the researchers found that poor students with growth mindsets performed just as well as wealthy students with fixed mindsets.

5 "Strikingly, students from low-income families (the lowest 10 percent) who had a growth mindset showed comparable test scores with fixed mindset students whose families earned 13 times more (80th percentile)," said the study, which was published in the *Proceedings of the National Academy of Sciences*, and co-authored by Dweck, Susana Claro, and David Paunesko, all of Stanford.

6 The problem is students from low-income families are much less likely to have growth mindsets. "At the extremes, students from the lowest-income families were twice as likely to endorse a fixed mindset as students from the top-income families and schools," according to the study.

Growth Mindset in Students—Deficit Ideology?

7 But is a focus on "growth mindset" just another way of blaming individual students for problems that are institutionalized and overwhelming? Is it another way of saying, hey, if you can't succeed, then there must be something wrong with you?

8 In his blog *The Becoming Radical*, Furman University education professor P. L. Thomas, a former South Carolina high school English teacher, points to the dangers

of "deficit ideology," or the belief that unsuccessful people lack something within themselves to be successful—like grit, or positivity. This kind of thinking discounts the effects of external forces, say racism or poverty, while also overlooking the benefits of wealth and privilege.

"Consequently, we routinely demand of children in the worst situations of life— through no fault of their own—that they somehow magically set aside those lives when they walk into school," Thomas points out. This may be an appealing idea, but it's something that most adults can't do, he adds. **9**

The problem, some advocates say, is not that the more than half of all American children who live in poverty have the wrong mindset. The problem is that more than half of all American children live in poverty. **10**

The researchers do address these concerns: "To be clear, we are not suggesting that structural factors, like income inequality or disparities in school quality, are less important than psychological factors. Nor are we saying that teaching students a growth mindset is a substitute for systemic efforts to alleviate poverty and economic inequality. Such claims would stand at odds with decades of research and our own data." **11**

Rather, they say, their work reveals the way structural inequalities can lead to psychological inequalities, and hopefully suggest ways that educators can more effectively support these students. **12**

How It Works in the Classroom **13**
Almost every teacher—98 percent—surveyed recently by the Education Week Research Center agreed that using growth mindset in the classroom can improve learning. And, importantly, nearly as many also say it will improve instruction.

The catch is that only about 20 percent strongly believe that they're good at fostering growth mindset in students, and they have even less confidence in their colleagues and administrators. Eighty-five percent said they would like to get professional development in this area. **14**

Since publishing her book, Dweck has identified a few ways that teachers are more likely to find success with using a growth mindset in their classes. For one thing, "a growth mindset isn't just about effort," she told *Education Week*. "Students need to try new strategies and seek input from others when they're stuck. They need this repertoire of approaches—not just sheer effort—to learn and improve." **15**

She also suggests that educators remember that effort is a means to an end, which is more learning. Effort is not the goal itself. "Too often nowadays, praise is given to students who are putting forth effort, but *not learning*, in order to make them feel good in the moment: 'Great effort! You tried your best!'" she writes. A better approach, she suggests: "When [students] are stuck, teachers can appreciate their work so far, but add: 'Let's talk about what you've tried, and what you can try next.'" **16**

Dweck also suggests that it's equally important to consider whether teachers themselves have a fixed, or growth, mindset, and to help them adopt a deeper, true growth mindset that will show up in their classroom practices. The key to this, she says, is acknowledging that we all are a mixture of fixed and growth mindsets, and we should watch carefully for our fixed-mindset triggers. **17**

After Reading: Reflect on the Text

Write responses to the following exercises using complete sentences.

6. Review your annotations and recall the lines from the reading you marked as interesting or thought-provoking or that you particularly agree with. Write down these lines and put quotation marks around them to indicate that they are the author's words. After the last quotation mark, write the author's last name and the text page number in parentheses. Then explain why you agree with the lines or find them interesting or stimulating.

7. Review your annotations and recall the lines from the reading that confused you or that you disagree with. Write down these lines and put quotation marks around them to indicate these are the author's words. After the last quotation mark, write the author's last name and the text page number in parentheses. Then explain why you find the lines confusing or disagree with them.

Read to Write Activity 1.3

Engage with the Reading

1. What did researchers find out about the link between poverty and a fixed or growth mindset? What did they find out about the link between students' mindsets and their achievement? Did these links surprise you? Why or why not?

2. The reading selection raises the question whether "a focus on 'growth mindset' [is] just another way of blaming individual students for problems that are institutionalized and overwhelming." What does this quote mean? Do you agree with the quote?

3. Do you have experience with or knowledge of schools in low-income neighborhoods versus those in wealthier communities? Using your knowledge or experiences, explain the differences between low-income and high-income schools and how or why different schools could influence student achievement.

4. Do you feel you come from a low-income family or a high-income family? Do you believe that your family's income influences your mindset as a student? Explain and give examples.

Vocabulary Strategy: Defining Key Terms in the Reading

The Vocabulary Strategy earlier in this chapter explained that authors may define key terms in the writing itself, right before or after the term. Review that advice before completing the Vocabulary Practice.

Vocabulary Practice

Each item below contains a quotation from the reading selection "Impact of Poverty on Students." Write a definition for each underlined word using the information in the sentences.

continued

Answers

6. Answers will vary. Encourage students to explain their thinking and link back to the text.

7. Answers will vary. Encourage students to explain their thinking and link back to the text.

Connect

Activity 1.3 can be found as a writing assignment in Connect.

Answers

1. The researchers found that low-income students are much more likely to have fixed mindsets; however, if poor students have a growth mindset, they can match the academic success of wealthier peers.

2. The quote suggests that problems with schools might be more to blame than the students' mindsets for the lack of achievement of students in poverty. Students may agree or disagree with this statement.

3. Answers will vary; encourage students to explain their thinking, give specific examples, and link back to the text.

4. Answers will vary; encourage students to explain their thinking, give specific examples, and link back to the text.

1. "In his blog *The Becoming Radical*, Furman University education professor P. L. Thomas, a former South Carolina high school English teacher, points to the dangers of '<u>deficit ideology</u>,' or the belief that unsuccessful people lack something within themselves to be successful—like grit, or positivity."

2. "The researchers do address these concerns: 'To be clear, we are not suggesting that <u>structural factors</u>, like income inequality or disparities in school quality, are less important than psychological factors. . . .'"

CHAPTER REVIEW

Key Terms

analyze To break down into parts to understand the whole.

brainstorm To discuss informally with others.

critical thinking The process of actively questioning arguments and evaluating evidence.

draft A version of a paper or other document.

evaluate To determine value or significance.

freewrite To write quickly and continuously in complete sentences but without regard to grammar and spelling errors.

outline A written plan for writing, separating main ideas from supporting points.

sinking in Reading slowly and carefully, usually to understand information.

skim To read or look over quickly, usually to find the main ideas.

synthesize To combine different ideas into a new whole.

text Any printed or written document, including textbooks, other books, articles, essays, and Web sites.

Chapter Summary

1. Successful college students read to learn, persist in the face of difficulties, and try various strategies for resolving confusion.

2. College writing requires time and effort; going through a process and practicing lead to more effective writing.

3. Being motivated and being interested to learn are keys to college success.

4. Successful college students believe that they can learn and have control over their learning.

5. College requires students to think critically about what they read and keep an open mind to new ideas.

6. Define key terms in a reading by looking for definitions in the text or at the end of the reading.

7. Read an infographic by understanding the title and considering the relationship between the text and visuals.

Apply What You Learned

Follow the instructions in each of the following exercises, using complete sentences for your responses.

1. Create a visual or find a picture that demonstrates at least one habit of successful college students. Write a brief summary for the visual or picture to explain the habit.

2. "Reading and Writing about an Infographic" includes an image that contrasts a growth mindset and a fixed mindset. Create an image that shows the habits of successful versus unsuccessful college students. Write a brief summary for the image to explain the habits.

3. Explain in writing what you plan to do to be successful in your college classes.

4. If you completed the survey (in Read to Write Activity 1.1) in the beginning of this chapter, look back over your answers and consider the information in this chapter. What reading, writing, and learning strategies will you use this semester in your college classes?

5. Reflect on your reasons and motivations for attending college. Why are you in college? What are your learning goals?

Works Cited

Academic Literacy: A Statement of Competencies Expected of Students Entering California's Public Colleges and Universities. Intersegmental Committee of the Academic Senates, 2002, senate.universityofcalifornia.edu/_files/reports/acadlit.pdf.

Beyeler, Julia. "Reluctant Readers: Case Studies of Reading and Study Strategies in Introduction to Psychology." *Teaching Developmental Reading: Historical, Theoretical, and Practical Background Readings,* edited by Norman A. Stahl and Hunter Boylan, Bedford/St. Martin's, 1998, pp. 301–16.

Shea, Rachel Hartigan. "Are You Ready for College?" *U.S. News & World Report,* 13 Sept. 2002.

Credits

2 | Active Reading and Writing

Look for these icons throughout the chapter. They signal key strategies to use in Read to Write Activities.

After reading this chapter, you will be able to

- Recognize reading and writing as processes.
- Preview and freewrite before reading.
- Identify the topic, thesis, and main ideas in a reading.
- Annotate and summarize a reading.
- Define words in context.
- Read and write about a pie graph.

Theme: What Is the Effect of Multitasking on Your Work or Learning?

Connect

Assign the LearnSmart Achieve topic "Reading to Understand Literal Meaning" for adaptive learning to accompany this chapter.

Multitasking refers to doing many things at the same time. Look at the photograph in Figure 2.1. How is the man multitasking?

Do you multitask? For example, while you are studying, do you also text on your phone or listen to music? Do you think multitasking makes you *more* productive—or *less* productive? In this chapter, you will read articles about how multitasking affects office workers and college students. You will learn strategies that will help you read with understanding. Specifically, because reading and writing are complementary processes, you will learn how you can use writing before, during,

FIGURE 2.1 Multitasking with Everyday Tasks

©Bananastock/Alamy Stock Photo

Class Activity

Search online for the *DaddyDoinWork.com* website to view a video of Doyin Richards, a father whose photo went "viral." Discuss the ways that parents are often required to multitask. Think about ways that students also multitask.

Class Activity

Before reading, brainstorm with students about what multitasking means and looks like.

Handout and Teaching Tip

Provide a blank "Before, During, and After Reading" graphic, in the Instructor's Resources, and have students write in strategies they currently use. Encourage them to add to their graphic organizers as they read through the chapter.

and after you read to aid your reading comprehension, help you think about your reading, and connect your reading to your life.

RECOGNIZE READING AND WRITING AS PROCESSES

College requires students to be active readers and skillful writers. As with any skill, such as playing a sport or drawing a picture, getting better takes practice. Good writing and good reading don't happen all at once. A *process* is involved.

This section focuses on the reading process. Strategic readers engage in many activities before, during, and after they read to be sure that they comprehend and think critically about what they read. Study Figure 2.2, which identifies some strategies readers can use during the reading process to understand the material. While this is not a complete description of *all* the things readers do, it is a good start.

Moreover, strategic readers rarely read just once. Often, a first reading helps them grasp the main idea or get an overview –the "big picture"–of the passage. Then a second reading may be more analytical or more focused. Even two readings may not be sufficient when readers are faced with understanding challenging or new material. The point is that the reading process is **recursive**; that is, it involves going back over what was read, sometimes many times.

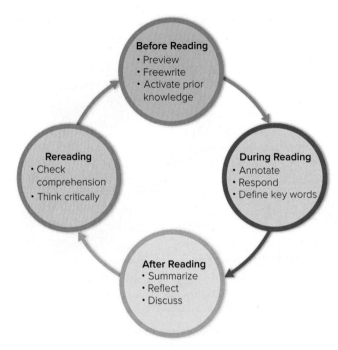

FIGURE 2.2 What Strategic Readers Do during the Reading Process

Much of what you learn in college comes through reading. When you are reading, you want to understand what you read: comprehension is an essential goal. Sometimes it is possible to read all the words on a page and still not truly comprehend what you have read. To explore this idea, try Read to Write Activity 2.1.

Read to Write Activity 2.1

Read for Comprehension 📖

First, read the following short passage, entitled "The Breakaway vs. the Peloton":

> At the pointy end of the peloton, Team Sky controlled the field. However, on the descent a breakaway formed. Relegated to Sky's slipstream, no others could bridge the gap. Finally, a rampaging chase group headed home but were unable to catch the five-man breakaway.

Now test yourself on the material you have read, and answer the following questions.

1. Who controlled the field?

2. What happened on the descent?

3. Who could bridge the gap?

4. How many men were in the breakaway?

5. Summarize the paragraph—that is, restate the main ideas using your own words.

Answers

1. Team Sky controlled the field.

2. A breakaway formed on the descent.

3. No one could bridge the gap.

4. Five men were in the breakaway.

5. The paragraph is about a cycling road race, in which five racers advance to the front of the pack to control and then win the race.

You were probably able to answer correctly questions 1-4 in Read to Write Activity 2.1 but had trouble with the last item, which asks you to **summarize** the paragraph, or restate the main ideas in your own words. Could you successfully summarize what the paragraph is about? Did you really understand what you read? Maybe you guessed that the passage is about a sport. Most likely, you did not really understand it—unless you know something about professional road race cycling. Maybe if you had done some background reading or had **prior**, or background, **knowledge** about cycling or had participated in a bike race yourself, the passage would have made more sense to you.

The point is that you can read all the words on a page and even successfully pass a test on a reading passage without processing and truly understanding what you read. When you are a college student, this kind of mindless reading does not serve your goals well. Instead, you will want to engage actively with your reading and understand what the author is saying. Writing about the reading in your own words can help you test your comprehension.

To sum up: College reading requires thinking. Read actively by engaging in the reading process and by using writing to test your comprehension.

PREVIEWING AND FREEWRITING BEFORE READING

Before you read, it is a good practice to preview the reading material. **Previewing** involves thinking about *what* you will be reading: the subject of the reading. It also involves thinking about *why* you are reading: the purpose for your reading. Think of previewing as a warm-up, like stretching before you exercise. Previewing prepares you mentally for the serious work of reading (see "Strategies for Previewing a Reading"). Furthermore, previewing can activate your prior knowledge (what you already know) on a topic so that you will better understand and remember what you read. The **topic** of a reading is the answer to the question *What subject is the reading about?* The answer can be expressed in a word or a phrase. For instance, the topic of this paragraph is previewing because that is the general subject of the paragraph.

Teaching Tip

Demonstrate how to preview by looking at the headings in the rest of Chapter 2 and anticipating the main ideas.

Strategies for Previewing a Reading

- Look at the *title* and the *headings* to get an overview of the topic.

- Read any *introductory* or *summary* material to identify the main ideas.

- *Skim*, or *glance quickly over*, the reading to get a feeling for its organization.

- Consider the *length* of the reading to estimate how much time you will need to read it.

- Recognize *why* you are reading the material to help you focus on your purpose as you read.

Handout

"Strategies for Previewing a Reading" is a reproducible handout in the Instructor's Resources.

When you preview, do not spend time reading the material. Instead, train yourself to glance at key places, especially the title, the headings, and the introductory headnote. Your goal when previewing is to get an overview of the reading and its *organization*—how the author has structured and presented the content. Then, after previewing, you can read carefully to understand the main ideas and study the topic in depth.

Another effective strategy for preparing to read is to freewrite about the topic. After previewing, you should have a general idea of the reading topic. Then the time is right to spend a few minutes freewriting—jotting down what you know about the topic quickly and continuously. The goal is simply to put your ideas down on paper. Do not worry about spelling mistakes or grammatical errors; your purpose is to get your brain thinking. Research shows that students who activate their prior knowledge before reading are more likely to understand and remember what they read.

Before you read the first article in this chapter, preview the content and freewrite about the topic by answering the "Before Reading" questions. The previewing questions are general—that is, you can apply them to most of your reading and in this way make previewing and freewriting a habit.

READING SELECTION

Connect

You will find a coordinated Power of Process assignment for this reading in your Connect course.

"DON'T MULTITASK: YOUR BRAIN WILL THANK YOU"

Complete the "Before Reading" and "During Reading" assignments. Then read the selection. Finally, complete the "After Reading" assignments.

 Before Reading: Preview; Identify Your Purpose; Recognize Prior Knowledge

Skim the reading "Don't Multitask: Your Brain Will Thank You," which follows. Then write answers to the following questions using complete sentences. Apply the tips after each question to help you answer the question.

1. What is the main topic of the reading?

    Tip: Look at the article title.

Answers

1. Multitasking (or not multitasking) is the topic.

2. Multitasking is not productive.

3. The reading is one continuous article meant to be read continuously and about two pages long.

2. Read the information in italics below the article title. What can you learn from it about the reading?

   Tip: Look for information that summarizes the reading.

3. How is the information organized? How long is the reading?

   Tip: Skim the reading and think about how the paragraphs are arranged. For instance, is the reading one continuous article, or is it divided into separate sections? Is the material meant to be read straight through, or are there graphs, illustrations, or other information that must also be read? How many pages long is the article?

4. What is your purpose for reading?

   Tip: Consider what your instructor expects you to do with the information. Do you have to know it for a test or use it in an essay? Must you apply it in some other way?

5. What do you already know about this topic? Freewrite about it for five minutes.

   Tip: Think about the topic. What comes to mind when you read the title?

 ## During Reading: Connect with the Text

Write responses to the following exercises using complete sentences.

6. As you read, mark any lines you find interesting or thought-provoking or that you particularly agree with. Explain why you agree with the lines or find them interesting or stimulating.

7. As you read, mark any lines that confused you or that you disagree with. Explain why you find the lines confusing or disagree with them.

Don't Multitask: Your Brain Will Thank You

By Issie Lapowsky

Inc.com, 8 April 2013

The following article appeared in Inc.com, *a monthly magazine that spotlights growing companies. Using information from two research studies, the author argues that workers who multitask are not as productive as those who focus their attention on one task at a time.*

---

4. The purpose of reading is to understand more about multitasking and how to apply reading strategies.

5. Answers will vary. Students might describe how, why, or when they multitask.

Answers

6. Answers will vary. Encourage students to relate their own experiences to specific passages in the reading that they agree with, or to explain what they find interesting.

7. Answers will vary. Encourage students to relate their own experiences to specific passages in the reading that they agree with, or to explain their confusion.

The ability to juggle work is a standard job requirement. 1

Researchers have another name for this supposedly desirable skill, however: 2
chronic multitasking.

If this sounds more like an affliction than a résumé booster, that's because 3
research has shown again and again that the human mind isn't meant to multitask.
Even worse, research shows that multitasking can have long-term harmful effects on
brain function.

In a 2009 study, Stanford researcher Clifford Nass challenged 262 college 4
students to complete experiments that involved switching among tasks, filtering
irrelevant information, and using working memory. Nass and his colleagues
expected that frequent multitaskers would outperform nonmultitaskers on at least
some of these activities.

They found the opposite: Chronic multitaskers were abysmal at all three tasks. 5
The scariest part: Only one of the experiments actually involved multitasking,
signaling to Nass that even when they focus on a single activity, frequent
multitaskers use their brains less effectively.

Multitasking is a weakness, not a strength. In 2010, a study by neuroscientists at 6
the French medical research agency Inserm showed that when people focus on two
tasks simultaneously, each side of the brain tackles a different task.

This suggests a two-task limit on what the human brain can handle. Taking on 7
more tasks increases the likelihood of errors, so Nass suggests what he calls the
20-minute rule. Rather than switching tasks from minute to minute, dedicate a
20-minute chunk of time to a single task, then switch to the next one.

His second tip: "Don't be a sucker for email." The average professional spends 8
about 23 percent of the day emailing, studies show. Inspired by that statistic, Gloria
Mark of the University of California, Irvine, and her colleague Stephen Voida
infiltrated an office, cut 13 employees off from email for five days, strapped heart
monitors to their chests, and tracked their computer use. Not surprisingly, the
employees were less stressed when cut off from email. They focused on one task
for longer periods of time and switched screens less often, thereby minimizing
multitasking.

Mark and Voida encourage business owners and their employees to check 9
emails a few scheduled times per day and turn email notifications off the rest of
the time. Adds Voida: "Quick questions are often better asked face to face or by
phone, where they don't add to the huge amount of email we're already dealing with."

 After Reading: Summarize; Reflect

Write responses to the following exercises using complete sentences.

8. To check your comprehension, rewrite the main ideas of the reading in
   your own words.

9. Review your annotations and then consider this: What ideas in the text
   are new to you? What ideas in the text conflict with what you already
   knew before you started reading?

Answers

8. Workers are expected to
multitask, but research
shows multitasking is not
truly possible and may be
detrimental. In one study,
"chronic multitaskers" did
not perform as well as those
who don't multitask.
Another study showed that
multitasking requires each
side of the brain to focus on
different activities. Better
than trying to multitask is to
focus on one thing at a time.

9. Answers will vary.
Encourage students to
reference the text and to
use specific examples to
support their thinking.

Read to Write Activity 2.2

Engage with the Reading

Write responses to the following exercises using complete sentences.

1. Research cited in the article reveals that people who frequently multitask do not work as effectively as nonmultitaskers when they attempt three activities at the same time or even when they focus on just one task. Why do you think individuals who multitask are less productive overall than those who do not?

2. Stanford University researcher Clifford Nass recommends the "20-minute rule"—that is, working on one task for 20 minutes and then switching to another task. How realistic do you think his advice is, especially for office workers?

3. Researchers also recommend checking e-mail at set times during the day rather than checking constantly. Is this good advice, in your view? Why or why not?

Connect

Activity 2.2 can be found as a writing assignment in Connect.

Answers

1. People who multitask may not be able to concentrate.

2. Being able to focus on one task for 20 minutes may depend on one's work environment.

3. This seems like good advice because workers could focus on one task—e-mail—and not multitask.

Vocabulary Strategy: Defining Words in Context in the Reading

Sometimes writers define a word by including a definition—set off by parentheses, commas, or dashes—in the sentence in which the word appears. Other times, writers give strong clues to the meaning of a word by providing examples. For their part, readers can make an educated guess about a word's meaning by considering the *context* of the writing—that is, by thinking about the meaning of the sentence in the work as a whole. When trying to understand an unfamiliar word, always look for clues to its meaning in the sentence in which the word appears—and also think about the larger context.

Vocabulary Practice

Write a definition for each underlined word from the reading selection, "Don't Multitask: Your Brain Will Thank You." Then look up the meaning of the word in a dictionary to check the definition. When you look up a word in a dictionary, do not simply accept the first definition given. Rather, read all the definitions carefully and look at how the word is used. Select the definition that fits the word in the context of the passage. Revise your own definition of the word if necessary.

Example: "<u>Chronic</u> multitasking could be making you less productive."

Answer: *Chronic* might mean doing something a lot because if someone multitasks a lot, he or she would not get much work done.

Dictionary Definitions of *chronic*:

1. Continuing or occurring again and again over a long period of time

2. Always present, such as habitually

continued

Revised answer: *Chronic* **means occurring again and again over a long period of time because that would lead to unproductive work.**

1. "Chronic multitaskers were <u>abysmal</u> at all three tasks."

2. "They focused on one task for longer periods of time and switched screens less often, thereby <u>minimizing</u> multitasking."

IDENTIFYING THE TOPIC, THESIS, AND MAIN IDEAS IN A READING

An important step in comprehending what you read is to locate the main ideas and the important information.

Topic versus Thesis

It is helpful to know the difference between a *topic* and a *thesis*. As we saw earlier in the chapter, the topic of a reading is a word or phrase that describes the reading's subject—what it is about. For instance, if you were asked the topic of the first reading in this chapter, you might answer "multitasking," because that is the general subject of the reading.

The **thesis** of a reading is an answer to the question *What does the author say about the topic?* The answer should be expressed in a complete sentence. For example, if someone asked you about the author's attitude toward the topic of the first reading, you might answer, "Multitasking can make it hard to think and concentrate." Often the thesis is referred to as the main idea of the reading. Figure 2.3 contrasts a topic with a thesis.

FIGURE 2.3 Topic versus Thesis

Topic	Thesis
Is the subject of the reading.	Combines the subject of the reading and the author's attitude toward that subject.
Is expressed in a word or phrase.	Is expressed in a complete sentence.
Example: multitasking	Example: Multitasking can make it hard to think and concentrate.

Identifying Main Ideas

Often writers break up the thesis (the overall main idea) and explain it in different parts of the writing. So in addition to locating the topic and thesis, you should determine the related main ideas the author has presented elsewhere in the reading.

Fortunately, the texts that you read in college are written to provide information. Therefore, the authors make the main ideas clear by giving strong clues. Knowing where to look for these main idea clues can help you recognize the crucial information. Study "Strategies for Locating Main Ideas" to understand where to locate the important ideas in a reading.

Strategies for Locating Main Ideas

Use the following clues in the reading itself.

- **Title and headings.** The title often helps identify an overall main idea in the reading, while a heading usually points to the main idea of a particular paragraph or section.

- **Opening sentence in a paragraph.** The first sentence of the paragraph often states its main idea, in which case it is called the *topic sentence*.

- **Last sentence in paragraph.** The closing sentence may sum up the main idea of a paragraph. In fact, sometimes the main idea of a paragraph is stated in both its opening and closing sentences or in both the opening and closing sentences of a section of the reading.

- **Examples.** Writers often use examples to explain important points and concepts. When you see an example, look for a main idea stated in the text right before or immediately after the example.

- **Repetition.** Writers sometimes repeat words or phrases to stress a main idea.

- **Key words.** Words that represent important concepts or subjects can help readers locate main ideas.

- **Highlighted words and phrases.** A special type style, such as bold or italic type, calls attention to important words and ideas.

Handout

"Strategies for Locating Main Ideas" is a reproducible handout in the Instructor's Resources.

Read to Write Activity 2.3

Read and Write about the Topic, Thesis, and Main Ideas

Review the reading "Don't Multitask: Your Brain Will Thank You" and then write answers to the questions that follow using complete sentences. Apply the tips after each question to help you answer the question. Identify the author or title of the article in your answers. See the Grammar and Style Handbook to learn one strategy for identifying the author or article in a sentence.

1. Identify the topic of the article.

   Tip: Titles often include words that represent the topic. Repeated words in the article can also be clues to the topic.

2. Identify a sentence in the article that states the thesis—the topic plus the author's attitude toward the topic. Write the sentence down and put quotation marks around it.

   Tip: Look for a sentence near the beginning or end of the reading that sums up the overall main idea.

Answers

1. In the article "Don't Multitask," the topic is multitasking.

2. According to the article "Don't Multitask" by Issie Lapowsky, "the human mind isn't meant to multitask."

continued

3. According to the article "Don't Multitask" by Issie Lapowsky, most people cannot effectively do two or more tasks at the same time.

4. According to the article "Don't Multitask" by Issie Lapowsky, "the human mind isn't meant to multitask." Lapowsky explains that "multitasking is a weakness, not a strength." In fact, "there is a two-task limit on what the human brain can handle."

---

3. State the thesis *in your own words*.

Tip: Imagine explaining to a friend what the article says about the topic.

4. Identify main ideas throughout the reading. Write down the main idea sentences and put quotation marks around these.

Tip: Look for sentences that contain the topic and important ideas about the topic. Sentences at the beginning or end of paragraphs often state main ideas.

WRITING WHILE READING: ANNOTATING AND SUMMARIZING

To involve yourself actively while reading, you can keep track of the main ideas by marking them in the text. To think meaningfully about what you read, you can write down your reactions to the text. These practices will help you stay focused on your reading.

Annotating a Text

Some students think that taking notes must involve extensively highlighting the reading with a brightly colored marker, but highlighting information often does not promote understanding and critical thinking. Other techniques for marking up a text may be more effective. Some research indicates that if students *selectively underline* key words or phrases, as well as *restate main ideas in their own words*, they will better understand what they read.

Although there is no one right way to mark a text, it is a good idea to develop a *system* for **annotating**, or taking notes, (see "Strategies for Annotating") and to understand the *purpose* of annotation.

Handout

"Strategies for Annotating" is a reproducible handout in the Instructor's Resources.

Strategies for Annotating

- **Write brief summaries in the margins.** It is important to write summaries in your own words rather than copy words or phrases from the reading. Using your own words will help you understand and remember what you have read. It will also help avoid unintentional *plagiarism*, a serious academic offense involving using someone else's words or ideas as if they were one's own. Summarize in a clear, concise manner so that you can reread your notes. Use abbreviations and symbols freely, as long as you will be able to remember them later.

- **List multiple ideas in a clear way.** For instance, if the text notes that there are "three causes," you could number the three causes; if the text describes causes and effects, you could use arrows to show the relationships.

continued

- **Note examples.** The text's examples not only promote understanding of concepts but also may be a useful way to demonstrate your knowledge on tests. Moreover, examples typically indicate that a main idea is close by in the reading, because if a concept is important, there is often an example to illustrate it. You can mark examples with a particular code, such as "EX."

- **Put key information into charts or graphs.** Pulling out important information from the text and organizing it is one way to make it your own. You may more clearly see the relationships among ideas, or among ideas and examples, in a chart or graph.

- **Jot down possible test questions.** If you are reading to prepare for a test, anticipate test questions. As you read, look for material that you believe will be on the test. If you can frame the information in the form of a question, do so as you are reading.

- **Note and seek clarification of confusing ideas.** You can mark unclear passages with a question mark. Ask your instructor during lecture or office hours to explain the concept, or get your classmates' help. Do not skim over important information; instead, work hard to make sense of it.

- **Underline key words and phrases.** After reading and annotating, underline key words and phrases in the text that will help you recall important information. Use your annotations in the margin to guide your selection of key phrases or sentences—that is, the ones that best sum up the important ideas.

- **Note your reactions.** If you have any questions, thoughts, associations, or responses concerning the reading, note them in the margin as you read so that you will not forget them. Reactions to the text may help you form questions, develop responses, or make connections among topics.

As you gain experience marking your texts, you may develop your own codes for annotating. For instance, you might highlight main ideas in color and circle examples. Whatever symbols or markings you use, be clear and consistent so that you will always know what your marks mean.

Summarizing a Text

An important part of annotating is to write brief summaries in the margin. As we saw earlier in this chapter, to summarize means to condense the information and to rewrite it in your own words. As Read to Write Activity 2.1, earlier in this chapter, demonstrates (the "Breakaway vs. the Peloton" paragraph), accurately summarizing a text is an important strategy for assessing comprehension. Moreover, an effectively written summary may be valuable in your own writing, for example, as background information on a topic or as evidence to support your original thesis.

"Strategies for Summarizing" is a step-by-step guide for writing summaries of main sections of a reading, using "Don't Multitask: Your Brain Will Thank You" as an example.

Handout

"Strategies for Summarizing" is a reproducible handout in the Instructor's Resources.

Strategies for Summarizing

The examples for these steps are from the reading selection "Don't Multitask: Your Brain Will Thank You" by Issie Lapowsky.

1. **Chunk the reading by dividing it into logical groups.** If the reading includes subheadings, the paragraphs under each subheading constitute a group. If there are no subheadings, look for connections between paragraphs to create logical groups.

   Example of chunking the reading: In "Don't Multitask," the first three paragraphs (or the first four sentences) introduce the reading and the topic of multitasking. Then the next two paragraphs describe a Stanford study on multitasking. Paragraphs 1–3 could be considered one chunk, and paragraphs 4 and 5 another chunk.

2. **Identify the main ideas in each section of the reading.** Look for clues to the main ideas, such as repeated words that express important concepts. Look in key places in the text, such as topic sentences or concluding sentences in paragraphs, for main ideas. Use headings or titles, too, as a guide to main ideas.

   Example of figuring out the topic from repeated words: The word *multitasking* appears in paragraphs 2, 3, 4, 5, 6, and 8.

   Example of finding the idea in a key place in text: The sentence "research shows that multitasking can have long-term harmful effects on brain function" comes at the end of the introduction and is the main idea of the reading.

3. **Focus on key words or phrases that exemplify the main idea.** No need to underline the entire sentence; rather, focus on the key concepts most important to the main idea. This technique will help you to condense the information.

   Example of main idea sentence with key words and phrases underlined: "Even worse, <u>research</u> shows that <u>multitasking</u> can have <u>long-term harmful effects</u> on <u>brain function</u>."

4. **Jot down the key words or concepts in your own words**. You don't have to write a sentence on the first attempt. Instead, write as much of the main ideas as possible in your own words. Use fresh words and new ways to rephrase the ideas. If you cannot replace key words or if phrases are especially well written, then you may include these in your summary with quotation marks around them.

   Example of key concepts written in own words:
   - Multitasking is bad for thinking.
   - Research proves that multitasking is not good in the "long term."

5. **Rewrite the important ideas in your own words in complete sentences.** It may take several attempts to write a summary sentence that is accurate and complete, and that uses your own words.

continued

Example summary, first draft: Multitasking can have bad effects on people's brains.

Comment: Too much like the original text. Rewrite using more of your own words.

Example summary, second draft: Research proves that multitasking is bad for thinking.

Comment: Better, but *bad* is vague and also implies judgment. Replace with a more specific and neutral word.

Example summary, final draft: Research proves that multitasking is detrimental to one's thinking.

Comment: Much better.

6. **Credit the source of the summary.** When you summarize other people's ideas, you must give them credit for their thinking. You can do this by either (a) writing the author and title of the reading at the beginning of your summary sentence or (b) including the author and page number in parenthesis after the summary sentence.

Example of crediting a source by citing the author and title of the reading at the beginning of the sentence: According to the article "Don't Multitask: Your Brain Will Thank You" by Issie Lapowsky, research proves that multitasking is detrimental to one's thinking.

Example of crediting the source by citing the author and page number in parenthesis after the sentence: Research proves that multitasking is detrimental to one's thinking (Lapowsky 34).

Study Figure 2.4, which provides annotations for the reading selection "Don't Multitask: Your Brain Will Thank You." The article was annotated after several readings. In the middle is the article.

- In the right margin of the article are brief summaries of the main ideas, which are highlighted in blue. The thesis is double-underlined.
- In the left margin are the reader's reactions ("responses") to the reading.
- Examples are clearly marked in the text (underlined) and in the right column ("EX"), where the relationship among ideas is explained.
- Definitions of unfamiliar words appear in the left margin, highlighted in yellow.

Notice that the annotations are consistent and well organized. They do not overwhelm the text. Rather, they selectively point out the thesis, the main ideas and examples, and the reader's reactions.

In the next section, you will have a chance to apply your writing strategies of freewriting and annotating. You will preview a reading; identify the thesis and the other main ideas; and take notes for the purpose of aiding your comprehension and developing a response to the readings.

Teaching Tip

FIGURE 2.4 Annotated Article

Have students develop a system (i.e., underline main ideas, check examples) to follow when annotating.

Responses	Annotated Article	Main Ideas
	Don't Multitask: Your Brain Will Thank You By Issie Lapowsky	_Thesis_ = Multitasking is not good for thinking.

Yes! Agree.
"chronic" = happening frequently or most of the time
"multitasking" = perform more than one activity at the same time
That sounds bad: multitasking has a harmful effect on thinking
	The ability to juggle work is a standard job requirement.
	    Researchers have another name for this supposedly desirable skill, however: chronic multitasking.
	    If this sounds more like an affliction than a résumé booster, that's because research has shown again and again that the human mind isn't meant to multitask. Even worse, research shows that multitasking can have long-term harmful effects on brain function.
	    In a 2009 study, Stanford researcher Clifford Nass challenged 262 college students to complete experiments that involved switching among tasks, filtering irrelevant information, and using working memory. Nass and his colleagues expected that frequent multitaskers would outperform nonmultitaskers on at least some of these activities.
		Main idea: People think multitasking is necessary, but research shows it can be bad for your thinking.
		
		EX: College students who were multitaskers did not do as well on tests involving memory and focus.

"abysmal" = extremely poor or bad	They found the opposite: Chronic multitaskers were abysmal at all three tasks. The scariest part: Only one of the experiments actually involved multitasking, signaling to Nass that even when they focus on a single activity, frequent multitaskers use their brains less effectively. Multitasking is a weakness, not a strength.	Main idea: Multitasking negatively affects people's thinking.
Sounds very efficient! But if people can do two things at once, isn't that multitasking?	In 2010, a study by neuroscientists at the French medical research agency Inserm showed that when people focus on two tasks simultaneously, each side of the brain tackles a different task. This suggests a two-task limit on what the human brain can handle. Taking on more tasks increases the likelihood of errors, so Nass suggests what he calls the 20-minute rule. Rather than switching tasks from minute to minute, dedicate a 20-minute chunk of time to a single task, then switch to the next one.	EX: Research shows that when people do two tasks, one side of brain deals with each task. Main idea: People can do no more than two things at one time. Better to focus on one task for a while, then switch to the other.
Good quote: e-mail can be a distraction Maybe e-mail is part of work?	His second tip: "Don't be a sucker for email." The average professional spends about 23 percent of the day emailing, studies show. Inspired by that statistic, Gloria Mark of the University of California, Irvine, and her colleague Stephen Voida infiltrated an office, cut 13 employees off from email for five days, strapped heart monitors to their chests, and tracked their computer use. Not surprisingly, the employees were less stressed when cut off from email. They focused on one task for longer periods of time and switched screens less often, thereby minimizing multitasking.	EX: Workers who don't check e-mail constantly are less stressed. Better to focus on one job for a longer period of time to be more productive.
I wonder what kind of work these people do.	Mark and Voida encourage business owners and their employees to check emails a few scheduled times per day and turn email notifications off the rest of the time. Adds Voida: "Quick questions are often better asked face to face or by phone, where they don't add to the huge amount of email we're already dealing with."	

READING SELECTION

"MULTITASKING MAY HURT YOUR PERFORMANCE BUT IT MAKES YOU FEEL BETTER"

Complete the "Before Reading" and "During Reading" assignments. Then read the selection. Finally, complete the "After Reading" assignments.

Before Reading: Preview; Freewrite

Skim the reading "Multitasking May Hurt Your Performance but It Makes You Feel Better," which follows. Write the answers to the following questions using complete sentences.

1. Do you multitask when you read or study? If so, why? If not, why not?

2. Read the title of the following reading and the information that immediately precedes the reading. Use these clues to predict what the reading will be about.

During Reading: Find the Main Ideas; Find Supporting Examples

3. Read the reading selection more than once. When you feel that you understand the material, annotate the text by underlining the thesis and the main ideas and by marking the supporting examples.

Multitasking May Hurt Your Performance but It Makes You Feel Better

Ohio State University, 30 April 2012

This article from the Ohio State University Web site describes research conducted by a faculty member and by a graduate student in Communications Studies. The researchers looked at when and why college students multitask. They concluded that students enjoy multitasking and make it a habit even when it does not help them study.

COLUMBUS, Ohio - People aren't very good at media multitasking—like reading a book while watching TV—but do it anyway because it makes them feel good, a new study suggests.   1

The findings provide clues as to why multitasking is so popular, even though many studies show it is not productive.   2

Connect

You will find a coordinated Power of Process assignment for this reading in your Connect course.

Answers

1. Answers will vary. Encourage students to provide specific instances of what they do when studying.

2. The article will be about multitasking, specifically how it makes people less productive but feel good.

3. Thesis is the opening sentence: "People aren't very good at media multitasking—like reading a book while watching TV—but do it anyway because it makes them feel good, a new study suggests."

   Main ideas include "multitasking often gave the students an emotional boost, even when it hurt their cognitive functions, such as studying"; "people show poorer performance on a variety of tasks when they try to juggle multiple media sources at the same time"; "participants were more likely to multitask when they reported an increase in cognitive needs (such as study or work) or habitual needs or both"; "the students reported that the multitasking was very good at meeting their emotional needs"; and "habits played an important role in the use of media multitasking."

Researchers had college students record all of their media use and other activities for 28 days, including why they used various media sources and what they got out of it. **3**

The findings showed that multitasking often gave the students an emotional boost, even when it hurt their cognitive functions, such as studying. **4**

"There's this myth among some people that multitasking makes them more productive," said Zheng Wang, lead author of the study and assistant professor of communication at Ohio State University. **5**

"But they seem to be misperceiving the positive feelings they get from multitasking. They are not being more productive—they just feel more emotionally satisfied from their work." **6**

Take, for example, students who watched TV while reading a book. They reported feeling more emotionally satisfied than those who studied without watching TV, but also reported that they didn't achieve their cognitive goals as well, Wang said. **7**

"They felt satisfied not because they were effective at studying, but because the addition of TV made the studying entertaining. The combination of the activities accounts for the good feelings obtained," Wang said. **8**

Wang conducted the study with John Tchernev, a graduate student in Communication at Ohio State. Their results appear online in the *Journal of Communication.* . . . **9**

Wang said many studies done in laboratory settings have found that people show poorer performance on a variety of tasks when they try to juggle multiple media sources at the same time: for example, going from texting a friend, to reading a book, to watching an online video. **10**

But surveys show that media multitasking is only becoming more popular. The question, Wang said, is why do people do so much multitasking if it actually impairs their performance? **11**

To answer that question, Wang said they had to move out of the laboratory and into real life. They recruited 32 college students who agreed to carry a cellphone-like device and report on their activities three times each day for four weeks. **12**

The participants reported on each media use (such as computer, radio, print, television) and subtypes (for computer use, whether they were web browsing, using social networking, etc.). They reported the type of activity, the duration, and whether any other activities were performed simultaneously (in other words, whether they were multitasking). **13**

They also provided their motivations for each activity or combination of activities from a list of seven potential needs, including social, fun/entertainment, study/work, and habits/background noise. For each need, they reported the strength of the need on a 10-point scale, and whether those needs were met on a 4-point scale. **14**

The results showed that participants were more likely to multitask when they reported an increase in cognitive needs (such as study or work) or habitual needs or both. **15**

That means, for example, that the students were more likely to multitask when they needed to study (a cognitive need). 16

But one of the key findings of the study is that this multitasking didn't do a very good job of satisfying their cognitive needs which actually motivate the multitasking in the first place, Wang said. That's probably because their other media use distracted them from the job of studying. However, the students reported that the multitasking was very good at meeting their emotional needs (fun/entertainment/relaxing)—interestingly, a need they weren't even seeking to fulfill. 17

In addition, the results showed that habits played an important role in the use of media multitasking. 18

"Our findings showed that habitual needs increase media multitasking and are also gratified from multitasking," she said. 19

This suggests that people get used to multitasking, which makes them more likely to continue. 20

"We found what we call a dynamical feedback loop. If you multitask today, you're likely to do so again tomorrow, further strengthening the behavior over time," she said. 21

"This is worrisome because students begin to feel like they need to have the TV on or they need to continually check their text messages or computer while they do their homework. It's not helping them, but they get an emotional reward that keeps them doing it. 22

"It is critical that we carefully examine the long-term influence of media multitasking on how we perform on cognitive tasks." 23

The study was supported by a grant from the National Science Foundation. 24

 ## After Reading: Summarize

Write responses to the following exercises using complete sentences.

4. Review your annotations of the main ideas; then summarize those ideas in your own words.

5. Review your annotations and summarize the thesis of the reading in one sentence in your own words. Identify the author or title of the reading in your sentence.

Pair and Share

Compare your annotations of the reading selection with those of a classmate. Focus on the annotations of the main ideas and examples. Did you locate the same main ideas? What clues did you use to find the main ideas?

Connect

Activity 2.4 can be found as a writing assignment in Connect.

Answers

1. Students might enjoy other activities, such as TV watching or music listening, more than studying or reading.

2. This sentence means that multitasking does not help students learn, even though studying may be why they multitask.

3. Students may not give up multitasking if they enjoy doing it.

Read to Write Activity 2.4

Engage with the Reading

Write responses to the following exercises using complete sentences.

1. The author reports that students who multitask while studying get an "emotional boost" and have more "positive feelings." Why do you think students feel good about multitasking? What might these positive feelings suggest about students' attitudes toward schoolwork?

2. The author writes that "one key finding of the study is that . . . multitasking didn't do a very good job of satisfying [students'] cognitive needs which actually motivate the multitasking in the first place." What does this mean? Explain in your own words.

3. If students realized that multitasking while studying was not helping them to learn, do you think they would stop watching TV or listening to music while studying? Explain your answer.

Pair and Share

Discuss your explanation of the study's key finding (exercise 2 in Read to Write Activity 2.4) with a classmate's explanation. Try to come to a consensus (that is, an agreement) about the meaning of this sentence.

Teaching Tip

Ask students to report out to the class their answers to the Pair and Share question.

Vocabulary Strategy: Defining Words in Context in the Reading

The Vocabulary Strategy earlier in this chapter explained that you can sometimes figure out the definition of a word by looking for clues in the writing. When you are trying to understand the definition of an unfamiliar word, always look for information on its meaning in the sentence in which the word appears, and also consider the larger context.

Vocabulary Practice

Write a definition for each underlined word. These words were selected from the reading "Multitasking May Hurt Your Performance but It Makes You Feel Better" because they are repeated. Two sentences for each word, from different places in the article, are given.

Answers

1. Media are different means of communicating information.

2. *Cognitive* relates to thinking.

1. "People aren't very good at <u>media</u> multitasking—like reading a book while watching TV—but do it anyway because it makes them feel good, a new study suggests."

   "The participants reported on each <u>media</u> use (such as computer, radio, print, television) and subtypes (for computer use, whether they were web browsing, using social networking, etc.)."

continued

2. "The findings showed that multitasking often gave the students an emotional boost, even when it hurt their <u>cognitive</u> functions, such as studying."

"The results showed that participants were more likely to multitask when they reported an increase in <u>cognitive</u> needs (such as study or work) or habitual needs or both."

READING AND WRITING ABOUT PIE GRAPHS

A *pie graph* (or circle graph) is so named because it looks like a pie that has been sliced up. Each "slice" in the pie graph represents a percentage or a numerical value. The size of a given slice corresponds to the fraction of the whole it represents. So a smaller slice represents a smaller percentage or number than a larger slice. By comparing the slices of the pie, readers can visualize the relationships among the values. Like other graphics, a pie graph can be a source of information to use when writing an essay, just as written texts are.

To read a pie graph

- Start with the title or caption to identify what overall information the graph is presenting.

- Read the information pertaining to each slice of the graph and compare the numerical values.

- Review the key or other explanatory information.

FIGURE 2.5 **Time Use on an Average Weekday for Full-Time University and College Students**

Source: Bureau of Labor Statistics; American Time Use Survey.

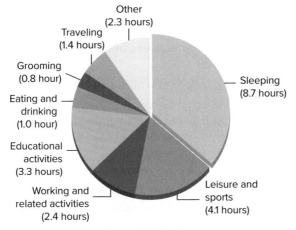

Total = 24.0 hours

Note: Data include individuals, ages 15 to 49, who were enrolled full time at a university or college. Data include non-holiday weekdays and are averages for 2010–14.

Answers

1. The topic is college students' time use.

2. Students spend most of their time sleeping.

3. Students spend the least amount of time on grooming.

4. Leisure and sports account for more time than working or than educational activities, so students spend more time enjoying themselves.

5. The graph does not make clear if students multitask.

Study the pie graph shown in Figure 2.5 and answer these questions:

1. What is the topic of the pie graph?
2. What activity do university and college students spend *most* of their time on each day?
3. What activity do college students spend the *least* amount of time on each day?
4. According to the information in the graph, do students spend more time working, studying, or enjoying themselves? Explain.
5. From looking at this graph, can you tell how much time students multitask? Why or why not?

CHAPTER REVIEW

Key Terms

annotating Marking, highlighting, or taking notes on a text.

previewing Quickly reviewing the content of a text before reading it.

prior knowledge Information that a reader already knows about a subject.

recursive Referring to a process that repeats or goes back over.

summarize Restate the main ideas in one's own words.

thesis The topic of a reading plus the author's opinion about that topic, expressed in a complete sentence.

topic The subject of a reading, expressed in a word or phrase.

Chapter Summary

1. Active reading is a process that involves understanding, writing, and thinking about what you read.
2. Previewing and freewriting before you read can prepare you mentally to do the serious work of reading.
3. Identifying the topic and then locating and marking the thesis and main ideas in a reading can help you to understand what you read.
4. Annotating by marking, taking notes on, and summarizing a text can help you actively read, learn, and respond to a text.
5. Consistently applying the writing strategies of freewriting and annotating while reading will aid your comprehension and help you develop a response to your reading.

6. You can define words by using context clues, such as definitions or examples in the reading.

7. To read a pie graph, start with the title and any caption. Then identify the information in each slice of the graph, and review the key as needed.

Apply What You Learned

Follow the instructions in each of the following exercises, using complete sentences for your responses.

1. List the writing strategies that best help you understand what you read. These could be strategies covered in this chapter or ones you have developed on your own.

2. What have you learned about multitasking from reading the articles in this chapter? How might you apply that knowledge to your own study habits or reading behavior? Give examples from the readings and/or from your own experience to explain.

3. Locate an article (not in this chapter) on multitasking. Read the article and annotate it, following the strategies in this chapter for locating main ideas and annotating a reading.

Credits

pp. 33–34: Lapowsky, Issie. "Don't Multitask: Your Brain Will Thank You." *Inc.*, 1 Apr. 2013. All rights reserved. Used with permission of The YGS Group; **pp. 43–45:** Grabmeier, Jeff. "Multitasking May Hurt Your Performance but It Makes You Feel Better." *Research and Innovation Communications*, The Ohio State University. All rights reserved. Used with permission; **p. 47:** From American Time Use Survey. Bureau of Labor Statistics, U.S. Department of Labor, www.bls.gov/tus/charts/students.htm.

Answers

1. Writing strategies that help with reading include summarizing the text, writing responses or reactions to the reading, underlining main ideas, and defining vocabulary words.

2. The readings in the chapter stress that it's not really possible and certainly not productive to multitask. Students should concentrate on their reading and not try to do other things, such as listen to music, watch television, or check their social media or cell phones, while studying.

3. Answers will vary.

Reading and Writing during the Writing Process

Look for these icons throughout the chapter. They signal key strategies to use in Read to Write Activities.

After reading this chapter, you will be able to

- Identify steps in the writing process.
- Define the purpose of a writing task.
- Read and write to choose a topic and generate ideas.
- Compose a rough draft.
- Revise, edit, and proofread with your reader in mind.
- Define unfamiliar words in context and check their meaning.
- Read and write about an illustration.

Theme: How Do Writers Write?

Connect

Assign the LearnSmart Achieve topic "The Writing Process" for adaptive learning to accompany this chapter.

Class Activity

Before students read the chapter, ask them to draw a picture of a writer. Then discuss their images and what they think writers do.

What do you picture in your mind's eye when you hear the word "writer"? You may—or may not—be surprised that writers are a diverse group of people. In Figure 3.1 are three writers, all of whom are successful, published authors and all of whom write different types of books for different readers for different reasons. Suze Orman is the author of many best-selling books about personal finance; Malcolm Gladwell has written several popular books about research in psychology; and Gene Luen Yang created an award-winning graphic novel for young adults.

What do you think writers do to write? Do they sit and think until ideas come into their heads and flow onto the paper? Not likely! As discussed in the chapter

"Introduction to College Reading and Writing," writing requires considerable time and effort. Author Suze Orman sums up her approach to writing:

> Writing is hard work, not magic. It begins with deciding why you are writing and whom you are writing for. What is your intent? What do you want the reader to get out of it? What do you want to get out of it? It's also about making a serious time commitment and getting the project done. (qtd. in Ryan 165)

FIGURE 3.1 Three Published Authors

From left to right: Suze Orman, Malcolm Gladwell, and Gene Luen Yang.
©s_bukley/Shutterstock; ©Araya Diaz/Getty Images; ©Jeff Malet/Jeff Malet Photography/Newscom

Orman's comments are sound advice not only for writing books but for writing in college. How do you feel about writing? How does writing help you as a college student?

In this chapter, we will consider what it means to be a writer and why writing is important. We will also examine the process most writers engage in, from the idea stage to a finished piece of writing.

AN OVERVIEW: IDENTIFYING STEPS IN THE WRITING PROCESS

Recall the reading process described in the chapter "Active Reading and Writing." Strategic writers go through a similar process as they write a paragraph, an essay, or any other text. Figure 3.2 illustrates the writing process.

As a strategic college writer, you should think and read before you write. You will want to write more than one draft. (Recall that a draft is an attempt at composing a complete piece of writing.) Often, you will compose a first draft to get ideas onto paper and then use subsequent drafts to organize and improve those ideas. You must apply your reading skills to evaluate the work carefully. Like the reading process, the writing process is recursive; as a strategic college writer, you may want to go over paragraphs or papers multiple times (and sometimes, painfully, back to the start) as you write.

FIGURE 3.2 The Writing Process

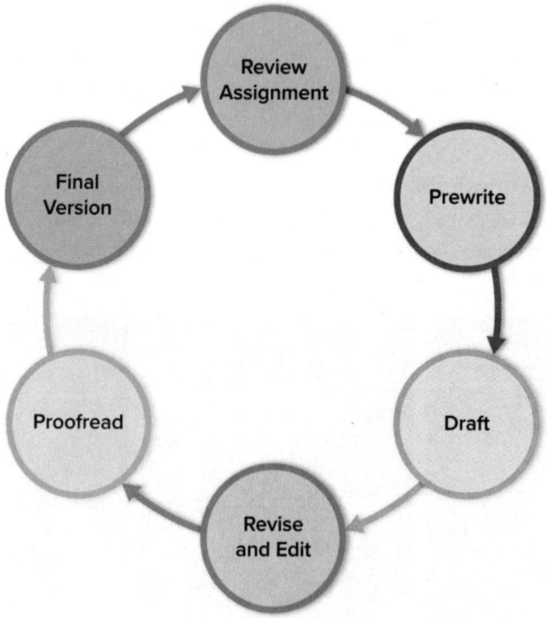

DEFINING THE PURPOSE OF A WRITING TASK

Writing can help you in college in many ways. It can help to clarify your thinking on a topic, understand what you have read, or remember what you heard in class. For instance, just as freewriting before reading activates prior knowledge of a topic, annotating a text while reading enables you to identify important ideas, and reflecting in writing after reading allows you to assess the author's main points.

Sometimes the writing you do in college will be for your own study purposes. For example, taking notes during class to remember important concepts or rewriting your notes to prepare for an exam might involve writing that only you will see.

Other times, instructors assign writing. Writing assignments may be designed for students' learning or to enable an instructor to see what students know or don't know. It's important to understand the purpose of assigned writing and therefore how to approach the assignment. We can place assigned writing into two broad categories:

- **Low-stakes writing**, which tends to be informal writing for your own learning.

- **High-stakes writing**, which is more formal writing that will typically be read and evaluated by an instructor.

In Figure 3.3, we review the features and purposes of these two types of writing.

Teaching Tip

Identify the assigned writing for the class as either low stakes or high stakes.

FIGURE 3.3 Low-Stakes versus High-Stakes Writing

Type of Writing	Low Stakes	High Stakes
Purpose	Writing to learn	Writing to demonstrate learning
Goal	Process information or discover ideas	Show mastery of material or original thinking
What It Looks Like	May be messy, disorganized, or contain errors	Is professional, polished, and proofread
Examples	• Jot down three things you learned in class. • Freewrite possible answers to a test question. • Explain the process you used to figure out a math problem. • Write a rough draft of a paper.	• Record a lab report in a biology class. • Compose a paragraph answer to a question on a midterm exam. • Put together a research paper in a history class. • Write an essay in an English class.
How It Is Assessed	• Typically not graded, but maybe assessed for completeness or for fulfilling requirements	• Typically graded

Whether you engage in low-stakes or high-stakes writing, take your writing seriously and put in your best effort. Low-stakes writing assignments often lay the groundwork for high-stakes writing assignments, so playing your A game during low-stakes writing can pay off with a quality piece of high-stakes writing.

The Read to Write activities in this chapter lead you through the process of completing a reading and writing assignment. Take a few moments now to read the topics in Read to Write Activity 3.1. Evaluate the topics. Which ones appeal to you? About which topics do you think you might have something to say?

Read to Write Activity 3.1

Evaluate Topics ⚬ⁿⁱ

To help you focus your reading and plan a piece of writing, review and evaluate the writing topics that follow by marking how interesting you find each one. Check "Interesting topic," "Maybe I would write on this topic," or "Can't relate to this topic" for each topic. By the end of this chapter, as you proceed through the Read to Write activities, you will have completed a brief essay, of about 250 words, based on one of these topics.

1. Some people love to write; others hate it. Some people enjoy creative writing, such as poems, songs, and blogs; others prefer informational writing, such as reports and research. Describe your feelings about writing. In your response, consider the following.

   • When do you like to write? Describe a situation when writing was enjoyable for you.

continued

- When is writing challenging for you? Are there times when you hate to write? Describe a situation when writing was difficult for you.

  ☐ Interesting topic
  ☐ Maybe I could write on this topic
  ☐ Can't relate to this topic

2. Describe your past experiences with writing in school. In your response, consider the following:
   - Describe one particularly good experience you had with writing in your past education (this could be in an English class or in another subject). Explain why it was positive.
   - Describe one particularly bad experience you had with writing in your past education and explain why it was unpleasant.

   ☐ Interesting topic
   ☐ Maybe I could write on this topic
   ☐ Can't relate to this topic

3. Describe your experiences with low-stakes and high-stakes writing assignments in school and what you learned from these assignments. In your response, consider the following:
   - Give an example of a low-stakes writing assignment you engaged in. Describe the assignment and to what degree it helped you to learn.
   - Give an example of a high-stakes writing assignment in school. Describe the assignment and to what degree it helped you to learn.

   ☐ Interesting topic
   ☐ Maybe I could write on this topic
   ☐ Can't relate to this topic

4. Describe your earliest memories with reading and writing, or your experiences with reading and writing growing up as a child. In your response, consider the following:
   - How did you learn to read or write? Describe what you remember about learning to read or write at home or at school and the feelings you associate with these processes.
   - What were reading and writing like in your family? Did family members read to you as a child or encourage you to write?

   ☐ Interesting topic
   ☐ Maybe I could write on this topic
   ☐ Can't relate to this topic

PREWRITING: CHOOSING A TOPIC AND GENERATING AND ORGANIZING IDEAS

Let's assume you have a writing assignment for a college class. Whether you are writing for yourself or for a graded assignment, getting started may feel like the hardest part. You must have an idea to write about; then you must think of something to say. It's easy to get stuck trying to come up with the perfect topic or even just *any* topic to write about. Strategic college writers know that beginning to write can be hard, and they have several strategies for getting started.

Choosing a Topic

Your writing topic may depend on your assignment, your instructor, or your class goals. Some instructors will give you general suggestions for writing and let you narrow down the topic. For instance, your instructor might ask you to select a common problem for college students and propose a solution. In this case, you could select any important topic to write about that is relevant to campus life—for example, the problem of maintaining a healthy weight and getting enough exercise or the challenges of studying and working while in college. Or the instructor might encourage you to write about whatever interests you most. With this type of assignment, you can select *any* topic, usually with instructor approval. See "Strategies for Selecting a Writing Topic" for ideas on choosing a compelling topic.

Strategies for Selecting a Writing Topic

- **Understand the requirements of the assignment. Can you select your own topic, or must you choose a topic the instructor has provided?**

  Example: Read to Write Activity 3.1, earlier in this chapter, presents four topics. If your instructor requires you to write about one of these topics, then you would need to select one of these to write about.

- **Select a topic you are interested in and would enjoy writing about.**

  Example: Read to Write Activity 3.1 asks you to evaluate topics based on your interest, so you could select a topic you marked as "Interesting." If you marked more than one topic as "Interesting," consider what you would most like to write about. For instance, if you enjoy writing poems, you might describe how poems are enjoyable but also challenging for you to write for topic 1.

- **Select a topic about which you have something thoughtful to write.**

  Example: Suppose you recently had a positive experience writing a paper in your English class because the topic inspired you, but a discouraging experience writing an in-class essay in history because you were anxious about the time pressure. These experiences could be discussed and analyzed for topic 2.

- **Check with the instructor to confirm that your topic is appropriate for the assignment before writing.**

  Example: If you enjoy writing and illustrating comics, you might ask your instructor if writing comic books would be appropriate for topic 1.

Handout

"Strategies for Selecting a Writing Topic" is a reproducible handout in the Instructor's Resources.

Generating and Organizing Ideas

Once you have a topic, you can start thinking about that topic and preparing to write. Writers typically do not write straight through their assignment from beginning to end; instead, many writers start with warm-up exercises—just as you might warm up before going for a five-mile run. This stage in the writing process is called **prewriting** (the prefix *pre-* means "before") because the thinking, reading, and writing prepare you to compose a first draft. Have you ever told a funny story to a friend and realized later that you could have added more details to make the story even better? Prewriting gives you the chance to think of more good ideas to use when you write the first draft. Prewriting can save time later in the writing process.

Let's imagine that you are taking a psychology course in which you are studying the effect of sleep on memory and learning. The instructor assigns the class to write on this topic: *Explain the relationship between sleep and learning.* You have to apply the information from class to yourself or to college students in general. How should you proceed? Here are some strategies you might use to generate ideas.

Review. Review your assigned readings, lecture notes, or class notes. Look for ideas, details, and examples related to the topic you are exploring. Take notes on ideas related to your topic or annotate the readings. Here is an example from a review of class materials.

Sample Annotated Text

Text	Your Notes
The National Sleep Foundation has found that 63 percent of college students, on average, do not get enough sleep. This causes 15 percent of students to fall asleep in class semi-regularly and lose 30 percent of the knowledge they have gained during the class time when paying attention.	*Good use of statistics to show lack of sleep interferes with learning*

Freewrite. Recall that *freewrite* means to write quickly and continuously. To help shape your ideas, you can write down everything you can think of on the topic. Do not worry about grammar or spelling; just get as many thoughts onto the page as you can. Some writers use a timer to motivate themselves to write for a certain length of time, such as ten minutes. When you have finished freewriting, review your work to look for any strong ideas you might use to develop your writing, as well as examples or details to support those ideas. Here is a partial example of freewriting.

Sample Freewriting

College students need sleep; that's because they work hard studying, and some even work, too—they have jobs. This means they get home late and stay up late studying, then have to get up and go to class . . .

List. Listing also involves putting ideas down on the page, but in a list form, such as a bulleted list. For instance, if you have to compare two things, you might list characteristics or examples of each. Notice in the following example how the writer begins to organize information by lining up contrasting details under each heading.

Sample Lists

Benefits of getting enough sleep	Drawbacks of not getting enough sleep
• Research shows rested brains think better and retain more information • Can pay attention in class and learn more • Feel better physically and emotionally	• Sleep deprivation makes people forgetful • Increases the chances of falling asleep during class and missing information • Makes people feel cranky, irritable

Create a Graphic Organizer. A **graphic organizer** is a visual representation of the relationships among ideas. It might use shapes or lines to show these connections. To get started writing, you might prefer a visual approach by putting ideas in a few words, with the connections shown between or among words or ideas. You can write the main idea in the middle of a page (take your pick—use a circle or square or any shape that works for you) and then link to supporting examples, details, and information in connected bubbles. Figure 3.4 shows an example of a graphic organizer.

FIGURE 3.4 Sample Graphic Organizer

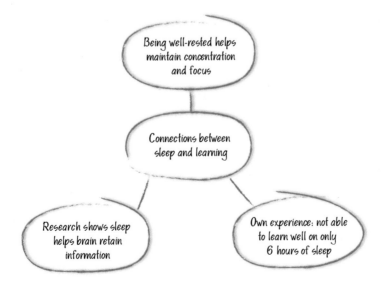

Outline. To begin organizing your ideas before writing, try outlining, which can be a successful strategy. An *informal outline* indicates in brief what you will include in the parts of your paragraph or paper—the beginning, middle, and end—as in the following example. Outlines show the main ideas, as well as the supporting information, often by indenting or numbering the support under main ideas.

Sample Informal Outline

Main Idea: Sleep is important for college students' success
- *Support: Research shows that well-rested brains function better*
- *Support: Example of working late and taking early morning class—not successful strategy*
- *Support: Example of changing work hours to get enough sleep and did better in class*
Closing: Sleep is critical to being a good student.

Discuss the Topic. To generate ideas, you could discuss the topic with classmates, family, or friends. You can suggest ideas and see what other people think about these—if they feel your ideas make sense or are interesting. You can brainstorm for examples to support your ideas, asking others whether the examples are effective or asking for further support.

Sample Discussion

Jenna: I'm writing a paper about how college students need to get enough sleep to do well academically. So, I'm thinking of using the time I was working the late shift at a convenience store as an example in the paper. Do you think this would work?
Luisa: I like that idea. I remember how you fell asleep in that 8 a.m. class one time! That story will really make the paper more interesting.

Read to Write Activity 3.2

Choose a Topic and Generate Ideas

Write responses to the following exercises using complete sentences.

1. Review your responses to Read to Write Activity 3.1 earlier in this chapter. Choose a topic to write about. What topic did you select, and why?

continued

Connect

Activity 3.2 can be found as a writing assignment in Connect.

2. Based on what you have read in this chapter, select one strategy for generating and organizing ideas. Use that method to generate ideas for the topic you chose. For inspiration, look at the graphic organizer that one student, Jane, created in response to topic 1 (Figure 3.5).

FIGURE 3.5 Jane's Graphic Organizer

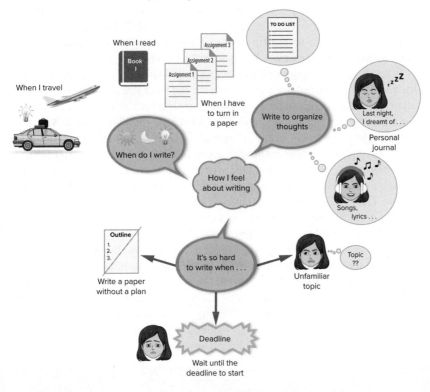

DRAFTING: WRITING MULTIPLE DRAFTS

Once you have chosen a topic, engaged in serious thinking, and dedicated prewriting time to that topic, you are ready to compose a draft—an attempt at creating a complete piece of writing. As in most stages of the writing process, there are various strategies—and no one "right way"—to compose a draft. Some writers like to write fluidly and discover their ideas during the process of drafting, while other writers prefer to think and plan carefully before attempting a draft. Of course, many writers fall somewhere in between. But we can call these two basic approaches to drafting either **discovery writing** or **planned writing**. Which approach best describes how you write a first draft?

If you prefer to engage in discovery writing, you may have a general idea of what you want to say, but use a draft to figure out what you *really* want to say. For instance, the American writer Joan Didion explains her drafting process as discovery writing: "I write entirely to find out what I am thinking, what I am looking at, what I see and what it means" (Popova). In a draft, you might explore ideas, test out examples, or experiment with approaches to the writing assignment. In contrast, if you tend to use a planned writing approach, you probably start with an outline or jot down key points you want to cover in the draft, then write to describe, elaborate on, or give examples of those ideas. Professor Yetta Goodman explains in the first reading selection in this chapter that she uses "an outline or organizational chart" to plan her professional writing.

In both approaches it is important to get the ideas down on paper, and to explain and support those ideas, but not be overly worried about spelling or grammar errors or making the writing sound polished. Refining your writing will come later in the writing process. Remember that drafting is primarily concerned with developing your ideas. In the next reading, "Rethinking the Writing Process," you will learn about different writers' approaches to writing. As you read, consider the strategies that professional writers use that you might apply to your own writing process.

READING SELECTION

Connect

You will find a coordinated Power of Process assignment for this reading in your Connect course.

"RETHINKING THE WRITING PROCESS"

The reading selection is formatted in APA (American Psychological Association) style and includes one source and therefore one reference. Complete the "Before Reading" and "During Reading" assignments. Then read the selection. Finally, complete the "After Reading" assignments.

 Before Reading: Preview; Predict

Look at the reading selection title and read the information that immediately precedes the reading. Then write answers to the following questions using complete sentences.

1. Based on your preview of the reading selection, what do you think successful writers might do to write?

2. Consider the title: Why might the selection make readers "rethink" the writing process?

 During Reading: Annotate; Make Connections

Write responses to the following exercises using complete sentences.

3. Mark any words, phrases, or sentences in the selection that you find interesting or thought-provoking or that you find particularly meaningful. Then explain why you find the text interesting or stimulating.

4. Mark any words, phrases, or sentences that confused you or that you did not find meaningful. Then explain why you find the lines confusing or irrelevant.

Answers

1. Successful writers read and write frequently, often every day.

2. "Rethinking the Writing Process" suggests that a reader might change his or her ideas of what writers do after reading about professional authors' comments on their own writing processes.

Answers

3. Answers will vary.

4. Answers will vary.

Rethinking the Writing Process:
What Best-Selling and Award-Winning Authors Have to Say

By Michael R. Sampson, Evan Ortlieb, and Cynthia B. Leung

Journal of Adolescent and Adult Literacy, 4 May 2016

The following selection is part of a longer article published in the May 4, 2016, issue of Journal of Adolescent and Adult Literacy, *an academic journal. Several professional authors were surveyed about their writing processes, including prewriting (note-making), drafting (textual evolution), revising, editing, and collaborating with other writers and readers. Some write fiction and others nonfiction.*

. . . What follows is a synthesized account of the participants' experiences in an attempt to explain how professional writers, including best-selling and award-winning authors, create quality writing . . .   1

Note-Making   2

A multitude of strategies for recording ideas prevailed, as some respondents indicated that they keep journals for recording their emergent thoughts regardless of time, location, or event. Having a way to record thoughts immediately was deemed quintessential to their writing process. Kimberly Willis Holt explained, "I always carry a small notebook with me, but I also keep a notebook for every book that I write. I'll include character sketches, plot graphs, calendars, and research." Others, such as Adrian Fogelin, add creative elements to their notebooks:

> I keep a traditional journal, writing in it every day, but at the top of the pages on which I record my day-to-day life, I log those small ideas, quotes, and thoughts that I may want to use in stories. Isolated at the top of the pages, they are easy to find.

The notebooks collect ideas in rough form, are particularly useful when traveling on day trips or vacations, and are less cumbersome than hauling a laptop.   3

Patricia McCormick wrote, "My notebook looks like the one from the character in *A Beautiful Mind* [by Sylvia Nasar]. Scraps of dialogue, random details, etc. No one would understand it but me." Writers who responded that they do not use journals had other means to collect materials.

In contrast to jotting down thoughts using pen and paper, an overwhelming majority of respondents indicated their preference toward computer-based writing to be efficient in word processing large amounts of text and/or during lengthy writing sessions, and some also write by hand. Jerry Spinelli mentioned that he used to compose both by hand and by computer: "Before I made the switch, I once wrote one book in the morning by hand and another at night by computer." Many of the authors remember when they used to write by hand but find the computer to be a much easier tool for writing today and find travel notepads ideal for recording and storing ideas. 4

Textual Evolution 5

The extent to which best-selling and award-winning authors use scripted outlines versus emergent ones varied widely depending on the writing task at hand. Most writers surveyed find that the story, content, or voice of each character reveals itself during the process of writing as opposed to before the drafting process. Jack Gantos shared, "I start with some sort of inspiration—some bit of story—and then discover and steer it as I'm writing." Per Joseph Bruchac, "At some point, the story always takes on a life—and a voice of its own." Jerry Spinelli aptly expressed, "Your wording [of the survey question] puts it perfectly. I interview the story, and when it starts talking back, I pay attention."

Bruchac wrote,

I sometimes wake up with a character's voice in my head. In other cases, especially historical fiction or books in which the main character is a real person, I do a great deal of research to get that voice right.

For Patricia McCormick,

It's like being an actor preparing for a role. You try to imagine a back story. You try to guess what the character might have in her purse, what he might eat for breakfast. The everyday details reveal a lot.

Setting is also tied to voice for Kristy Kiernan: "The characters and setting dictate the voice for me." Yetta Goodman noted that "even in professional writing, I change my voice depending on my audience: teachers, researchers, academicians, etc." 6

"Preplanning too much deadens that voice for me," said Adrian Fogelin, who also finds that "the energy that propels the story is generated by the act of writing. If I had to preplan my books, they would never get written." Writing a novel is a process of discovery for Kimberly Willis Holt: "I usually know the beginning and the ending when I start a book. Everything else I discover as I write." Jerry Jenkins also described the unfolding of the plot as a process of discovery: "I am from the Stephen King school: Put interesting characters in difficult situations and write to find out what happens." King (2015) affirmed this stance that the character, not the author, tells the story through this dialogue in his novel *Finders Keepers*: "A good 7 novelist does not lead his characters, he follows them. A good novelist does not create events, he watches them happen and then writes down what he sees. A good novelist realizes he is a secretary, not God" (p. 170).

The academic writers surveyed start with an outline or plan, but they also add and change ideas once they start writing. Yetta Goodman commented that with professional writing, "I do know that ideas shift and change as I am writing even when I have an outline or organizational chart that I follow." The outline or plan may be in their mind before they begin writing, as with Thomas Gunning: "I may have a general idea of the piece if it is nonfiction. Often I will plan the piece in my head for a day or more before I start writing." Some writers use different processes for writing different genres, as in this response from an anonymous writer: 8

> In screenplays or contemporary novels, I do an outline. But in writing historical fiction, I find I work best with a loose structure; then, as I do research, the history I unearth often suggests plotlines or characters that take the story in unexpected directions. If I find the plot turns unexpectedly, I figure the readers will, too.

Revision 9

Textual evolution also requires author reflection and revision. The number of revisions that writers make to their manuscripts varies from none to more than 10, with most authors making four to 10 revisions per piece of writing and others making more than 10. The many iterations and revisions that these highly successful authors make to their manuscripts are in stark contrast to the writing process that occurs in schools.

Some writers use self-created systems for revising. Sol Stein uses a "lockstitch technique," revising and revisiting what he has written throughout the writing process. Yetta Goodman said, 10

> It is hard to specify. I rewrite segments of my text over a long period of time, so I can't count separate revisions. It goes on continually until I believe I'm ready to send articles or books to the publishers.

> Randy Wayne White

> revise[s] daily. I rewrite the previous two chapters (at least) each workday before pressing ahead. By the end of the book, there have been numerous rewrites. Learn to cut! Be tough on yourselves. You can't be a competent writer without being a good editor.

Editing 11

Although the long-standing debate over whether to edit during or after writing will press onward, an overwhelming majority of those surveyed edit on the fly, but the big edit comes when the writing is complete and ready to be shared with others. Professional journalist Roy Peter Clark shared, "As I'm writing, I edit and proofread as I draft, but in a more disciplined way at the end of the process." Kristy Kiernan responded that she edits "as I'm writing. I'm a decent natural grammarian and speller, so I tend to write pretty clean first drafts when it comes to those things."

Research

12

Data revealed a split between authors in favor of doing research, ranging from minimal to extensive, before beginning the writing process. Whereas some writers exclusively use library and Internet resources for their research, most of the writers surveyed carry out research by interviewing and visiting the site where their story is set, in addition to reading and using the Internet. Almost all stated that they use secondary sources (e.g., books, library resources, the Internet). Jerry Jenkins shared that "nonfiction has to be unbelievable; fiction believable. The definitions have switched. That means heavy research, regardless of the discipline." Randy Wayne White explained,

> Whether writing fiction or nonfiction, if a reader catches you in a factual error, you've forfeited some of the book's credibility. However, there is a danger of continued research becoming an excuse for not confronting the more difficult work of writing.

Many writers, including Alan Brennert and Roy Peter Clark, continue to research until their book is finalized. Even when writers research the topic and characters, they may begin the story based on personal knowledge or experiences. For Mark Reibstein, "the story has to come from something I know, then I research as the story develops. Ideally, the research gives the story new direction and depth without undercutting the original intention, spirit, or plot essentials."

13

Collaboration

14

Although the majority of the writers in this sample are not members of a writers' group, many wish they were. Patricia McCormick's writers' group "meet[s] every week. I think of my group as true collaborators." Jane Yolen's writer's group is composed of eight colleagues and friends. Adrian Fogelin said that she "ha[s] been part of a writing group for perhaps 14 years." David Schwartz is also in a writers' group:

> Those of us in the group who have had the most success, and therefore are often away from home, find it hardest to attend meetings and as we (as a group) have gotten more successful, we've been finding it harder to even schedule meetings. A sad irony, as we all continue to benefit from meeting.

A slight majority of the writers surveyed do not share their work with an audience before it is published, and those that do tend to share with a loved one rather than the final intended audience. Kristy Kiernam answered, "Yes. When I think I'm finished, I have three or four alpha readers." Yet, most authors do not share. Kimberly Willis Holt elaborated, "A mere disappointed look from someone can freeze me up. I'm a better writer than oral storyteller." Randy Wayne White expressed strong feelings about why a work in progress should not be shared: "No. Absolutely not. Committees build bridges; individuals write books. Talking about a story burns creative energy that should be reserved for the actual work."

15

Challenges

16

The plot is the most challenging obstacle that these professional writers face. Adrian Fogelin shared, "Creating the large structure of the plot is most difficult for me—as I think it is for many writers. The big picture, which is plot, can be intimidating." An anonymous writer noted, "Weaving an interesting, engaging plot has been the hardest thing for me." Jerry Spinelli shares plot plus one more: "None of these so much as plot. Stuff a hundred pages in what Eve Bunting calls 'the miserable middles.' And then there's my greatest fear: being boring." Academic writers Yetta Goodman and Thomas Gunning both mentioned condensing as their greatest obstacle; per Goodman, "Condensing, deadlines. I find everything I write challenging. I worry a lot about my voice and my audience." In Gunning's textbooks, he tends to write too much and has to cut. Lee Bennett Hopkins concurred with Goodman that deadlines are a challenge: "Meeting deadlines. Mostly because my travel schedule has become so intense." For Sol Stein, it is quality: "Preserving literary values in a marketplace that has different values." Randy Wayne White responded, "Dialogue, word/story fluency, deadlines. For me, all aspects of writing are challenging. It wasn't easy when I started, and it has only gotten harder. Good writing is the selective elimination of details."

Reference

King, S. (2015). *Finders keepers*. New York, NY: Pocket.

After Reading: Identify Audience; Identify Purpose

Write responses to the following exercises using complete sentences.

5. Consider the audience: Who are the intended readers of this text? What clues helped you identify the audience?

6. Think about the purpose: Do the authors want the audience to be informed, instructed, or persuaded? What clues in the text helped you figure out the purpose?

Read to Write Activity 3.3

Engage with the Reading

Write responses to the following exercises using complete sentences.

1. Review your annotations from exercise 3 under "During Reading," and select some aspects of the writing process that professional authors engage in that you can identify with. In your own words, explain those aspects of the writing process and why you feel they apply to you.

2. Review your annotations from exercise 4 under "During Reading," and select some aspects of the writing process that professional authors engage in that you do not find useful or suitable. In your own words, explain those aspects of the writing process and why you don't find them useful or suitable.

3. Look back over your annotations and your answers to exercises 1 and 2 above. Then describe your own writing process, how it is similar to or different from those of professional writers, and how you might change your writing routine to improve it.

Answers will vary.
Encourage students to use
their own vivid and specific
examples and details.

Pair and Share

With a classmate, compare your responses to exercise 3 in Read to Write Activity 3.3. Discuss how your writing processes are similar and different, why your individual writing processes work for you, and how your writing processes might be more effective.

Vocabulary Strategy: Defining Unfamiliar Words and Checking Their Meanings in the Reading

Writers often provide a definition or a context clue for words that might be unfamiliar to the reader. But what should you do if there is a word you don't know and the context doesn't provide adequate information for you to decipher the meaning of the word? You can look at any examples used in the writing to see whether they give a strong clue to the meaning of a word. Sometimes, though, a writer's examples do not give enough information and you need to make a best guess about a word's meaning. If you can guess the meaning of a word and get the gist of the reading, then do so and read on. Later you can confirm the meaning of the word by looking it up in the dictionary (see "Vocabulary Strategy: Building Dictionary Skills" in the chapter "Writing about Reading" for tips about using a dictionary).

Vocabulary Practice

Write a definition for each underlined word from reading selection 1, "Rethinking the Writing Process." Then look up the meaning of the word in a dictionary to check the definition.

Example: ". . . some respondents indicated that they keep journals for recording their <u>emergent</u> thoughts regardless of time, location, or event."

My guess: *emergent* means "sudden"

Dictionary definition: *emergent* means "newly formed" or "arising unexpectedly"

Answers

1. *Quintessential* means an important part of something.

2. *Iterations* means repetitions of a process.

3. *Collaborators* are people who work with others.

4. *Alpha* means the most powerful.

1. "Having a way to record thought immediately was deemed <u>quintessential</u> to their writing process."

2. "The many <u>iterations</u> and revisions that these highly successful authors make to their manuscripts are in stark contrast to the writing process that occurs in schools."

3. "'. . . I think of my group as true <u>collaborators</u>.'"

4. "'When I think I'm finished, I have three or four <u>alpha</u> readers.'"

READING AND WRITING ABOUT ILLUSTRATIONS

An *illustration* (for example, a drawing) can help readers understand an idea or concept. For instance, an illustration, even one that uses simple drawings, can show an important concept or bring an idea to life.

To read an illustration

- Start with the title, if the illustration has one, to understand what overall information or idea the illustration is presenting.

- Study the picture and consider what it means, especially in relation to the title.

- Read any text and consider how the text relates to the illustration.

- Review any captions (writing that explains the illustration).

Look closely at the illustration shown in Figure 3.6. Write answers to the following questions using complete sentences.

1. What is the topic of the illustration?

2. What do the three stick figures and the arrows connecting them represent?

3. What is the significance of the words and arrows in the bubble below the stick figures?

4. From what source did the information in this illustration come?

5. How does this illustration connect with ideas about the writing process that you have read in this chapter?

Answers

1. The topic is writing or rewriting.

2. The figures are writers creating drafts; the arrows show the progress from first to second to third draft.

3. The graph in the bubble shows the more drafts written, the better the quality of writing.

4. The information comes from the book *On Writing Well*.

5. The illustration reinforces that many drafts are needed to produce good writing.

FIGURE 3.6 The Essence of Writing Is Rewriting

Source: Doug Neil; *Thegraphicrecorder.com.*

Connect

Activity 3.4 can be found as a writing assignment in Connect.

Read to Write Activity 3.4

Write a First Draft

Follow the directions for each exercise below.

1. When you are writing a first draft, do you generally feel more comfortable engaging in discovery writing or planning before writing? Explain.

2. Review your writing topic and prewriting (from Read to Write Activity 3.2). Build on your prewriting by writing a first draft. Give yourself permission to write without worrying about grammar or spelling or correctness; know that you can revise and improve your writing later. For inspiration, review one student's first draft in response to topic 1, shown in Figure 3.7.

FIGURE 3.7 Sample First Draft

To be honest, writing has never been interesting to me. I always catch myself talking more than putting things down on the paper. However, after my last year in middle school, I realized I should find a better way to keep my thinking together. Since then, I started to write a lot. Of course, at first, it was just for fun purposes. I wrote songs when I feel like my crush turned his head and looked at my direction. I wrote down some crazy dreams in the morning after I woke up, because I thought that one day I can publish them; but turned out, those dreams were from a movie I saw before bed last night. I wrote down my mom's grocery list and put it in her purse before she went out to the store; and of course, those things on the list are my favorite treats. When I made my way to high school, I realized I could write to improve my grades at school. I began to put more efforts into turning my dreams journal into a personal journal. I began to create to-do list for myself, so I will not forget any important things I have to get done. I began to write longer songs with more meaningful lyrics, mostly about positivities because we can never get enough of those. After maintaining my writing habit throughout high school, I moved to college and started to be familiar with "assignments". That is when I realized I have to write in some cases, no matter if I want to or not. I wrote more and more after I purchased a smartphone. I wrote on the bus, in the car, on an airplane; whenever something comes up to my mind, I wrote it down on my phone. In addition, I like to highlight and mark my books with a lot of colors and margins notes. A colorful book will help me more when I

continued

FIGURE 3.7 **Sample First Draft** (*continued*)

need to find a piece of evidence I will need in my paper. However, writing has its own challenges when it comes to college writing. It is hard to look at a blank page on a computer knowing that the words count for this paper is two thousand words. Writing is impossible without a plan. To me, the word "deadline" always has one meaning: I'm dead if I waited till the due day to start writing my paper. Last but not least, being unfamiliar with the topic that I was assigned for is also a difficulty for me. In order to write about something I have never heard before, I should do some researches before thinking about the topic. The thinking process is only fun, when I make up questions and ask myself to answer them.

REVISING, EDITING, AND PROOFREADING: REREADING YOUR WRITING WITH YOUR READER IN MIND

Writers go through multiple drafts before completing a finished work. For instance, in her book *Bird by Bird: Some Instructions on Writing and Life*, author Anne Lamott describes the process of writing a terrible first draft to get her ideas down on paper. She then improves her first draft to create a better second draft and finally a third draft that is publishable. When Lamott writes her first draft, she hopes no one will read it. When she develops her subsequent drafts, she reads her writing carefully. She thinks about how someone else might read her writing. In other words, she starts shaping her writing for a reader. We call this "writing with a reader in mind." In this way, Lamott is continuing the writing process by revising, then editing and proofreading her writing.

Revising for Content and Organization

Revising involves focusing on the content of the writing—the ideas, examples, or details; the organization; and the logical flow. When revising, writers think about the "big picture" of their writing, such as whether their writing has a clear focus, their ideas are supported by evidence or examples, and their organization makes sense. Revising often means making big changes in the first draft. For instance, a writer might take out a paragraph or move it to another part of the writing. He or she might add—or remove—details or examples or even completely rewrite the introduction or conclusion. As you reread and revise your paper, ask yourself questions like those shown in "Strategies for Revising."

Teaching Tip

Locate and share with students Anne Lamott's advice about writing first drafts from her book *Bird by Bird*.

Handout

"Strategies for Revising" is
a reproducible handout in
the Instructor's Resources.

Strategies for Revising

1. Does your writing respond to the assignment? If not, can you change it to respond to the topic, or do you need to start all over again?

2. Does the writing have a clear focus or point to make? Can you underline a sentence or two in the paper that sums up your main idea?

3. Can you develop the ideas with more examples, details, or information from the readings? If so, add more support to the writing.

4. Do ideas progress logically from one section to the next and from one sentence to the next? If not, can sections or sentences be logically connected with transitions?

5. Are there any parts of the paper that seem out of place or not relevant? Can you move these to other places in the paper, or should you take them out?

6. Is there more you can say on the topic? If so, add more sentences or paragraphs.

Review Figure 3.7, which is a first draft written by a student who is responding to topic 1 about how she feels about writing. Then, look at Figure 3.8, a second draft, in which the writer revised her first draft to improve the content. Notice that she crossed out unnecessary information and added specific examples and details (marked in purple ink). She also clarified the organization by changing the order of information and by adding transitions (also in purple).

FIGURE 3.8 Sample Second Draft

To be honest, writing has never been interesting to me; when I was young, 1

I always ~~catch~~ _caught_ myself talking more than putting ~~things~~ _words_ down on the paper.

I had energy to ran around, but had none to sit down and write. Later on in

life, I figured that writing had a lot of benefits. I was able to organize my

thoughts, think more careful before making something happen, and most impor-

tantly, I was able to express myself.

After my last year in middle school, I realized I should find a better 2

way to keep my ~~thinking~~ _ideas_ together. ~~Since then,~~ I started to write, a lot.

~~Of course,~~ At first, it was just for fun purposes. I wrote songs when I feel

like my crush turned his head and looked at my direction. I wrote down ~~some~~ _my_

crazy dreams ~~in the morning~~ after I woke up, because I thought that one day I

~~can~~ _could_ publish them; ~~but~~ turned out, those dreams were from a movie I saw before

bed last night. I wrote down my mom's grocery list and put it in her purse

continued

FIGURE 3.8 Sample Second Draft (*continued*)

before she went out to the store; and of course, those things on the list are my favorite treats. When I made my way to high school, I realized I could write to improve my grades at school. I began to put more efforts into turning my dreams journal into a personal journal. I began to create to-do lists for myself, so I ~~will~~ ^{would} not forget any important things I have to get done. I began to write longer songs with more meaningful lyrics, mostly about ~~positivities~~ ^{positivity} because we can never get enough of ~~those~~ ^{it}. After maintaining my writing habit throughout high school, I moved to college and started to be familiar with "assignments". That ~~is~~ ^{was} when I realized I ~~have~~ ^{had} to write ~~in some cases~~, no matter if I wanted to or not. I wrote more and more after I purchased a smartphone. I wrote on the bus, in the car, even on an airplane; whenever something comes up to my mind, I wrote it down on my phone. In addition, I liked to highlight and mark my books with a lot of colors and margins notes. A colorful book will be more helpful to me ~~more~~ when I need to find a piece of evidence ~~I will~~ needed ~~in~~ ^{for} my paper. However, writing has its own challenges when it comes to college writing. Being unfamiliar with the topic that I was assigned for ~~is~~ ^{was} also a difficulty for me. In order to write about something that I have never heard before, I should do some researches before thinking about the topic. It is hard to write when you look at a blank page on a computer knowing that the words count for this paper is two thousand words and you have nothing in mind. Writing is impossible without a plan or an outline. It is just like the 80/20 rule. If you put 80% of your effort to do the thinking process, then you would only need 20% of your effort to start writing. On the other hand, ~~To me,~~ the word "deadline" always has one meaning to me: I'm dead if I waited untill the due day to start writing my paper. We cannot wait till time runs out, and hope for some miracle. As writing requires some thoughtful thinking, it also requires some time, too. ~~The thinking process is only fun, when I make up questions and ask myself to answer them.~~

Writing is not as hard as some people think it is. Only when you have no ideas of what you are writing about, or you do not give yourself enough time to write, that's when everything gets harder. At the end of the day, writing is not only about getting that good grade at school, but it is also a tool to sharpen our thoughts.

3

Read to Write Activity 3.5

Revise a First Draft

Follow the directions for each exercise below.

1. Study Figure 3.7 ("Sample First Draft") and Figure 3.8 ("Sample Second Draft") and notice the changes between the drafts. Writing that was removed is crossed out, while writing that is added is in purple. Why do you think the writer made the changes she did? How do they improve the draft? Do you agree with the changes that the writer made? Are there parts of the writing you would have kept in or taken out that the writer did not? Explain your answer.

2. Review your first draft from Read to Write Activity 3.4. Revise your first draft paying close attention to content and organization.

Pair and Share

- With a classmate, compare your answers to exercise 1 in Read to Write Activity 3.5. Discuss what changes—changes that were made or should have been made—would most improve the first draft.

- Exchange your second draft with a classmate. Make suggestions to each other about which parts of the writing to keep and which parts to take out, as well as where to add information or where it is not needed. Also, make suggestions about the organization: how to reorganize or make the organization clearer.

The following reading selection, an interview with the writer Mike Rose, explores ideas about writing process and, in particular, how he feels about writing and strategies for drafting. Pay close attention to Rose's suggestions for revising his writing and how reading plays a key role in his writing process.

READING SELECTION

Connect

You will find a coordinated Power of Process assignment for this reading in your Connect course.

"WRITING AS A PROCESS: AN INTERVIEW WITH MIKE ROSE"

Newspaper and magazine articles such as the following reading selection sometimes include interviews with experts, authors, or other knowledgeable people. If an interview is recorded verbatim—that is, word for word—the reporter will indicate who is speaking before the words. Often quotation marks are not used; instead, the speaker's name or initials are included before their words.

Complete the "Before Reading" and "During Reading" exercises. Then read the selection. Finally, complete the "After Reading" exercises.

 ## Before Reading: Recognize Prior Knowledge

Look at the reading selection title and read the information that immediately precedes the reading. Then write responses to the following using complete sentences.

1. Do you think that writing is hard work? That it is fun? Or is it sometimes both or neither? Explain your answer.

2. What role do you think reading plays in the writing process? For instance, do writers have others read their writing? Do writers read to improve their own writing? Explain.

 ## During Reading: Annotate; Make Connections

Write responses to the following exercises using complete sentences.

3. Mark any text you find interesting or thought-provoking or that you particularly agree with. Then explain why you agree with the text or find it interesting or stimulating.

4. Mark any text that confused you or that you disagree with. Then explain why you find the text confusing or disagree with it.

Answers

1. Answers will vary. Encourage students to see the joys or rewards of writing.

2. Writers read their own work critically and also have others read their writing to get constructive feedback.

Answers

3. Answers will vary.

4. Answers will vary.

Writing as a Process: An Interview with Mike Rose

By Tina Arora

InterActions: UCLA Journal of Education and Information Studies, 2010

Mike Rose began his academic career as a working-class student, the son of Italian immigrants, but eventually became a professor at the University of California at Los Angeles. He has written many articles and books about college students, especially about the challenges new college students face and their potential to be successful.

TA: You enjoy writing and publishing and you did say that you ask your students to look at the jewels that are present at their feet and write about what they're involved in. Where does this enthusiasm come from or what motivates you?

MR: That's a really good question. You know, there's times when the writing is a joy, but, more often, it's not. It's, it's difficult, taxing, work that seems to slam me constantly up against my limitations. My limitations as a thinker, the limitations of my knowledge, the limitations of what I can do with language, all of my own insecurities. But writing for me is driven, in a way, because it's a means that I have to try to explore and express, a means to explore something that bothers me, or something that I think is not right or wrong-headed. Writing is my toolkit to pursue those issues. If I were a lawyer, I would have the law and the courts. If I were a physician, I would

1

2

probably be doing certain kinds of medicine in certain kinds of communities. But the toolkit that I have at my disposal is this ability to write, something I have developed over many, many, many years of practice.

When I was a young man, I wrote poetry, I had these fantasies of becoming a poet. 3 Now, I was never a very good poet, but I think I learned a lot about the craft of writing by doing it, and then I carried that skill into my professional and academic writing. Caring about style, worrying about the sound of the language as well as what ideas the language is trying to convey. In fact, there's not a separation between the sound of the language and the ideas it conveys. If I can hit the right pitch with the language, then that advances the idea all the more. And conversely, if the ideas are shoddy, the idea isn't carefully wrought, then the language is going to fall apart, for me, anyway.

I wish I could tell you that writing is pure pleasure, that I sit down at the desk at 8 4 in the morning, and the next thing I know it's 5 in the evening, and I've had this blissful day lost in thought. But, no, it's not at all like that. If somebody had a little camera on me, and they traced out the patterns of my writing day, there would be dozens upon dozens of times when I'm getting up from the chair and going to the refrigerator, and getting up from the chair and going for a walk, and getting up from the chair and trying desperately to think of anybody I can call.

TA: So, it is similar to what other people go through. . .   5

MR: It is. . .it is what many students who I've worked with go through. There's no 6 difference. I guess I'm just committed to it. I know that if I stick at it long enough, something will come out of it. Plus, I have to say, over the years, I've been blessed enough to cultivate a large number of people who I can trust to give me honest feedback. I purposefully make sure I have a diversity of readers, people who come at the world in a different way from the way I do so that I can get all the feedback I can. If I'm writing about particular people like in the book *Possible Lives: The Promise of Public Education in America*, then, of course, they became part of the critical loop as well. I would send them the stuff I wrote and we would begin this exchange about the material, which then would lead to further discussion.

So that's my writing process. It's probably similar to a whole lot who are gonna be 7 reading this interview. It has its moments of pleasure and moments where the words do seem to come, but it has many more moments of just being stymied and going back to your books and trying to find the right train of thought, and getting up to get a snack, and waking up in the middle of the night with an idea and scribbling on a notepad only to look at it in the morning and realize it's not such a great idea after all. That's just the way it is.

TA: What do you believe is the efficient way to train research apprentices/student 8 researchers in understanding writing and becoming effective and prolific writers?

MR: We've created here in the department of Social Research Methodology these two 9 writing classes, one for professional writing and one for people who want to write for broader audiences. So, I'm a firm believer that you really can learn a lot about how to do this work, do it better and do it with more grace. But, as I was just saying a moment ago, that doesn't guarantee that it's going to be easy or effortless, I mean I don't think any good performance is. There's no good performance in any domain that doesn't come without its cost, its pain and difficulty.

I think that young researchers, first of all, can put themselves in situations where they can learn more about the craft involved both in framing their research projects and writing about them. They can do that through courses. And they can do that through aligning themselves with a very good editor who's not just going to edit for them but teach them as well. They also can go out of their way to find those other people, their peers or mentors, who respond well to their writing and form relationships with them where they read each other's writing. 10

I'm also a firm believer in reading good stuff. When you find authors who write well in your discipline or people who just write well, a favorite novelist, read them and read them like a writer, rather than reading them like a reader. In other words, read them with an eye to figuring out what it is they do that makes their writing work so well. You read them analytically, you read them with an eye to stealing a trick or two. So I think there are a lot of things that students can do to help themselves become better writers. 11

And also, as I was talking about earlier, remember that writing is hard for everybody, I do think sometimes that students carry in their minds the assumption that for other people composing is an effortless enterprise, this effortless activity, when, in fact, it is difficult for everybody. I think just even understanding that up front keeps you at the keyboard rather than allowing yourself to give into the feeling of inadequacy, thinking that it's only you who are going through this awful stuff. It's more the norm than you think. 12

After Reading: Find Supporting Details

Write responses to the following exercises using complete sentences.

5. Rose says that although sometimes "writing is a joy . . . more often . . . it's difficult, taxing, work." What details in the text show that writing is a joy? What details in the text show that writing is hard work?

6. Rose states that students can "learn a lot" about how to write well. What details in the reading describe what students should learn about writing?

Read to Write Activity 3.6

Engage with the Reading

Write responses to the following exercises using complete sentences.

1. Rose mentions that he appreciates having a "diversity of readers" who can give him "honest feedback" on his writing. Why do you think having different kinds of people read and respond to a writer's work is helpful?

2. Review your annotations and select a sentence or two that you find thought-provoking—either because you agree with Rose or because you disagree. Explain why you agree or disagree.

3. Compare your process for writing to Rose's. For instance, do you feel writing is hard work or that it is a joy, or both? Do you like to get feedback from lots of different people? Do you read to get ideas? Explain.

Answers

5. Rose suggests writing is pleasurable when "the words do seem to come," but it's also frustrating because often he gets stuck thinking about what to write or how to say it. He also suggests writing takes "many, many, many years of practice" to write well.

6. Rose says "reading good stuff" can make writers see what makes good writing. Students should also seek out "a very good editor" and "read each other's writing." They should also know that "writing is hard for everybody."

Answers

1. Rose suggests that because different people have different perspectives, they might see things he does not.

2. Answers will vary. Encourage students to quote the author's words.

3. Answers will vary. Encourage students to compare how they use feedback or how they work to Rose's activities.

Connect

Activity 3.6 can be found as a writing assignment in Connect.

Pair and Share

With a classmate, compare your answers to exercise 3 in Read to Write Activity 3.6. Explain the differences and similarities between your writing processes and Rose's writing process.

Answers

1. *Convey* means to communicate or express.

2. *Shoddy* means poorly done or made.

3. *Cultivate* means to become friendly with.

4. *Stymied* means to stop from doing something.

Vocabulary Strategy: Defining Unfamiliar Words and Checking the Meaning in the Reading

The Vocabulary Strategy earlier in this chapter described how to use context clues to guess the meaning of a word and then use a dictionary to check the meaning. Review that advice before completing the Vocabulary Practice.

Vocabulary Practice

Write a definition for each underlined word from the reading selection, "Writing as a Process." Then look up the meaning of the word in a dictionary to check the definition.

1. "In fact, there's not a separation between the sound of the language and the ideas it <u>conveys</u>."

2. "And conversely, if the ideas are <u>shoddy</u>, the idea isn't carefully wrought, then the language is going to fall apart, for me, anyway."

3. "Plus I have to say, over the years, I've been blessed enough to <u>cultivate</u> a large number of people who I can trust to give me honest feedback."

4. "It has its moments of pleasure and moments where the words do seem to come, but it has many more moments of just being <u>stymied</u> and going back to your books and trying to find the right train of thought, and getting up to get a snack, and waking up in the middle of the night with an idea and scribbling on a notepad only to look at it in the morning and realize it's not such a great idea after all."

Editing Sentences and Proofreading for Errors

Editing your writing involves focusing on the "little details," such as sentences and words, checking that these are clear and that they make sense. **Proofreading** means reading your writing carefully, looking for errors, such as grammar or punctuation mistakes, and correcting these. Examples of what you might do to edit your writing include the following:

- Rewriting sentences to be clear or correct.
- Combining sentences to make the writing more concise.
- Selecting new words to make ideas more clear or vivid.

In *Bird by Bird: Some Instructions on Writing and Life*, the writer Anne Lamott explains this stage as "the dental draft, where you check every tooth" (25–26), or rather, when you check every word and sentence to be sure it is clear and correct and effectively expresses your ideas.

Strategies for Editing and Proofreading

- **Read your paper slowly and out loud.** Be sure you are reading what is on the page and not what is in your head. Put your finger under each word as you read. You might notice that you accidentally left out a word or maybe typed the same word twice.

- **Read your paper several times.** It is not possible to catch everything with one reading. Read through your paper first for clarity of sentences, then again for word choice, and a third time to check grammar, spelling, and punctuation.

First reading: Read each sentence carefully and think about whether it is clearly and correctly written. Will a reader understand what you mean in that sentence? Are there vague words that can be replaced? Know that readers will encounter your writing one sentence at a time, so each sentence must make sense and advance your ideas. If a sentence does not "sound right," then stop, mark it, and try to fix it. Try rewriting the sentence several different ways. Also consider whether the sentence needs to be moved to another part of the essay or maybe taken out.

Second reading: Read your writing thinking about the words. Ask yourself whether words are well chosen to say exactly what you mean. Avoid vague words (*really, sort of, very, many*); use specific, precise, and vivid words or details. Look particularly at the nouns and verbs in the sentences. Most often, strong writing uses specific nouns and active verbs. For instance, rather than write that Naomi's childhood was traumatic (*traumatic* is a vague noun), you could be more specific about why her childhood was traumatic: *Naomi was eleven years old when she dived into a lake and hit her head on a rock.* (*Traumatic* was replaced with more specific nouns and description.)

Third reading: Check the grammar, punctuation, and formatting. For instance, you might circle each piece of punctuation to check that it is appropriate. Be sure you have followed your instructor's guidelines for setting up the writing, including heading or formatting.

Finally, after correcting sentences, words, or other errors, give your essay one last read through to be sure the writing makes sense and is correct.

Handout

"Strategies for Editing and Proofreading" is a reproducible handout in the Instructor's Resources.

Editing and proofreading come in the final stages of the writing process. Review "Strategies for Editing and Proofreading" for suggestions about how to edit and proofread your paper.

Study Figure 3.9, in which the student edited her second draft and proofread it for errors. She carefully read her paper, looking for ways to improve the words and sentences; also, she searched for errors, such as correct verb tense. Changes are highlighted in blue.

FIGURE 3.9 Sample Third Draft

When I was young, writing was never interesting to me. ~~To be honest, writing has never been interesting to me; when I was young,~~ I always ~~catch~~ caught myself talking more than putting ~~things~~ words down on the paper. I had energy to ~~ran~~ run around, but had none to sit down and write. Later on ~~in life,~~ I figured that writing had a lot of benefits. I was able to organize my thoughts, think more carefully before making a decision ~~something happen,~~ and most importantly, I was able to express myself. 1

After my last year in middle school, I realized I should find a better way to keep my ~~thinking~~ ideas together. ~~Since then,~~ I have started to write a lot since then. ~~Of course,~~ At first, it was ~~just~~ only for fun purposes. I wrote songs about what I felt like when my crush turned his head around and looked ~~at~~ in my direction. I wrote down ~~some~~ my crazy dreams ~~in the morning~~ after I woke up, because I thought that one day I ~~can~~ could publish them; ~~but turned out,~~ Ironically, those dreams were from a movie I saw the night before ~~before bed last night.~~ I wrote down my mom's grocery list, and put it in her purse before she went ~~out~~ to the store; of course, those things on the list ~~are~~ were my favorite treats. When I made my way to high school, I realized I ~~could~~ should write to improve my grades at school. I began to put more effort into turning my dreams journal into a personal journal. I began to create to-do lists for myself, so I ~~will~~ would not forget any important things I ~~have~~ had to get done. I began to write longer songs with more meaningful lyrics, mostly about ~~positivities~~ positivity because we ~~can~~ could never get enough of ~~these.~~ it After maintaining my writing habit throughout high school, I moved to college and started to be familiar with "assignments". That ~~is~~ was when I realized I ~~have~~ had to write ~~in some cases,~~ no matter if I wanted to or not. I wrote more and more after ~~I purchased~~ purchasing a smartphone. I wrote on the bus, in the car, and even on ~~an~~ the airplane; whenever something ~~comes~~ came to ~~ind,~~ mind, I wrote it down on my phone. In addition, I liked to highlight and mark my books with a lot of colors and margin notes. A colorful book will be more helpful to me ~~more~~ when I need to find a piece of evidence ~~I will needed~~ in for my paper. However, writing has its own challenges when it comes to college writing. Being unfamiliar with the topic that I was assigned ~~for is~~ was also a difficulty for me. ~~In order to~~ To write about something that I have never heard before, I should do some ~~researches~~ research of before ~~thinking about~~ analyzing the topic. It is hard to write when you look at a blank page on a computer knowing that the words count for this paper is two thousand words and you have nothing in mind. Writing is impossible without a plan or an 2

continued

FIGURE 3.9 **Sample Third Draft** (*continued*)

outline. It is ~~just like~~ *similar to* the 80/20 rule. If you put 80% of your effort into doing the thinking process, then you would only need 20% of your effort to start writing. On the other hand, ~~To me,~~ the word "deadline" always has one meaning to me: I'm ruining the paper if I wait unti~~ll~~ the due day to start writing ~~my paper.~~ *it* We cannot wait till time runs out, and hope for some last-minute miracle. As writing requires some thoughtful thinking, it also requires some time, too. ~~The thinking process is only fun, when I make up questions and ask myself to answer them.~~

Writing is not as hard as some people think it is. Only when you have no ideas   3
of what you are writing about, or you ~~do~~ *are* not ~~give~~ *giving* yourself enough time to write, that's when everything gets harder. At the end of the day, writing is not only about getting that good grade at school, but it is also a tool to sharpen our thoughts.

Read to Write Activity 3.7

Edit and Proofread a Second Draft

Follow the directions for each assignment.

1. Go back to Figure 3.9 ("Sample third draft"). The additions in the second draft are in purple, and the additions in the edited and proofread third draft are in blue. Writing that was removed is crossed out. What changes were made in the third draft (blue)? Why do you think the writer made the changes she did? How do the changes improve the draft? Do you agree with the revisions the writer made? Explain your answer.

2. Review your second draft (from Read to Write Activity 3.5). Revise your second draft, paying close attention to the sentences and words.

Answers

1. Changes in the third draft (blue) tend to be word choice, transitions, and grammatical corrections. The changes make the writing more coherent and unified, as well as more articulate and correct.

2. Encourage students to read their drafts out loud, listen for problem spots, and then revise for clarity and correctness.

Pair and Share

- With a classmate, compare your answers to exercise 1 in Read to Write Activity 3.5. Discuss which changes—changes that were made or should have been made—most improve the second draft.

- Exchange your third draft with a classmate. Make suggestions to each other about which parts of the writing to edit or revise or correct. Also make suggestions about the sentences and the words.

CHAPTER REVIEW

Key Terms

discovery writing approach Drafting by starting with a general idea and then writing to figure out what to say.

editing A final stage in the writing process in which writers focus on improving the clarity and logic of sentences and words.

graphic organizer A visual representation of the relationships among ideas.

high-stakes writing Formal writing that will typically be read and evaluated by others.

low-stakes writing Informal writing for study or learning purposes.

planned writing approach Drafting by starting with an outline or key points and then writing to describe, elaborate on, or give examples of those ideas.

prewriting Thinking, reading, and writing as preparation to compose a first draft.

proofreading Reading writing carefully to correct errors in grammar, spelling, or punctuation.

revising A stage in the writing process in which writers focus on improving the ideas and organization of the writing.

Chapter Summary

1. Strategic college writers use a recursive writing process—circling back through writing process steps as necessary.

2. Assigned writing in college falls into two broad categories: (a) low-stakes writing, which tends to be informal writing for your own learning, and (b) high-stakes writing, which means more formal writing that will typically be read and evaluated by an instructor.

3. After evaluating and choosing a topic that is appropriate to the assignment, the writer can employ various prewriting strategies—reviewing class materials, freewriting, listing, creating a graphic organizer, outlining, and discussing—to generate ideas and launch the writing process.

4. A draft is an attempt to create a complete piece of writing, when the writer is most concerned about getting ideas down onto paper, whether by discovering ideas as he or she writes or planning and then writing.

5. Revising a draft involves focusing on the content, such as the ideas, examples, or details, and the organization, including the logical flow of the writing.

6. Editing a draft requires focusing on sentences and words, checking that these are clear and that they make sense.

7. Proofreading means reading the writing carefully, looking for errors, such as grammar or punctuation mistakes, and correcting these.

8. When you encounter an unfamiliar word when reading, guess the meaning using context and then confirm the meaning of the word by looking it up in the dictionary.

9. An illustration can help readers understand an idea and can be used by writers as information in a paper.

Apply What You Learned

Follow the instructions in each of the following exercises, using complete sentences for your responses.

1. Create an illustration that shows Mike Rose's writing process or that shows your writing process.

2. What have you learned about the writing process from reading the articles in this chapter or from reading the chapter itself? How might you apply that knowledge to your own writing? Give examples from the readings, from your own experience, or from both to explain.

3. How does reading help someone become a better writer? For instance, when should writers read, or how should they read, during the writing process? Give examples from this chapter or from your own experience, or from both.

Connect

"Apply What You Learned" can be found as a writing assignment in Connect.

Works Cited

Lamott, Anne. *Bird by Bird: Some Instructions on Writing and Life*. Anchor, 1995.

Popova, Maria. "'It's an Aggressive, Hostile Act': Joan Didion's Thoughts on Writing." *The Atlantic,* 17 Oct. 2012, www.theatlantic.com/entertainment/archive/2012/10/its-an-aggressive-hostile-act-joan-didions-thoughts-on-writing/263679/.

Ryan, Kevin. *Write Up the Corporate Ladder: Successful Writers Reveal the Techniques That Help You Write with Ease and Get Ahead*. AMACOM, 2006.

Credits

SPOTLIGHT ON STUDENT WRITING

Annotating and Evaluating Student Writing

Connect

Assign the LearnSmart Achieve topic "Revising" for adaptive learning to accompany this Spotlight material.

As you have learned, reading and writing require time, effort, and practice. Successful students take charge of their learning, using such strategies as annotating a piece of writing for thesis, main ideas, and examples and using the writing process to create multiple drafts, to revise, and to edit. You can apply these same strategies to student writing.

In this Spotlight section, you will practice reading and writing skills that will enable you to evaluate any piece of writing, including your own writing and the writing of other students. You will apply annotation skills to student writing, with an eye toward revising and editing. Specifically, you will review strategies for annotating a piece of writing and then practice reading and evaluating student writing.

ANNOTATING TO UNDERSTAND AND EVALUATE STUDENT WRITING

Teaching Tip

Emphasize that it's difficult to read with two purposes in mind. Even most experienced readers, such as teachers, read texts, including student papers, more than once.

Teaching Tip

Consider describing your own approach to reading and marking student papers.

Annotating your own writing can help you to better understand the structure of your writing and evaluate how effective it is. You might also read and annotate a classmate's piece of writing to provide that person with feedback to improve his or her paper. An effective strategy when reading to annotate is to read the paper at least two times.

- During your *first reading*, focus on understanding the main ideas and examples to ensure that the purpose and organization of the writing are clear.

- As you do your *second reading*, focus on evaluating the paper by assessing the strengths of the writing or considering what could be improved. Note what is effective about the writing so that the writer will retain those parts, but also point out where the writing is weak so the writer can revise and improve those parts.

After each reading, you will want to annotate the writing. Here are some strategies for successful annotations:

First Reading: Annotations for Comprehension

- Note the title to identify the topic.
- Underline main ideas, such as the thesis or concluding statements, to discover the paper's organization.
- Mark examples to determine the support for the main ideas.
- Write brief summaries of main ideas and examples in the margin to reinforce your comprehension of the writing.

- Look for places in the paper where the writing is effective and label those places with words such as "Good" or "Strong."

- Be specific about what is effective. For instance, rather than writing "Good example," you can write "Good example of how you worked hard in school to be successful."

- Look for places in the paper where the writing could be improved and label those places using words such as "Unclear" or "Confusing." Avoid judgmental terms like "Bad" or "Boring."

- Be specific about what is not effective. For instance, rather than writing, "Confusing sentence," you can write, "I don't understand why you mention your dog eating your homework or how that relates to failing math."

- Ask questions if you are not sure whether the writing is effective. For instance, you might ask a question about how the paper is formatted or whether the writer needs to use examples from the reading.

ANNOTATING SAMPLE STUDENT PAPERS

This Spotlight section includes two sample student papers for you to read and think about. The first student paper is marked so you can see an example of effective annotations. The second paper is not marked; you can use it to practice annotating.

The students responded to a specific writing prompt. After reading Carol Dweck's article "Brainology," students had a choice of prompts to write about, including the following.

> **Writing Prompt:** *Carol Dweck's research indicates that students with growth mindsets are more successful academically than students with fixed mindsets. Based on your experience and observations, do you agree that a growth mindset leads to greater academic success than a fixed mindset?*

The two student papers—Alejandra Jimenez's "The Good, the Bad, and the Math" and Veronica Alvarez's "Involuntary Resignation"—were written in response to this prompt. For this assignment, which was the first paper due in the course, students were encouraged to explain Dweck's ideas about fixed and growth mindset and to use their own experiences or observations to reflect on Dweck's ideas. As you read, notice how the students respond very differently to Dweck's ideas and how each uses her own experiences to support her response.

The first paper, by Jimenez, is annotated by a reviewer. First, the reviewer read the paper to understand the writer's thesis, main ideas, and examples. Then the reviewer reread the paper to evaluate the strengths and weaknesses of the writing. Notice there are annotations on the paper

Class Activity

An alternative to having students review the first annotated student paper is to have students practice annotating *both* papers. The first student paper can be reproduced without the annotations and given to students. See the Instructor's Resources for a clean copy of Jimenez's paper.

Teaching Tip

"Brainology" can be found in Chapter 1, "Introduction to College Reading and Writing."

itself, on the right margin, and on the left margin. Here is an explanation of these annotations:

- **Annotations on the paper.** The thesis and main ideas are highlighted in blue. Additionally, the thesis is double-underlined on the paper. Examples are underlined, to indicate where an example begins.

- **Annotations in the right margin.** The title, thesis, and main ideas are summarized in the right-hand column to check comprehension. Examples are indicated with the abbreviation "EX" and briefly summarized.

- **Annotations in the left margin.** Responses to the paper, such as what is effective, what is not clear, or questions the reader had, appear in the left column.

Notice the paper is not overly marked up. Writing too many comments can be overwhelming and counterproductive for the reviewer and for the writer. Instead, most reviewers strive to highlight the main ideas and examples and to include a few well-chosen comments that focus on the most important aspects of the writing. Review this annotation strategy by studying Jimenez's paper. Then practice reading and annotating by applying these strategies to the second student paper, which is not annotated.

STUDENT PAPER 1
About the Author

Alejandra Jimenez
©Alison Kuehner

Alejandra Jimenez is majoring in child development and hopes to become a kindergarten teacher. She loves to read and to figure out how the ideas in a book connect with each other. She says it is not hard to write a paper if you create a basic outline, have notes, and are organized. After that, writing a paper is just a matter of putting the words down on the page. While she admits that writing papers is time consuming and that she does not always enjoy writing, Jimenez likes the feeling of accomplishment when she is done.

Jimenez 1

Alejandra Jimenez

Professor Kuehner

English 151RW

20 September 2015

The Good, the Bad, and the Math

In Carol Dweck's article, "Brainology: Transforming Student's Motivation to Learn," she states that people have different types of learning mindsets; "fixed" or "growth" mindset. With her research, she has found that many students have a "fixed" mindset, which is when the student believes that he or she cannot change or enhance their intelligence. They think that they either have an innate intelligence or they do not. In contrast to a "fixed mindset," people with a "growth" mindset believe that they can improve their intelligence through hard work and perseverance. Dweck claims that having a growth mindset can make a person do better academically than someone with a fixed mindset. I agree that people with a growth mindset do better academically than those with a fixed mindset because a person with a growth mindset wants to learn and improve, while a person with a fixed mindset gets held back. The amount of times I have heard students say that they are "bad at math" is a grand one. Unfortunately, I was one of them. I had a fixed mindset in math. I for one thought I would never improve in math but with enough effort and a growth mindset, I did.

Dweck states that people with a fixed mindset "worry about how much . . . intelligence they possess." They think that the amount of intelligence they have cannot be altered. They believe that what they have is all they are going to get. They do not seem to believe that they can reach their full potential. They give up right away without even trying. This is exactly what I thought when it came to math. Every year I dreaded my math class

Fun title!

*Good explana-
tions of fixed and
growth mindsets*

*Is it OK to use
"I" in the paper
or in the thesis?*

*Clearly sets up
focus on math in
rest of paper*

*Be more specific
about "people"—
maybe say
"students"*

*Strong quotes in
this paragraph*

*Title suggests
topic: math and
growth and fixed
mindsets*

*Thesis responds
to the prompt—
agrees with
Dweck*

*EX: how she
changed from
fixed to growth
mindset; connects
fixed mindset to
herself in math*

*EX: quote from
Dweck*

*Main idea: has a
fixed mindset in
math*

because it was the only class I felt behind in. Everyone else seemed to fully understand the material except for me. All I could think was, "They get it, you do not, and there is nothing you can do about it." I felt embarrassed. I decided not to try in math at all so people would think that the only reason I was failing was because I would not do my work and not because I did not understand the material. Little did I know that with a growth mindset and perseverance I could change all of that.

EX: quote to show a fixed mindset

EX: not trying, not doing work

Dweck also states that people with a growth mindset "understand that even Einstein wasn't Einstein until he put in years of focused hard work." People with a growth mindset know they will not be as smart as, say, Einstein right away, but they know that they do have the potential to become very intelligent. They are motivated by this; they want to have the feeling of accomplishing something. They do not mind all the hard work they have to put in because they want to reach their full potential, and in the end, that is the main goal. It is as Jane Austen once wrote, "The distance is nothing when one has a motive. . . ." What I think this quote means is that no matter how long it takes people to accomplish something, it should not matter because they have this strong motivation to get to their destination. I feel that they do better academically because they do not believe that they are bad at something, they just feel that they need to improve. This was a turning point for me.

Clear explanation of Dweck's growth mindset

EX: quote from Dweck

Is it necessary to write "I think"?

EX: quote from Austen

Main idea: Switches from fixed to growth mindset

In my math class I began to realize that many of the students were not "good" at math because they were born with that natural ability; it was due to the fact that they put all the effort they had into getting a better grade. This made me want to try my hardest the rest of the year. Every day in my class, I would ask questions and ask for help. Whenever there was a chance for extra credit, I would take it. I would constantly do practice tests every day. By the end of the year, I had received a B in the class and I was proud of myself. It felt great to finally have a high grade in math. I did not stop there however. Knowing that I was capable of getting a B, I decided to aim for a

Very good point! Hard work is necessary to learn math

Effective details about what a growth mindset looks like

EX: working hard and asking questions

EX: getting a good grade

Strong sentence

higher grade. To this day I am working on getting an A in my math class. Even if I do not get a high grade right away, I know that I am able to achieve it as long as I put effort into it.

Main idea: with a growth mindset, did well in math

   In the end, my experience has led me to the conclusion that a growth mindset can definitely lead to academic success. With a fixed mindset, I did not achieve anything. On the other hand, with a growth mindset, I became "good" at math. Dweck demonstrates that a fixed mindset should not be a limitation but rather be motivation to develop a growth mindset. Having a fixed mindset can negatively affect academic achievements if one feels incapable of reaching his or her goal, but with enough willpower, it can change from a weakness to a strength.

Main idea: growth mindset and improvement in math reinforces the thesis

STUDENT PAPER 2

Now it is your turn to read and annotate a student paper. Use the annotation strategies and the examples of annotations on Jiminez's paper to guide you as you review Alvarez's paper.

Before Reading: Predict

Complete the following using complete sentences.

1. Consider the title of the paper. How do you think the student will respond to Dweck's ideas? For instance, do you think she will agree or disagree with Dweck?

During Reading: Annotate; Evaluate

Complete the following exercises.

2. As you read, underline the writer's thesis and main ideas. Then briefly summarize these in the margins. Identify the examples.

3. What do you think are the most effective aspects of Alvarez's paper? Be specific by referencing words or sentences, examples, or paragraphs that you feel are especially strong and jotting down why.

4. Are there any parts of the paper you feel could be improved? If so, identify these specifically by referencing words or sentences, examples, or paragraphs and noting how these could be stronger.

Veronica Alvarez
©Alison Kuehner

Veronica Alvarez is the first person in her family to attend college. In fact, she encouraged her mother to follow in her footsteps and to take college English classes! Her first language is Spanish; she lived with her family in Mexico for eight years when she was in elementary and middle school. Alvarez is a psychology major and would like to work with students. Her advice to her peers is to stay on top of assignments, for instance, writing down all the important due dates in a planner at the beginning of the semester. Veronica says classes may be hard in the beginning, but if students put in the time and effort, they can be successful.

Handout

Sample annotated version of Alvarez's essay is in the Instructor's Resources.

Student Paper

Alvarez 1

Veronica Alvarez

Professor Kuehner

English 151RW

15 February 2016

Involuntary Resignation

In the article "Brainology," author Carol S. Dweck states that by having a fixed mindset we have less probabilities of being successful rather than the ones with a growth mindset. But . . . is this true? Can we guarantee that we will be successful by having a growth mindset? I admit I do agree with Dweck's observations of both mindsets: putting in effort and challenging ourselves with new things to increase our intelligence (growth mindset) is indeed more beneficial for us compared to convincing our mind that intelligence is a talent that we either have or not (fixed mindset). However, throughout my life, I have observed and known many people that started with a growth mindset and ended up converting into a fixed mindset. How is this possible? After experiencing high school in two different countries—Mexico and United States—I was able to notice that those who switched into a fixed mindset did not do it because they wanted to, but because they realized that they had no other option and gave up. In some places, putting effort into learning and being academically successful is still not enough. In Mexico, for example, if students do not have enough money to attend and actually graduate from a prestigious school, even if they have a growth mindset, there is a very low possibility that they will achieve their dream job . . . or any job. Having a growth mindset does not guarantee our success.

When I read the article "Brainology" for the first time, I was amazed by the author's splendid explanation about fixed and growth mindsets. I enjoyed reading it so much that I decided to read it a second time, but this time there was a specific sentence that caught my attention in which author Dweck described the fixed mindset in a student: "They don't want to make mistakes and feel dumb—and, most of all, they don't want to work hard and feel dumb. So they simply retire." After reading this, it made me think for a moment. Do students really retire because they have a fixed mindset and don't want to feel "dumb," or because they lost the motivation to keep studying? But really, both mindsets can drop out of school because of lack of motivation—not only fixed mindsets. After studying the first two years of high school in Mexico, I realized that there are many bright minds that are being wasted there; so many students with a growth mindset that, because of life circumstances, do not get to be as successful as they could. In order to obtain success, in whatever place that we happen to live in, we need money to attend a college or university. Of course, there are many financial aids and scholarships that can help students to not drop out because of their economic problems. However, being a student without enough resources to attend a distinguished school becomes quite more complex when they live in Mexico; if they do not come from a wealthy family, it is almost impossible to even think of getting a degree in whatever major that it is that they want to study. It is at this point that growth mindset students start to assimilate the crude reality of not being able to keep studying, and, therefore, not obtaining the job they aspire to. Their motivation to study and keep putting effort into school soon comes to an end, and everything related to school seems simply pointless since they know they will be unable to accomplish their dreams. These students did not retire because they did not want to make mistakes or feel "dumb," neither because they did not work hard enough . . . but because their opportunities of becoming successful were too low to come true. They were forced to have a fixed mindset.

After reading "Brainology" for a third time, I was able to notice that Dweck briefly talks about changing fixed mindsets into growth mindsets, but does not talk about growth mindsets turning into fixed mindsets. Does it seem too impossible for that to happen? To change a positive mind into a negative one? Believe me it is possible. Those students in Mexico with growth mindsets and shallow economic income became an involuntary fixed mindset; they once had motivation and wanted to learn; they wanted to succeed and not give up, but were never given the opportunity to prove so. Living in Mexico was a great experience, but unfortunately it is very easy to change a student's mentality into a fixed mindset over there. I remember having a growth mindset before moving from California to Mexico. Attending school was an adventure full of new and fresh experiences for me, I enjoyed learning new things everyday, and the fact that I was getting good grades out of it was just a bonus. As I begin my sophomore year in high school, I started to realize how my life would be if I stayed in Mexico. At that point all I knew was that I had to graduate high school there and that I had to find a way to be successful without worrying my parents economically. Thinking about my future gave me anxiety and made me cry for days; I did not know what was going to happen after graduating high school. The only way I could keep studying was if I attended a college that was two hours away from my house; nonetheless, it was almost impossible to get accepted, and acceptance still did not guarantee students they would get a decent job after. The stress was unreal; it got to the point in which I did not care anymore. No matter how much effort I put into school, money always came in first. I realize now that I started having a fixed mindset; I had no motivation at all and school started to be more of a load than an enjoyment. This should have not been an exception for me to stop having a growth mindset, but again, the possibilities of being successful in these circumstances are almost nonexistent—it can make a student lose interest in school very easily. Moving back to the U.S. was truly a blessing; once again I have a growth mindset and all the intentions of putting as much effort as I can on my studies and future.

In conclusion, we cannot base our success on whatever our mentality is; situations and issues in our life can make our mindset change even if we do not expect it to. A growth mindset student can lose motivation for school in any moment just like a fixed mindset: they both face the same risks of giving up. As I said in the beginning, I agree with Dweck that growth mindsets have more possibilities of succeeding than a fixed mindset, but it does not guarantee that they will indeed accomplish their academic dreams or get the job they aspire to. Growth mindset students can face major complications that can be more than they can handle, forcing them to give up and change into a fixed mindset. They did not stop trying because they were lazy or afraid of challenges, but because they lost the motivation that made them want to learn. The truth is, we can change our mentality and change it again and therefore cannot expect all growth mindsets to succeed and think always the same, nor does it mean that all fixed mindsets retire because they are afraid and think their intelligence is limited. Our life and mentalities have a background that is too complex to be defined by whether we succeed because we are smart or we do not succeed because we are not.

After Reading: Summarize; Evaluate

Complete the following exercises.

5. Review your annotations and write down what you feel are the two or three main strengths of the essay, as well as any areas that need improvement.

6. Did you have any questions about the writing? If so, write these down.

7. Do you feel Alvarez demonstrates a good understanding of Carol Dweck's ideas? Why or why not?

8. Do you feel Alvarez responds with her own original ideas and critical thinking to Dweck's ideas? Why or why not?

READING AND ANNOTATING FOR PEER REVIEW

An important strategy for becoming a strong reader, a skillful writer, and a critical thinker is to test your ideas by getting feedback from others. Writers often ask readers they trust to give them advice, such as what is working well, what is not clear, or what could be improved in the writing. For instance, in the chapter "Reading and Writing during the Writing Process," Mike Rose explains how he relies on "a diversity of readers" to give him "honest feedback" on his writing. "The College Reading and Writing and Learning Survey" in the chapter "Introduction to College Reading and Writing" includes "ask the instructor or a tutor to read my draft and give me feedback" as a strategy choice. This valuable feedback can be considered and then used to revise or edit the paper. The process in which writers share their work with classmates and provide constructive criticism is called *peer review*. (A peer is someone of equal standing, so your fellow classmates are your peers.) A valuable part of the writing process, peer review requires careful reading, thoughtful writing, and critical thinking to provide the most effective, useful feedback. You can use the same annotation strategies discussed in this chapter to review your classmates' writing. That is, you can read to understand the writer's main ideas and examples and then read again to indicate strengths of the paper and where the writing could be improved.

Peer review involves at least two people: the writer of the paper that is being reviewed and the reader of the paper whose job it is to provide feedback. Each person must perform his or her role as best as he or she can by trying to do the following.

Strategies for Readers Giving Feedback

- **Stay focused.** Consider the assignment and whether the writing achieves the goal of the assignment.
- **Understand the writing.** Identify the writer's thesis and main ideas, as well as the examples.

- **Provide positive feedback.** Focus on strong aspects of the writing—anything you think the writer does well, such as clearly stating a main idea, giving support for ideas, writing clear sentences, or using original thinking.
- **Offer constructive criticism.** Reflect on how the writing could be improved—anyplace the writing is not strong, such as where the writer does not respond to the topic, strays from the main point, does not clearly explain the ideas from the reading, or writes unclear sentences.

Strategies for Writers Receiving Feedback

- **Read and reflect.** Consider the reader's comments and be sure you understand what these mean; ask for clarification if need be.
- **Own your paper.** Focus on feedback you believe reflects valid strengths or weaknesses of your writing. You do not need to accept all criticisms as valid; use your own good judgment and remember this is your paper.
- **Apply feedback.** Use feedback to improve your writing. If you can build on your strengths, then do so. If you can revise weak parts, then make changes.

Spotlight Activity: Practicing Peer Review

If you completed a writing assignment for your class, exchange your writing with a classmate. Read and annotate each other's papers to understand and evaluate the writing.

Apply What You Learned

1. If you have read "Brainology," did reading the two sample student papers change your mind about Carol Dweck's ideas about fixed and growth mindset? Why or why not? If you have not read "Brainology," did the two student essays cause you to be interested in reading about Dweck's ideas? Explain.

2. Write a response to the Writing Prompt that was the basis for the two sample student papers in this Spotlight section. To do this, you will need to read Carol Dweck's "Brainology," if you have not already done so, and consider your own academic experiences in light of Dweck's ideas.

3. If you are currently working on a piece of writing for your English class or for any other subject, annotate the writing. Identify the main ideas and examples; then review the writing, looking for areas of strength and places where the writing could be improved. Use your annotations to help you improve the writing.

4. Answers will vary;
students may have learned
a consistent system for
annotating student papers
with feedback on the left
and outlining on the right.
The value of annotations is
to understand the structure
of the paper, as well as the
strengths and weaknesses
of the writing. Students
should be able to apply
these annotation skills to
their own writing or to any
writing they must read for
work or school.

4. What have you learned from this section about annotating writing, examining the annotated sample student paper, and annotating a student paper? For instance, what is valuable about annotating writing? What have you learned about how to effectively annotate? How might you use these reading and annotation skills in your college career or in your life?

Pair and Share

Review your written responses to prompts 1, 2, and 4 in the Apply What You Learned activities. Choose one response and exchange responses with a classmate. Read and annotate each other's papers to evaluate and give feedback on the writing.

PART TWO

Essential Elements of College Reading and Writing

Writing · **Reading** · **You** · **Engaging** · **Thinking**

Look for these icons throughout the chapter. They signal key strategies to use in Read to Write Activities.

After reading this chapter, you will be able to

- Identify the parts of a paragraph.
- Shape your writing to your purpose and audience.
- Write an effective paragraph with a topic sentence, supporting sentences, and a closing sentence.
- Revise paragraphs for unity and coherence.

Connect

Assign the LearnSmart Achieve topic "Generating Ideas" for adaptive learning to accompany this chapter.

Class Activity

Show the infographic in Figure 4.1 and use questions in text to start a discussion about procrastination.

Teaching Tip

Reading an infographic is covered in Chapter 1.

Theme: How Can We Deal with Procrastination?

Do you ever get distracted from a task you should be attending to? Do you sometimes put off what you could do right away? If so, you are *procrastinating*—delaying doing something because you do not feel like doing it.

In this chapter, you will read about procrastination—at school, at work, and in your personal life. You will consider what causes procrastination and how to manage it. This chapter also takes a look at paragraph structure, and you will write a paragraph about procrastination.

Figure 4.1, "Procrastination Buster," shows an *infographic*—a visual presentation of information combining text and pictures—that illustrates strategies to prevent procrastination. Each colored line identifies, in bold type, a strategy for dealing with procrastination. What are some of these strategies? What message or meaning do you take away from this graphic?

FIGURE 4.1 Procrastination Buster

What is the purpose of the cluster of graphics at the end of each colored line?

Source: Learning Fundamentals http://learningfundamentals.com.au/resources/

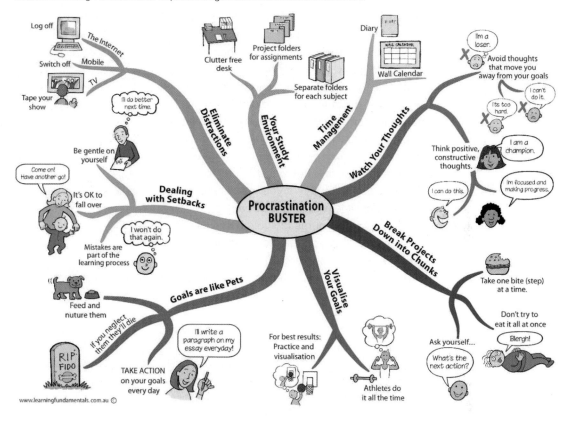

IDENTIFYING THE PARTS OF A PARAGRAPH

In your college courses, you may be asked to write a paragraph—perhaps on an exam, perhaps as a writing assignment. At work, you might be required to write an email, a report, or a letter. These situations demand writing clearly and with focus. Knowing how to compose a good paragraph is the key.

A paragraph may either stand alone or be part of a longer work, such as an essay or a report. A stand-alone paragraph usually concentrates on one main idea, which is typically expressed in a **topic sentence**. The main idea is then developed by the other sentences in the paragraph, called **supporting sentences**, that provide more information about the main idea. A writer can support the main idea in different ways, such as by providing examples and details, relating a story, or giving explanations. Sometimes, a paragraph ends with a **closing sentence** that wraps up the main point of the paragraph. To understand paragraph structure in writing, study the sample paragraph in Figure 4.2, which was written by a college student to advise other students how to avoid procrastination.

Class Activity

Ask students what they know about paragraphs. For instance, what are the parts of a paragraph?

Teaching Tip

Discuss when it is appropriate to use the first-person "I" or second-person "you" in writing. Consider audience and purpose.

FIGURE 4.2 Sample Annotated Paragraph

Sample Paragraph	Annotations
<u>Procrastination has a tricky way of sneaking up on you</u>. One minute you're searching for a word you don't know in your textbook; then the next thing you know, <u>you're halfway through season 5 of *The Office*</u>. Once you get <u>onto the Internet</u>, there are so many possible distractions that make it nearly impossible to remain focused on the current task. An <u>innocent online thesaurus</u> check in the midst of a grueling essay can metamorphose into hours lost to <u>online shopping and *YouTube*</u> if you're not careful. Oftentimes, it is wise to pull out a <u>paper dictionary or thesaurus</u> to avoid being sidetracked from your mission, and best to <u>avoid screens</u> during break periods. While working, some find it a distraction to even know their phone is within arm's reach, so it can be very beneficial to <u>put away electronics</u> until the job is done. To avoid procrastinating you need to avoid situations where you will be easily tempted to stop working. The key to successful distraction-free work is foreseeing distractions before they occur—and ensuring they will not be present in your workspace.	*Topic sentence focuses the paragraph on the challenges of dealing with procrastination.* *Supporting sentences provide details and examples to show how easy it is to procrastinate.* *Supporting sentences suggest solutions to distractions.* *Closing sentence wraps up the paragraph by suggesting writers need to anticipate and avoid electronic temptations.*

Before you read the articles about procrastination in this chapter, review the paragraph prompts in Read to Write Activity 4.1 and identify one that could be the basis of a paragraph you might write. **Prompts** are the directions for writing that indicate what topic to write about and how to write about that topic. Keep your chosen prompt in mind as you read and annotate the articles and answer questions about them.

Read to Write Activity 4.1

Choose a Prompt for a Paragraph on Procrastination

Select one of these prompts to help focus your reading and plan a paragraph about procrastination as you navigate through this chapter.

1. Suppose you are enrolled in a psychology or student success course. On the midterm exam, the instructor asks students to write a paragraph explaining

continued

one major cause of procrastination. In the paragraph, identify an important reason for procrastination and provide at least two specific examples to illustrate the reason.

2. The college newspaper will be publishing a feature story about procrastination. The editor has asked you to write a one-paragraph column providing solutions for procrastination. Present what you feel is the best solution for procrastination in a paragraph aimed at college students.

3. Management has identified procrastination as a problem in your workplace. Workers are not always completing their tasks on time or are rushing to meet deadlines at the last minute. Your manager notices that you do not seem to have a problem with procrastination and therefore asks you to write a short (one-paragraph) memo to your colleagues suggesting how they can best avoid procrastination.

4. Imagine that the designer of Figure 4.1, "Procrastination Buster," wants a written text to accompany the image. You have been assigned to write an explanation of the graphic. Select one of the strategies in the graphic and write a paragraph explaining how a person would implement that strategy. Feel free to provide examples and details that are in the graphic, as well as others that are not.

5. Write a paragraph addressed to students in your English class persuading them not to wait until the night before a writing assignment is due to start working on it.

6. Write a paragraph addressed to students in your English class describing specific steps they can take to prevent procrastination when completing assigned reading or homework.

You are about to read a news article, "Why Your Brain Loves Procrastination." This article begins by explaining why people tend to procrastinate. Before you begin reading, take a few minutes to become familiar with the topic by completing the "Before Reading" activities.

READING SELECTION

"WHY YOUR BRAIN LOVES PROCRASTINATION"

Newspaper articles tend to have shorter paragraphs than other types of writing, such as magazine articles and academic essays. As a result, a main idea in a news article might be developed over several paragraphs. Keep this point in mind as you read the article "Why Your Brain Loves Procrastination" and as you look for the thesis and topic sentences.

Connect

You will find a coordinated Power of Process assignment for this reading in your Connect course.

Complete the "Before Reading" and "During Reading" exercises. Then read the selection. Finally, complete the "After Reading" exercises.

 ## Before Reading: Recall Prior Knowledge; Predict

Write your answers to the following questions using complete sentences.

1. Do you think of yourself as someone who procrastinates or someone who gets things done right away? Explain.

2. Look at the title and read the italicized information before the reading. What do you think the reading will have to say about procrastination?

 ## During Reading: Find the Main Ideas

Practice annotating by completing the following exercise.

3. As you read, mark the thesis and main ideas.

Why Your Brain Loves Procrastination

By Susannah Locke

Vox, 8 December 2014

The first part of this article is composed by one person—Susannah Locke—and includes written paragraphs. Locke then interviews Timothy Pychyl, who has conducted research and written a book on procrastination. This second part of the article is an interview. Notice that the author's initials (SL) and the interview subject's initials (TP) indicate who is speaking.

Most people procrastinate from time to time. And most of the time it's not so harmful: putting off doing the laundry for a few days or 15 minutes here and there, lost in Facebook.   1

But procrastination can also create huge problems for many people—at work, at school, and at home. Consider all the people who keep meaning to start saving for retirement, for example, but never do it. Or people with obesity or diabetes who constantly tell themselves: "I'll start eating right tomorrow"—but never do it. Roughly 5 percent of the population has such a problem with chronic procrastination that it seriously affects their lives.   2

None of it seems logical. How can people have such good intentions and yet be so totally unable to follow through? Conventional wisdom has long suggested that procrastination is all about poor time management and willpower. But more recently, psychologists have been discovering that it may have more to do with how our brains and emotions work.   3

Procrastination, they've realized, appears to be a coping mechanism. When people procrastinate, they're avoiding emotionally unpleasant tasks and instead doing something that provides a temporary mood boost. The procrastination itself then causes shame and guilt—which in turn leads people to procrastinate even further, creating a vicious cycle.   4

But getting a better understanding of why our brains are so prone to procrastination might let us find new strategies to avoid it. For example, psychologist Tim Pychyl has co-authored a paper showing that students who forgave themselves for procrastinating on a previous exam were actually less likely to procrastinate on their next test. He and others have also found that people prone to procrastination are, overall, less compassionate toward themselves—an insight that points to ways to help. 5

Pychyl, a professor at Carleton University in Ottawa, Canada, has been studying procrastinators for some 19 years. I talked to him about why people procrastinate and how they can learn to stop: 6

Susannah Locke: What are the biggest misconceptions about procrastination? 7

Tim Pychyl: When a procrastinator thinks about themselves, they'll think, "Oh, I have a time management problem" or "I just can't make myself do it. There's a problem with my willpower." And when other people think about procrastinators, they use that pejorative term: "They're lazy." 8

But psychologists see procrastination as a misplaced coping mechanism, as an emotion-focused coping strategy. [People who procrastinate are] using avoidance to cope with emotions, and many of them are non-conscious emotions. So we see it as giving in to feel good. And it's related to a lack of self-regulation skills. 9

I can simplify that and say that psychologists recognize we all have a six-year-old running the ship. And the six-year-old is saying, "I don't want to! I don't feel like it!" 10

SL: What are you discovering about how procrastinators' brains work? 11

TP: Recently we've been doing research that relates to the work on "present self"/"future self" because what's happening with procrastination is that "present self" is always trumping "future self." 12

Hal Hershfield has done some really great research on looking at how we think about "future self." He's shown that in experimental settings, if someone sees their own picture digitally aged, they're more likely to allocate funds to retirement. When [the researchers] did the fMRI studies, they found our brain processes present self and future self differently. We think of future self more like a stranger. 13

My graduate student Eve-Marie Blouin-Hudon just did three studies, and what she looked at is our ability to imagine the future self. She measured people's self-continuity. You'd see circles representing present self and future self and choose how much to overlap them. Some people see these selves as completely distinct, and some people see them totally overlapping. The people who see the present and future self as more overlapping have more self-continuity and report less procrastination. 14

She's doing a study right now using an imagery intervention. So she's going to have students think of an image of themselves at the end of the term. And the hypothesis is that those students who engage with this imagery of future self will then procrastinate less. We [think] that people will make less procrastinatory choices now because they'll realize that "It's me in the future we're talking about, here. I'm going to be under the gun." 15

SL: What's the most surprising thing to you about procrastination? 16

TP: I think the most surprising thing that I'm still grappling with is that for many 17
people, the experience of procrastination doesn't match the definition that most of
us are working with: a voluntary delay of an intended action despite knowing you're
going to be worse off for the delay. If you speak to people, they'll tell you that it
doesn't feel voluntary: "I feel like I have no control over it." For some people, it feels
totally involuntary, like they can't help themselves.

SL: What's your one biggest tip for stopping procrastination? 18

TP: One of my pet expressions is "Just get started." And it's important you don't say 19
"Just do it"—that's overwhelming. But just get started.

    Whenever we face a task, we're not going to feel like doing it. Somehow adults 20
believe that their motivational state has to match the task at hand. We say, "I'm not
in the mood."

    Our motivational state rarely matches the task at hand, so we always have to 21
use self-regulation skills to bring our focus to it. So at first, it will be "Okay, I
recognize that I don't feel like it, but I'm just gonna get started."

SL: What's the evidence that just beginning a task, even in a very small way, makes 22
it easier to follow through?

TP: We know from psychological research by [Andrew] Elliot and others that 23
progress on our goals feeds our well-being. So the most important thing you can do
is bootstrap a little progress. Get a little progress, and that's going to fuel your well-
being and your motivation.

    Back in the 1990s, I put pagers on students and paged them [eight times a day 24
for five days before an academic deadline]. And when they finally started working
on the project, empirically we found that they didn't see it as difficult or as stressful
as earlier in the week.

    So their perceptions of the task changed. There's lots of reasons to think that 25
that's what happens to us when we get started.

SL: But what about getting distracted? 26

TP: [Peter] Gollwitzer and his colleagues for years have shown us that 27
implementation intentions make a huge difference to even deal with things like
distractions.

    Implementation intentions take the form of "If, then." "If the phone rings, then 28
I'm not going to answer it." "If my friends call me to say we're going out, I'm going to
say no." So you've already made this pre-commitment.

    You can use implementation intentions to keep yourself focused: "If I've 29
finished this part of the article, then I'm going to immediately turn my attention to
reading the next part."

SL: Can people really overcome procrastination? 30

TP: I guess I'm a living case. When I was an undergraduate, I procrastinated a lot. 31
And now that I understand procrastination, I just have no room to wiggle.

    Because it's all about self-deception—you aren't aware that it's going to cost 32
you, but you are. When there's no more self-deception and you face yourself, . . .

[y]ou're either going to do it, or you're not going to do it. I really like my life, and I like to make time for the things that are important to me.

[Robert] Pozen, who's written a book on extreme productivity, has the OHIO rule: only handle it once. And I'm like that with email. I look at that email and say "I can reply to it now, or I can throw it out," but there's not much of a middle ground. I'm not going to save it for a while.   33

And so if I can deal with it in two minutes—this is David Allen's work—I deal with it.   34

I used to procrastinate, and now I don't because I got all these wicked strategies. And it's every level: some of it's behavioral, some of it's emotional, some of it's cognitive. And now my biggest challenge is how do I teach my kids this. That's really hard.   35

Further Reading

Jaffe, E. (2013, March 29). Why wait? The science behind procrastination, a review of the contemporary research. *Observer, (29)*4. Retrieved from https://www.psychologi-calscience.org/observer/why-wait-the-science-behind-procrastination

Pychyl, T. A. (2013). *Solving the procrastination puzzle: A concise guide to strategies for change.* New York, NY: TarcherPerigee.

 ## After Reading: Summarize; Reflect on the Text

Write responses to the following exercises using complete sentences.

4. Review your annotations (from exercise 3 in "During Reading"). Then write the thesis and main idea in your own words; in other words, summarize the reading. Cite the source of the information by writing the title of the reading at the beginning of the summary.

5. What does it mean that procrastination is a "coping mechanism" that creates a "vicious cycle"? Does procrastination truly help people cope with their tasks?

6. What have researchers learned about procrastination by understanding how people see their "present self" in relation to their "future self"? Explain.

Answers

4. According to the reading "Why Your Brain Loves Procrastination," procrastination may feel good in the moment, but people should start on tasks and have strategies to deal with procrastination.

5. In a "vicious cycle," people avoid things they don't want to do by putting them off, but that makes them feel bad, which makes them avoid doing those things even more.

6. If we can imagine what we will be like in the future, we can accomplish present tasks.

Read to Write Activity 4.2

Engage with the Reading

Write responses to the following exercises using complete sentences.

1. The article suggests various ways people can avoid procrastination— "imagery intervention," "just get started," "implementation intentions," and "the OHIO rule." Select one of these strategies. Briefly summarize the strategy and then explain how you might apply it to a deadline you have coming up in the next week or month.

2. Do you agree that procrastination is counterproductive? Write a paragraph in which you describe an experience you had with procrastination.

Answers

1. Answers will vary. Example: OHIO means "Only handle it once." If I respond to a text as soon as I see it, then it's done.

2. Answers will vary.

Class Activities

Students explain how they figured out the thesis statement and what clues in the reading they used. Student pairs create a poster summarizing one procrastination strategy and illustrating how it could be applied. Students can talk about their posters and/or do a "gallery walk" to look at others' posters.

Pair and Share

- Compare the thesis and main ideas you identified in the reading (question 3) with those that a classmate identified. Did you locate the same thesis and main ideas?

- Compare your answer to question 1 in Read to Write Activity 4.2 (the strategy you identified to deal with procrastination and how you would apply it) with your classmate's answer. Discuss why you picked the strategy you did and how you feel it would be useful.

Vocabulary Strategy: Analyzing Words

Sometimes you can look at an unfamiliar word and figure out its definition by analyzing the word. This strategy works if you know the meanings of key parts of the word. The key parts include the *prefix* (a letter or letters at the beginning of a word that indicate a particular meaning) and the *root* (the core of the word that creates the basic meaning). In the word *reread*, for example, *re-*, meaning "again," is the prefix and *read* is the root. So *reread* means "to read again." As a second example, in the word *semicircle*, *semi-*, meaning "half," is the prefix, and *circle* is the root, so *semicircle* means "half a circle."

Vocabulary Practice

The table that follows lists some prefixes and roots and gives their meanings. In the numbered items following the table, write a definition for each underlined word from the reading selection "Why Your Brain Loves Procrastination," using word analysis and context clues from the sentence that will help you understand the meaning of the word.

Prefix	Meaning
mis-	wrong, mistaken
in-	not, within

1. "What are the biggest <u>misconceptions</u> about procrastination?"

2. "But psychologists see procrastination as a <u>misplaced</u> coping mechanism, as an emotion-focused coping mechanism."

3. "For some people, it feels totally <u>involuntary</u>, like they can't help themselves."

Teaching Tip

Using context clues is covered in Chapter 2.

READING AND WRITING ABOUT SIDEBARS

A *sidebar* presents information in a box that appears alongside a more detailed discussion of a particular topic. Sidebars are common in textbooks and magazine articles. Their purpose is to provide information to supplement or to highlight aspects of the main reading, including examples, research, and illustrations that can aid understanding. Sidebars can be useful sources of support in written work.

The sidebar shown in Figure 4.3 is from the textbook *Peak Performance: Success in College and Beyond* by Sharon Ferrett (2015). Reading the sidebar will give you a concrete sense of what characteristics define a procrastinator. You might find information in the sidebar with which to describe a procrastinator in your writing.

To read a sidebar, do the following:

- First consider how the information relates to the primary reading.
- Read the sidebar as you would any other text: from top to bottom and from left to right.
- Consider the relationship between the sidebar text and any featured illustrations, such as graphs, diagrams, and photographs.

Study the sidebar and answer these questions:

1. What is the title of the sidebar? What is the sidebar explaining?

2. Read the sidebar text and look at the photograph. How are the text and this illustration connected? What do you think is the purpose of the photograph?

3. After studying the sidebar, describe in your own words some characteristics of a procrastinator.

Answers

1. The title is "Am I a Procrastinator?" The sidebar explains what procrastinators do.

2. The photograph suggests the reader should think about the statements given in the sidebar.

3. A person who procrastinates avoids work and makes excuses or feels anxious about doing this.

FIGURE 4.3 **Am I a Procrastinator?**

Source: Sharon Ferrett; *Peak Performance: Success in College and Beyond*; McGraw-Hill Education, 2015.

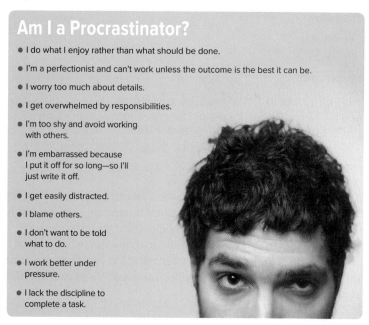

SHAPING YOUR WRITING TO YOUR PURPOSE AND AUDIENCE

As a reader, you should always determine an author's **purpose** and **intended audience**: why he or she is writing and for whom the piece is written. As a reader, this knowledge will help you understand what information is included and why. It will also help you respond critically, as you consider whether the writer achieved his or her purpose and wrote appropriately for the audience.

As a writer, too, you will need to consider your purpose and audience. In his book *Write Up the Corporate Ladder: Successful Writers Reveal the Techniques That Help You Write with Ease and Get Ahead*, Kevin Ryan quotes the author Suze Orman explaining how writing "begins with deciding why you are writing [purpose] and whom you are writing for [audience]" (165). For instance, you might be writing just for your own learning (low-stakes writing), or you might be writing to demonstrate your learning (high-stakes writing). Since low-stakes writing may be read only by you, it may not be as organized or as clearly written as high-stakes writing, which is aimed at readers. If you are writing for a reader, you must select the most appropriate information to support your points and determine the best strategy for convincing your readers that what you say is true or reasonable.

Teaching Tip

See Chapter 3 for a more extensive quotation from Suze Orman.

Purpose

Four categories of writing goals that are typically found in college-level readings can help you understand the purpose of a reading and think about your own purpose when you write. These goals are

- To inform.
- To instruct.
- To argue.
- To persuade.

To inform means to tell, explain, or give information. A news article that explains what *procrastination* means and describes situations in which people procrastinate is an example of writing to inform.

To instruct means to teach or to give directions or instructions. A student handbook that offers specific suggestions for avoiding procrastination is an example of writing to instruct.

To argue means to establish the truth—or likely truth—of a claim. A research report might argue that people procrastinate not because they are lazy but instead because procrastinating makes them feel good in the short term.

To persuade means to convince the reader to change his or her mind or to take action. An essay that encourages student writers not to wait to start writing until the night before a paper is due, and that gives reasons why, is an example of writing to persuade.

Class Activity

Ask students to think about who reads their writing. Who is their audience? Brainstorm a variety of audiences they might write for at work and at home and how that might change their writing.

Intended and Specific Audience

A starting point for understanding the intended audience for a piece of writing is to consider whether the target reader is a novice (a beginner) or an expert (an experienced or knowledgeable person) on the topic. For instance, newspaper articles are usually written for general, nonexpert readers. High-level scientific articles, on the other hand, are likely to be written for experts in a particular field of science.

It is also useful to think about the *specific audience*–the subset of readers to whom the material is directed. For example, the specific audience for a chemistry lab manual is chemistry students, and for a statistics textbook it is students in a statistics class. Sometimes readers can get clues about the specific audience by looking at who the writer is and where the writing is published. For instance, a student writing in the school newspaper is probably writing mainly for other students. A doctor publishing an article in a medical journal is likely to be writing for other doctors or health professionals. For some publications, such as magazines, it may be helpful to know who the readers typically are. For example, *The Atlantic*, a magazine focused on cultural and political affairs, is aimed at a college-educated audience, whereas *Sports Illustrated*, with a focus on professional sports, tends to appeal to sports fans. If you are not sure about the audience for a publication, you can ask a librarian or your instructor or do a little research to find out more about the publication's target readership.

Your instructor may provide information about how to think about your audience. As a student writer, you will often be writing for that instructor or for an academic audience in general. In such cases, your instructor may tell you to assume that your reader is an educated person. Or your instructor may tell you to assume that your reader is someone who is not familiar with the topic or with the assigned readings, as a way to encourage the development of your ideas. Still other times, the instructor may present an assignment with a specific target audience. For instance, in Read to Write Activity 4.1, each writing task includes clues that will help you, as a writer, determine the audience and purpose. For one example, review the sample prompt shown here. In this sample, the underlined words identify purpose and the highlighted words identify audience. Pay close attention to the directions for each writing assignment and ask your instructor for clarification if you are unsure about the audience.

Sample Annotated Prompt

Prompt	Annotations
1. Suppose you are enrolled in a psychology or student success course. On the midterm exam, the instructor asks students to write a paragraph explaining one major cause of procrastination. In the paragraph, identify an important reason for procrastination and provide at least two specific examples to illustrate the reason.	*Audience:* The clue "midterm exam" indicates the writing will be read and graded by the instructor. *Purpose:* The words *identify* and *illustrate* suggest the writer should inform the reader about procrastination.

Connect

Activity 4.3 can be found as a writing assignment in Connect.

Answers

1. The intended audience is college students.

2. The purpose is to instruct students how to work productively by avoiding distractions.

3. Answers may vary, but students may appreciate the specific details the writer gives, such as using a paper dictionary, to keep focused on the task at hand.

4. The writer achieves her purpose, especially when she concludes the paragraph by telling readers not to put themselves in the way of distractions.

5. The audience for prompt 1 is the instructor of the psychology class; for prompt 2, college students; for prompt 3, work colleagues; for prompt 4, general audience; for prompt 5, students in English class; and for prompt 6, students in English class. In all the prompts, the audience is stated, except for prompt 4.

6. The purpose for prompt 1 is to inform ("identify" and give "two specific examples"); for prompt 2, to persuade ("best solution"); for prompt 3, to persuade ("how best"); for prompt 4, to inform ("explanation"); for prompt 5, to persuade ("persuading"); and for prompt 6, to inform ("specific steps"). The clue words are quoted for each prompt.

Connect

Activity 4.4 can be found as a writing assignment in Connect.

Teaching Tip

Prewriting strategies are covered in Chapter 3.

Read to Write Activity 4.3

Recognize Audience and Purpose

Review the sample annotated paragraph in Figure 4.2 and the text that precedes it. Write your answers to the following questions in complete sentences.

1. Who is the paragraph's intended audience?

> ☐ **Tip:** Consider who the author is and why the paragraph was written.

2. What is the author's purpose?

> ☐ **Tip:** Think about the details in the supporting sentences and the message in the closing sentence to understand the purpose.

3. How do you think most of the intended readers would respond to this paragraph? Explain.

4. Do you think the writer achieved her purpose? If so, why? If not, why not?

5. Review Read to Write Activity 4.1. Who is the intended audience for each prompt? What clues in the prompt did you use to determine the audience?

> ☐ **Tip:** Read each prompt carefully to determine if the intended audience is identified.

6. In Read to Write Activity 4.1, what is the purpose for each paragraph prompt? What clues in the prompt did you use to determine the purpose?

> ☐ **Tip:** Read each prompt carefully, looking for clues that suggest the purpose of the writing.

Read to Write Activity 4.4

Generate Ideas for a Paragraph

Review Read to Write Activity 4.1. Then write your answers to the following questions using complete sentences.

1. Which Read to Write Activity 4.1 paragraph prompt did you choose for your paragraph-writing activity? Why?

2. Review the following prewriting strategies: reviewing your assigned readings, lecture notes, or class notes; freewriting; listing; creating a graphic organizer; outlining; or discussing. Select one strategy for generating and organizing ideas. Use that method to generate ideas for the prompt you chose in Read to Write Activity 4.1.

Pair and Share

- With a classmate, discuss the paragraph prompt you each selected in Read to Write Activity 4.1. Share why you chose the prompt you did.

- With a classmate, compare the strategies given in Read to Write Activity 4.4 that you used to generate ideas for your prompt. Which methods were most helpful for producing good ideas? Can you think of more ideas that could be included in your paragraphs?

DRAFTING: WRITING AN EFFECTIVE PARAGRAPH

Teaching Tip

Walk students through the steps of writing a strong paragraph to help develop their own writing on the topic of procrastination.

Let's assume you have selected a writing topic, completed some reading on it, and done some prewriting. This section describes a step-by-step process that will help you get started on your first draft for a strong paragraph. Each step focuses on one part of the paragraph. Several of the examples in the following steps come from the article "Classroom Resources for Addressing Procrastination" by Dominic J. Voge, which provides information to help students succeed in their college classes and appears on the McGraw-Hill Center for Teaching and Learning Web site.

Creating a Topic Sentence

Because a paragraph is focused on one main idea, that idea must be clear to readers. A topic sentence provides this clarity. The topic sentence typically includes the topic of the paragraph and the writer's attitude toward that topic. Keep in mind that an effective topic sentence, such as the following example from Voge's article, states the topic of the paragraph specifically enough so that all the supporting information directly relates to it.

> **EFFECTIVE TOPIC SENTENCE:** To overcome procrastination, it's critical to stay motivated for productive reasons.

This topic sentence identifies the topic of the paragraph: overcoming procrastination. It also gives the writer's attitude toward the topic—that staying "motivated for productive reasons" is "critical."

In comparison, here are two ineffective topic sentences. The first one is too general, and the second one is too specific.

> **TOO GENERAL:** There are many ways to overcome procrastination.

This statement is so general that readers will not know what to expect in the paragraph. To begin with, the phrase "many ways" is broad and nonspecific. It would be better to state exactly *one* way to avoid procrastination. On the other hand, a topic sentence can also be too narrow, or specific:

> **TOO SPECIFIC:** My friend was motivated to do well in his kinesiology class because he wants to become a physical therapist.

This statement is so specific that it does not allow the writer to develop and support the idea with more information. Also, if the assignment is to write about college students, then focusing on only one person might be too limiting for a body paragraph. This sentence might be a better supporting sentence in a paragraph about how or why students can stay motivated in their college classes.

Supporting the Main Idea

Teaching Tip

See Chapter 8 for more on types of support.

Teaching Tip

Brainstorm with students about different types of support and organization for the same topic sentence.

Writers can support the topic sentence in a paragraph in various ways, and different approaches might appeal to different readers. So writers often find it effective to include different types of support to be convincing. For instance, facts and statistics can demonstrate real and accurate support for a topic sentence. Quotations from experts can lend credibility to a writer's own ideas. An explanation of how or why something works can help readers think through a topic.

The types of support you use to organize your writing will depend on the controlling idea of the paragraph. For instance, if you want to describe why procrastination is a problem and propose a strategy for overcoming it, the order of your supporting sentences might be first to describe the problem and then to offer a solution.

Study "Strategies for Using Paragraph Patterns" to learn different ways to organize a paragraph.

Handout

"Strategies for Using Paragraph Patterns" is a reproducible handout in the Instructor's Resources.

Strategies for Using Paragraph Patterns

- **Analogy.** Make a comparison between two very different things. Present the familiar first and then the unfamiliar.

- **Cause/Effect.** Explain a cause and/or explain the effect that the cause produces. You can organize the information to present causes first, then effects, or effects followed by causes.

- **Classification.** Separate the topic into groups, or explain the various parts of a topic. Proceed by grouping information and explaining the logic behind that grouping.

- **Comparison/Contrast.** Show how two subjects are similar (compare) or different (contrast). Present information first about one subject and then about the other subject, or move back and forth in the writing between the two subjects.

- **Definition.** Provide a detailed definition of a key term. Present the term, explain its meaning, and give an example.

- **Description.** Provide specific details about what something looks, feels, tastes, smells, or sounds like so that the reader can visualize or imagine it. Organize information in a particular order, such as from top to bottom, if describing an object, or in chronological sequence (time order), if describing an event.

- **Example (or illustration).** Illustrate a point with one or more examples. Examples might proceed from the most obvious or most typical to more complex or unusual.

- **Narration.** Tell a story or an anecdote. Write chronologically from beginning to end.

- **Process.** Explain, step by step, how something works or is done. Organize the writing so as to follow a sequence of steps, such as what should be done first, second, and third.

Note that a writer might use more than one type of support in a body paragraph. For instance, suppose a writer wants to support the main idea that working in a place where others are also working can lead to productivity. To support this main idea, the writer might explain why the idea is true, as well as offer specific examples or details to show how it is true. The following two sample paragraphs, adapted from Voge's article, show how a writer might use cause/effect and example as support in a paragraph.

Supporting Sentences Using Cause/Effect	Annotations
"Productive reasons" means reasons for learning and achieving that lead to positive, productive, satisfying feelings and actions. These reasons are in contrast to engaging in a task out of fear of failing, or not making your parents angry, or not looking stupid, or doing better than other people to "show off." While these are all reasons—often very powerful ones—for doing something, they are not productive since they evoke maladaptive, often negative feelings and actions.	*Definition of "productive reasons"* *Contrast to non-productive reasons* *Effect of non-productive reasons*
Supporting Sentences Using Examples	**Annotations**
For example, if you are concerned with not looking dumb, you may not ask questions, delve into new areas, try new methods, or take the risks necessary to learn new things and reach new heights. A good way to put positive motives in motion is to set and focus on your goals. Identify and write down your own personal reasons for enrolling in a course and monitor your progress toward these personal, intrinsic goals as well as your grade goal.	*Example of strategies to avoid "looking dumb"* *Example of more effective strategies*

Closing the Paragraph

Often it is useful to end a paragraph, especially a lengthy paragraph or one that gives complicated information, by reinforcing the paragraph's main idea. A *closing sentence*, one that sums up the main point of the paragraph without repeating the topic sentence, can serve this reinforcing function. Here are the closing sentences from Voge's article:

> **EFFECTIVE CLOSING SENTENCES:** Remember to focus on your reasons and your goals. Other people's goals for you are not goals at all, but obligations.

These sentences end the paragraph by reinforcing the main idea that avoiding procrastination requires finding productive reasons. Notice that the sentences do not repeat the paragraph's main idea but rather bring the paragraph to

Teaching Tip

Provide students a sample paragraph without the closing sentence; have them compose a closing sentence; then share in groups or with the class.

a satisfying end. Here is an example of a closing sentence that is ineffective because it is repetitive.

> **INEFFECTIVE CLOSING SENTENCE:** In conclusion, it's important to stay motivated to avoid procrastination.

If the topic sentence is "To overcome procrastination, it's critical to stay motivated for productive reasons," then stating the same idea in the same words at the end of the paragraph is repetitious and to be avoided. Readers will remember your words; it is more effective to use fresh language.

The following concluding sentence is ineffective because it does not stay on the topic.

> **INEFFECTIVE CLOSING SENTENCE:** Overcoming procrastination can be hard work, but it is worth it.

If the topic sentence is "To overcome procrastination, it's critical to stay motivated for productive reasons," then concluding that writing is worth the "hard work" goes beyond the scope of the paragraph. It does not simply sum up the main idea of the paragraph.

To see how the topic sentence, supporting sentences, and closing sentences work together to create a paragraph, study Figure 4.4, "Model of an Effective Paragraph." This paragraph is adapted from Voge's article.

FIGURE 4.4 Model of an Effective Paragraph

To overcome procrastination, it's critical to stay motivated for productive reasons. Productive reasons mean reasons for learning and achieving that lead to positive, productive, satisfying feelings and actions. These reasons are in contrast to engaging in a task out of fear of failing, or not making your parents angry, or not looking stupid, or doing better than other people to "show off." While these are all reasons—often very powerful ones—for doing something, they are not productive since they evoke maladaptive, often negative feelings and actions. For example, if you are concerned with not looking dumb, you may not ask questions, delve into new areas, try new methods, or take the risks necessary to learn new things and reach new heights. A good way to put positive motives in motion is to set and focus on your goals. Identify and write down your own personal reasons for enrolling in a course and monitor your progress toward these personal, intrinsic goals as well as your grade goal. Remember to focus on your reasons and your goals. Other people's goals for you are not goals at all, but obligations.

Read to Write Activity 4.5

Evaluate a Paragraph

Review the model paragraph in Figure 4.4 and answer the following questions.

1. Do you feel the writer has an effective topic sentence? Why or why not?

2. Do you feel the writer has effective supporting sentences? Why or why not?

3. Do you feel the writer has an effective closing sentence? Why or why not?

4. Notice that the writer of the model paragraph uses *you* to address readers directly. Do you feel the use of second person (*you*) is appropriate given the author's intended readers (college students) and her purpose for writing (to give advice about how to avoid procrastination)?

Read to Write Activity 4.6

Draft a Paragraph

Follow the directions for each exercise.

1. Review your paragraph prompt and prewriting (from Read to Write Activity 4.4). Focus on a main idea. Write a topic sentence.

2. Review your prewriting and select appropriate support, such as examples, facts, or explanations, for your paragraph. Consider the different patterns of paragraph development. Select a pattern or patterns and write supporting sentences for your topic sentence.

3. Review your topic sentence and supporting sentences and write a closing sentence.

Pair and Share

With a classmate, exchange the paragraph you developed for Read to Write Activity 4.6 and evaluate each other's paragraph. Are the topic sentence, supporting sentences, and closing sentence effective? Why or why not?

REVISING PARAGRAPHS FOR UNITY AND COHERENCE

After you write a first draft of your paragraph, take the time to reread and revise it. To revise a piece of writing involves looking at its organization and supporting sentences and improving those aspects of your work. When revising, you might add or remove supporting sentences; you might move sentences around or substitute new words or new information.

Proceed systematically through the paragraph:

- First, consider the topic sentence. Check that this key sentence is on track—not too broad, not too specific, but clear about the topic and your attitude toward it.

- Then check that all the supporting sentences in the paragraph relate to the topic sentence. If they do, you have written a **unified** paragraph.

- Also check that the paragraph is **coherent**—that the ideas are presented in a logical order that will read smoothly. You want readers to move effortlessly from one idea or example to the next. The objective is to make your writing flow smoothly from one sentence to the other.

Apply the following strategies for developing coherence in your paragraphs. The examples are written by a psychology student writing a paragraph about sleep and learning, the same topic used in the prewriting examples earlier in Chapter 3 "Writing and Reading during the Writing Process."

Strategy 1: Keep the Focus of Your Sentences on the Topic of the Paragraph

If the paragraph is about sleep and learning, then include *sleep* or *learning* in most sentences. Doing this ensures that most sentences will focus on what the paragraph is about.

> Sleep is an important ingredient to help college students learn better. According to researchers, sleep helps the brain consolidate and retain information.

Strategy 2: Link the End of One Sentence to the Beginning of the Next Sentence

If you end a sentence by writing about one topic, then begin the next sentence by writing about the same topic. In this way, you link ideas from one sentence to the next.

> My first semester of college, I had a job that required me to work late and a class that required me to get up early. Rising at 6:30 a.m. to get to an 8:00 a.m. class on time meant that I was not well rested or in a mood to pay attention in class.

Strategy 3: Use Transitional Words and Phrases to Show the Relationships between Ideas

Transitional words and phrases, also known as **transitions**, show the relationship among ideas in a piece of writing. Selecting appropriate transitional words can help readers see the connection among ideas.

> Many college students do not get enough sleep. In fact, the National Sleep Foundation estimates that 63% of college students are regularly sleep deprived.

As you read and reread your paragraph, and as you revise and rethink the information, use the checklist in "Strategies for an Effective Paragraph" to remind yourself of how the parts of a paragraph should work together to create a unified and coherent whole.

Strategies for an Effective Paragraph

1. Does the paragraph have a clear topic sentence?

   _____ Yes, the topic sentence identifies the topic and the writer's attitude.

   _____ No, the topic sentence is too broad.

   _____ No, the topic sentence is too narrow.

2. Does the paragraph have sentences that appropriately support the topic sentence?

   _____ Yes, the supporting sentences all relate to the topic sentence and are coherent.

   _____ No, some supporting sentences are not related to the topic sentence.

   _____ No, some supporting sentences are not coherently organized.

3. Does the paragraph have a satisfying closing sentence?

   _____ Yes, the closing sentence wraps up the paragraph's main idea.

   _____ No, the closing sentence does not wrap up the main idea.

Handout

"Strategies for an Effective Paragraph" is a reproducible handout in the Instructor's Resources.

Read to Write Activity 4.7

Revise a Paragraph for Unity and Coherence

Review your paragraph from Read to Write Activity 4.6 and complete the following exercises.

1. Check that each sentence in the paragraph relates to the topic sentence. Revise as needed by changing, adding, or deleting sentences.

2. Check that the paragraph is coherent. Revise as needed by moving around sentences, adding transitions, or rewriting sentences.

3. Review one of the two model paragraphs in this chapter (Figure 4.2 or Figure 4.4) using the checklist in "Strategies for an Effective Paragraph." How effective is each part of the paragraph—topic sentence, support, and closing sentence?

Connect

Activity 4.7 can be found as a writing assignment in Connect.

Pair and Share

Exchange your paragraph with a classmate. Use the "Strategies for an Effective Paragraph" checklist to review each other's paragraph. Check carefully to determine if the paragraph is unified and coherent.

CHAPTER REVIEW

Key Terms

closing sentence A sentence that wraps up the main idea of the paragraph.

coherent Characteristic of a paragraph in which ideas are presented in a logical order.

intended audience For whom an author writes, such as for novice readers or experts.

prompt The directions for writing that indicate what to write about and in what particular way.

purpose The reason an author writes, such as to inform, to instruct, to argue, or to persuade.

supporting sentences Sentences in a paragraph that provide more information about the main idea.

topic sentence A sentence that states the main idea of a paragraph.

transitions Words or phrases that show the relationship among ideas in a piece of writing.

unified Characteristic of a paragraph in which all the supporting sentences relate to the topic sentence.

Chapter Summary

1. A paragraph focuses on one main idea and includes a topic sentence, supporting sentences, and usually a closing sentence.

2. Before writing, a writer needs to consider his or her writing purpose—to inform, to instruct, to argue, or to persuade—and the intended audience for the work.

3. The essential steps for drafting a paragraph are creating a topic sentence, supporting the main idea, and closing the paragraph.

4. Writers use several strategies to develop unity and coherence as they draft and revise their work.

5. Knowing the meanings of word parts can help a reader analyze and define a word.

6. When reading a sidebar, consider its relationship to the main text and to any other graphics.

Apply What You Learned

Follow the instructions in each exercise, using complete sentences for your answers.

1. Avoiding procrastination can help students be more productive and happy learners. Think of another important strategy, habit, or skill that college students need to be successful or engaged with their learning. Write a paragraph addressed to students in your English class explaining that strategy, habit, or skill.

2. Write a paragraph addressed to your instructor explaining what you learned from reading this chapter about writing paragraphs or about procrastination.

3. Now that you have learned more about procrastination, what, if anything, will you do to change your work, study, or personal habits? Explain using information from the readings in the chapter, as well as your own experiences.

Work Cited

Ryan, Kevin. *Write Up the Corporate Ladder: Successful Writers Reveal the Techniques That Help You Write with Ease and Get Ahead.* AMACOM, 2006.

Credits

5 | Reading and Writing Essays

Look for these icons throughout the chapter. They signal key strategies to use in Read to Write Activities.

After reading this chapter, you will be able to

- Analyze essay structure.
- Identify purpose and audience in a writing prompt.
- Analyze words to identify definitions.
- Read and write about tables.
- Draft a tentative thesis and essay plan.
- Write an effective essay introduction.
- Compose essay body paragraphs
- Write a strong concluding paragraph.
- Revise and edit to improve an essay draft.

Theme: Why Is Sleep So Important?

Statistics show that many college students do not get the recommended eight hours of sleep each night. Figure 5.1 shows a poster created for a University of Arizona educational campaign to encourage students to get enough sleep. Read the text on the poster. What reasons does it give students to get sufficient sleep? What suggestions does the poster make to help students sleep better? What does the photo on the poster imply about how a good night's sleep makes a person feel?

FIGURE 5.1 Go to Bed!

According to this poster, why might a person need to get a good night's sleep?

Source: "Freshmen Face Sleep Problems; Education Helps"; The University of Arizona, Campus Health Service, 2011.

In this chapter you will read about sleep—in particular, why it is important to get a good night's rest. You will read a student essay and a news article about sleep. As you work through the chapter, you will learn what an essay is and, in the process, you will have an opportunity to develop and write your own essay on sleep.

ANALYZING ESSAY STRUCTURE

In this chapter, we focus on reading and writing essays. An **essay** is a piece of writing that expresses an author's point of view on a topic. Essays are the most typical and fundamental type of student writing. You will learn the basic essay structure first by reading and examining essays and then by writing an essay yourself.

Class Activity

Ask students what they know about essays. What are the parts of an essay?

Essay Parts and Their Purpose

Much in the same way that paragraphs have three parts—a topic sentence, supporting sentences, and a closing sentence—essays usually have three basic parts: an introduction (beginning), a body (middle), and a conclusion (end). Each part serves a particular purpose. Here is an overview of how each part of an essay works:

1. The **introduction**

   - Draws readers in and makes them want to read the essay.

   - Clearly establishes the topic, or subject, of the essay.

   - Presents the writer's **thesis statement**, a sentence that sums up the main idea of the essay and states the writer's opinion on the essay topic.

2. The **body** explains, supports, and develops the thesis. Each **body paragraph**

   - Has a clear main idea, stated in a *topic sentence*.

   - Includes supporting sentences that providing personal examples, quotations from readings, or researched information.

   - Ends with a *closing sentence* that sums up the paragraph's main idea.

3. The **conclusion**

   - Briefly summarizes or synthesizes the information presented in the body of the essay.

   - Ends with a final thought for readers and gives a sense of closure.

Teaching Tip

See Chapter 4 for review of body paragraphs, including topic sentences, supporting sentences, and closing sentences.

A Published Student Essay

Figure 5.2 shows a sample essay with annotations entitled "To Sleep or Not to Sleep: That Is the College Student's Eternal Question," written by an undergraduate student. The essay, published in the online journal *Grey Matters* at the University of Washington, illustrates the different parts of an essay.

As you read the essay in Figure 5.2, you will notice parentheses follow some sentences. In the parentheses are the names of authors whose ideas or words are used in that sentence in the essay. Typically, a page number would also appear in the parenthetical citation after the author's name; however, since the sources are found online, no page numbers are needed. At the end of the essay is a works cited page that provides more information about the author's work. This citation style is called MLA (Modern Language Association) style and is often used in English classes. However, because the essay is a published paper, it does not have the full MLA heading it would have if it were submitted to an instructor for a class assignment. Know that different disciplines use different citation styles to fulfill the important requirement that writers give credit to the sources of information they use in their papers.

FIGURE 5.2 **Published Student Essay**
Source: Courtney Roberts; "To Sleep or Not to Sleep"; *Grey Matter*, Nov. 2013.

Roberts 1

Courtney Roberts

23 November 2013

To Sleep or Not to Sleep: That Is the College Student's Eternal Question

Ironically, I am currently in Odegaard, the University of Washington's 24-hour library, writing an article about sleep deprivation at one in the morning. As I am writing, I am wondering how many of my classmates are planning to take advantage of the library's hours to pull an all-nighter to cram for their midterms tomorrow. College students have been identified as a population group especially affected by sleep loss (an estimated 73% of students) (Buboltz et al.), which I am quite confident any college student or graduate would agree with. Sometimes, particularly around final examinations, it seems that sacrificing a couple hours of sleep is the only way to earn the "A." However, many years of research have shown that sleep deprivation is detrimental to cognitive ability (Buboltz et al.).

Sleep improves your cognitive ability by facilitating learning and memorizing new information in two ways. First, sleep aids restorative processes in the brain. When we are sleep deprived, we are not able to focus our attention as well—which we all know from personal experiences like trying to sit through a lecture the day after a long night (Smith and Lapp). Last month, the Nedergaard lab at the University of Rochester Medical Center published a groundbreaking paper in *Science* regarding the mechanism behind the restorative function of sleep. Their research shows that the restorative function of sleep is a result of a heightened ability to clear out the day's built-up, potentially neurotoxic waste from the interstitial space in the central nervous system (Xie et al.). During sleep there is a 60% increase in the interstitial space, causing a significant increase in the rate of convective exchange of cerebrospinal fluid with interstitial fluid (Xie et al.).

The heading identifies the author and the date of paper.

A catchy title identifies the paper's topic and draws in the reader.

The introductory paragraph sets the essay topic (sleep), gets the reader's attention (with personal details), and states the thesis (double-underlined and highlighted).

Page numbers to this and the Smith and Xie parenthetical citations should be added.

The first body paragraph includes a topic sentence (highlighted), provides supporting information (from research), and ends with a closing sentence (how sleep rejuvenates the brain).

Roberts 2

This then leads to an increase in the clearance of ß-amyloid, a protein that is the main component of amyloid plaques and associated with diseases such as Alzheimer's (Xie et al.). Clearing out these potentially toxic waste products thus allows our brains to be rejuvenated in the morning (Xie et al.).

Second, sleep is thought to help with memory consolidation ("Sleep"). There are three different steps in memory processing: acquisition, consolidation, and recall ("Sleep"). During acquisition, new information is introduced into the brain ("Sleep"). Consolidation refers to the stabilization of the memory and recall to the ability to access the information after it has been stored ("Sleep"). Both acquisition and recall only occur while we're awake; however, research has suggested that memory consolidation takes place during sleep ("Sleep").

There is no known mechanism of memory consolidation during sleep currently; however, many researchers think that specific characteristics of brainwaves, such as slow wave and rapid eye movement sleep, are associated with the formation of different types of memory ("Sleep"). One example comes from a study performed by Smith and Lapp. Smith and Lapp monitored honors psychology students during summer break and the consecutive weeks following final examinations during winter break. After final examinations, there was an increase in the number of rapid eye movements during the fifth REM period of sleep from the number made during summer break. These results suggest that an increase in the number of rapid eye movements during 5th period REM sleep—not the length of time spent in REM—accompanies extensive learning (Smith and Lapp). Other such correspondences between different sleep brainwave characteristics and types of learning have also been demonstrated (Smith and Lapp). It is quite likely that different types of learning and memorizing are accompanied with different changes in brainwave characteristics ("Sleep").

In addition, the study by Smith and Lapp also reported another interesting finding. When asked how well they thought they performed on the study's test, the sleep deprived students rated their performance

The second body paragraph includes a topic sentence, *supporting sentences (to explain how memory works), and a closing sentence (linking memory consolidation to sleep).*

The third body paragraph includes a topic sentence, *supporting sentences (from research studies), and a closing sentence (to explain the theory).*

The fourth body paragraph provides supporting sentences (from a study) and a topic sentence (that sleep deprivation harms performance and judgment).

significantly higher than non–sleep deprived students. Yet, the sleep deprived students still performed significantly worse than their counterparts (Smith and Lapp). A proposed explanation is that since the students were sleep deprived, they had to expend more effort to complete the task, which caused the students to think that they had performed better since they had tried harder. From this, the researchers proposed that many students are unknowingly sabotaging their own performance by choosing to sleep-deprive themselves before a complex cognitive task (Smith and Lapp).

All the research so far points to sleep being necessary for optimal cognitive ability. But, so what? We're still college students, and we're still going to have the same incredible amount of work and activities as always. It's the eternal problem of the college student. Yet, when students contemplate the question of "to sleep or not to sleep?" the research shows that sleep should be chosen over the extra couple of hours of studying.

The concluding paragraph briefly synthesizes information in the essay (sleep is necessary) and ends with a final thought to provide closure (students should get more sleep).

A works cited page at the end of the essay gives sources used in the essay in MLA style.

Works Cited

Buboltz, Walter C., Jr., et al. "Sleep Habits and Patterns of College Students: A Preliminary Study." *Journal of American College Health*, vol. 50, no. 3, 2001, pp. 131–35, doi:10.1080/07448480109596017.

"Sleep, Learning, and Memory." Division of Sleep Medicine at Harvard Medical School, 2007, healthysleep.med.harvard.edu/healthy/matters/benefits-of-sleep/learning-memory.

Smith, C., and L. Lapp. "Increases in Number of REMS and REM Density in Humans Following an Intense Learning Period." *Sleep*, vol. 4, no. 14, 1991, pp. 325–30, www.ncbi.nlm.nih.gov/pubmed/1947596.

Xie, Lulu, et al. "Sleep Drives Metabolite Clearance from the Adult Brain." *Science,* vol. 342, no. 6156, 18 Oct. 2013, pp. 373–77, doi:10.1126/science.1241224.

IDENTIFYING PURPOSE AND AUDIENCE IN A WRITING PROMPT

Teaching Tip

See Chapter 3 for more on choosing a topic.

Sometimes you will be given a choice of topics for a writing assignment. Other times you will be assigned a specific topic. In either situation, it is important to understand the essay assignment so you can successfully complete the task.

Recall that **prompts** are the directions for writing assignments giving the topic and specific directions for how to write about the topic. An essay prompt may consist of more than one sentence. Some statements or questions in a prompt may help you think about the topic. Some may give examples of what you might write about. Others may be the specific directions or your purpose for writing. It is important to read the prompt carefully and annotate its main points so that you fully understand what is required. Consider the following prompt.

> PROMPT: College faculty are considering the question "When should classes start in the morning?" Write an essay to present at a faculty meeting that explains when classes should begin in the morning and why this start time would be beneficial for students.

The question in the prompt—"When should classes start in the morning?"—asks you to think about the topic. The second statement—"explains when . . . and why"—gives the purpose for writing. As you carefully read a prompt, look for key words that

- Identify the *purpose* for writing (to inform, to instruct, to argue, or to persuade).
- Indicate the *audience.*
- Describe the *subject* of the essay.

You can remember these key features with this memory device:

PAS = **P**urpose, **A**udience, **S**ubject

Think about making a "pass" over the prompt, and underline or highlight the important words that help you understand the assignment. An annotated version of the sample prompt might look like this:

Sample Annotated Prompt

Essay Prompt	Annotations
Prompt: College faculty members are considering the question "When should classes start in the morning?" Write an essay to present at a faculty meeting that explains when classes should begin in the morning and why this start time would be beneficial for students.	*Purpose* = Explain when classes should begin and give reasons why; to persuade *Audience* = College faculty *Subject* = College classes and start time

In this chapter, you will read an essay written by a college professor about sleep. Before and while you read, review the essay prompts in Read to Write Activity 5.1 to think about how *you* might write about the topic of sleep.

Read to Write Activity 5.1

Choose a Prompt for an Essay on Students and Sleep

Select one of the prompts that follow to help you focus your reading and plan an essay about sleep as you navigate through this chapter.

1. What happens when people, especially college students, don't get enough sleep? Describe the effects of lack of sleep on a student's study, work, or personal life. Write your essay directed at your fellow students.

2. The college staff wants to know, "What can colleges do to encourage students to get enough sleep?" Write an essay to present to faculty, staff, and administrators at your college's health center explaining your perspective on this question.

3. Write an essay for your college newspaper giving advice to your fellow students about what college students can do to be sure they get enough sleep. In your essay, identify some activities that might be keeping students from getting enough sleep, such as working, using social media, or studying late at night, and suggest solutions for dealing with these obstacles.

4. Write an essay to be published in the *Chronicle of Higher Education*, a publication for college faculty and administrators, explaining the main reasons why college students do not get enough sleep. Write the essay from a student's point of view.

5. As a project for your health class, write an essay persuading students that getting a good night's sleep is in their best interest and describing ways to get enough sleep. Imagine this essay will be e-mailed to every student on campus as part of a back-to-school health campaign in the beginning of the fall semester.

6. In her article "Forget A's, B's, and C's—What Students Need Is More Zzzz's," which appears later on in this chapter, Mary A. Carskadon quotes the slogan of the energy drink Red Bull: "Nobody ever wishes they'd slept more during college." She argues that this is bad advice to give to college students. Write an essay aimed at fellow college students in which you agree or disagree with the comment, "Nobody ever wishes they'd slept more during college."

continued

7. The published student essay (Figure 5.2) concludes that when college students consider whether or not to sleep, "Sleep should be chosen over the extra couple of hours of studying." Write an essay aimed at fellow college students in which you explain when it might be acceptable or necessary for students to choose *not* to sleep so they can engage in some other activity. Be specific about when, why, and what students might do instead of sleeping, and justify those choices.

Read to Write Activity 5.2

Annotate an Essay Prompt 📖 📝

Answer

Students should clearly identify the key parts of the prompt: Purpose, Audience, and Subject.

Complete the following exercise: Review the essay prompt you selected in Read to Write Activity 5.1. Annotate the prompt, identifying the essay's PAS—purpose, audience, and subject.

You are about to read "Forget A's, B's, and C's—What Students Need Is More Zzzz's." This article begins with the author taking issue with a Red Bull advertising campaign message about sleep.

READING SELECTION

Connect

You will find a coordinated Power of Process assignment for this reading in your Connect course.

Teaching Tip

Let students know if or when it is acceptable to use "I" in their own writing.

"FORGET A'S, B'S, AND C'S—WHAT STUDENTS NEED IS MORE ZZZZ'S"

As you read, you will notice that the author, Mary A. Carskadon, uses the pronoun *I* (also called *first person*) to refer to herself. Sometimes students are told not to use *I* in academic writing because the focus should be on the subject, not on the writer. However, some writers use *I* to state their opinion or present their personal experience. Judge whether the use of *I* in the essay is effective given the audience and purpose of the essay.

Before you start reading, take a few minutes to become familiar with the topic by completing the "Before Reading" activity. Then complete the "During Reading" and read the selection. Finally, complete the "After Reading" questions and activities.

Before Reading: Predict; Identify Audience

Write the answers to the following questions using complete sentences.

1. Read the title of the reading selection and the italicized information preceding the essay. What do you think is the essay's topic?

2. Consider the author and the work in which the essay was published. Who do you think might be the intended audience?

3. Freewrite on the topic of whether college students get enough sleep, using your own experiences or what you know, have learned, or have read.

Answers

1. The title suggests the topic is college students and sleep.

2. The publication suggests the audience is college faculty.

3. Encourage students to think about themselves as well as other students.

During Reading: Find Main Ideas; Find Support

Practice annotating by completing the following activity.

4. As you read, mark the thesis and main ideas. If the thesis is not directly stated, write it in your own words.

5. As you read, identify the support for the main ideas.

Answers

4. The thesis is implied: Research shows sleep is important for college students.

5. In paragraphs 3, 4, 7, 8, 9, and 10, the topic sentence is first. In paragraph 6, the topic sentence is mid paragraph.

Forget A's, B's, and C's—What Students Need Is More Zzzz's

By Mary A. Carskadon

The Chronicle of Higher Education, 20 November 2011

The author, Mary A. Carskadon, is a professor of psychiatry and human behavior at Brown University and studies sleep in young people. Her essay was published in The Chronicle of Higher Education, *a source of information for college faculty and administrators. Carskadon argues that students, for the sake of their physical, mental, and academic well-being, need to resist temptations and slogans aimed at getting them* not *to sleep.*

Some advertisers routinely entreat us to undermine our health, but rarely through overt attacks on healthy behavior. When one such unhealthful message assaulting sleep reached my university's campus this fall, I began to hear about it from offended and sympathetic colleagues. One saw it in her freshman daughter's dorm. Another saw it in a campus convenience store. The makers of the energy drink Red Bull advised students that "Nobody ever wishes they'd slept more during college." 1

Decades of studies about the neurological and psychiatric importance of sleep in teens and young adults indicate that this "advice" is rubbish. Unlike the drink maker's aluminum cans, it should never be recycled. 2

In adolescents—and younger college students, according to recent data from my lab—sleep is a neurologically important process during which the fast-growing brain becomes better organized. Many neural connections forged earlier in life 3 during rapid growth are pruned away if they are no longer needed, and new pathways are established to the parts of the brain that are responsible for such things as planning, organizing, and abstract thinking.

Adequate sleep has implications not only for proper brain development but also for immediate behavior and safety. The list of negative outcomes associated with insufficient sleep goes well beyond merely feeling tired. A recent study of college students in Texas indicated that 16 percent of the participants reported falling asleep at the wheel. A study published by a researcher in my lab, Kathryn Orzech, found that college students who report inadequate sleep also report lower grades and more trouble with coursework. Still other studies have found an association between poor sleep and elevated alcohol use. The literature also supports associations between poor sleep and depressed mood and poorer physical health. 4

Any one of those outcomes should be enough to make a student wish he or she had slept more in college. 5

To be fair to the advertiser and its fun-loving sentiment, there really are a lot of opportunities for college students to have a good time. If students were getting enough sleep, they probably would miss out on some fun. But many studies, including Orzech's, have found that on average, young college students are not within shouting distance of the amount of sleep clinicians believe to be healthy. I tell my students that they should get about eight and a half hours of sleep every night, but a recent study found that students on average are getting nearly an hour less than that. I'll make that more explicit: College students should sleep more. 6

The well-substantiated finding that adolescents go to bed later and later as they age is not the fault of advertising. In fact, it is quite natural for older teens to stay up later—about 90 minutes or so—than younger ones. But the need for sleep doesn't change. Unfortunately, because many high schools start too early and assign a lot of homework, teens lose sleep simply because they are caught between two immutable forces: biology and the school schedule. That's probably why one lesson that college students learn quickly is to avoid early classes. 7

Other activities limit sleep as well, including texting, tweeting, and Facebooking in bed, which can keep students awake by producing light and causing social stimulation. (Studying late at night also involves light, although it is surely not as stimulating as is social networking.) Once teens get to college, whatever help their parents still provided to set a bedtime, or at least to encourage sleep, is no longer available. Students are left to exercise their judgment about when to sleep, and their decisions are based more on what to do while awake than when to sleep. 8

Advertising slogans that mock the choice for healthy sleep, and then deliver on that message with such chemical stimulants as caffeine, are certainly not helping. Caffeine is no more a substitute for sleep than are Cliffs Notes for reading original works of literature. 9

What will help, though, is education. Working with her former colleagues at the University of Arizona, Orzech found that a campus advertising campaign costing a mere $2,500 helped improve the sleep of about 10 percent of the students who saw it. It is also important to staff health- and psychological-services offices with people who are aware of the importance of sleep. 10

Although they suffer because of it, many students can at least get by with not getting enough sleep. But it is especially important that those who are struggling academically, medically, or psychologically receive guidance on how to improve their sleeping habits. 11

Students (and parents and educators) who think that sleep is directly related to mental health, academic performance, and personal safety will be better armed when faced with competing pressures, such as advertising. 12

Perhaps we'll someday hear of students referring to an "all-nighter" to describe their sleep rather than their lack of it. 13

 ## After Reading: Map the Text

Refer to the reading selection as you answer the following questions using complete sentences.

6. Review your annotations to determine which paragraph or paragraphs make up the introduction to this essay. How does the writer use the introduction to get your interest? Does she succeed in making you want to read the essay? Why or why not?

7. Review your annotations to determine which paragraph or paragraphs make up the body of this essay. Do the body paragraphs provide enough information to convince you of the thesis? Which pieces of support do you find most convincing?

8. Which paragraph or paragraphs make up the conclusion to this essay? Does the conclusion give the writer's opinion on the topic and end thoughtfully? Explain.

Answers

6. The first two paragraphs constitute the introduction. The first paragraph draws readers in with the Red Bull ad, and the entire second paragraph states the thesis.

7. Paragraphs 3–11 are the body paragraphs. Answers may vary, but the research studies, such as those in paragraph 4, should be convincing because they are factual evidence.

8. The last two paragraphs create the conclusion. Paragraph 12 synthesizes information in the body; the last paragraph leaves readers with a final thought.

Read to Write Activity 5.3

Engage with the Reading

Write responses to the following exercises using complete sentences.

1. "Forget A's, B's, and C's—What Students Need Is More Zzzz's" mentions an advertisement by Red Bull that suggests students would lose out on fun if they slept. Should colleges allow advertisements for consumer products on campus, especially if the product might be harmful to students? Why or why not?

2. "Forget A's, B's, and C's—What Students Need Is More Zzzz's" mentions an educational advertising campaign on the University of Arizona campus that seemed to be successful in persuading students to get more sleep. Should colleges use advertising to influence students' behavior? Why or why not?

3. What is your feeling about getting enough sleep? How does your own experience support or not support Carskadon's ideas?

Answers

1. Answers will vary. Encourage students to give support, such as examples or facts, for their opinion.

2. Answers will vary. Encourage students to give support, such as examples or facts, for their opinion.

3. Answers will vary. Encourage students to give support, such as examples or facts, for their response to Carskadon.

Read to Write Activity 5.4

Prewrite after Reading

Complete the following exercises.

1. Using the topic you selected for Read to Write Activity 5.1, do some freewriting, brainstorming, or listing about that topic by jotting down ideas from the reading that you agree or disagree with.

2. For each idea from the reading you listed in exercise 1, think of examples or details from your own experiences or observations to respond to the reading and to support why you agree or disagree. An example follows.

Sample Listing and Response

> *Mary A. Carskadon focuses on college students not getting enough sleep because "they probably would miss out on some fun."*
> - *I disagree somewhat. Yes, college students often don't get enough sleep, but that's because they are working a job to pay tuition or they have family obligations.*

Vocabulary Strategy: Analyzing Words

Sometimes you can figure out a word's definition through word analysis. This strategy works if you know the meaning of key parts of the word. These include a *prefix* (a letter or letters at the beginning of a word that indicate a particular meaning) and a *root* (the core of the word, which creates the basic meaning).

Vocabulary Practice

Write a definition for each underlined word from the reading selection, "Forget A's, B's, and C's—What Students Need Is More Zzzz's." Use word analysis by referring to the following table, along with context clues from the sentence, to understand the meaning of the word.

Prefix	Meaning
in-	not, within
neur-	relating to a nerve, or to the nervous system
psych-	mind, soul

Suffix	Meaning
-ology	study of

continued

1. "Decades of studies about the <u>neurological</u> and <u>psychiatric</u> importance of sleep in teens and young adults indicate that this 'advice' is rubbish."

2. "Many <u>neural</u> connections forged earlier in life during rapid growth are pruned away if they are no longer needed, and new pathways are established to the parts of the brain that are responsible for such things as planning, organizing, and abstract thinking."

3. "The list of negative outcomes associated with <u>insufficient</u> sleep goes well beyond merely feeling tired."

4. "A study published by a researcher in my lab, Kathryn Orzech, found that college students who report <u>inadequate</u> sleep also report lower grades and more trouble with coursework."

5. "But it is especially important that those who are struggling academically, medically, or <u>psychologically</u> receive guidance on how to improve their sleeping habits."

Answers

1. neurological = related to the nervous system; psychiatric = science related to mental and emotional disorders

2. neural = related to nerves or the nervous system

3. insufficient = not adequate, not sufficient

4. inadequate = not adequate, not enough

5. psychologically = related to the study of the mind and behavior

READING AND WRITING ABOUT TABLES

A *table* contains textual or numerical information that is typically organized in columns and rows. Tables appear frequently in research articles and sometimes in textbooks. Their purposes include presenting raw data that are discussed in a main reading and providing information to supplement such a reading. For example, a table might display data from a study, statistics from research, or factual information.

Tables are useful tools for clarifying and supporting a main idea in a reading. In this way, they can aid reading comprehension. They can also serve as a source of supporting information for a writer in a paper. In this way, they can serve as evidence for a thesis. The following table comes from a research article entitled "Causes and Consequences of Sleepiness among College Students." The table can help you understand what keeps college students from getting a good night's sleep and provide support in your own writing to explain why students do not get enough sleep.

To read a table, follow these steps:

- First, look at the title to understand the focus of the content.
- Next, study the organization. Note that headings usually run across the top of the table and labels (if present) often appear on the sides.
- Then read the information in the table.

Look closely at the table shown in Figure 5.3. Write answers to the following questions using complete sentences.

FIGURE 5.3 Challenges to Good Sleep Hygiene in College Students

Source: Shelley D. Hershner and Ronald D. Chervin; "Causes and Consequences of Sleepiness among College Students"; *Nature and Science of Sleep,* vol. 6, 2014; pp. 73–84.

Technology	Substances	College Scheduling and Activities
TV, computer, or video games before bed	Caffeine and energy drinks	Variable class schedules from day to day
Cell phones on overnight	Alcohol use	Late night socializing
Frequent exposure to light before bed	Stimulant use	Early or late obligations

1. What is the title of the table? What is the table explaining?

2. Read the table text and notice how the information is organized. What is the relationship between the bold text and the normal text? How are they connected?

3. After studying the table, explain in your own words why many college students do not get a good night's sleep.

4. Review your selected essay topic (from Read to Write Activity 5.1). What information from Figure 5.3 might you use in an essay on your selected topic?

DRAFTING A TENTATIVE THESIS AND AN ESSAY PLAN

You have chosen an essay topic, carefully read and annotated the prompt, and done some prewriting and reading on the topic. You feel ready to begin writing. Where do you start?

Tentative Thesis

Writers often produce many *drafts* (attempts at writing) before completing a final essay. To get started on your first draft, you can try writing a **tentative thesis** (or **working thesis**), your first effort at a thesis statement that will guide the initial draft. Your thesis will most likely change as you write the paper, but a working thesis will provide a focus to get you started. It may be a general statement of the topic and your approach to the topic, as the following sample tentative thesis shows:

SAMPLE TENTATIVE THESIS: College students do not get enough sleep.

In this tentative thesis, the subject is *college students and sleep;* the words *do not get enough* express the writer's attitude. However, the thesis is general. It does not state why college students do not get enough sleep, why this might be a problem, or even if there is a particular group of students who suffer more than others from lack of sleep.

Keep your purpose and audience in mind as you develop your thesis. For instance, Courtney Roberts, in her essay "To Sleep or Not to Sleep," uses research to *inform* readers that sleep deprivation leads to impaired cognitive ability. If you are writing about what colleges can do to encourage students to get enough sleep, you might *persuade* college administrators to take specific actions to improve students' quantity of sleep. Also consider your audience: for whom are you writing? Further refine your tentative thesis with your audience and purpose in mind. Here's an example.

> **REVISED TENTATIVE THESIS STATEMENT—INFORMATIVE:** Many years of research have shown that sleep deprivation is detrimental to cognitive ability.

This tentative thesis is informative because it explains why lack of sleep harms people's ability to think clearly; the explanations are supported by research and evidence.

> **REVISED TENTATIVE THESIS STATEMENT—PERSUASIVE:** The campus student health center should inform students about the benefits of getting sufficient sleep.

This tentative thesis is persuasive because it urges the campus student health center to take action to ensure students are better educated about sleep.

Essay Plan

After you have selected a topic and written a tentative thesis, the next step is to generate ideas for your essay. Then you can review those ideas with an eye to identifying the ones you can use. In particular, give attention to which ideas relate to the purpose of the essay and what support will appeal to your audience. For instance, college administrators who are interested in the experiences of many students might be persuaded by research or statistics, while students who are interested in their own behaviors and health might respond better to personal examples.

You can choose one or more of the following prewriting strategies: reviewing your assigned readings, lecture notes, or class notes; freewriting; listing; creating a graphic organizer; outlining; or discussing. Often it is useful to use several prewriting strategies to generate more ideas. For instance, Figure 5.4 shows a graphic organizer that includes details from the reading selection ("Forget A's, B's, and C's—What Students Need Is More Zzzz's"), details from the "Published Student Essay" (Figure 5.2), information from the table "Challenges to Good Sleep Hygiene in College Students" (Figure 5.3), and ideas from freewriting about the essay topic.

For a first draft, you might want to plan a three-part organization featuring these elements:

- Introduction (a beginning), in which you first present the topic and state your main idea (the thesis).
- Body (a middle), in which you provide support for your thesis.
- Conclusion (end), in which you conclude the main points of the essay.

Class Activity

Students compare thesis statements in groups to anticipate the main points of a paper based on its thesis statement.

FIGURE 5.4 Graphic Organizer: Whether Students Get Enough Sleep

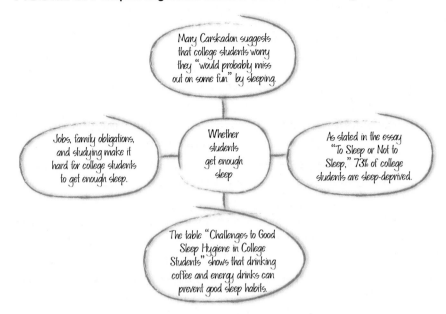

Class Activity

Students create posters with their informal outlines; other students include comments about what is effective and suggestions for improvement on sticky notes.

Then you can think about how you will flesh out each part of the essay. At this stage in the writing process, you might take your prewriting and your notes from annotated readings and create an essay plan, a rough outline to organize your thinking. A plan, such as the one shown here, will change as you write and develop the essay but should provide a launching point for your first draft.

Sample Essay Plan

Tentative Thesis: College students, especially those at community colleges, do not get enough sleep because many are juggling work, school, and a family life.

Body Paragraph 1: Working students have a hard time getting enough sleep.

Body Paragraph 2: Studying can interfere with getting a good night's sleep.

Body Paragraph 3: Family life can keep some students up late.

Body Paragraph 4: Social activities can also keep some students up late.

Conclusion: Lots of demands—academic, career, family, and social—keep students from getting the sleep they need.

Read to Write Activity 5.5

Write a Tentative Thesis and an Essay Plan

Complete the following exercises.

1. Create a graphic organizer that includes details from the reading selection, Figure 5.2, and Figure 5.3, and any ideas from brainstorming, freewriting, or listing related to your essay topic. Put your main idea in a center circle, and add links to connecting circles that have supporting examples, details, and information. See Figure 5.4 for an example.

2. Using your graphic organizer, write a tentative thesis statement.

3. Create a plan for your essay using your tentative thesis and the information in your graphic organizer. Include notes for each part of the essay: introduction, body paragraphs, and conclusion.

Connect

Activity 5.5 can be be found as a writing assignment in Connect.

Teaching Tip

Suggest students include reasons to support the thesis.

Answers

1. Suggest that students emulate the sample graphic organizer and include some information from each of the various sources in the text—the sample student paper, the reading selection, and the table—as well as their own ideas.

2. Encourage students to develop their thesis, as per the examples in the text.

3. Students can use key words from their thesis statements to build an essay plan, as well as part of their graphic organizer.

WRITING AN EFFECTIVE ESSAY INTRODUCTION

When readers pick up an essay, they do not necessarily know what the essay will be about. It is the job of the essay's introduction to ease readers into the paper—to help them move from the world around them into the world of the essay. Writers have various strategies for starting essays. Not all strategies work well in all situations, but knowing the different options can lead to a successful approach.

Sensible Strategies for Introductions

Writers know that they have only one chance to make a good first impression on their audience. So the very beginning of the essay must demonstrate that the work has valuable content and must engage readers' interest. The examples below show the opening sentences in possible introductions. (The writer would need to follow these opening lines with additional sentences to fully develop the paragraph.) These time-honored strategies for crafting strong introductions include:

- **Introduce and summarize source text(s).** Academic writing often requires analysis of texts read in class or located through research. In this case, it is a good move to name the sources in the introduction. Give the title of the text, state the author's full name, and briefly summarize the text. Note that after stating the full name, you should refer to the author only by his or her last name.

EXAMPLE: According to Mary A. Carskadon, a professor at Brown University and author of the article "Forget A's, B's, and C's—What Students Need Is More Zzzz's," most college students do not get enough sleep. Carskadon explains that the average college student sleeps seven and a half hours each night, when students should be getting eight and a half hours to be fully rested.

Class Activity

Before assigning this section, brainstorm with students ways to begin an essay.

- **Give background information.** Imagine that your readers are educated but not necessarily familiar with the topic. In the introduction, briefly tell them what they need to know about the topic to understand the essay. For instance, you might explain key terms or important ideas, state authoritative opinions or findings about the topic, or provide factual information.

EXAMPLE: Scientists who have studied sleep have developed different theories to explain why sleep is necessary for people. Researchers believe that sleep may serve various purposes, such as recharging the brain, releasing important hormones, consolidating learning, and repairing cells.

- **State an interesting fact or statistic.** While reading about the topic in preparation for writing, you perhaps came across a fact or statistic that sparked your interest. You might use this detail to get your readers interested in the topic, too.

EXAMPLE: A recent study published in the *Journal of Adolescent Health* shows that 70% of college students receive less than the recommended eight hours of sleep per night.

- **Ask a provocative question.** Questions can make readers think. Asking a thought-provoking question, one that does not necessarily have an easy answer, can be a good way to pique your readers' interest in the topic and encourage them to read on to find the answer.

EXAMPLE: Sleep takes up almost one-third of a person's life. When people sleep, they are not apparently doing anything productive—not eating or drinking, not working or playing. So why do people sleep? What purpose does sleep serve in people's lives?

- **Tell a story.** Describing your own experience can help readers personally connect with the topic. You can tell a story about something that happened to you or to someone you know, or you might describe what happened to a person you read or heard about in relation to the topic.

EXAMPLE: My first semester in college, I had a brilliant plan. I would take all my classes in the morning and therefore have afternoons free to study and evenings to hang out with friends. The only problem with this plan was my friends liked to stay up late, and I had to get up early for a math class that met at 8:00 a.m. Halfway through math, I would find my eyelids closing and my head drifting toward the desk. It was embarrassing to be caught by the professor napping, and worse news for my grade point average.

- **Begin with a quotation.** A quotation can be from a world-famous person, from a campus figure, or in some cases even from your grandmother, as long as it clearly relates to the topic. Quotations pull readers in and help them think concretely about the topic.

EXAMPLE: The American novelist and journalist E. W. Howe once said, "There is only one thing people like that is good for them; a good night's sleep." Yet most Americans do not get a good night's sleep.

Introductions to Avoid

Just as there are many effective strategies for writing introductions, there are also strategies that do not grab readers' interest and are therefore best avoided. The beginning of a possible introduction is shown in the examples below.

- **Providing unnecessary dictionary definitions.** Although you will inevitably need to define or explain some important terms in an essay, avoid defining terms that readers know. Also resist giving dictionary definitions that do not help readers understand the essay's thesis, as in the following example.

AVOID: According to Merriam-Webster's dictionary, *sleep* means "the natural state of rest during which your eyes are closed and you become unconscious." College students are often sleep deprived.

- **Making sweeping generalizations.** Sometimes students are taught to start with a general idea and work down to a specific idea (their thesis) in the first paragraph. Although this can be a reasonable strategy, beginning with a statement that is *too* broad may not provide a sufficiently clear connection to the topic.

AVOID: Sleep is a big problem in the world today. Every day there are many people who do not get enough sleep.

- **Stating the obvious.** Assume that your readers are an educated audience. If you start out by stating what readers should already know, readers will not be excited about reading the rest of the essay.

AVOID: Sleep is very important in a college student's life. If students do not get enough sleep, they will feel tired.

Read to Write Activity 5.6

Read and Write Introductions

1. Review the first paragraph of the essay "To Sleep or Not to Sleep" in Figure 5.2. What strategy does the writer use in the introduction? Might you use a similar strategy to begin your essay? Explain.

2. Review the first paragraph of "Forget A's, B's, and C's—What Students Need Is More Zzzz's" and your response to exercise 6 from the reading selection's "After Reading" activity. What strategy does the writer, Mary A. Carskadon, use to begin her essay? Might you use a similar strategy to begin your essay? Explain.

3. Review your notes from Read to Write Activities 5.2, 5.4, and 5.5. Select one of the sensible strategies for writing an introduction and compose an introduction for your own essay.

4. Review your notes from Read to Write Activities 5.2, 5.4, and 5.5. Select one of the sensible strategies for writing an introduction—a different one from what you used in exercise 2—and compose another introduction for your essay.

Answers

1. The writer gets the reader's interest with a personal example of studying in the library; students could use a personal example related to sleep.

2. The author opens with a quote from a Red Bull ad. Students could use a quote to start an essay.

3. Suggest students use a familiar strategy.

4. Recommend students use a strategy they have never tried before.

5. Prompt students to look for strategies to avoid when deciding which introduction is most effective.

Teaching Tip

Tell students that writing two introductions is a good way to experiment with different possible introductions. The Pair and Share activity will help them select a strong introduction.

Teaching Tip

Ask students to volunteer to read aloud promising introductions.

> ### Pair and Share
>
> With a classmate, exchange and read your two introductions (from exercises 3 and 4 in Read to Write Activity 5.6). Explain which introduction you find more effective and why.

WRITING BODY PARAGRAPHS

Body paragraphs are the heart of any essay. As a reader, you will examine body paragraphs carefully, looking for supporting information. As a writer, you will use body paragraphs to support your thesis and convince readers that what you say is true. You can use the basic paragraph structure—topic sentence, supporting sentences, and closing sentence—to develop body paragraphs in an essay. You can also use the various paragraph patterns—analogy, cause-effect, classification, comparison-contrast, definition, description, example (or illustration), narration, and process—to organize information.

Teaching Tip

This paragraph pattern is also known as PIE—point, information (or support), and explanation—and is explained in more detail in Chapter 6.

Academic writing often follows a pattern that represents a particular way of thinking about main ideas and support. Academic essay writers accordingly aim to do several things in a body paragraph:

- To present the *main point*, often in a topic sentence.
- To give *support* for the main idea, such as examples, details, quotations, facts, and statistics.
- To provide an *explanation* for how the support illustrates the main idea.
- To provide a *closing sentence* that sums up the main idea.

Study the following example to understand how a paragraph can use different kinds of support for its topic sentence.

Sample Body Paragraph

Body Paragraph	Annotations
One reason why many students don't get enough sleep is that they work. College costs money, so students need to work to pay tuition or buy books. Students don't always have control over their work schedules or may need to work at night in order to take classes during the day. For example, my best friend works at a shop in the mall. She works from six o'clock until closing time, which can be ten on weekdays or eleven on weekends. Then she has to stay after the store closes to straighten up the shelves, do inventory, and lock up. She often does not get home until after midnight. Other students take on extra hours at work during the holiday season in November and December, which is also when term papers and final exams are coming up. Extra hours at work and extra work at school mean less time to sleep.	*Topic sentence* *Support: Explanation* *Support: Specific example with details* *Support: General example* *Closing sentence*

Read to Write Activity 5.7

Read and Write Body Paragraphs

1. Review the body paragraphs of the essay "To Sleep or Not to Sleep" in Figure 5.2 at the beginning of this chapter. Might you use similar paragraph structures in your essay? Explain.

2. Review the body paragraphs in the reading selection ("Forget A's, B's, and C's—What Students Need Is More Zzzz's") and your answer to question 7 in the "After Reading" activity for the reading. Might you use similar paragraph structures in your essay? Explain.

3. Review your notes from Read to Write Activities 5.2, 5.4, and 5.5. Try writing a body paragraph for your essay. Begin with a topic sentence, provide support and explanation for that topic sentence, and include a closing sentence.

4. Review your notes from Read to Write Activities 5.2, 5.4, and 5.5. Select a paragraph pattern—analogy, cause-effect, classification, comparison-contrast, definition, description, example (or illustration), narration, and process—for writing a body paragraph. Use a different pattern than you used for exercise 2 in this activity. Write another body paragraph for your essay.

5. Review your notes from Read to Write Activities 5.2, 5.4, and 5.5. Write as many more body paragraphs as you need to develop the ideas for your essay.

Connect

Activity 5.7 can be found as a writing assignment in Connect.

Answers

1. Paragraphs begin with topic sentences, except the second paragraph, which ends with a topic sentence.

2. Students should group single-sentence paragraphs with other paragraphs to better see the topic sentences and support.

3. Students can annotate their paragraphs to show the support and explanation.

4. Students may need to use different support with a different pattern.

5. Students should select the most effective paragraph pattern and write as many body paragraphs as they need to support their thesis.

Pair and Share

With a classmate, exchange your body paragraphs (from exercises 3, 4, and 5 in Read to Write Activity 5.7). Suggest more strategies to develop the main ideas in each body paragraph, such as with information from readings or with more examples or details.

WRITING A STRONG CONCLUSION

Class Activity

Before reading this section, brainstorm with students ways to end an essay.

The last paragraph of the essay should help readers arrive at a satisfying conclusion. It should communicate a reason why the information in the essay is important. As a reader, look to the conclusion to pull together the essay's main ideas. As a writer, use your conclusion to help readers see the value of the information in the essay.

Sensible Strategies for Writing a Conclusion

The conclusion is the writer's opportunity to have the final say on the essay topic. A strong conclusion leaves the reader feeling satisfied that the topic has been explained well and positive about having read the paper. Choose from these strategies for creating a conclusion that hits the mark:

- **Ask yourself, "So What?"** A good way to end your essay is to consider the question "So what?" In other words, why is your topic important? Why does it matter? Answer questions like these in the last paragraph.

- **Come full circle.** Look back at your introduction to get inspiration for the conclusion. For instance, if you began with a story, you might end with the resolution of that story. If you started with a question, you might end with the answer.

- **Synthesize.** Often a conclusion can be more specific about the main idea of the essay than the introduction can be. After presenting information and support in the body paragraphs, you can pull these details together—*synthesize* them—in the final section, explaining clearly and concisely how the support reinforces the main idea.

- **Go beyond.** Although your conclusion should not introduce completely new ideas into the essay, you *can* suggest that readers think about the logical consequences of the ideas you presented. For instance, if the essay analyzed a problem, the conclusion may suggest a solution. If the essay looked at an issue, the conclusion might help readers come to a new understanding of that issue. A thoughtful conclusion might even help readers connect the important ideas in the essay to their own lives.

Conclusions to Avoid

Some strategies for ending essays should be avoided because they are not interesting or effective. Some are listed here.

- **Summarizing by unnecessarily repeating information.** Often students are instructed to summarize the essay or to repeat the thesis in the conclusion. Although it is possible to do so effectively, simply repeating what you have already stated can be boring or unnecessary.

- **Being vague or indecisive.** You might weaken your main idea if you undercut your argument by making an unhelpful qualifying statement such as "Everyone can have a different opinion on this topic." If you have asserted a thesis and supported that thesis, then stick by it to the end.

- **Introducing new ideas or new support.** Important ideas and support belong in the body paragraphs, not in the conclusion. If you find yourself developing a new idea with supporting evidence, consider writing another body paragraph before composing the conclusion.

Connect

Activity 5.8 can be found as a writing assignment in Connect.

Read to Write Activity 5.8

Read and Write Conclusions

Complete the following exercises.

1. Review the conclusion of the essay "To Sleep or Not to Sleep" in Figure 5.2. What strategy did the writer use? Might you use a similar strategy to end your essay? Explain.

continued

2. Review the conclusion of the reading selection, "Forget A's, B's, and C's—What Students Need Is More Zzzz's," and your response to exercise 8 in the "After Reading" activity for the reading. Might you use a similar strategy to end your essay? Explain.

3. Review your notes from Read to Write Activities 5.2, 5.4, and 5.5. Select one of the sensible strategies for writing a conclusion and compose a conclusion for your own essay.

4. Select one of the sensible strategies for writing a conclusion—a different one from what you used in exercise 3—and compose another conclusion for your essay.

Pair and Share

With a classmate, exchange your two conclusions (from exercises 3 and 4 in Read to Write Activity 5.8). Explain which conclusion you find more effective and why.

REVISING AND EDITING TO IMPROVE AN ESSAY DRAFT

The first draft is usually the beginning of an essay writing assignment. Experienced writers know that they must reread and rewrite their first draft several times until their paper meets the expectations of the assignment and of their readers, as well as of themselves as writers. After composing a first draft, writers should take a break—for an hour or even a day—and then reread the draft with fresh eyes.

Revising a draft involves looking at its organization and support to resolve problems in these areas. When you are reading your essay to revise, be sure the various sections do what they are supposed to do:

- First, determine whether the essay has a clear thesis and the draft stays focused on the thesis.

- Next, look at the body paragraphs to determine whether they have topic sentences and closing sentences related to the thesis. In addition, information in each body paragraph should relate closely to the topic sentence and thereby support it in a compelling way.

- Finally, check that the essay has an introduction that establishes the topic and captures the reader's interest and that the draft ends with a satisfying conclusion.

Use the checklist in "Strategies for an Effective Essay" to help you focus on the various parts of the draft, ask critical questions, and take care of any problems.

Answers

1. The writer synthesizes the information and leaves the reader with a final thought.

2. The author "comes full circle" because she uses a quotation at the end, as she did at the beginning.

3. Suggest students use a familiar strategy.

4. Recommend students try a new strategy.

Teaching Tip

Tell students that writing two different conclusions is intended for them to experiment with possibilities. The Pair and Share activity will help them select a strong ending.

Teaching Tip

Remind students that the writing process is described in Chapter 3.

Handout

"Strategies for an Effective Essay" is a reproducible handout in the Instructor's Resources.

Strategies for an Effective Essay

1. Does the essay have a clear thesis?
   _____ Yes.
   _____ No. (Describe how the thesis could be clearer.)

2. Does the essay have an introduction that sets the topic for the paper and attracts the reader's interest?
   _____ Yes.
   _____ No. (Describe how the introduction could be improved.)

3. Do the body paragraphs have clear topic sentences and closing sentences?
   _____ Yes.
   _____ No. (Identify where the topic sentences or closing sentences could be clearer.)

4. Do the body paragraphs include compelling supporting information?
   _____ Yes.
   _____ No. (Explain why not.)

5. Does the essay have a satisfying conclusion?
   _____ Yes.
   _____ No. (Explain why not.)

Teaching Tip

To distinguish strengths from weaknesses, students can use different colors (i.e., blue and black) to write comments on drafts.

Class Activity

Students can use the sample student papers in the Spotlight on Student Writing to practice commenting on papers.

Teaching Tip/Connect Activity

Ask students to annotate the revised draft, highlighting and explaining improvements to the draft.

Another strategy for revising is to read your draft and write comments in the margins. Alternatively, you can ask a trusted individual, such as a tutor or a knowledgeable classmate, to do so. During the first reading of a first draft, take care to examine the thesis, the body paragraphs and supporting evidence, and the introduction and conclusion for effectiveness. Focus on positive aspects of the essay, unclear parts, and specific areas needing improvement. The essay draft in Figure 5.5 has been annotated with comments to help with revision.

If you read and assessed your own draft, you should review the comments and make changes to improve the writing. If someone else read and commented on your draft, evaluate the comments thoughtfully before acting. You might have received some helpful suggestions for improving the essay. However, you might also have received feedback that is unclear or does not serve the purpose of your paper. In short, as the author, *you* need to decide how best to revise your writing. Take the comments that make sense and will improve the draft, and revise accordingly. Finally, read your draft carefully to edit the sentences and words, and to proofread for correctness. After revising, continue the writing process to polish your paper.

Figure 5.6 shows a revision of the draft essay in Figure 5.5 that takes into account the comments in Figure 5.5.

FIGURE 5.5 Draft of an Essay, with Comments

Essay Draft	Comments on Draft
Sleep is important for college students. According to Mary A. Carskadon, a professor of psychiatry and human behavior at Brown University, college students who do not get enough sleep "report lower grades and more trouble with coursework." There are many reasons why college students do not get enough sleep.	Good to include a quotation in the beginning to show importance of sleep.
Ironically, students who do not get enough sleep report lower grades, but that might be because students have to study. Often they study late into the night, and that keeps them from getting a good night's sleep. Although it's not the best thing to do, some students stay up the night before a test cramming or stay up the night before a paper is due writing their essay. Staying up until the wee hours of the morning means that they lose sleep. Students may also drink coffee or energy drinks to keep themselves awake. So in an attempt to get good grades, students may actually be getting poorer grades because they are depriving themselves of sleep.	Thesis: Include more evidence that students don't get enough sleep?
	Could be more specific: identify reasons?
	Make this the topic sentence?
	Include more evidence or details in paragraph to show how poor study habits interfere with sleep
	This detail seems out of place.
	Nice concluding sentence that sums up the dilemma for students.
When they are not studying, students like to spend time with their friends and socialize. No longer in high school, college students can stay up as late as they like. And the temptation when everyone else is talking, partying, having a good time is to join in the fun. There's no parent to tell the student when to be home or go to bed. So students often lose track of time in the quest to have fun. Plus some students work. Not all students can party. They have to work to support themselves and help pay for school and this adds stress to their lives and makes them lose sleep.	Make topic sentence more clearly related to sleep?
	Maybe write a separate paragraph about how work makes students sleep-deprived?
One solution to the problem of students not sleeping enough was pointed out in the article "Forget A's, B's, and C's— What Students Need Is More Zzzz's." The article stated that at the University of Arizona an advertising campaign helped students understand the need for sleep. A little bit of sleep can go a long way toward making students feel better and get better grades. Maybe more schools should help educate students about good sleep habits.	Good idea to reference the reading at the end and to give a solution.
	Conclusion could be stronger, more definite statement about sleep.

FIGURE 5.6 Revised Draft of an Essay

According to Mary A. Carskadon, a professor of psychiatry and human behavior at Brown University, the average college student gets seven and a half hours of sleep each night when he or she should be getting eight and a half. This shortage of sleep can be a serious problem, causing students to "report lower grades and more trouble with coursework," according to one research study. Other studies find that a lack of sufficient sleep is related to poor physical health and to serious problems like depression. Given these issues, why don't college students get enough sleep? The answer is that for so many students, juggling work, school, and a family life, a good night's sleep is the last priority.

One reason why many students don't get enough sleep is that they work. College costs money, so students need to work to pay tuition or buy books. Students don't always have control over their work schedules or may need to work at night in order to take classes during the day. For example, my best friend works at a shop in the mall. She works from six o'clock until closing time, which can be ten on weekdays or eleven on weekends. Then she has to stay after the store closes to straighten up the shelves, do inventory, and lock up. She often does not get home until after midnight. Other students take on extra hours at work during the holiday season in November and December, which is also when term papers and final exams are coming up. Extra hours at work and extra work at school mean less time to sleep.

Ironically, often students do not get enough sleep because they have to study. Although it's not the best thing to do, some students stay up the night before a test cramming or stay up the night before a paper is due writing their essay. Other more responsible students, like my friend who works at the mall, may be able to study only after they come home from work. That means staying up until two or three in the morning to complete their reading and assignments. To keep themselves awake, these students may drink coffee or energy drinks, which then make it hard to go to sleep. Indeed, a research article titled "Causes and Consequences of Sleepiness among College Students" cites "caffeine and energy drinks," as well as "stimulant use," as factors that prevent college students from having a good night's sleep. In an attempt to achieve good grades, students may actually be getting poorer grades because they are depriving themselves of sleep.

When they are not studying, students like to spend time with their friends or family. Indeed, "late-night socializing" is noted as a challenge to good sleep in the research study on "Causes and Consequences of Sleepiness among College Students." This makes sense given that younger students right out of high school can stay up as late as they like.

continued

These students may be tempted to hang out and party, to have a good time. After all, part of the college experience is late-night bull sessions and freedom from parents who set the rules for getting home and going to bed. So students often lose sleep in the quest to have fun.

Not all students can party, though. Some students have a family they are responsible for. The same research study notes that "early or late obligations" are factors that cut into sleep. Students who are parents might have to get up early to prepare children for school. Then, in the evenings, student parents might need to pick up their kids, feed them dinner, help them with homework, and put them to bed before they can hit the books themselves. Whether having fun with friends or being a good parent, students are people with personal lives that can sometimes make them choose that over sleep.

College students face lots of demands, including academic, career, and social, that keep them from getting the sleep they need. It's hard to juggle all these demands. Plus, sleep is not something that most people admit they want to do. As Mary Carskadon cited in her article, Red Bull's slogan is "Nobody ever wishes they'd slept more during college." Until students put sleep as a high priority on their to-do list, it's unlikely that most college students will get the eight and a half hours of sleep they need each night.

Read to Write Activity 5.9

Read to Revise a Draft

Use the essay you wrote for the Read to Write Activities in this chapter to complete the following exercises.

1. Study Figures 5.5 and 5.6 and notice the changes between the first draft and the revised draft. Why do you think the writer made the changes she did? How do they improve the draft? Do you agree with the changes that the writer made? Are there parts of the writing you would have kept in or taken out that the writer did not? Explain your answer.

2. Use "Strategies for an Effective Essay" to revise your essay by reading your draft and completing the checklist.

3. Read your essay and your comments on it. Mark parts of the draft that are effective or ineffective. Focus on concerns such as organization, coherence and unity of body paragraphs, and effectiveness of the introduction and conclusion, but not on grammar and spelling.

4. Read your essay again, focusing on the sentences, word choice, and correctness. Make any changes needed to improve the writing.

Connect

Activity 5.9 can be found as a writing assignment in Connect.

Answers

1. Answers will vary. The second draft is better developed with more details and references to the readings. It is also more clearly organized as each body paragraph has a clear topic sentence and closing sentence.

2. Students can use different colors (e.g., black = areas to improve; blue = strong points) to comment on their drafts.

Teaching Tip

For help with revising and editing, students can review "Strategies for Revising" and "Strategies for Editing and Proofreading" in Chapter 3

Pair and Share

- Give your essay draft to a classmate or someone else you trust and ask that person to complete the checklist in "Strategies for an Effective Essay."

- Give your draft to a classmate or someone else you trust and ask that person to write comments on it, looking at what is effective or not and making suggestions for improvement. Have your reader focus on the thesis, organization, and support, not on grammar and spelling.

CHAPTER REVIEW

Key Terms

body The middle section of an essay, which explains, supports, and develops the thesis.

body paragraph A paragraph in the middle of the essay that provides support for the essay's thesis.

conclusion The end of an essay, in which the writer summarizes the information presented in the body of the essay or gives final thoughts.

essay A piece of writing consisting of several paragraphs that expresses an author's point of view on a particular topic.

introduction The beginning of an essay, which establishes what the essay is about, sets the tone, gets the reader's interest, and introduces the thesis statement.

tentative (working) thesis An initial thesis statement that guides a writer during drafting.

thesis statement A sentence that gives the topic of the essay and the writer's opinion on the essay topic.

Chapter Summary

1. Essays, which are the most typical type of student writing, consist of an introduction, a body, and a conclusion.
2. Before you write an essay, it is a good practice to carefully read and annotate the prompt to ensure you understand the subject, audience, and purpose of the assignment.
3. To get started writing a first draft, you may find it helpful to compose a tentative thesis and create an essay plan.

4. An effective introduction sets the essay topic, gets the reader's attention, and states the thesis.

5. Each body paragraph includes a topic sentence and closing sentence and provides essential supporting information.

6. The essay's conclusion should communicate why the information in the essay is important and help readers feel satisfied about the ideas and their value.

7. Revising a draft involves rereading and rewriting with the goal of improving the writing.

8. Sometimes a word can be defined through analysis of the word parts.

9. Reading a table requires looking at the title, understanding the organization, and examining the information.

Apply What You Learned

Follow the instructions in each exercise.

1. Locate an essay about sleep in your college library. Identify the essay's introduction, body, and conclusion by annotating the work. If it is not feasible to annotate the essay, determine which paragraphs compose the different parts of the essay by referring to them by paragraph numbers.

2. Evaluate the essay about sleep that you found in the library (from exercise 1). Using complete sentences, comment on how effective the essay's introduction, body paragraphs, and conclusion are. Explain your evaluations.

3. Now that you know the importance of sleep, what, if anything, will you do to change your sleep routine? Explain using information from the readings in the chapter, as well as your own experiences.

Answers

1. Students can annotate using different colors for the different essay parts. They can also identify the introduction and conclusion strategies.

2. Students can use the checklist or annotate the essay to help with their evaluation.

3. Students can write an essay on this topic.

Credits

p. 119: "Go to Bed!" The University of Arizona-Campus Health Service. All rights reserved. Used with permission; **p. 121:** Roberts, Courtney. "To Sleep or Not to Sleep: That Is the College Student's Eternal Question." *Grey Matters*, 23 Nov. 2013. Copyright © 2013 Grey Matters Inc. Used with permission; **p. 127:** Carskadon, Mary A. "Forget A's, B's, and C's–What Students Need Is More Zzzz's." *The Chronicle of Higher Education*, 20 Nov. 2011. All rights reserved. Used with permission of The YGS Group; **p. 132:** Hershner, Shelley D., and Ronald D. Chervin. "Causes and Consequences of Sleepiness among College Students." *Nature and Science of Sleep*, vol. 6, 2014, 73–84.

6 | Writing about Reading

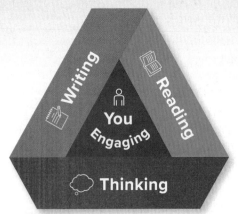

Look for these icons throughout the chapter. They signal key strategies to use in Read to Write Activities.

After reading this chapter, you will be able to

- Choose a topic for readings-based writing.
- Summarize a text.
- Quote from a text.
- Categorize and outline information from texts.
- Write a readings-based paragraph using PIE structure.
- Write an essay incorporating information from texts.
- Use the dictionary to define words in context.
- Read and write about a line graph.

Theme: What Is the Value of a College Education?

Connect

Assign the LearnSmart Achieve topic "Integrating Source Material into a Text" for adaptive learning to accompany this chapter.

This chapter's theme explores the question, what is the value of a college education? One way to think about this question is to consider how much attending college costs. Many students must work to make money, or they borrow money in the form of loans, to pay for a college education. They may wonder if going into debt is worthwhile. How does the infographic in Figure 6.1 illustrate this theme? To get at this question, first read the text in the black rectangle in the middle of the graphic and then examine the text in the white rectangles. What does this visual say about the level of student loan debt in the United States?

FIGURE 6.1 Student Loan Debt

Source: Graphic by *Bloomberg Businessweek*; data from College Board/Sallie Mae/Census/
NCES/FRBNY.

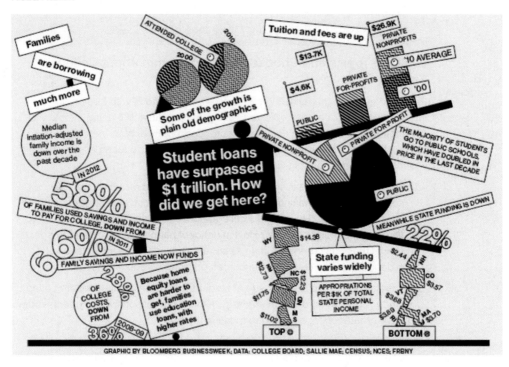

GRAPHIC BY BLOOMBERG BUSINESSWEEK; DATA: COLLEGE BOARD; SALLIE MAE; CENSUS; NCES; FRBNY

Why is student loan debt so high? What details and facts support the reasons
student loan debt is high?

In this chapter, you will read texts to understand more about student debt.
Then you will write an essay presenting facts and opinions about student debt that
you gained from your reading. In the process, you will learn how to summarize and
quote information from readings to use in your writing.

CHOOSING A TOPIC FOR
READINGS-BASED WRITING

Reading forms the basis for much of college writing, and indeed you will often be
called on to think about and write about texts you read. When you write about
what you read, you are basically saying, "This is what I read and learned; this is
what I understand about the topic." But also, your instructors may expect you to do
more than simply repeat what you learned from assigned readings. They assume
you will be able to explain ideas in the readings or relate these to other situations.
They may require you to evaluate or give your opinion about what you read. They
may want you to synthesize or organize information in original ways.

As you read about student debt in this chapter, think about how you might approach writing an essay on the topic of college debt. The prompts in Read to Write Activity 6.1 offer ideas for composing your essay.

Read to Write Activity 6.1

Evaluate Topics and Choose a Writing Prompt about College Student Debt

Read and evaluate the following topics on a scale of 1 to 3, with 1 being an interesting topic, 2 being a topic you feel neutral about, and 3 being a topic you are not interested in. Using complete sentences, briefly explain your level of interest in each topic. Then select the topic you plan to use for an essay you will write. Explain why this topic appeals to you.

1. Your economics class is studying the advantages and disadvantages for college students of taking on educational debt. The class is considering these specific questions: How might a college education benefit students' lives, careers, or earning potential? How might debt harm students' future prospects or limit their choices in life? In an essay, argue whether the advantages of a college education outweigh the burden of taking on educational debt.

2. Your class will discuss the issue of student debt, specifically, Why are college students taking on debt? In an essay, explain the reasons why students today have greater college debt than those in the past.

3. Interview students at your school about their debt and read interviews of debt-burdened students at other colleges. Select several students to profile in an essay for the school newspaper describing the situation of debt at your college and at other schools.

4. Your political science class is examining how laws affect people's lives. Because student debt has reached an all-time high, politicians have proposed various plans to help students reduce their debt. Explain at least three different governmental plans or legislative proposals to reduce student debt.

5. In your psychology class, you have learned that different people may have different reactions to similar situations. For example, many students take on debt to get themselves through college; for some, being in debt might be stressful, but for others, it might relieve stress. In an essay, explain how college students might react to and feel about debt and why.

Pair and Share

With a classmate, discuss the topics you were interested in and that you selected in Read to Write Activity 6.1. Explain why you each chose the topic you did.

SUMMARIZING FROM A TEXT

The first reading selection in this chapter—"The Average American Has This Much Student-Loan Debt"—discusses the magnitude of student loan debt in America. The reading also compares student loan debt with other types of household debts, such as credit card debt and mortgages. You will want to read carefully to understand the issues and take notes on the reading to help you write an essay.

Importance of Note-Taking

Imagine you are assigned to write an essay explaining the seriousness of student loan debt. Which parts of the reading selection might you focus on? Suppose instead that the assignment is to write an essay proposing ways to reduce student loan debt. Which parts of the reading would you focus on? It would make sense to pay attention to the facts and statistics showing how much loan debt Americans carry if your purpose for writing is to explain the seriousness of debt. On the other hand, focusing on programs to relieve student loan debt would make sense if your goal is to propose ways to reduce debt. The essay prompt and your purpose for writing will determine the parts of a reading to which you pay the most attention.

Once you select the parts of a reading that are most relevant to your purpose, you will want to take notes from those parts. **Taking notes** means recording information that is related to the essay prompt. The time you spend reading, thinking about, and taking notes on your readings will pay off in the form of an effective essay—one that you will feel good about writing, that will be meaningful and interesting for you as a student.

Take notes during or immediately after reading, when the ideas are freshest in your mind. The notes should include important information from each reading that will help you respond to the essay prompt. Researchers have found that students who take extensive notes while reading and who think through the information write higher-quality papers than do students who take few notes or who copy directly from sources into their papers. Moreover, students report that taking notes on their reading helps them organize their thinking, understand the issues and complexities surrounding the topic, and make connections across readings. So think of notes as an opportunity to learn from and to reflect on the information in your readings.

One way to take notes is by summarizing information from the reading.

Summarizing as a Note-Taking Strategy

To aid your understanding of a reading and to use that reading in your essay, you can rely on one important writing strategy: summary. To create a **summary**, you restate information from the reading in your own words. Moreover, a summary condenses information and focuses on main ideas. Also, a summary is shorter than the original passage.

When you summarize information, you must keep careful records of where you found the information. When you use your own words to take notes, you must always identify the source of that information, such as the author or the title of the reading. Taking the time and effort to restate information in your own words means

Teaching Tip

Review "Strategies for Summarizing" in Chapter 2.

Teaching Tip

You may wish to direct students to the Documentation Resource Guide for strategies to cite sources.

that you will have parts of your essay already written when you start drafting. You can incorporate summarized information into your essay for these purposes:

- To prove or support a point.
- To explain ideas.
- To maintain a consistent style and tone.
- To preserve the flow of thought.

When and How to Summarize

A summary is useful when you want to make information more compact. For instance, if you read several sentences or paragraphs that include relevant information, you might restate that information concisely in your own words to highlight the most important points. Let's say, for example, that you read about how student loan debt has increased in recent years, in "The Average American Has This Much Student-Loan Debt," and you want to explain the rise in debt but do not want to include all the details from the reading. You might restate the most appropriate parts in your own words. What follows is a passage from the reading and several examples of summaries.

> **ORIGINAL PASSAGE:** In addition, Americans' outstanding student-loan debt is heavily weighted toward recent graduates, who have had to borrow more to keep up with rising tuition costs. According to the website *Student Loan Hero*, the average Class of 2016 graduate has $37,172 in student-loan debt, over $10,000 more than the average borrower.

> **EFFECTIVE SUMMARY:** *The Motley Fool* reports that because the cost of college has gone up, the average student in 2016 borrowed approximately $10,000 more than students borrowed in prior years.

> **COMMENT:** This summary restates the idea that students "have had to borrow more to keep up with rising tuition costs" (Frankel 156) by rephrasing these words ("because the cost of college has gone up"). It also includes the idea that "the average Class of 2016 graduate has $37,172 in student-loan debt, over $10,000 more than the average borrower " by stating that "the average student in 2016 borrowed approximately $10,000 more than students borrowed in prior years." In this way, the summary shortens the original passage but captures its main ideas. Finally, the summary is introduced with a reference to *The Motley Fool*, which is the original source of the information.

Writing a good summary can be challenging and may require several tries. Practice is essential. When first attempting to summarize, you may find that your writing is vague or inaccurate or that it includes unnecessary details, as these next examples of summarizing the original passage illustrate.

> **VAGUE SUMMARY:** *The Motley Fool* reports that students owe more debt.

> **COMMENT:** Although this summary is accurate, it does not specify which students have the increased debt and how much more they owe.

> **BETTER:** *The Motley Fool* reports that students graduating in 2016 owe about $10,000 more in student loan debt than earlier graduates did (Frankel 156).

A summary must be completely accurate to the original source.

> **INACCURATE SUMMARY:** According to *The Motley Fool*, student loan debt is a serious problem.

> **COMMENT:** This summary incorrectly states that the reading claims that student loan debt is "a serious problem." However, the original passage makes no statement about whether or not student loan debt is serious. In fact, later in the reading, the author claims that credit card debt is "much more dangerous" (Frankel 156) than student loan debt.

> **BETTER:** According to *The Motley Fool*, student loan debt is on the rise (Frankel 156).

An effective summary omits unnecessary details—details that do not contribute to the main ideas of your essay. Here's another excerpt from the article.

> **ORIGINAL PASSAGE:** The roughly 23.2 million households with student loans have an average outstanding debt of $49,905. . . .

> Keep in mind that these are the *household* debt statistics, and that many households have more than one student-loan borrower. According to a *ValuePenguin* report, which used data from the New York Federal Reserve, the average outstanding balance per student-loan borrower is $26,700.

> **OVERLY DETAILED SUMMARY:** A story from *The Motley Fool* reports on student loan debt as well as auto loans, credit card debt, mortgages, and any other debt. It points out how often more than one person in a household is counted when calculating student loan debt per household. So whereas the average household debt for student loans is $49,905, each student in a household owes about $26,000 in debt.

> **COMMENT:** This summary includes many details from the original passage, but it is not clear how certain details, such as the other debt *The Motley Fool* reports on, help readers understand student debt.

> **BETTER:** *The Motley Fool* reports the average household debt for student loans is $49,905; however, the average student in each household owes about $26,000 (Frankel 156).

"Strategies for Writing an Effective Summary" restates the key steps to keep in mind when summarizing.

Strategies for Writing an Effective Summary

1. **Read the passage carefully.** Be sure you understand all the words and ideas. I think we need to add a step about taking notes, since the whole section prior to this box is about notetaking!

2. **Take notes on the reading.** Restate in your own words important ideas and information in the reading related to your writing purpose.

3. **Compose the summary without looking at the original passage.** Staring at the page while writing may make it difficult to use your own words to restate ideas. Instead, review your notes.

Handout

"Strategies for Writing an Effective Summary" is a reproducible handout in the Instructor's Resources.

continued

4. **Identify the most important parts.** For instance, if your purpose is to understand why students have debt, focus on a student's expenses or reasons for taking on loans.

5. **Consolidate details.** For instance, paying for rent, buying books, and paying tuition might be collected in the broad category "college expenses."

6. **Begin your sentence with different words.** Avoid following the same sentence structure or word order as the original passage; rewrite in a different style by starting your sentences in a different way.

7. **Check for unintentional plagiarism.** If you use three or more words in a row from the original passage, either quote them or rewrite them in your own words.

8. **Check for accuracy.** Be sure that details are correct and you have not changed the meaning when using your own words.

9. **Revise as needed.** Plan to rewrite, revise, and edit, because rarely is the first draft of a summary clear, accurate, and well written.

10. **Identify the source.** Use key words or phrases in every sentence in which you summarize information from a reading. Let readers know where you obtained that information by identifying the author or the title of the reading.

READING SELECTION

"THE AVERAGE AMERICAN HAS THIS MUCH STUDENT-LOAN DEBT"

As you read, look for information you might use in your own essay about college students and debt (see the essay prompt you chose in Read to Write Activity 6.1). Complete the "Before Reading" and "During Reading" assignments. Then read the selection. Finally, complete the "After Reading" assignments.

 ### Before Reading: Recognize Prior Knowledge; Predict

Write responses to the following exercises using complete sentences.

1. Do you feel that borrowing to fund a college education is a wise investment or a risky decision? Explain.

2. Skim the reading, looking at the subheadings. What are the main topics of the reading selection?

Answers

1. Students may feel that they will be able to get a job that pays better or is more rewarding with a college degree, so their education will pay off in the long run.

2. The reading will discuss the average American household debt, the increase in student loan debt, whether student loan debt is worse than credit card debt, and whether student debt will continue to increase.

During Reading: Annotate; Summarize

Complete the following exercise.

3. Chunk the reading according to the subheadings; then write a one-sentence summary of each section of the article.

The Average American Has This Much Student-Loan Debt

By Matthew Frankel

The Motley Fool, 25 June 2017

This article appeared on The Motley Fool, *a Web site that is devoted to financial news and personal investing advice. The term* motley fool *refers to a Shakespearean character, a common person who dressed like a jester or fool but used his wits to entertain or to outsmart others. The motto of the* Motley Fool *Web site is "to educate, amuse & enrich."*

As of the fourth quarter of 2016, Americans owed a total of $1.31 trillion in student-loan debt—more than for auto loans ($1.16 trillion) or credit card debt ($779 billion). Since there are approximately 126 million households in the United States, this translates to an average of $10,397 in student-loan debt per household. **1**

However, this doesn't tell the whole story, since fewer than 19% of households owe any money on student loans at all. The roughly 23.2 million households with student loans have an average outstanding debt of $49,905. **2**

The Average American Household's Debt **3**

According to "NerdWallet's 2016 American Household Credit Card Debt Study," the average American household carried a total of $99,836 in debt as of the fourth quarter of 2016. However, keep in mind that this includes households with no debt at all. The average American household that has any type of debt owes a total of $134,643.

The four major types of debt, in order from greatest total amount to least, are mortgages, student loans, auto loans, and credit cards. Here's a rundown of how much the average American owes on each type of debt, and how many households have each type. **4**

Type of Debt	Total Debt	Average per Household	% of Households with This Type	Average per Household with This Type of Debt
Mortgages	$8.48 trillion	$67,301	38.2%	$176,222
Student loans	$1.31 trillion	$10,397	18.4%	$49,905
Auto loans	$1.16 trillion	$9,206	31.8%	$28,948
Credit cards	$779 billion	$6,183	36.9%	$16,748
Any debt	$12.58 trillion	$99,836	74.1%	$134,642

Data source: "Nerdwallet's 2016 American Household Credit Card Debt Study." Calculations and chart by author.

The Average American's Student-Loan Debt

Keep in mind that these are the *household* debt statistics, and that many households have more than one student-loan borrower. According to a *ValuePenguin* report, which used data from the New York Federal Reserve, the average outstanding balance per student-loan borrower is $26,700.

In addition, Americans' outstanding student-loan debt is heavily weighted toward recent graduates, who have had to borrow more to keep up with rising tuition costs. According to the website *Student Loan Hero*, the average Class of 2016 graduate has $37,172 in student-loan debt, over $10,000 more than the average borrower.

Student-Loan Debt Has Ballooned in Recent Years, but Is Slowing Down

It's no secret that student-loan debt has skyrocketed in recent years. In fact, the total has grown by 186% over the past decade alone.

However, it looks like the growth of student-loan debt may be finally starting to slow down. Although it grew by 6.3% in the most recent one-year period for which complete data is available, this is actually the slowest growth rate since *NerdWallet* began tracking student-loan debt in 2003. To put this into perspective, consider that from 2003 to 2010, U.S. student-loan debt grew at an *average* rate of 17.9% per year.

Is America's Student-Loan Debt Really Worse Than Its Credit Card or Auto-Loan Debt?

To be fair, comparing student loans to auto loans and credit cards isn't exactly an apples-to-apples comparison. In all honesty, I think Americans' $779 billion in credit card debt is somewhat *worse* than their $1.31 trillion in student loans.

For starters, student loans tend to have much lower interest rates than credit cards. My outstanding student loans average about 6% interest, while my credit cards average about 15%. It's 150% more expensive for me to borrow on my credit cards than it was to borrow for my education. This alone makes credit card debt much more dangerous, especially if it's carried for a long time. Plus, student-loan interest can be tax-deductible.

In addition, there are programs in place to make it easier for student-loan borrowers to pay their debt that simply don't exist with other forms of debt. Repayment options such as the Pay As You Earn program keep payments affordable for working graduates, and forgive any remaining balance after a certain amount of time. Last I checked, my mortgage and credit card lenders didn't offer similar programs (although that would certainly be nice).

There are also deferment and forbearance options for borrowers who are experiencing financial hardships. And there are forgiveness programs, such as the Teacher Loan Forgiveness program and the Public Service Loan Forgiveness program, which wipe any remaining debt away after a specified period of employment (five years of teaching, or a decade in certain public-service jobs).

To be clear, I'm not saying that American student-loan debt isn't too high, or isn't getting worrisome. I think ballooning student-debt levels are a problem that needs to be solved. Rather, I'm saying that when you read headlines like "Student debt is nearly twice the size of credit card debt," take them with a grain of salt. Credit card debt, especially, is a much more dangerous form of debt for most Americans to carry.

Will the Student-Debt "Bubble" Continue to Grow? 13

Unless there's a serious change in the magnitude of available student-loan forgiveness programs, it's almost certain that student-loan debt will continue to grow. Inflation is a natural economic process, so college costs *should* rise over time, just not at the rates we've seen over the past few decades. And higher college costs will naturally translate into larger student loans.

The better question is: Will student debt grow at a healthy and sustainable 14
pace, or will it balloon out of control and create a nationwide student-debt crisis, as many experts fear?

 ## After Reading: Reflect on the Text

Write answers to the following questions using complete sentences.

4. What information or ideas in the reading are new to you? In other words, what did you learn about student debt from the reading?

5. Are there any ideas or information in the reading that conflict with what you already knew before you started reading? Explain.

Pair and Share

- With a classmate, compare your answers to exercise 4 in the "After Reading" activity. Discuss what you learned from reading the article.

- With a classmate, compare your answers to exercise 5 in the "After Reading" activity. Discuss what information in the reading conflicts with what you know.

Read to Write Activity 6.2

Engage with the Reading

Complete the following exercises:

1. The reading begins by stating that the average student loan debt per household is $10,397, but then immediately states that this fact "doesn't tell the whole story." What does the author mean? What is a more accurate picture of student loan debt?

2. The author states twice that credit card debt is "much more dangerous" than student loan debt. What support does the author give for this statement? Do you agree that credit card debt is more problematic than student loan debt?

Answers

4. Answers will vary. Students might find that the size of household student loan debt is new information.

5. Answers will vary. Students might feel the article's assertion that credit card debt is more "dangerous" than student-loan debt conflicts with their thinking.

Connect

"After Reading" questions can be completed in Power of Process.

Answers

1. The author means that the average does not show how many households carry debt or what the actual average debt per person is. A more accurate view is that less than 19% of households have student loan debt but the average owed is $26,700 per person or $49,905 per household.

2. The author points out that interest on credit card debt is much higher than on student loan debt and there are no options or programs to pay off credit card debt on account of financial hardship. Students may agree or not that credit card debt is more problematic.

Read to Write Activity 6.3

Summarize from a Reading

Using the essay topic you selected in Read to Write Activity 6.1, locate one part of "The Average American Has This Much Student-Loan Debt" to summarize in support of the prompt. Using complete sentences, write an appropriate summary following the guidelines in "Strategies for Writing an Effective Summary."

Pair and Share

Compare the summary you created for Read to Write Activity 6.3 with that of another student in the class. Check that your summaries are effectively written and relate to your chosen prompt.

Vocabulary Strategy: Building Dictionary Skills

Sometimes the meaning of a word cannot be figured out through context clues or word analysis. In these situations, use a dictionary to find the word's meaning. When you look up a word in a dictionary, do not simply accept the first definition given. Rather, read all the definitions carefully and look at how the word is used. Select the definition that fits the word in the context of the passage.

Vocabulary Practice

Select the dictionary definition that best fits the meaning of the underlined word in the context of the sentence from "The Average American Has This Much Student-Loan Debt."

1. "Since there are approximately 126 million households in the United States, this <u>translates</u> to an average of $10,397 in student-loan debt per household" (Frankel 155).
   a. To change words from one language into another language
   b. To explain (something) in a way that is easier to understand
   c. To have the same meaning

2. "[T]he average <u>outstanding</u> balance per student-loan borrower is $26,700" (Frankel 156).
   a. Extremely good or excellent
   b. Not yet paid
   c. Continuing to exist

3. "The better question is: Will student debt grow at a healthy and <u>sustainable</u> pace, or will it balloon out of control and create a nationwide student-debt crisis, as many experts fear?" (Frankel 157)
   a. Capable of being used without being completely used up
   b. Involving methods that do not completely use up natural resources
   c. Able to last or continue for a long time

READING AND WRITING ABOUT A LINE GRAPH

A *line graph* may be used to show how much something has changed over a period of time. For example, a line graph can show how temperature has gone up or down over several weeks or how enrollment at your college has gone up or down over several years.

To read a line graph, do the following:

1. Read the title and any captions to find out the subject of the graph.

2. Check the labels along the bottom of the graph, called the *x axis*. Do the labels indicate time periods or some other factor?

3. Check the labels along the left side of the graphic, called the *y axis*. What factors do these labels indicate—amounts of money? numbers of people? quantities of goods?

4. Construct a "how" question that incorporates the labels on the x and y axes. For example, ask, "How did *enrollment* [y axis label] at my college change from *2015* to *2019* [x axis labels]?"

5. Find the spot on the line graph that provides the information you seek.

Applying what you learned about reading a line graph, answer these questions concerning the graph in Figure 6.2:

1. What information does the graph show? Explain in your own words.

2. Based on this graph, what in 2017 constitutes the majority of nonhousing debt?

3. Based on this graph, how much did student loan debt rise from 2004 to 2017?

4. How might you use information from the graph in an essay explaining student loan debt?

FIGURE 6.2 Household Debt (Excluding Housing Costs)

Source: "Household Debt and Credit Report" 2017; Center for Microeconomic Data, Federal Reserve Bank of New York Consumer Credit Panel/Equifax.

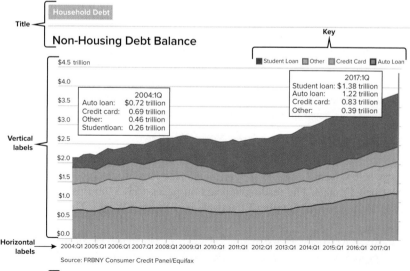

Answers

1. The graph shows household debt, not including housing-related debt (mortgages). Household debt includes student loans, credit card debt, car loans, and other debt.

2. Student loan debt in 2017 is the largest area of debt.

3. The graph shows that student loan debt has risen from about $0.26 trillion in 2004 to around $1.38 trillion in 2017.

4. This information could be used to show how student loan debt has increased and constitutes the majority of debt for households.

Read to Write Activity 6.4

Summarize from a Line Graph

Using the same essay topic you selected in Read to Write Activity 6.1, locate one part of the line graph in Figure 6.4 to summarize in support of the prompt. Write a summary of the graph information you selected using "Strategies for Writing an Effective Summary," which appears earlier in this chapter.

QUOTING FROM A TEXT

A **quotation** results when you copy words, phrases, or sentences exactly as written and enclose them in quotation marks. Like a summary, a quotation can support a point or elaborate on an idea.

When and How to Quote

So why use a quotation rather than a summary? In some circumstances, such as the following, directly quoting is more appropriate than using your own words:

- The original is particularly well written in clear, concise, or catchy language.
- The original passage uses key words or important phrases.
- You want to capture a person's precise words—for instance, because that individual is an expert or has firsthand knowledge about the topic.

Keep the following guidelines in mind when you are quoting someone directly:

- Copy the quotation exactly as written in the original; do not change the word order, spelling, or anything else.
- Enclose the borrowed material in quotation marks.
- Provide context when you introduce the quote: that is, identify the speaker and the situation. so readers understand the quotation.
- Always incorporate the quote into a sentence that you compose; a quote should not stand alone as its own sentence.
- Add a citation in parentheses at the end of the sentence to indicate the source. In MLA style, the citation should include the author's last name and page number, or just the page number if the author's name has been used previously in the sentence. If required by your instructor, include a works cited entry at the end of the paper for your source.

Integrating Quotations into Your Writing

For additional tips on quoting, study the following examples based on an original passage, below, from "The Average American Has This Much Student-Loan Debt" by Matthew Frankel. The reading appears on pages 155–57 in this chapter. Also refer to "Strategies for Quoting Effectively in a Written Work." The MLA works cited entry for the entire reading follows.

> Frankel, Matthew. "The Average American Has This Much Student-Loan Debt." *Writing to Read, Reading to Write*, edited by Alison Kuehner, McGraw-Hill Education, 2019, pp. 155–57. Originally published in *The Motley Fool*, 25 June 2017, www.fool.com/retirement/2017/06/25/the-average-american-has-this-much-student-loan-de.aspx

ORIGINAL PASSAGE: My outstanding student loans average about 6% interest, while my credit cards average about 15%.

EFFECTIVE QUOTATION THAT IDENTIFIES THE SPEAKER: Matthew Frankel explains that his "student loans average about 6% interest" whereas his "credit cards average about 15%" (156).

COMMENT: The writer introduces the quotation in his or her own words by explaining who is speaking.

ORIGINAL PASSAGE: I'm saying that when you read headlines like "Student debt is nearly twice the size of credit card debt," take them with a grain of salt. Credit card debt, especially, is a much more dangerous form of debt for most Americans to carry.

EFFECTIVE QUOTATION THAT IDENTIFIES THE SPEAKER AND THE SOURCE: *The Motley Fool* suggests readers should think critically about newspaper headlines with titles such as "Student debt is nearly twice the size of credit card debt" because credit card debt might be more difficult to pay off in the long term (Frankel 156).

COMMENT: The writer introduces the quotation in his or her own words by explaining the source of information and what the situation is.

Like summarizing, quoting well takes practice. At first, you may make the mistake of using overly long quotes, neglecting to integrate quotes, or not making quotes fit grammatically into your own sentences.

UNNECESSARILY LONG QUOTATION: *The Motley Fool* says, according to "The Average American Has This Much Student-Loan Debt," "When you read headlines like 'Student debt is nearly twice the size of credit card debt,' take them with a grain of salt" because "credit card debt . . . is a much more dangerous form of debt for most Americans to carry" (Frankel 156).

COMMENT: The quotation takes up most of the sentence. The first part of the quotation and the last part could be more effectively expressed in the writer's own words, as in the example "Effective Quotation That Identifies the Speaker and the Source," above.

Effective quotations are clearly integrated into your own writing.

UNINTEGRATED QUOTATION: Matthew Frankel describes his debts. "My outstanding student loans average about 6% interest, while my credit cards average about 15%."

COMMENT: Notice how the quotation is a sentence of its own, not introduced or integrated into a sentence composed by the writer. Moreover, the source of the quote is not completely identified.

BETTER: In describing his own experience, Matthew Frankel, in "The Average American Has This Much Student-Loan Debt," says, "My outstanding student loans average about 6% interest, while my credit cards average about 15%" (Frankel 156).

Quotations need to fit grammatically into the sentence in which they appear.

UNGRAMMATICAL QUOTATION: Frankel writes about student loan debt "My outstanding student loans average about 6% interest, while my credit cards average about 15%" (Frankel 156).

COMMENT: Although the quotation is integrated into the sentence, the quoted words do not fit smoothly or grammatically into the sentence. An example of a quotation used grammatically is shown in "Effective Quotation That Identifies the Speaker and the Source" on the previous page.

GRAMMATICAL QUOTATION: Writing about his own experience with debt, Frankel says that his student loans "average about 6% interest, while [his] credit cards average about 15%" (156).

To make a quotation fit grammatically into your sentence or to shorten a quotation, you may need to modify the language of the original text. You can make modifications in two ways:

1. If you remove words or phrases from the original text, use ellipses (. . .) to indicate where text was omitted.

2. If you must clarify information, such as a pronoun reference, or modify a word to make it fit grammatically into your sentence, such as change a verb tense, you can replace the unclear or ungrammatical word in the original with a more appropriate word in brackets ([ ]).

In the example that follows, ellipses indicate where words were removed; brackets signal that the verbs *think* and *needs* were altered to ensure a consistent point of view in the sentence.

ORIGINAL PASSAGE: To be clear, I'm not saying that American student-loan debt isn't too high, or isn't getting worrisome. I think ballooning student-debt levels are a problem that needs to be solved.

EFFECTIVE QUOTATION THAT SHORTENS AND CLARIFIES INFORMATION: The author of *The Motley Fool* article "think[s] ballooning student-debt . . . [is] a problem that needs to be solved" (Frankel 156).

It's time to put what you have learned to work. In the reading and activities that follow, you will practice selecting information from a reading by taking notes that involve summarizing and quoting relevant information. "Strategies for Quoting Effectively in a Written Work" summarizes how to use quotations.

Handout

"Strategies for Quoting Effectively in a Written Work" is a reproducible handout in the Instructor's Resources.

Strategies for Quoting Effectively in a Written Work

- Copy a quotation exactly as written in the original passage, including word order and spelling.
- Enclose the quotation in quotation marks.
- Introduce the quotation by providing context. Include other relevant information to help readers understand the background to the quotation.
- Identify the source of the quote by naming the author and/or title of the reading from which the quotation is taken.
- Always integrate the quote into a sentence of your own; never let a quote stand alone.

continued

- Use as much or as little of the quotation as needed to support your point. You can shorten quotations by eliminating words and adding spaced dots, or an ellipsis (. . .).

- If the quotation does not fit grammatically into your writing, modify a word (for example, change the verb to a different tense) and use brackets ([ ]) to indicate a change.

- Add a citation in parentheses at the end of the sentence to indicate the source. In MLA style, the citation should include the author's last name and page number.

READING SELECTION

"86 PERCENT OF COLLEGE STUDENTS VIEW HIGHER EDUCATION AS A GOOD INVESTMENT"

Complete the "Before Reading" and "During Reading" assignments. Then read the selection. Finally, complete the "After Reading" assignments.

 ### Before Reading: Recognize Prior Knowledge

Write answers to the following questions using complete sentences.

1. Do you view higher education as a good investment? Why or why not?

2. The article's title claims that a large majority of college students believe higher education is a "good investment." How do you think those students might define "good investment"? What are they getting for their money? Why might other students (14%) feel that college is *not* a good investment?

 ### During Reading: Annotate; Summarize

Complete the following exercises.

3. As you read, look for information you might use in your own essay about college students and debt (see Read to Write Activity 6.1 for the essay prompt you chose). Annotate the reading by marking potential quotes for an essay.

4. As you read, look for information you might use in your own essay about college students and debt. Take notes by summarizing information from the reading.

Connect

You will find a coordinated Power of Process assignment for this reading in your Connect course.

Answers

1. Students may feel that college is a good investment because they will become a better-educated person or they can be a role model to their children.

2. Good investment might mean making more money after college, or it could mean having a more fulfilling life.

Answers

3. Answers will vary.

4. Answers will vary.

86 Percent of College Students View Higher Education as a Good Investment

By Elise Rich

The Journal, 21 November 2012

The Journal *is the college newspaper for Webster University in Missouri. This article was published online about six months after student debt reached an all-time high of $1 trillion in March 2012.*

———————————————

When Brittany Marta graduated from college in May 2010, she owed $50,000 to the University of Missouri. Now a stay-at-home mom, Marta said she has not used her art history undergraduate degree for a specific job, but she does not regret her education. Marta believes education is not just about getting a job, but becoming a better person intellectually. 1

"School on the university level helped me develop my reasoning capabilities and use logic and rational explanations to explain my point of view," Marta said. "I am using all of the skills I gained and the person I became to raise my two children and give them opportunities in the future." 2

American college students currently hold nearly $1 trillion in student loan debt. The Institute for College Access and Success reports that two-thirds of 2011 college seniors graduated with student loan debt, with approximately $26,600 per borrower. Despite the debt, a Pew Research study reports 86 percent of college graduates say college was a good investment. 3

According to a 2007 College Board study, college graduates earn approximately $20,000 more per year than those who hold just a high school diploma. The study also reports college graduates are more likely to receive employer-provided benefits. 4

Zach Brengard, a former Webster University student, was pursuing a Bachelor of Fine Arts in painting at Webster. But Brengard decided to leave Webster in 2010 when a job opportunity in tattooing became available. 5

"Once I had an opportunity to do what I had planned to do when I graduated, I figured I'd might as well take it," Brengard said. 6

Brengard works in Las Vegas as a tattoo artist and is happy with his decision to leave school. He said he enjoyed his time at Webster, but felt his job experience has been just as beneficial in his development as an artist. 7

Peter Thiel, co-founder of PayPal, a system that allows money to be transferred via the Internet, and billionaire venture capitalist, said he believes there are times when college is not always necessary. 8

In a May 2012 *60 Minutes* interview with Morley Safer, Thiel said if a person wishes to pursue a career which requires a specific credential, then college is required. But if training or accreditation is not necessary for employment, students should think hard about whether college is worth the investment. 9

"We have a society where successful people are encouraged to go to college. But it's a mistake to think that that's what makes people successful," Thiel said. 10

Tracy Johnson, owner of SweetTpieS Dessert Studio in Festus, [Missouri,] graduated from Jefferson College in 1991. She said her business degree helped 11 with the accounting aspect of her own business. Johnson also said her experience as a real estate agent and her work in retail prepared her more than her degree. Johnson said she believes the best training for an entrepreneur is to shadow a professional in the field.

"Shadow someone successful with a proven track record—especially in the field you are looking for," Johnson said. 12

There are several nontraditional options besides a four-year degree. Technical schools provide specialized job training with competitive wages. 13

According to Ranken Technical College salary information, the average yearly wage for a graduate with three to four years of experience is $40,000 to $60,000. Ranken Technical College President Stan Shoun said despite the country's economic troubles, graduates are able to find jobs in their chosen career fields. 14

"In some areas such as machining, the demand is greater than the number of graduates," wrote Shoun in Ranken's 2012 fiscal report. 15

Nick Fowler graduated from Linn State Technical College with an associate degree in applied science in powersports technology. He graduated with less than $15,000 in student loan debt. Fowler said he was able to use the Missouri A+ Program, which partly financed his college education. 16

Fowler secured a job with Mungenast St. Louis Honda Motorsports before he graduated in 2009, but he was laid off within six months. Fowler was able to get work as a security guard after being laid off, but was disappointed he was not using his degree. 17

"At first I thought my degree was a waste of time because I couldn't find work in my career field," Fowler said. "But I recently got rehired this August at Mungenast St. Louis Honda MotorSports, so I can't complain." 18

After Reading: Find Main Ideas; Find Supporting Details

Write responses to these exercises using complete sentences as appropriate.

5. What is the main idea of the article? What clues in the reading helped you identify the thesis statement?

6. What information supports the main idea? Is there any information that contradicts the main idea?

7. The article features quotations from various people throughout. Select one quote and explain what important idea it supports.

8. Information is reported in the writer's own words throughout the article. Select one piece of such information and explain what important idea it supports.

Answers

5. The main idea of the reading is that most "college graduates say college was a good investment." The main idea is in the title and in a statement near the beginning of the reading.

6. The Pew Research study supports this main idea, given that 86% of college students feel college was a good investment. However, Peter Thiel is quoted as saying that college is not always needed to advance in one's career.

7. According to Brittany Marta, a stay-at-home mother, "School on the university level helped me develop my reasoning capabilities and use logic and rational explanations to explain my point of view." In other words, Marta feels her college education was a good investment because it made her a better thinker.

8. The author points to a College Board study that shows college graduates earn more money than high school graduates to argue that college can be a good investment.

Answers will vary. Remind students to use "Strategies for Quoting Effectively" when completing the exercises.

Read to Write Activity 6.5

Engage with the Reading

Complete the following exercises using complete sentences.

1. The reading quotes different people's views about getting a college education. Select one quote that you can identify with and explain why you can relate to that person's point of view.

2. Select one quote from the reading selection that you do not identify with and explain why you disagree with that person's point of view.

Read to Write Activity 6.6

Summarize and Quote from a Text

Write responses to the following exercises using complete sentences.

1. Review your annotations from "During Reading" exercise 3. Using what you have learned in this chapter, write a sentence that appropriately integrates a quotation from the reading that supports your essay prompt.

2. Review your annotations from During Reading exercise 4, then write an appropriate summary related to your essay prompt. Follow the tips for writing an effective summary.

Pair and Share

- Compare the sentence containing a quotation that you wrote for Read to Write Activity 6.6 with the sentence written by another student in the class. Check that each sentence effectively integrates the quotation and relates to the prompt.

- Compare the summary you created from Read to Write Activity 6.6 with that of another student in the class. Check that your summaries are effectively written and relate to the prompt.

Vocabulary Strategy: Building Dictionary Skills

The Vocabulary Strategy earlier in this chapter explained how to select the most appropriate dictionary definition of a word by using context clues. When trying to understand the meaning of an unfamiliar word, read all the dictionary definitions carefully, look at how the word is used, then select the definition that fits the word in the context of the passage.

continued

Vocabulary Practice

Select the dictionary definition that best fits the meaning of the underlined word from "86 Percent of College Students View Higher Education as a Good Investment" in the context of the sentence.

1. "In a May 2012 *60 Minutes* interview with Morley Safer, Thiel said if a person wishes to pursue a career which requires a specific <u>credential</u>, then college is required."
   a. Something that warrants credit or confidence.
   b. A document showing that a person is qualified to do a particular job.
   c. A government letter of introduction for a new ambassador.

2. "But if training or <u>accreditation</u> is not necessary for employment, students should think hard about whether college is worth the investment."
   a. Giving official authorization or approval of.
   b. Sending (someone, such as an ambassador) to act as an official representative.
   c. Certifying (a school or college) as meeting all formal official requirements of academic excellence, curriculum, facilities, and so on.

Answers

1. B is the correct definition.
2. A is the correct definition.

CATEGORIZING AND OUTLINING INFORMATION FROM READINGS

Before you draft any readings-based essay, it is crucial that you review and organize your notes with your writing purpose squarely in mind. Take care to create your own organizational plan rather than simply repeating the structure of the readings or writing a summary of each article. In this way, you can convincingly tell readers what you have learned about the essay topic and make your writing your own.

Categorizing Information

A good way to start planning your essay is to create your own categories of information and to group related ideas within those categories. First, review your annotations and notes on the readings to identify information that addresses the essay prompt. Let's say your prompt directs you to write about the advantages of a college education versus the disadvantages of student debt. You might begin by organizing information from the readings into the two broad categories of "Advantages" and "Disadvantages." Then, within each category, you can group related ideas. For instance, some advantages (such as getting a well-paid job and having access to an employee benefits plan) may have to do with accumulating wealth and could be grouped in that general way. Other advantages (such as learning about the world and making new contacts) might have to do with gaining personal satisfaction and may be grouped accordingly. Note that not everyone will categorize the advantages and disadvantages in the exact same ways.

Always be sure your classification of information includes separate and distinct categories. For instance, creating one category about how debt is a financial burden and another category about how debt keeps people from making major purchases might not be ideal because the categories are closely related.

The following list shows how a student might categorize notes by eliminating repeated ideas and grouping together some items. The student could then add numbers to reflect the order of ideas to be used in the paper.

Taking on Debt to Pay for College	
Advantages	**Disadvantages**
(3) College is a great personal experience. ~~Get to have interesting times and meet new friends.~~ *(Part of "great personal experience")* *(2)* College grads make more money, so loans are worthwhile. *(1)* Some parents can't afford college for their kids.	*(1)* You need to take any job just to pay off the debt. *(2)* Debt hurts society in general. ~~Debt ties you down.~~ *(Repeats first item)*

Creating an Outline

After categorizing your notes, you may want to develop a blueprint for your paper by outlining your essay. An **outline** is a plan for writing.

Writers use different types of outlines. Outlines can be as informal as a bulleted list of ideas. Informal outlines often include some phrases and incomplete sentences to express ideas and support.

Outlines can also be *formal*. Formal outlines use Roman numerals (I, II, III, and so on) to identify major headings and capital letters (A, B, C, and so on) to represent minor headings. Formal outlines typically feature complete, full sentences. A full-sentence formal outline includes a thesis statement, topic sentences, and support for each topic sentence, all written in complete sentences, as the example in Figure 6.3 illustrates. A formal outline is a tool you can use to begin writing key parts of the paper because it already contains the thesis statement and the topic sentences. You can also use the formal outline to check that you have supporting information for each body paragraph. If you do not have enough supporting material, you can do more reading to locate support, or you can revise the topic sentences to fit the support better. Notice that the formal outline in Figure 6.3 incorporates additional sources on college debt beyond the sources in this chapter.

FIGURE 6.3 Formal Outline

Essay prompt: Discuss the pros of a college education vs. the cons of student debt.

Purpose for writing: Explain the advantages of a college education vs. disadvantages of college students taking on debt.

Intended audience: Professor and classmates

I. Introduction

    A. Thesis statement: Although taking on debt to pay for college can limit a student's options after graduation, most students who

continued

acquire debt benefit because of greater earning potential, better job opportunities, and the personal satisfaction that comes with a college degree.

II. Advantages of student loans

    A. Loans allow poor students who otherwise could not afford higher education to attend college.

        1. Tiffany Brown had to take out loans to get through college when her father was ill. (New York Daily News)

        2. Christina Chaise grew up poor and needed loans to get through college. (New York Daily News)

    B. College graduates benefit monetarily in the long run; therefore student loans can be a good investment in their future.

        1. College graduates earn more money over the years than people who do not graduate from college. (quotes from The Journal and Bloomberg Businessweek)

        2. College graduates are less likely to be unemployed than nongraduates. (statistics from the US Bureau of Labor)

    C. Not only can attending college be a good investment financially, but college graduates also benefit personally.

        1. Brittany Marta feels that college made her "a better person intellectually." (The Journal)

        2. A Pew Research study shows that 86% of college graduates believe "college was a good investment." (The Journal)

III. Disadvantages of student loans

    A. Debt is not all good. For one thing, debt can limit students' choices after graduation.

        1. Tiffany Brown still lives at home and is not sure she can attend law school because she already has so much student debt. (New York Daily News)

        2. Christina Chaise is worried about taking on more debt to finish graduate school. (New York Daily News)

    B. Student loan debt burdens individuals and also hurts the economy by increasing overall consumer debt.

        1. Nineteen percent of households have student loan debt and those households owe almost $50,000. (Frankel, The Motley Fool)

        2. Individual student loan debt has increased sharply in recent years, from $26,700 to $37,172. (Frankel, The Motley Fool)

        3. Senator Kirsten Gillibrand says that student loan debt is "dragging down our economy." (New York Daily News)

IV. Conclusion: Although debt (and college) is not for everyone, student loans can allow some students to fulfill their dreams and accomplish their goals in life.

Read to Write Activity 6.7

Organize Notes and Create an Outline

Review your answers to Read to Write Activities 6.1, 6.3, 6.4, and 6.6.

1. Read this chapter's reading selections ("The Average American Has This Much Student-Loan Debt" and "86 percent of College Students View Higher Education as a Good Investment") and take fresh notes with your essay prompt in mind. Compose summaries and include quotations related to the prompt.

2. Review your notes and annotations on the readings from Read to Write Activities 6.3, 6.4, 6.6, and from exercise 1 in Read to Write Activity 6.7. Organize the information into categories.

3. Develop an outline for an essay. Use your organized information to create an outline, either informal or formal. You may use the sample outline in Figure 6.3 as a guide.

Pair and Share

Exchange outlines (exercise 3 from Read to Write Activity 6.7) with a classmate. Review each other's outlines and check that there are quotes and summaries from the readings that relate to the thesis and main ideas of the essay. Point out any support you feel is not well connected to a main idea. Also, make any suggestions for including more quotes or additional summaries your classmate might have missed that would support the main ideas.

Teaching Tip

To supplement the readings in this chapter, ask students to bring to class an article related to student loan debt. Alternatively, students could locate the readings listed in the works cited page in the sample essay, Figure 6.7.

WRITING A READINGS-BASED BODY PARAGRAPH USING PIE STRUCTURE

A body paragraph typically includes a topic sentence, supporting information, and a closing sentence. When you are writing an essay based on *readings*, the supporting information in a body paragraph comes from those readings in the form of quotations or summaries. Because the support comes from readings, you may need to explain to your readers *how* the information supports the main point of each paragraph. The PIE paragraph structure is a useful model to follow.

PIE stands for "Point, Information, Explanation." In a body paragraph, *point* is the main idea, usually revealed in the topic sentence. *Information* includes the support, such as quotations and summaries. *Explanation* means the connection between the point and the information, usually an explanation of how the information supports the main idea. Following the PIE paragraph structure helps readers understand what a writer is saying and why. Figure 6.4 provides an example of a body paragraph written according to the PIE format.

FIGURE 6.4 Annotated PIE Paragraph

PIE Paragraph	Annotations
For many students, going into debt to pay for college is stressful. According to the Institute for College Access and Success, 66% of students who graduate from college owe money, and the average amount a student owes is $26,700, as reported by Matthew Frankel in *The Motley Fool* (156). In 2016, debt for the average college graduate with loans rose to over $37,000 (Frankel 156). This is a lot of money for a student who may not yet have a job. Students may worry about whether they can pay off their debt. Even for students with a job, making student loan payments can be challenging. According to *Bloomberg Businessweek*, one former student, Christina Mills, who works for a nonprofit, took out loans to pay for college and law school. Mills said she "just went into the car and started sobbing" when she found out that her monthly payments would be $1400. Another college graduate, Christina Chaise, is quoted in the *New York Daily News* as saying that the amount of money she needs to borrow to pay for college "scares" her. Going into debt can be nerve-wracking when it's not clear how to repay the loans.	*Point* *Information (summary)* *Explanation* *Information (quotations)* *Explanation*

Read to Write Activity 6.8

Write a PIE Paragraph

Review your work for Read to Write Activities 6.3, 6.4, 6.5, and 6.7 and complete the following exercises.

1. Using the PIE structure, write a paragraph based on the readings in this chapter and in response to the essay prompt you selected in Read to Write Activity 6.1.

2. Annotate your paragraph by identifying which sentence or sentences are the point, which include information, and which are explanations.

Pair and Share

Exchange your PIE paragraph (from Read to Write Activity 6.8) with a classmate. Identify the point, information, and explanation in each other's paragraphs.

Researchers who studied college students in an introductory psychology class found that students who waited until the night before a paper was due—and who did not spend much time reading or thinking about their sources—did not write effective papers. One student not only earned a low grade but also came close to writing a plagiarized paper because she copied so much information directly from the readings. On the other hand, students who spent time reviewing, thinking about, and reading their sources and notes; who were careful to acknowledge the sources of information and to attribute quotes; and who planned, outlined, and revised their essays wrote good papers.

Let's examine an effective readings-based essay (see Figure 6.5). As you read, ask yourself, what specific strategies for composing a successful essay has the writer applied?

FIGURE 6.5 A Successful Readings-Based Essay

Essay	Annotations
According to Matthew Frankel's article in *The Motley Fool,* Americans owe more than $1 trillion in student loan debt (Frankel 155). That means Americans owe more money in student loans than they do on their credit cards or car payments (Frankel 155). The average college graduate owes approximately $27,000 in student loans; however, the debt burden has increased in 2016 to around $37,000 per graduate, as reported by Frankel (156). What these statistics suggest is that young people must carefully consider whether it is worthwhile to go into debt to get a degree. What are the advantages or disadvantages of taking out student loans to finance an education? On the one hand, taking on debt to pay for college can limit a student's options after graduation. On the other hand, students can benefit from greater earning potential, better job opportunities, and the personal satisfaction that comes with a college degree.	*Introduction with statistics for background and interest* *Thesis: Specifies disadvantages and advantages of debt*
An important reason student loans exist is to enable anyone to get a college education. For instance, the *New York Daily News* profiled Christina Chaise, a graduate of Columbia's Teachers College, who grew up poor, living in public housing in New York City (Friedman). She needed loans to get through college, as well as to	*Topic sentence: 1st advantage summarized* *Summarized examples of students*

Essay	Annotations
attend graduate school. For students like Chaise, whose families cannot help them pay for higher education, student loans are a way to get a degree. Sometimes unexpected events, such as family troubles or illness, can mean that students must take out loans. For instance, Tiffany Brown, also profiled in the *New York Daily News* article, graduated from Queens College in New York and had to take out loans to get through college when her father was ill (Friedman). So loans allow poor or disadvantaged students who otherwise could not afford higher education to attend college.	*Explanation* *Summarized information* *Closing sentence*
Not only do loans help students attend college and graduate, but college graduates benefit monetarily in the long run from getting a degree. In this way, a loan can be a good investment in a student's future. College graduates earn more money over the years than people who do not graduate from college. The Bureau of Labor Statistics reported in 2017 that workers with a bachelor's degree earned a median wage of $1,173 a week compared with high school graduates' $712 median weekly earnings ("Employment Projections"). Moreover, college graduates get jobs more easily than nongraduates. Again, the Bureau of Labor Statistics reported in 2017 that young people with a bachelor's degree had an unemployment rate of 2.5%, compared with 4.6% for those with only a high school diploma or a G.E.D. ("Employment Projections"). So getting a job and getting a well-paying job are more likely with a college degree.	*Topic sentence: 2nd advantage* *Explanation* *Summarized information* *Summarized information* *Closing sentence*
Not only can attending college be a good investment financially, but college graduates also benefit personally. Webster University's *The Journal* interviewed Brittany Marta, who was an art history major and is now a stay-at-home-mother. Marta feels that college made her "a better person intellectually" (qtd. in Rich 164). As she explains, "School on the university level helped me develop my reasoning capabilities and use logic and rational explanations to explain my point of view" (164). Marta may not be employed in the traditional sense, but she feels she and her family benefit from her college degree, despite the fact she owes $50,000 to the University of Missouri. Moreover, *The Journal* cited a Pew Research study that shows 86% of college graduates believe "college was a good investment" (qtd. in Rich 164). Yes, a college degree can be an investment in getting a good job, but it can also mean developing critical thinking skills or learning more about the world and about oneself.	*Topic sentence: 3rd advantage* *Example of student and quotations* *Explanation* *Example of study with quotation* *Closing sentence*

Essay	Annotations

However, taking on debt, even to finance college, has real disadvantages. For one thing, debt can limit students' choices after graduation. Even though Tiffany Brown has a job as the project coordinator with the New York Public Interest Research Group, she still lives at home and is not sure she can attend law school because she already has so much student debt (Friedman). Similarly, Christina Chaise is worried about taking on more debt to finish graduate school (Friedman). Another college graduate, Christina Mills, interviewed by *Bloomberg Businessweek*, has to make monthly payments of $1,400 a month (Coy). When she found out that her loan payments would be more than her take-home pay, she says, "I just went into the car and started sobbing" (qtd. in Coy). Clearly, some students suffer from debt: they worry how they can pay off their loans and fear taking on more debt, even if the money would help them go further in school or with their careers.

    Topic sentence: 1st disadvantage

    Summarized example

    Summarized information; quotations

    Explanation

    Closing sentence

Student loan debt is not just a personal matter. Loan debt also hurts the economy by increasing overall consumer debt. Senator Kirsten Gillibrand of New York State, who is working on legislation to lower interest rates on student loans to help students pay off their debts faster, claims that student loan debt is "dragging down our economy," according to the *New York Daily News* (qtd. in Friedman). That's because even if college graduates are employed and earning money, much of their income goes to paying off their loans. That, in turn, means students aren't buying cars or houses or taking vacations. Instead of going to stimulate the economy, their earnings go to pay off their loans.

    Topic sentence: 2nd disadvantage

    Summarized information; quotations

    Explanation

    Closing sentence

Debt, like college, is not for everyone. Student loans have real costs—costs to students who have to pay off their debts and costs to society. As Arne Duncan, a former education secretary, states in a *Bloomberg Businessweek* article, "Obviously if you have no debt that's maybe the best situation" (qtd. in Coy). Still, many would agree that getting a college degree is worthwhile. Student loans can allow some students, especially low-income students, to fulfill their dreams and accomplish their goals in life. While no debt is the best debt, in the words of former Secretary Duncan, student loan debt is "very good debt to have" (qtd. in Coy). It's money well spent.

    Conclusion: Brief summary; memorable quotations

Works Cited

Coy, Peter. "Student Loans: Debt for Life." *Bloomberg Businessweek*, 18 Sept. 2012, www.bloomberg.com/news/articles/2012-09-18/student-loans-debt-for-life.

"Employment Projections." United States. Department of Labor. Bureau of Labor Statistics, 27 Mar. 2018, www.bls.gov/emp/ep_chart_001.htm.

Frankel, Matthew. "The Average American Has This Much Student-Loan Debt." *Writing to Read, Reading to Write*, edited by Alison Kuehner, McGraw-Hill Education, 2019, pp. 155–57. Originally published in *The Motley Fool*, 25 June 2017, www.fool.com/retirement/2017/06/25/the-average-american-has-this-much-student-loan-de.aspx

Friedman, Dan. "Americans Owe $1.2 Trillion in Student Loans." *New York Daily News*, 17 May 2014, www.nydailynews.com/news/national/americans-owe-1-2-trillion-student-loans-article-1.1796606.

Rich, Elise. "86 Percent of College Students View Higher Education as a Good Investment." *Writing to Read, Reading to Write*, edited by Alison Kuehner, McGraw-Hill Education, 2019, pp. 164–65.

Read to Write Activity 6.9

Write an Essay Based on Readings

Answers will vary.

Review your work for the Read to Write Activities 6.3 through 6.8 when completing these exercises.

1. Draft an essay based on the readings in this chapter and in response to the essay prompt you selected in Read to Write Activity 6.1.

2. Check your essay draft to be sure you have used summaries effectively. Refer to "Strategies for Writing an Effective Summary."

3. Check your essay draft to be sure you have handled quotes effectively. Refer to "Strategies for Quoting Effectively in a Written Work."

4. Revise your draft as needed.

Pair and Share

Exchange your essay draft (from Read to Write Activity 6.9) with a classmate. Check that the summaries and quotes are used effectively in the writing to support the thesis. Point out any areas where the writing could be improved.

CHAPTER REVIEW

Key Terms

outline A plan for an essay showing the relationship among the main ideas and the support.

quotation The result of copying words, phrases, or sentences exactly as written and enclosing them in quotation marks.

summary A restatement of information to condense it to the main ideas.

taking notes Recording information that is related to the essay prompt.

Chapter Summary

1. College students often write about what they read and must demonstrate their understanding of a topic.

2. Two important steps in preparing to write a readings-based paper are to select the parts of the readings most relevant to your purpose and to take notes with the essay prompt in mind.

3. Summarizing information from readings can help you explain and support a topic in writing.

4. Quoting experts or experienced people from readings is another strategy for supporting your topic, as well as elaborating on your ideas.

5. A good way to start planning your essay is to create your own categories of information, to group related ideas within them, and to use this information to create an outline.

6. Using the PIE (point-information-explanation) paragraph structure can help you include information from readings in an organized way to support a main idea.

7. Students who read and think about their sources and notes, who painstakingly acknowledge their sources and attribute the quotes they use, and who plan and revise with care write better papers than those who do not.

8. When looking up a word in a dictionary, you should read all the definitions carefully and select the one that fits the word in the context of the passage.

9. A line graph can be read by understanding the title, checking the labels on the x and y axes, and knowing what the line(s) represent.

Apply What You Learned

1. Locate an article (not in this chapter) in the college library about the value of a college education. Read and annotate the article. Then select information from the article to develop into a PIE paragraph. Quote and summarize the information, and acknowledge your sources.

2. Locate an article (not in this chapter) in the college library on the topic of your choice. Read and annotate the article. Then select information from the article to develop into a PIE paragraph. Quote and summarize the information, and acknowledge your sources.

3. Do you have student loan debt? If so, how do you feel about your debt after reading the various selections in this chapter? Compare your experiences with debt to comments in the reading selections or to any of the information presented in the chapter.

Credits

p. 149: Data: College Board, Sallie Mae; Census; NCES; FRBNY. Used with permission of Bloomberg L.P. Copyright© 2017. All rights reserved; **pp. 155–157:** Frankel, Matthew. "The Average American Has This Much Student-Loan Debt." *The Motley Fool*, Jun. 25, 2017. Used with permission of The Motley Fool; **p. 159:** Reproduced with permission from Federal Reserve Bank of New York, *Quarterly Report on Household Debt and Credit*, Feb. 2018. Available at https://www.newyorkfed.org/microeconomics/hhdc.html; **pp. 164–165:** Rich, Elise. "86 percent of College Students View Higher Education as a Good Investment." *The Journal of Webster University*. All rights reserved. Used with permission.

SPOTLIGHT ON STUDENT WRITING

Reading and Analyzing Student Writing

We have seen how to use summaries and quotations in a piece of original writing. In addition, we have looked at essay structure, including how to read for and write strong introductions, effective body paragraphs with main ideas and support, and satisfying conclusions. These reading and writing strategies are at the core of academic writing in which students are often asked to reflect on and write about assigned readings in paragraphs and papers.

In this Spotlight section, you will have a chance to reinforce your understanding of how summaries and quotations from readings are incorporated into paragraphs and essays to build a strong piece of writing. First, you will examine an annotated student paper to see how the student uses textual evidence, such as quotes and summaries, to support his thesis. Then you will have an opportunity to annotate a second essay to practice analyzing student writing. To analyze means to break down into parts in order to understand the whole. By analyzing student writing, you can learn how the parts of a paper fit together to make a successful, complete essay. Finally, you can apply these same reading, annotating, and analysis strategies to your own paper or to your classmates' writing to determine the effectiveness of paragraphs and essays that incorporate readings in writing.

ANALYZING PARAGRAPH AND ESSAY STRUCTURE AND USE OF EVIDENCE

Annotating a piece of writing can help you understand the writer's ideas and also how the writer delivers those ideas. In other words, you can learn about the content and the structure of a piece of writing. By analyzing a writing's structure, you can also learn strategies to use in your own writing. For instance, in your reading, you may have noticed how a writer acknowledges a source by including the author's name or the title of the reading at the beginning of a sentence before quoting information. You can use this same strategy in your own writing to acknowledge a source before a quotation.

Recall that when you are reading a text to annotate it, an effective strategy is to read the paper at least two times. The first reading is to understand the writer's message. Then, during the second reading, you can examine the writing analytically to understand what makes it work. Think of doing the following:

- During the *first reading*, focus on understanding the thesis, main ideas, and examples. This focus will ensure that the purpose, organization, and main ideas of the writing are clear to you.

- During the *second reading*, focus on analyzing how the different parts work together. For instance, determine where the introduction ends and where the body of the paper begins. Notice how the body paragraphs develop the argument. Consider where the conclusion starts.

After each reading, you will want to annotate the writing to analyze the parts. Here are some strategies for successful annotations.

First Reading: Annotations for Comprehension

- Note the title to understand the topic.
- Underline main ideas, such as the thesis, topic sentences, or concluding statements, to discover the paper's organization.
- Mark examples, quotes, and summaries to determine the support for the main ideas.
- Write brief summaries of main ideas and examples in the margin to reinforce your comprehension of the writing.

Second Reading: Annotations for Analysis

- Identify the introduction and consider if it establishes the topic, gets the reader's attention, and states the thesis.
- Examine the body paragraphs and determine whether these have topic sentences that relate to the thesis and relevant supporting information, such as quotations and summaries.
- Identify the conclusion and consider whether it explains why the information in the essay is important and whether it comes to a satisfying end.
- Determine if evidence is used effectively, such as whether support is relevant to the main ideas and thesis, quotes are integrated grammatically, and summaries are specific and detailed.
- Look at the title and assess if it effectively represents the focus of the paper.

ANNOTATING AND ANALYZING STUDENT PAPERS

This Spotlight section includes two student papers for you to read and think about. The first student paper is annotated so you can see an example of effective analytical annotations. The second paper is an opportunity to practice analytical annotations.

Each student responded to a specific writing prompt on the topic of happiness. To understand what makes people happy, especially the role that wealth plays in happiness, students read various articles and were given a choice of prompts to write about. Matthew Ricafrente's essay "The Key to Happiness" is a response to the following prompt.

Teaching Tip

The theme of happiness and the related readings appear in Chapter 7, "Writing to Respond to Texts."

Writing Prompt A: *What makes people happy human beings? For instance, does it make people happy to have money or to give money away? Is happiness determined by how people live their lives or by the people with whom they spend time? Does happiness involve doing meaningful work or experiencing pleasure? In your essay, explain what defines happiness and what makes people happy.*

Jingting Chen's essay "Buying Happiness" deals specifically with the question of whether money makes people happy. She writes in response to the following prompt:

Writing Prompt B: Mail Online, *reporting on a Pew Research Center study, asserts that "more money does make you happier." Is this true? For instance, does earning more money make people happier? Are wealthy people happy people? Is there some point at which making more money does not contribute to happiness? Does how people use their money make a difference in their happiness? In your essay, discuss to what extent money makes people happy.*

The essay directions include this additional requirement:

Requirement: *In this essay, you will create an argument and use evidence from readings, videos, or graphs for support. You should draw on at least two of the resources (the articles, graphs, and videos provided) to support your answer. You may also include your own or other people's experiences.*

The students' papers were written about midway through the course. Students had two hours to write their essays in class, and they could refer to the texts as they wrote their papers. For that reason, students were required to cite quotations using parenthetical citations but not to create a works cited page. As you read, notice how each student states his or her thesis and uses evidence, including examples, explanations, and quotes from readings and graphs, and from his or her own experiences, to support the thesis.

The first paper, by Ricafrente, is annotated as follows. First, the paper was read for an understanding of the writer's thesis, main ideas, and examples. Then the paper was read to analyze the parts of the essay. Notice there are annotations on the paper itself, in the right margin and in the left margin. Here is an explanation of these annotations.

- **Annotations on the paper.** The thesis is double-underlined, and both the thesis and the paragraph main ideas are highlighted in blue on the paper. Support is underlined to indicate where the evidence begins.

- **Annotations in the right margin.** The title, thesis, and main ideas are summarized in the right-hand column to demonstrate comprehension. The introduction and conclusion are identified as essay parts. Main ideas and support are distinguished in the body paragraphs to establish the relationship between thesis, main ideas, and support.

- **Annotations in the left margin.** The different parts of the paper are analyzed with brief comments, such as whether the introduction sets the topic and gets the reader's attention, whether body paragraphs have support from the readings, and whether the conclusion brings the paper to a satisfying close.

Review this annotation strategy by studying Ricafrente's paper. Then practice reading, annotating, and analyzing by applying these strategies to the second student paper, which has not been annotated.

STUDENT PAPER 1

About the Author

Matthew Ricafrente
©Alison Kuehner

Matthew Ricafrente was born in the United States, but his parents are from the Philippines, and he identifies as Filipino-American. His first language is Tagalog; he learned English when he started school. Matthew began his college career as a psychology major but switched to music, because music is his passion. He can play the clarinet, the guitar, and the piano and is a self-confessed "band nerd" and jock (basketball is his sport). His advice to students is to really do the reading—read the material over and over. Then write about what you are passionate about. Finally, revise. It might be tedious to rewrite, but if you sit on a draft, read it over, think about it, and manage your time, you will be able to produce writing you care about.

Annotations for Analysis

How Can the Writing Be Improved?

Annotations for Comprehension

Identify the Thesis, Main Ideas, and Support.

Ricafrente 1

Matthew Ricafrente

Professor Kuehner

English 151 RW

9 October 2016

The Key to Happiness

According to Gallup's Poll circa 2013, research suggests "nearly 60 percent of all Americans today feel happy, without a lot of stress or worry" (3). Everyone wants to be happy; however, the research suggests that the percentages of happy and unhappy people are approximately the same. People live their entire lives pursuing happiness, but many are unable to find true happiness. How can this be? What is the key to fulfilling ultimate happiness? According to various articles, graphs, and discussions regarding happiness, the key to happiness is found through a balance of wealth, how one spends money, self-fulfillment through experiences and success, and assisting others.

Money, viewed as society's most sought-after resource, has proven more than just a correlation to a person's happiness; moreover, money causes happiness. In a study entitled "How Happy Are You?" conducted by the University of Michigan, the graph suggests that with an increase of income, an increase in happiness also occurs. For example, there is a 10% increase in happiness when comparing individuals with an income of $100k–150k to $150k–250k. Furthermore, the study implies that 100% happiness is achieved when an individual earns more than $500k annually. In addition, Ellie Zolfagharifard and Ollie Gillman,

Title indicates topic is happiness

First paragraph is introduction

Introduction ends with the thesis, which responds to the prompt and gives reasons why people are happy.

Start of body

Topic sentence: Money causes happiness.

Support: Summarized information from graph shows how the rise in income connects to a rise in happiness.

Good strategy to begin with a quote about happiness.

The statement that the percentages of happy and unhappy people are the same is contradicted by the opening quote.

Thoughtful questions pull the reader into the paper and the thesis.

Clear topic sentence that connects to first point in thesis.

Source of information—title of study and where research was conducted—is effectively identified.

Good specific details from the graph to support the main idea.

Source of information—author and title of article—is effectively identified.

authors of the *MailOnline* article "More Money Does Make You Happier," write, "The study [by the Pew Research Center Poll] confirmed that rises in national income are closely linked to personal satisfaction" (2). Although the phrase, "money can buy happiness," has been an age-old adage that many have come to believe, studies have put an end to any doubts. Researchers and psychologists have concluded that money can truly buy an individual's happiness.

There is truth behind the idea that money causes happiness; however, additional research reveals that there is more to having money that makes one happy. Author Olivia Goldwill of the *Quartz Online* writes that "there is indeed a link between spending money and happiness" and then adds that "life satisfaction increases with spending—but only if people use money in line with their personality type" (1). Goldwill references research from the University of Cambridge that states that classified personality traits in the study of psychology, such as "openness, conscientiousness, extraversion, agreeableness, neuroticism" (1), give individuals different preferences to spending money that provoke a person's true happiness. For example, an extraverted individual has a tendency to feel happier when spending money on activities involving others such as going to a bar and attending a sporting event or concert. In contrast, an introverted person will find more happiness spending money on activities that provide isolation and detachment such as buying a book to read at the bookstore or renting a movie to watch alone at home. Overall, spending money geared towards a person's personality preference is the key to utilizing money as a way to feel happy.

Well-chosen quote from the reading to support the main idea.

Clear closing sentence—but how do we know money causes happiness and isn't just correlated with happiness?

Effective transition sentence—main idea of previous paragraph (money causes happiness) linked to new idea (there is more to happiness).

Source of information—author and title of article—is effectively identified.

Skillfully identifies when the author references other research.

Examples are specific and detailed; these show how personality connects to spending money and to happiness.

Support: Quote from research study shows the relationship between increased wealth and increased happiness.

Closing sentence reinforces idea that money is linked to happiness.

Opening sentence hints at the main idea of the paragraph.

Support: Quotes from author show that people need to spend money according to their personality to be happy.

Support: Summary of examples shows how spending money according to one's personality can make people happy.

Closing sentence serves as the topic sentence and reinforces the idea that spending money according to one's personality is what makes for happiness.

Understanding the relationship between money and happiness is important to maximize life's resources, but it is even more important to consider that achieving ultimate happiness does not simply rely on money itself. Andrew Blackman, author of the article "Can Money Buy You Happiness?" claims "life experiences give us more lasting pleasure than material things" (6). Blackman further explains society's misbelief that material goods are more valuable because they last longer in comparison with an experience's short-term effect on an individual. However, after a later reevaluation, people involved in the study claimed that "experiences actually provided better value." Furthermore, according to Viktor Frankl, a Jewish psychiatrist and neurologist in Vienna who was interned at Auschwitz during the Nazi invasions of the 1940s, people who knew and understood their life "meaning" determined whether or not they truly made the most out of their lives. Frankl explained that knowledge of one's life purpose was "the difference between those who had lived and those who had died [in the Nazi concentration camps]" (Smith 2). In relation to happiness, Frankl writes, "Happiness cannot be pursued; it must ensue. One must have a reason to 'be happy'" (qtd. in Smith 3). And that "reason to be happy" is an individual's life "meaning." In support of Frankl's ideas and beliefs, Emily Esfahani Smith, author of *The Atlantic* article "There's More to Life Than Being Happy," expands upon the benefits of life purpose and writes, "Research has shown that having purpose and meaning in life increases overall well-being and life satisfaction, improves mental and physical health, enhances resiliency, enhances self-esteem, and decreases the chances of depression" (3). Overall, life experiences and living with a purpose is just as important, if not more, than the money an individual makes or how that individual spends it.

Conclusion effectively pulls in the word "key" from the title of the paper.

To conclude, why then is the key to happiness so important? Without knowledge of what truly causes happiness, one can live a lost life valuing superficial material goods in our world. For example, a misunderstanding of the value of money can occur. One might believe that money is the only source of happiness, which inevitably leads to a corrupt and selfish lifestyle that does not provoke true and ultimate happiness. Knowing the key to happiness allows individuals to live their lives on a guided path with proper motives and incentives. It promotes a balanced approach to what society values and expands the perspective of what is truly meaningful in life. All in all, knowing and understanding the key to happiness and its importance and implementation into one's life leads to a fulfillment of the longing for happiness that nearly everyone hopes to achieve by the end of his or her lifetime.

Start of conclusion

Question asking why understanding happiness is important leads into conclusion.

Conclusion sums up ideas in the paper, such as how money contributes to happiness but is not the only source of happiness.

Conclusion could be more specific about what makes for a meaningful or happy life— what are "proper motives" and "incentives"? How do people find "meaning" in life?

Concluding sentence wraps up essay by explaining that happiness and fulfillment are important in life.

STUDENT PAPER 2

Now it is your turn to read and annotate a student paper. Use the annotation strategies and the examples of annotations on Ricafrente's paper to guide you as you review Chen's paper.

 Before Reading: Predict

Write answers to these questions using complete sentences.

1. Review Writing Prompt B. What does the writer need to do in her writing to create a successful paper?
2. Read the "Requirements" for the essay assignment. What does the writer need to do, in addition to addressing the prompt, to create a successful paper?

Answers

1. The writer needs to explain to what extent money makes people happy.

2. The writer must include at least two of the resources (the articles and graphs provided) to support the thesis.

During Reading: Annotate

Complete the following exercises.

3. As you read, annotate the writer's thesis and main ideas. Also mark the evidence used to support the thesis. Identify the introduction, body of the paper, and conclusion.

4. As you read, analyze how effective the thesis, main ideas, and support are.

About the Author

Jingting Chen
©Alison Kuehner

Jingting Chen is majoring in business administration and aspires to become an accountant. Her parents did not go to college; her older sister is the first in her family to attend college. She was born in Fujian, China, and she moved from China to Guam and then to the United States. Her first language is Mandarin Chinese. Jingting finds peer review helpful and encourages students to get their essays read by others to make their writing stronger. She also suggests creating a schedule to stay on top of college assignments.

Student Paper

Chen 1

Jingting Chen

Professor Kuehner

English 151RW

9 October 2016

Buying Happiness

Zolfagharifard and Gillman, authors of "More Money Does Make You Happier," explain that money is one factor in happiness by providing data from the Pew survey that shows more people in a richer place have higher satisfaction for their lives than people in a poor area (215). It is true that more money can easily make many people happy whether they are poor or rich. Money is a necessary item in today's society. Without money, individuals' essential needs are difficult to obtain, and without these basic needs, it is difficult to gain happiness too. When livelihood is difficult, pure money can make people happy because that symbolizes a comfortable life. Even after obtaining a livelihood, money still supports people to be happy. Money can create happiness by buying surprises, such as gifts, or by purchasing experiences and time. Money does bring people happiness because it satisfies their basic needs and can be exchanged into something that makes them happy.

For people who have a difficult life, happiness comes with money because it can support their essential needs. For example, if people do not have food to eat or clothes to wear, they would not have a high satisfaction in their lives. Many studies prove the relationship between income and happiness, which indicates rich people are happier than poor people who could not support their lifestyles. In the graph "How Happy Are You?" Betsey Stevenson and Justin Wolfers, professors at the University of Michigan, indicate that more income makes individuals happier (203). This chart shows that 35% of people who earn less than 10k feel very happy, and 44% feel fairly happy, but still 21% are not happy. In contrast, the group that has an income of more than $500k are 100% very happy. Another graph also shows a similar idea, but it focuses on the wealth of different countries instead of personal income. "Life-Satisfaction" is the title of the graph based on a Pew Research survey, which involved 47,643 participants in 43 countries (Zolfagharifard & Gillman 200). It supports the idea that money makes people have a higher satisfaction in their lives by giving data that shows people's life satisfaction ratings in different countries. For example, in the Pew survey, more than 60% of people in the United States, a wealthy country, rate their life satisfaction at least seven out of ten, but in Bangladesh, a poor country, only 36% of individuals rate seven or higher in satisfaction. All these data show that more money does bring happiness to people and wealthy people have a high possibility to be happy people.

On the other hand, many people argue that money does not bring happiness to people. For example, the figure, "How Happy Are You?" shows that individuals who earned $40k to $50k have a less "very happy" rate and a higher "not too happy" rate than people who made $30k to $40k (203). This drop in happiness might be caused by "adaption," which is a theory described by Sonja Lyubomirsky, a psychology professor at the University of California, Riverside (Blackman 4). Professor Lyubomirsky explains that one significant reason that people are not always happy with what they have is they adapt to what they have. It could be that as people who earned $40k to $50k adapt to what they have, they raise their aspirations; they want to make more money and be upper class. But, if they do not achieve upper class status, they are not very happy.

Although many people who can afford a comfortable lifestyle adapt to what they have, money still can bring them happiness, such as buying experience, gifts, and time. Buying experiences means using the money to travel or participate or play. People who want happiness should buy experiences instead of goods. Ryan Howell, a professor at San Francisco State University, explains that experiences can make people happier than material goods because experiences and the memory of experiences last forever, while material goods don't. While buying experiences is a good idea, people also can use their money to buy a gift for others. In her experiment, Professor Dunn, an associate professor of psychology at the University of British Columbia, found out that people will become happier when they give money away rather than spend it on themselves. The experiment is to hand out money to people and tell them to either spend it on themselves or someone else. The result of this research shows that people who spent on others were happier than those who spent it on themselves. Also, Professor Dunn talks about how buying time can make people happy by using the money to buy quality time. For example, a person can pay someone else to do the work that he or she does not like and use the time to do something he or she does like. These studies teach people how to use money to create happiness, which indicates that money does bring people happiness if they use it in their favor. Money can make people happy even if they already have a comfortable life because it helps people get what they want.

Money can make people happy because it secures people's needs and wants. Needs are necessary to support an individual's life. Wants are things that are not necessary for living but give people intrinsic value. Why does this matter? The answer is happiness is important since it is a positive emotion that affects people's behaviors. People should know that although money can bring happiness, money does not equal happiness. Money itself cannot make people happy, but what it can give us is what makes people happy, such as living supplies, experiences, gifts, and time.

 ## After Reading: Analyze the Writing

Complete the following exercises.

5. What is the writer's thesis? Is it clearly written?
6. Consider the introduction. Does it get your attention and establish the topic of the paper?
7. Examine the body paragraphs. Do the main ideas support the thesis? Does the writer use sources and summaries effectively to support the main ideas?
8. Do you feel the conclusion brings the essay to a logical and satisfying end?
9. Do you feel the student effectively responds to the writing prompt? Why or why not?

8. The conclusion both sums up the main ideas in the essay and considers why the issue of money and happiness is important.

9. The student effectively responds to the prompt because the thesis addresses the prompt and the writer uses more than the required two sources to support the thesis.

Answers

5. The thesis is the last two sentences in the introduction; it clearly lays out the main points of the paper, such as how using money to buy time or gifts and support basic needs, leads to happiness.

6. The introduction focuses the paper immediately on the question of whether money creates happiness.

7. The main ideas of the body paragraphs support the thesis by focusing on using money to buy essentials, to buy gifts, or to buy time to increase happiness.

ANNOTATING AND ANALYZING FOR PEER REVIEW

In addition to annotating to understand and evaluate student writing, you can also annotate and analyze to provide feedback for yourself or for other students. For instance, you can use "Checklist for Analyzing an Essay," shown here, to review and revise your own paper. Or you can exchange papers with a classmate and complete the checklist as a way to provide feedback.

Checklist for Analyzing an Essay

- Does the introduction establish the topic, get the reader's attention, and state the thesis?

- Do body paragraphs have topic sentences that relate to the thesis?

- Do body paragraphs contain relevant supporting information, such as quotations or summaries, from the readings?

- Is evidence used effectively to support the main ideas? Is there a logical connection between the evidence and the main idea of a paragraph?

- Are quotes integrated grammatically into sentences? Is there context for each quote? Is the source of the quotation acknowledged?

- Are summaries specific and detailed? Is the source of the summary identified?

- Does the conclusion explain why the information in the essay is important and bring the essay to a satisfying end?

- Does the title effectively represent the focus of the paper?

Spotlight Activity: Practice Peer Review

1. If you have completed an essay for your English class, read and annotate your paper to analyze your writing. You might also use "Checklist for Analyzing an Essay" to check the effectiveness of your writing.

2. If you have completed an essay for an English assignment, exchange your paper with a classmate. Read and annotate the paper; then use "Checklist for Analyzing an Essay" to provide feedback by answering each question about your classmate's paper.

3. Write a response to one of the writing prompts that formed the basis for the student papers in this section. To do this, you will need to read research or articles about happiness so you can incorporate quotes and summaries into your writing.

4. Exchange your writing from exercise 3 with a classmate. Read and annotate each other's papers. Use the "Checklist for Analyzing an Essay" to check the effectiveness of each other's writing.

Apply What You Learned

1. Did you feel that one of the student papers was more convincing than the other, or were they equally effective? Explain your answer.

2. If you are currently working on a piece of writing for any subject, annotate and analyze the writing. Identify the main ideas and examples; then review the writing to examine the introduction, body paragraphs, use of support, and conclusion. Use your annotations to help you analyze and improve the writing.

3. What have you learned about analyzing student writing from reading this section, examining the annotated student paper, and annotating a student paper?

4. What have you learned about writing an effective essay using readings from studying the two student papers in this section?

Pair and Share

Discuss your answers to question 1 in Apply What You Learned. What did you feel was effective about the two student papers? Did you agree that one essay was more effective, or were they equally effective?

Answers

1. Both papers use a variety of sources to support their thesis statements and do not use personal experience. In this way, both are academically appropriate and make strong arguments.

2. Answers will vary.

3. Answers will vary. Students might have learned to read their writing more carefully and think about how the parts fit together.

4. Answers will vary. Students may have observed how the students introduce and integrate quotes and summaries into their paragraphs for support.

PART THREE

Reading and Writing about Texts

7 | Responding to Texts

Look for these icons throughout the chapter. They signal key strategies to use in Read to Write Activities.

After reading this chapter, you will be able to

- Read critically to respond in writing.
- Identify types of support.
- Use an encyclopedia or a dictionary to define terms.
- Read and write about a bar graph.
- Use the SOS organizational pattern—summary, opinion, and support.
- Draft a response essay.
- Organize and develop body paragraphs.

Theme: What Makes People Happy?

Connect

Assign the LearnSmart Achieve topic "Planning and Organizing" for adaptive learning to accompany this chapter.

Class Activity

Use the chapter theme question "What makes people happy?" as a brainstorming or freewriting activity.

Are you happy? If so, what makes you happy? If not, why not? In the last decade, researchers have been studying questions like these and arriving at conclusions about what makes people happy.

Abraham Maslow, an American psychologist, developed a theory to explain human happiness, with the ultimate goal being *self-actualization*, or fulfillment of one's potential. Maslow posited that people need to fulfill basic needs, such as the need to sleep or eat, and then they will strive to fulfill other needs, such as the need to be loved or to belong to a community. The infographic in Figure 7.1 represents Maslow's hierarchy, or ranking, of needs. Consider the key words at each level as well as the pictures. What does each level represent?

FIGURE 7.1 **Maslow's Hierarchy of Needs**

In this chapter, you will read about research on happiness. The articles consider whether money makes people happy and whether having possessions or engaging in particular experiences produces happiness. You will have a chance to read and think about these issues and write a response presenting your own ideas.

READING CRITICALLY TO RESPOND IN WRITING

A **response essay** is a common college assignment. Often its goal is to encourage reflection and critical thinking. An instructor in a health science class might ask students to reflect on an author's opinion that health care professionals must understand their patients' cultural backgrounds; an instructor in a communication course might ask students to respond to a journal editorial claiming that social media facilitate bullying; a political science instructor might ask students to comment on an article arguing that social media can mobilize people in a political campaign. Outside the classroom, film reviews, newspaper editorials, political debates, and online opinion pieces are also typically responses to others' ideas. These writings are an attempt to persuade people to think carefully about which ideas are sound and which are not.

Readers often read a text recursively—that is, they read it more than once, depending on their purpose. For instance, if a text is complex, an experienced reader may read it several times in order to understand it.

When you are reading with the goal of responding in writing, an effective strategy might be to read the text at least three times. For the first (overview) reading, your goal is to look for the main ideas and support. Then, in your second

Handout

"Strategies for Reading to Respond to a Text" is a reproducible handout in the Instructor's Resources.

reading, you might analyze how effectively the author supports those ideas. Your third reading might focus on how you respond to the material as a reader: do you agree or disagree with the author's ideas? Use "Strategies for Reading to Respond to a Text" to review these steps.

Teaching Tip

Review reading strategies from earlier chapters in the book: "Strategies for Critical Thinking" in Chapter 1 and "Strategies for Locating Main Ideas" in Chapter 2.

Strategies for Reading to Respond to a Text

When you read to respond, you should read the text several times, with each reading targeting one of these goals:

1. Identify and summarize the author's main ideas.

2. Analyze the support the author uses to convince readers of the main ideas.

3. Respond by considering to what extent you agree or disagree with the author's main ideas.

Class Activity

To introduce types of support, provide students with the four terms and their definitions. Then ask students to match examples given on these pages with the terms. Finally, assign the reading in this section: Tell students to check their answers as they read.

IDENTIFYING TYPES OF SUPPORT

In addition to finding and annotating for main ideas when reading to respond, take care also to locate the support an author provides. Authors use support to convince readers that their main points are believable. Support can come in different types; knowing these types will help you respond critically to the reading.

Although there are different ways to categorize support, we will use four basic types, as identified by Professor Jennifer Hurley of Ohlone College. Hurley calls these "the four Es of support": factual evidence, expert testimony, explanation, and examples. Most successful writers use a mixture of these different types of support to make their ideas convincing.

Teaching Tip

Explain to students that terms for support may vary, but these are typical terms they may encounter in other classes.

Factual Evidence

Factual evidence refers to grounds for belief based on the use of facts or statistics. A **fact** is a statement that can be proved true or false. For example, the statement "The Pew Research Center conducted a survey in October 2014" is a fact. Why? This information can be checked, and it is either true or false. A **statistic** is a particular type of fact, one that is expressed in terms of numbers. The statement "Nearly 60 percent of people living in the UK [United Kingdom] rate their happiness as at least a seven out of 10" is a statistic because it uses a percentage ("nearly 60 percent") and a numerical rating ("seven out of 10") to express a fact.

Expert Testimony

Expert testimony is the use of the words or ideas of an *expert*—a person or organization with experience, knowledge, skill, and/or training in the subject or content area. The testimony can be a *direct quote* (the expert's exact words in quotation marks) or a *paraphrase* (a restatement of the expert's ideas). For instance, at the end of an article about happiness and meaning in life, an author quotes the famous psychiatrist Carl Jung as saying, "The least of things with a meaning is worth more in life than the greatest of things without it" (qtd. in Smith). Quoting Jung is support for the idea that a meaningful life is more important than a happy life.

Explanation

Explanation involves expressing reasons why an idea is true. Explanation requires strong critical thinking or logical reasoning. Some common methods of explanation follow:

- To use logic.
- To imagine the possible consequences of certain actions.
- To point out flaws in another person's argument.
- To make an analogy (a comparison) between two concepts.

For instance, to explain why people in rich countries are only slightly happier than people in less affluent societies, the Pew researchers whose work is showcased in the reading selection "More Money *Does* Make You Happier" speculate that after a certain point, increasing income does not make as much of a difference in life satisfaction (Zolfagharifard and Gillman 200). In this way, the researchers provide an explanation for the data showing that people in wealthy countries scored only a few percentage points above people in not-so-wealthy countries on a life satisfaction scale.

Examples

An **example** is a specific case that supports or illustrates the main idea or other ideas. Writers use examples to make writing clear and vivid; examples can also add emotional appeal. Examples may come from the author's own experience or observations or from an outside source, such as research or a reading. For instance, at the end of the reading selection "More Money *Does* Make You Happier," the authors include examples of two survey participants who comment on whether they feel money makes them happy (Zolfagharifard and Gillman 200). These examples of real people and their honest comments spark the reader's interest and help explain the survey results.

In addition to reading and rereading a text to identify the main ideas and support, reading with your purpose in mind can help you take notes and prepare to write about what you read. To this end, review the essay prompts in Read to Write Activity 7.1 for help in thinking about your writing goal as you read. Then put your reading skills to the test as you read—and reread—the first article about what makes people happy.

Read to Write Activity 7.1

Analyze Prompts for Responding to a Text on Happiness

Read and rate the essay prompts below in order of interest to you. As you read through the chapter, keep your selected prompts in mind, as you will need to plan an essay on one of these.

1. The first reading selection in this chapter, "More Money *Does* Make You Happier," reports on the Pew Research Center's international survey of life

Connect

Activity 7.1 can be found as a writing assignment in Connect.

continued

satisfaction. The title of that reading gives the conclusion that "more money *does* make you happier" (Zolfagharifard and Gillman 199). Write an essay directed at your classmates in which you summarize the survey findings. State whether you agree or disagree that more money does make people happier, and why.

2. At the end of the reading selection "More Money *Does* Make You Happier," two individuals are quoted. One says, "Money can't secure happiness," and the other says, "Money can buy lots of happiness" (qtd. in Zolfagharifard and Gillman 200). Write a response to either person, stating that you either agree or disagree about whether money can buy happiness. Explain your view.

3. In the second reading selection in this chapter, "Can Money Really Buy Happiness?" John Grohol concludes, "Money can buy you happiness, as long as you give some of the money away, or use it for an experience rather than buying a product" (207). Do you agree that giving money away or spending money on experiences can make you happier than keeping money or buying material possessions? Write a response to Grohol in which you agree or disagree with his conclusion, and give reasons for your response.

READING SELECTION

"MORE MONEY *DOES* MAKE YOU HAPPIER"

Connect

You will find a coordinated Power of Process assignment for this reading in your Connect course.

Complete the "Before Reading" assignment. Then read the selection while you complete the "During Reading" activities. Finally, complete the "After Reading" assignments.

 Before Reading: Ask Questions; Identify Audience

Write responses to the following exercises in complete sentences.

1. Consider the title of the essay, and freewrite about the relationship between money and happiness. Why might more money "make you happier"?

2. Review the information that immediately precedes the reading. Who is the intended audience? What clues help you identify the audience?

Answers

1. Students might consider how much money they need to live on and how much having more money could increase their happiness.

2. The article is written for a British audience. The publication is a clue.

During Reading: Annotate; Find Main Ideas; Find Support

Write responses to the following exercises using complete sentences.

3. Annotate the reading by marking main ideas and support for the main ideas in the right margin. Identify the following types of support: factual evidence, expert testimony, explanation, and examples. (NOTE: Not all articles include all four types of support.)

More Money *Does* Make You Happier

By Ellie Zolfagharifard and Ollie Gillman

MailOnline, 30 October 2014

This news article, published online by a British news organization, reports on an international survey about happiness. The survey asked people in 43 countries to rate their happiness on a scale of 0 to 10, with 0 representing the most miserable life and 10 the best life. The results found that people in wealthy countries tend to be happier with their lives than people in poor countries, which inspired the headline "More Money Does Make You Happier."

More money does make you happier, with people from rich countries like Britain saying they are happier than citizens of poorer nations.   **1**

Nearly 60 percent of people living in the UK [United Kingdom] rate their happiness as at least a seven out of 10, higher than most other rich countries. However, some wealthy nations, including France and Japan, are still miserable, with barely half of their citizens happy with their lives.   **2**

Morale has dropped slightly in the UK, the report by the Pew Research Center, in Washington, [DC,] found. The number of people saying they were satisfied with their life dropped [one percentage point,] from 59 percent to 58 percent, in the last seven years.   **3**

Germany saw a rise of 13 percent in the same time, possibly because Germans were less affected by the economic downturn than other Western nations. Meanwhile, only 43 percent of people surveyed in Japan said they were satisfied with their lives, while slightly more than half of the French said they were happy.   **4**

The only developed nations to have higher satisfaction levels than the UK were the U.S. and Israel, while the lowest ratings were found in Egypt, Kenya, and Tanzania. Emerging markets in Asia saw the biggest rise in citizens' satisfaction over the seven-year period, the global survey suggested. Levels of self-reported well-being in fast-growing nations like Indonesia, China, and Malaysia now rival those in the U.S. and Europe, who traditionally topped the happiness charts.   **5**

And women in particular are growing more satisfied with their lifestyles as a result, the research found.   **6**

The study confirmed that rises in national income are closely linked to personal satisfaction. The pollsters asked people in 43 countries to place themselves on a   **7**

Answers

3. The main idea is in the first sentence: "More money does make you happier . . ."

Factual evidence: Many statistics such as: 60% of people in the UK rate their happiness at least 7 out of 10.

Expert testimony: None. *Explanation:* "But the data also suggested that there is a limit to how much happiness money can buy."

Examples: Ngyuen Thi Mai and Tony Wong, quoted at the end of the article, could be considered examples.

"ladder of life," with a scale from 0 to 10 and the top rung [10] representing the best possible life and the bottom the worst. Pew carried out the same survey in 2002 and 2005 in most of those countries, enabling researchers to look at trends over time.

But the data also suggested that there is a limit to how much happiness money can buy. For example, 56 percent of Malaysians rated their life a "seven" or higher on the ladder, significantly more than the 36 percent in Bangladesh, a poor country. Yet the public in Germany, which has far higher gross domestic product per capita than Malaysia, expressed a life satisfaction level of 60 percent, just four [percentage points] more than Malaysia. **8**

While wealth appears to contribute to happiness, other research has indicated it is far from the only factor. Women tend to be happier than men, for example, and unmarried and middle-aged people tend to report lower levels of well-being than married and younger people, respectively. **9**

The Pew survey [was] based on 47,643 interviews in 43 countries with adults 18 and older between March and June. It found that people in emerging and developing economies prioritize a few essentials in life, including their health, their children's education, and safety from crime. Fewer people in those economies said Internet access, car ownership, free time, or the ability to travel is very important in their lives. **10**

The survey saw significant gains in personal satisfaction in Indonesia, where 58 percent of those polled placed themselves on the seventh-highest rung of the "ladder of life" or above, up from 23 percent in 2007 [and in] Malaysia, where 56 percent put themselves in that same upper range, up from 36 percent seven years ago. In Vietnam, which wasn't included in the 2007 survey, 64 percent said they were on the seventh-highest rung or above. The Associated Press asked people in those three nations what they thought of the findings. **11**

"Money can't secure happiness," said Nguyen Thi Mai, 66-year-old retired teacher from Vietnam. "There are people who don't have any money, but they lead a happy life because family members love and respect each other. But there are rich families where husbands and wives often quarrel and children are addicted to drugs." **12**

"Money can buy lots of happiness for me because I am very materialistic," said businessman Tony Wong in Malaysia. "But that's not the only thing that makes me happy. Money is number one on my top five list, followed by health, family, dogs, and friends." **13**

After Reading: Summarize; Reflect on the Text

Write responses to the following exercises using complete sentences.

4. Review your annotations of the main ideas. Write a brief summary of the reading.

5. What is the purpose of this article? How do you know?

6. Review the reading again, and annotate by jotting down your reactions to the ideas and support in the left margin.

Answers

4. Possible summary: In the article "More Money *Does* Make You Happier," the authors report on data from an international survey showing that people in wealthy countries tend to be happier than people in poor countries.

5. The article is informative, designed to explain the data from the survey. The large amounts of data and factual statements are clues.

6. Answers will vary.

Read to Write Activity 7.2

Engage with the Reading

Complete the following exercises.

1. The reading begins by stating that "people from rich countries like Britain [say] they are happier than citizens of poor nations" (Zolfagharifard and Gillman 199). What support in the article confirms this statement? Is there any support that contradicts this statement?

2. In the middle of the reading, the authors note that "other research has indicated that [wealth] is far from the only factor [that contributes to happiness]" (Zolfagharifard and Gillman 200). What other factors, according to the reading, influence people's happiness?

3. At the end of the reading, the authors quote two individuals: a teacher from Vietnam who says "Money can't secure happiness," (qtd. in Zolfagharifard and Gillman 200) and a businessman from Malaysia who says "Money can buy lots of happiness" (qtd. in Zolfagharifard and Gillman 200). Which person's opinion do you agree with more? Give support for your answer.

Pair and Share

- With a partner, discuss your responses to exercises 1 and 2 in Read to Write Activity 7.2. Together, make a list of what support from the article shows that people in rich countries are happier than people in poor countries and what evidence, if any, shows that other factors contribute to happiness.

- With a partner, discuss your responses to exercise 3 in Read to Write Activity 7.2. Try to see the merits of both quotations and think of support for either opinion.

Read to Write Activity 7.3

Prewrite for Writing Prompt 1 or 2

Review prompts 1 and 2 in Read to Write Activity 7.1. Select one prompt and do some prewriting on the topic. You may also refer to your responses to the "After Reading" exercise or to Read to Write Activity 7.2 to get ideas.

Vocabulary Strategy: Using an Encyclopedia to Define Terms

Figuring out the definition of unfamiliar words and phrases while you are reading—by using context clues, word analysis, or the dictionary—can improve your comprehension. Sometimes, though, these strategies are not enough to explain the meaning of an unknown word or phrase. In such cases, you may need to consult an encyclopedia, such as *Scholarpedia* or the *Encyclopedia*

Answers

1. Support that happiness is tied to wealth: people from wealthy countries, such as the UK and the United States, report high levels of happiness.

Support that contradicts includes fewer than half the people in Japan and France are happy.

2. Other factors include gender, age, and marital status.

3. Students might agree with Nguyen that happiness is dependent on love and good relationships. Other students might agree with Wong, citing that money can secure important things in life, such as a college education or a good home.

Class Activity

After pairing and discussing, students could write their lists on the board or on a poster to share with the whole class.

Teaching Tip

Demonstrate how to search for words online via Scholarpedia and *Encyclopedia Britannica* on a computer with an overhead projector.

continued

Britannica, for background knowledge about the word. Often looking up a word in an encyclopedia and reading the opening paragraph can provide enough information to help you understand its meaning.

Vocabulary Practice

The sentences in this exercise come from the reading selection "More Money *Does* Make You Happier." Look up the underlined phrases in an encyclopedia—either print or online. For an online source like the *Encyclopedia Britannica*, type the phrase into the site's search engine. Read the encyclopedia entry and then write a brief definition of the phrase.

1. "Germany saw a rise of 13 percent in the same time, possibly because Germans were less affected by the <u>economic downturn</u> than other Western nations" (Zolfagharifard and Gillman 199).

2. "Germany saw a rise of 13 percent in the same time, possibly because Germans were less affected by the economic downturn than other <u>Western nations</u>" (Zolfagharifard and Gillman 199).

3. "The only <u>developed nations</u> to have higher satisfaction levels than the UK were the U.S. and Israel, while the lowest ratings were found in Egypt, Kenya, and Tanzania" (Zolfagharifard and Gillman 199).

4. "<u>Emerging markets</u> in Asia saw the biggest rise in citizens' satisfaction over the seven-year period, the global survey suggested" (Zolfagharifard and Gillman 199).

5. "Yet the public in Germany, which has far higher <u>gross domestic product</u> per capita than Malaysia, expressed a life satisfaction level of 60 percent, just four [percentage points] more than Malaysia" (Zolfagharifard and Gillman 200).

READING AND WRITING ABOUT A BAR GRAPH

A *bar graph* compares related data in a visual display by using the height or length of rectangles to represent numerical values or characteristics. A bar graph has an x axis (information labels across the bottom of the graph) and a y axis (information labels along the side of the graph). It might also have a *key* that explains information in the graph, such as the meaning of different colors.

To read a bar graph, follow these steps:

- Start with the title to identify the graph's focus.
- Read the labels on each axis.
- Review the key, if available.
- Look at the bars to understand the amount or quantity of each set of information.

Now consider the following questions:

1. What information does the graph in Figure 7.2 compare?
2. Which group is most happy?
3. Which group is least happy?
4. What conclusion can you draw about the relationship between happiness and income in the United States?

FIGURE 7.2 **A Bar Graph**

Source: Betsey Stevenson and Justin Wolfers; "Subjective Well-Being and Income: Is There Any Evidence of Satiation?"; University of Michigan.

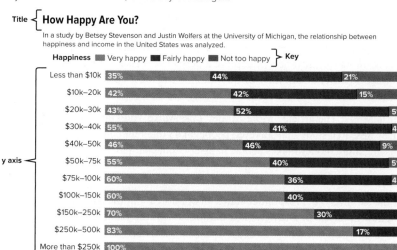

Note: Some categories may not equal 100% due to rounding.

Read to Write Activity 7.4

Prewrite about Visuals

Reread the prompt you chose for Read to Write Activity 7.1. Review the bar graph in Figure 7.2 and the graphic in Figure 7.1 at the beginning of this chapter. Consider what information might support your topic. Do some prewriting to add more ideas or support to your topic.

USING THE SOS ORGANIZATIONAL PATTERN

When you are assigned to write an essay in which you must respond to a reading, you might find it difficult to develop your own original thoughts. Having a specific strategy for writing a response can be valuable. One approach is to respond to the author's *main ideas.* You can respond by stating whether you agree or disagree with those ideas and why.

To compose an effective response, many writers find this organizational pattern useful, whether they are writing a paragraph or an essay:

1. Write a brief *summary.*

2. State an *opinion.*

3. Offer *support* for that opinion.

You can remember this pattern by the shorthand SOS, which stands for "**S**ummary, **O**pinion, **S**upport."

Teaching Tip

The student papers in "Spotlight on Student Writing: Annotating and Evaluating" are models of writing to respond, as both students write in response to Carol Dweck's article "Brainology."

Summary

A response usually begins with a brief summary of an idea or example from the source to which the writer is responding. The summary may be necessary because some readers may not be familiar with the original source. Yet even if readers have read the original text, a summary both refreshes their memory of the main ideas and focuses the writer's response. In place of a summary, the responder might choose to quote (for instance, to capture a person's precise words). The responder must judge whether a summary or quotation is the most compelling way to introduce the main idea from the reading.

Teaching Tip

See Chapter 6 for more on using quotations.

SUMMARY: The article "More Money *Does* Make You Happier" reported on a Pew Research study that surveyed people in 43 different countries and found that having more money makes people happier (Zolfagharifard and Gillman 199).

Opinion

After the summary, the responder states an opinion about the source—for instance, saying how much he or she agrees or disagrees with the main ideas. The responder's opinion can be stated indirectly, as in the assertion "Those who feel money buys happiness are misguided." Or it may be expressed directly, for example, by writing "I agree" or "I disagree."

However, whether it is appropriate to use the first-person pronoun (*I*) in your own writing will depend on the assignment, your audience, and your instructor's directions. Be aware that in academic writing, the first person is often thought to be inappropriately informal, as well as unprofessional.

OPINION: Money cannot always make people happy.

Another consideration when giving an opinion is to **qualify** your response to a main idea, which means to modify, limit, or restrict it. In other words, you might believe that the author's idea is correct in certain situations but not in others. For example, you might agree that money makes people happy, but only up to a certain point. Once people have enough income to eat well, live comfortably, and support their family, more money may not make for more happiness. Think carefully about whether you agree or disagree with an author's idea and to what extent.

QUALIFIED OPINION: Money allows for a certain level of material comfort but cannot make people truly happy in their personal lives.

Support

In your response, you must also provide support for your own ideas. In fact, most of a written response should be devoted to supporting ideas with facts, statistics, examples, explanations, and/or expert testimony. For instance, if you believe that money contributes to personal happiness, you might use *factual evidence*, such as statistics from surveys, to show that wealthier people report greater happiness than poor people do. Or you might use an *example* of a person who is well off and happy. You might further *explain* how money can buy a student a good education, allow a family to go on a vacation, or enable a young couple to purchase a home, all of which can contribute to personal happiness.

> **SUPPORT:** In the Pew survey, people in some wealthy countries, such as France and Japan, indicated that "barely half of [them are] happy with their lives" (Zolfagharifard and Gillman 199). In contrast, people of some less well-off countries, such as Malaysia, indicated that more than half of them are happy. These survey results show that there is not a simple connection between having money and being happy. As a teacher who is quoted at the end of the article explains, "There are people who don't have any money but they lead a happy life because family members love and respect each other. But there are rich families where husbands and wives often quarrel and children are addicted to drugs" (qtd. in Zolfagharifard and Gillman 200).

Once you have gone through the steps of summarizing the main idea, giving your opinion about the main idea, and then supporting your opinion, you can put these elements together to create a response paragraph.

Sample Response Paragraph

The article "More Money Does Make You Happier" reported on a Pew Research study that surveyed people in 43 different countries and found that having more money makes people happier. However, this conclusion is misleading, because money cannot always make people happy. For instance, in the Pew survey, people in some wealthy countries, such as France and Japan, indicated that "barely half of [them are] happy with their lives" (Zolfagharifard and Gillman 199). In contrast, citizens of some less well-off countries, such as Malaysia, indicated that more than half of them are happy. These survey results show that there is not a simple connection between having money and being happy. As a retired teacher at the end of the article explains, "There are people who don't have any money but they lead a happy life because family members love and respect each other. But there are rich families where husbands and wives often quarrel and children are addicted to drugs" (qtd. in Zolfagharifard and Gillman 200). Money may not make people happy with their families or their personal lives. As we know from the Beatles, money can't buy us love.

Figure 7.3 summarizes the SOS organizational pattern. Look for the SOS pattern when you are reading a response, and use it to write a response. Be aware, though, that these three elements do not always appear in this exact order.

Handout

Figure 7.3 is available in the Instructor's Resources as a reproducible handout.

FIGURE 7.3 SOS Response Organizational Pattern

Summary
A brief summary of, or quotation illustrating, the main idea to which the responder is reacting.

Opinion
A statement of whether and to what extent the responder agrees or disagrees with the main idea.

Support
Evidence for the responder's opinion, such as the four **Es** of support: factual **e**vidence, **e**xpert testimony, **e**xplanations, and **e**xamples.

READING SELECTION

Connect

You will find a coordinated Power of Process assignment for this reading in your Connect course.

Answers

1. Encourage students to be specific about how or when money can or cannot buy happiness.

2. The reading is partly informative because the author reviews research studies, but also persuasive because he includes his own ideas about the research.

3. Opinion in paragraphs 1 & 2; Summary in paragraphs 3 & 4; Opinion in paragraph 5; Summary in paragraphs 6 & 7; Opinion in paragraph 8; Support in paragraph 9; Opinion in paragraph 10.

Teaching Tip

Refer students to Figure 7.3 as they read and annotate.

"CAN MONEY REALLY BUY HAPPINESS?"

Complete the "Before Reading" assignment. Then read the selection while you complete the "During Reading" activities. Finally, complete the "After Reading" assignments.

 Before Reading: Ask Questions; Identify Purpose

Write responses to the following exercises using complete sentences.

1. Consider the title of the essay, and freewrite to answer the question "Can money really buy happiness?"

2. Consider the information that immediately precedes the article: When you read the text, will you be instructed, informed, or persuaded, or some combination of these purposes?

 During Reading: Identify Text Organization

Write responses to the following exercise using complete sentences.

3. As you read and reread, annotate the article's organizational pattern. In particular, identify where in the reading the author (a) summarizes or quotes from other readings or other people's ideas to which he is responding, (b) gives his opinion, and (c) supports his opinion.

Can Money Really Buy Happiness?

By John Grohol

PBS This Emotional Life

On his blog post, the author, a psychologist, discusses research related to the connection between money and happiness. He both summarizes that research and responds to it with ideas of his own. Grohol is on the editorial board of the journal CyberPsychology & Behavior *and is a founding member of the Society for Participatory Medicine.*

It turns out that whoever said money can't buy you happiness was wrong. 1

Money can buy you happiness, as long as you give some of the money away, or 2 use it for an experience rather than buying a product.

Dunn and colleagues (2008) conducted three studies that examined the 3 relationship between Americans' spending habits and their self-reported happiness. The first study was a national survey conducted on 632 Americans that asked respondents to detail their income and spending habits. The participants were also asked to rate their general happiness level.

Teaching Tip

Check *YouTube* for videos featuring Dunn talking about her research to share with students.

The researchers found that two things were significantly correlated with greater 4 general happiness levels—higher income and spending on gifts for other people or money given to charity. Although past research has been inconsistent in its finding that people who are rich generally are happier than people who are less well off, more recent research finds that the wealthy are indeed considerably happier than those with average or poor incomes (Lucas & Schimmack, 2009).

One could argue, "Well, hey, of course having more income can make you 5 happy. . ." But maybe it's related to either the dollar amount given or the fact that people who are more likely to give money to others or to charity are just inherently happier people by character. So the researchers set out to examine those hypotheses in two separate follow-up experiments.

In a small, second study, 16 employees were asked about their general 6 happiness levels before and after receiving their annual bonus. No matter what the size of the actual bonus, employees who spent more of their bonus money on others or charity reported greater general happiness levels than those who spent more of it on themselves.

Finally, in a third study of 46 people, researchers discovered that participants 7 who were directed to spend a small amount of money on others (either $5 or $20) reported greater feelings of happiness than those who were directed to spend the same amounts on themselves. Again, the dollar amount didn't matter.

The third study suggests that even when the choice isn't ours, we still feel the 8 happiness effects of giving away money to others—even when the actual value is small.

Other recent research sheds more light on the relationship between happiness 9 and money, too. For instance, Nicolao et al. (2009) found evidence that confirmed previous research that we are also generally happier when we spend money on experiences—like a vacation—rather than material things. But here's the catch—we're happier only when those experiences are positive (not so much when they are negative).

So indeed, money can buy you happiness—as long as you give some of it away. 10 A good thing to keep in mind this holiday season.

References

Dunn, E. W., et al. (2008). Spending money on others promotes happiness. *Science, 319*(5870), 1687–1688.

Lucas, R. E., & Schimmack, U. (2009). Income and well-being: How big is the gap between the rich and the poor? *Journal of Research in Personality, 43*(1), 75–78.

Nicolao, L., Irwin, J. R., & Goodman, J. K. (2009). Happiness for sale: Do experiential purchases make consumers happier than material purchases? *Journal of Consumer Research, 36*(2), 188–198.

After Reading: Summarize

Complete the following exercise.

4. Review your annotations and write a brief summary of the reading using complete sentences.

Read to Write Activity 7.5

Engage with the Reading

Write responses to the following exercises using complete sentences.

1. Do you agree with the author's assertion that money can buy happiness "as long as you give some of the money away, or use it for an experience rather than buying a product"? Why or why not? What support can you give for your opinion?

2. At the end of the article, the author points to research indicating people are "happier when [they] spend money on experiences—like a vacation—rather than on material things." Do you agree with this finding? What support can you give for your opinion?

3. The second research study included 16 people; the third study had 46 participants. Do you think that studying 16 or 46 people is a sufficient number on which to base conclusions about most people? Explain why or why not.

4. Which reading do you find more convincing—"More Money *Does* Make You Happier" or "Can Money Really Buy Happiness?" Explain your answer.

- With a partner, discuss your answers to exercises 1 and 2 in Read to Write Activity 7.5. Brainstorm and list support for whether either giving money away or using money to buy experiences can make people happy.

- With a partner, discuss your responses to exercise 4 in Read to Write Activity 7.5. Brainstorm and list support to show how convincing each article is.

Read to Write Activity 7.6

Prewrite for Writing Prompt 3

Review prompt 3 in Read to Write Activity 7.1, and do some prewriting on the topic. You may also refer to your answers to the "After Reading" exercise or to Read to Write Activity 7.5 to get ideas.

Vocabulary Strategy: Using an Encyclopedia or a Dictionary to Define Terms

Often looking up an unfamiliar word or phrase in an encyclopedia and reading the opening paragraph provides enough information to help you understand its meaning.

Vocabulary Practice

When should you use an encyclopedia like *Encyclopedia Britannica*, and when should you use a dictionary to understand unfamiliar words? Try this test: Look up the underlined words in the numbered items that follow, which come from the reading selection "Can Money Really Buy Happiness?" Use both an encyclopedia (print or online) and a good dictionary (such as *Merriam-Webster* online). Read the definitions for the words from both sources, determine which source provides a clearer definition that fits the word in context, and write your own brief definition, stating which source you used.

1. "Dunn and colleagues (2008) conducted three studies that examined the relationship between Americans' spending habits and their <u>self-reported</u> happiness" (Grohol 207).

2. "The researchers found that two things were significantly <u>correlated</u> with greater general happiness levels—higher income and spending on gifts for other people or money given to charity" (Grohol 207).

3. ". . . [P]eople who are more likely to give money to others or to charity are just <u>inherently</u> happier people by character" (Grohol 207).

4. "So the researchers set out to examine those <u>hypotheses</u> in two separate follow-up experiments" (Grohol 207).

Answers

1. *Self-report* indicates that research participants select a response without the researcher intervening. Encyclopedia.

2. *Correlated* indicates that two things are related. Dictionary.

3. *Inherently* means the quality of belonging to the basic nature of someone or something. Dictionary.

4. *Hypotheses* means explanations for events or phenomena. Encyclopedia.

Read to Write Activity 7.7

Generate Ideas and Draft a Response Paragraph

Review the two reading selections in this chapter and complete the following exercises, using complete sentences where appropriate.

1. Which one idea from the two readings do you find *most* convincing? Explain why and give support for your opinion in the form of factual evidence, expert testimony, explanation, and/or examples from either of the two readings.

2. Which one idea from the two readings do you find *least* convincing? Explain why and give support for your opinion in the form of factual evidence, expert testimony, explanation, and/or examples from either of the two readings.

3. Review your prewriting from Read to Write Activities 7.2 through 7.6 and consider your answers to questions 1 and 2 immediately preceding. Then reread the prompt you chose in Read to Write Activity 7.1. Explain why you chose that topic and what you might say about it.

4. Keeping in mind the prompt you selected, write a paragraph using the SOS organizational pattern. In your paragraph, respond to one of the main ideas from one of the reading selections. You can use your response to exercise 1, 2, or 3 in this activity as the basis of your paragraph.

Pair and Share

- Exchange your SOS paragraphs from Read to Write Activity 7.7. Read each other's paragraphs and identify the summary, the opinion, and the support.

- Read your SOS paragraphs from Read to Write Activity 7.7 and analyze the paragraph by asking these questions: (1) Is the *summary* accurate and detailed? (2) Is the *opinion* clearly stated? (3) Is the *support* sufficient and convincing?

DRAFTING AN ESSAY IN RESPONSE TO A TEXT: APPLYING THE SOS ORGANIZATIONAL PATTERN

Just as you can use the SOS (summary, opinion, support) pattern to write a response paragraph, you can apply the SOS pattern when writing essays.

For instance, just as you can begin your written response paragraph by summarizing or quoting a main idea from the reading, in an essay, you can use the introduction to summarize the ideas to which you will respond. You will want to present the author's idea in an *objective* manner—that is, in factual statements rather than in statements based on your own opinions. This step demonstrates that you accurately understand the author's idea.

Then, as your thesis statement, respond to the reading's idea by stating your opinion clearly and in a way that separates your idea from that of the author. You can indicate indirectly whether you agree or disagree by writing a statement such as "More money can buy happiness, but only if the money is spent wisely." Alternatively, if it is appropriate to use first person in your writing, you can state directly "I agree" or "I disagree."

Next, support your own ideas in body paragraphs, devoting most of your response to this part of your essay. For instance, if you agree (or disagree) with the author, provide support of your own (factual evidence, expert testimony, explanation, and/or examples) for your ideas. If you believe that the author's support is, or is not, convincing, then explain why. In the body paragraphs, you may need to quote or summarize more material from the original source.

Finally, end with a conclusion that summarizes the main points of your response and leaves readers with a sense of closure.

Read to Write Activity 7.8

Draft a Response Essay

Review your work from Read to Write Activities 7.2 through 7.7. Then select one of the essay prompts from Read to Write Activity 7.1 and draft a response essay.

Answer

Encourage students to review their notes and answers to exercises before drafting an essay.

Following the SOS pattern can help you develop the first draft of a response essay. Once you have completed a draft, you will want to review it and revise as needed. The checklist in "Strategies for Writing a Response Essay" outlines the elements of an effective written response to a reading.

Strategies for Writing a Response Essay

____ Does the essay summarize or quote a main idea from the text?

____ Does the essay clearly state an opinion about the main idea?

____ Does the essay give factual evidence, expert testimony, explanations, and/or examples for support?

____ Is the essay logically organized (with an introduction, body paragraphs, and a conclusion)?

____ Are the sentences clearly written, and are the transitions from one idea to the next smooth and logical?

____ Has the writing been revised for unity and coherence, and proofread for errors?

Handout

"Strategies for Writing a Response Essay" is a reproducible handout in the Instructor's Resources.

Class Activity

Before students see Figure 7.4, present this sample response essay (you can find an unannotated version in the Instructor's Resources) and ask students to evaluate it. Then students can compare their evaluations to the annotated Figure 7.4.

Review the draft of a response essay in Figure 7.4. The draft has been annotated at the left to point out places where the draft is successful or where it might be improved. On the right margin are annotations to identify the thesis, main ideas of the body paragraphs, and support to indicate ways the draft could be made more effective.

FIGURE 7.4 Draft of a Response Essay

Annotations for Analysis	Response Essay	Annotations for Comprehension

Good idea to start with a catchy quote—but introduce quote and add a parenthetical citation. State opinion without using "I"?
 	
Start sentences with specific words, not "there."
 	
Good lead-in to the essay.
 	
Who is "they"? Name the source.
 	
Specific details from the survey are appropriate.
 	
Integrate quotation
 	
Provide more support in this paragraph—maybe an example to show rich vs. poor people's happiness.
 	
Be specific about the article, the survey, the other researcher.
 	
Avoid using "you," which sounds informal.
 	
Provide more support in this paragraph—maybe an example.
 	
Make first sentence stronger. Cite author and source of the "interesting article."
	"Money can buy lots of happiness for me because I am very materialistic," businessman Tony Wong stated. I don't agree with Mr. Wong, because money can only buy certain things, like material possessions, which might make you happy in the short term but not in the long term. There's lots of evidence that money does not buy people happiness or give people meaning in their life.
	
	    First of all, there was a poll that showed that people in rich countries were happier than people in poor countries. They surveyed people in 43 countries and asked them to rate their personal satisfaction on a scale of 1 to 10, with 1 being an unhappy life and 10 a very happy life. People in places like the United Kingdom and the United States scored high, while people in places like Egypt and Kenya scored low. "The study confirmed that rises in national income are closely linked to personal satisfaction." There is evidence from other studies, though, that money isn't everything that makes a person happy.
	
	    The same article says that "while wealth appears to contribute to happiness, other research has indicated it is far from the only factor." For instance, the same survey showed that women are usually happier than men and that married people are happier than single people. Another researcher points out that giving money away or using money to buy an experience, like a vacation, will make people happy. So it's not just that money can make you happy, it also depends on who you are or how you spend that money.
	
	    A very interesting article made a distinction between a happy life and a meaningful life. It turns out that people who have a meaningful life are healthier than people who have a happy life. *Happy* in this case is defined as "feeling good," and
		Introduction
		Support: Quote suggests money makes people happy.
		
		Thesis
		
		Main Idea: Rich people happier than poor
		
		Support: Facts from poll
		
		Support: Quote to explain money isn't the only factor.
		Support: Facts that women and married people are happier.
		
		Main Idea: More than money makes people happy.
		
		Support: Quote to define happiness vs. meaning.

Annotations for Analysis	Response Essay	Annotations for Comprehension
Clear definitions of important terms.	*meaningful* is defined as "doing good" or "being good." This makes sense, because people can feel rewarded about giving their money away or doing good things for other people. It seems that these would be more important than just making yourself feel good.	*Support: Explanation why meaning is important.* *Main Idea: Meaning more important than happiness*
Nice idea to mention Tony Wong again at end.	So, if you are very materialistic, like Tony Wong, then perhaps money can make you happy, but if you want to feel good about yourself and have a more enriching life, then how you use your money is more important than having money.	*Conclusion: Not money, but how one uses money is important to happiness.*

Read to Write Activity 7.9

Check Your Draft

Review your draft using the checklist in "Strategies for Writing a Response." Note what areas you feel are strong and what areas you feel need improvement.

Answer

Answers will vary. Encourage students to annotate their drafts.

Pair and Share

Exchange your draft with a partner. Give one another feedback by each writing comments in the margins of the draft. Point out passages that are working well and places where the writing might be improved. Make specific and helpful comments.

ORGANIZING AND DEVELOPING BODY PARAGRAPHS

Earlier in this chapter, you learned that a response essay typically follows the SOS (summary-opinion-support) organizational pattern. It is also important to know that, as in most essays, the parts of a response essay are an introduction, body paragraphs, and a conclusion. Furthermore, each paragraph should have a topic sentence, use complete sentences, and include transitions.

For all essay types, including response essays, you need to make good decisions about which ideas you will respond to first, second, third, and so on, in the body paragraphs. In a response essay, you are building a case for your position in relation to the text to which you are responding. You want to proceed with your case in a logical order. Here are some strategies for ordering your body paragraphs to ensure a successful outcome.

Teaching Tip

Consider starting to introduce the idea of argumentative essays, covered in Chapter 8, by noting the similarities for students.

Chronological Order

Some essays are best organized in **time order**, also called **chronological order**. Among these are **narrative essays**, those that tell a story. Opting for a chronological order might also make sense for a response essay. For instance, if you are composing a response to a series of surveys about people's happiness, you might write about the earliest surveys in the first few body paragraphs and then use later paragraphs to examine how subsequent survey results have changed, and why.

Climactic Order

Another organizational strategy, especially for argumentative or persuasive essays, is **climactic order**, which involves beginning the body paragraphs with the weakest point and working up to the strongest point. An essay using climactic order builds to a *climax*—a high point—and leaves readers with a powerful last impression. For instance, in an argument claiming that money can buy happiness, you might point out in the first body paragraph how money can put food on the table. In the second body paragraph, you might explore how money can pay the rent and other living expenses. These early body paragraphs lead into paragraphs on what you might argue is money's most important benefit: funding an education. In turn, you might say, putting money into education can lead to a satisfying career that can create lifelong meaning and happiness. By ending with money's key benefit (paying for an education), the one most likely to produce both a happy and a fulfilling life, you have built up to your most compelling point.

Climactic order can also be employed in reverse. Sometimes it is effective to begin an essay with a powerful point to get the reader's attention or to impress upon the reader the importance of the topic. For example, beginning an essay with examples of how the lack of money sometimes forces people to choose between two important things—such as buying essential prescription medicines and paying the rent—might also be an effective organization for illustrating how having money can help people lead happier lives.

Simple-to-Complex Order

With **simple-to-complex order**, you begin your body paragraphs with a point that should be easy for readers to grasp and then proceed in later paragraphs to more difficult points. This way, you start readers on familiar ground before introducing complexity. Notice that the reading selection "More Money *Does* Make You Happier" begins with the straightforward idea that more money makes people happier. However, as the article progresses, it is clear that this equation is not so simple: people in rich countries are sometimes only a little bit happier than their counterparts in developing countries. Moreover, wealth is not the only factor in determining happiness, because women tend to be happier than men. In this way, the reading proceeds from the most obvious to the least obvious points.

Development of Depth and Detail

Whereas *order* refers to the sequence of paragraphs in an essay, particularly the body paragraphs, *development* refers to the depth of information within paragraphs, particularly the body paragraphs. Whether they are writing a response essay or some other type of essay, most beginning writers make the mistake of not providing enough factual evidence, expert testimony, explanations, or examples to support their ideas. In fact, the most convincing essays often include a variety of evidence drawn from the four Es of support. Notice, for example, that the reading selection "More Money *Does* Make You Happier," while providing a lot of *factual evidence* in the form of information and statistics from a Pew Research Study, also *explains* the results of the study (why people in some countries are more or less happy) and provides *quotations* from ordinary people about the survey results. Thus, this short article uses several types of support.

Read to Write Activity 7.10

Revise Body Paragraphs for Order and Development

Review your work from Read to Write Activities 7.8 and 7.9, including your essay draft, to complete the following exercises.

1. Consider whether the body paragraphs in your essay draft are in an effective order. What order did you use? Would revising the order make the essay more effective?

2. Review your essay draft and judge whether there is sufficient support throughout and especially in each body paragraph. Recall the four Es of support and consider how you might use them to strengthen your support. Are there places in the essay where more specific information can be added to bolster your support?

Figure 7.5 shows how the response essay in Figure 7.4 could be revised to be more effective.

FIGURE 7.5 Revised Response Essay

Money Can't Buy Happiness

An article first published in the British news source *The Daily Mail* in October 2014 reported on an international survey revealing that people from rich countries described greater levels of satisfaction with their lives than did people from poor countries. The article's title, "More Money *Does* Make You Happier," implies that being rich equates with being happy (Zolfagharifard and Gillman 199). However, that title is misleading: while having money can make a person happy, other evidence suggests how people spend their money or whether people have meaning in their life is more important than being rich.

The international survey, conducted by the Pew Research Center, questioned people in 43 countries and asked them to rate their personal satisfaction on a scale of 0 to 10, with 0 being a miserable life and 10 a very happy life. People in places like the United Kingdom and the United States, where incomes are high, scored high, while people in places like Egypt and Kenya, where incomes are low, scored low. Because of this connection, "The study confirmed that rises in national income are closely linked to personal satisfaction" (Zolfagharifard and Gillman 199). In other words, rich people seem to be happier people.

However, in this same article there is evidence that questions this simple connection. The authors explain: "The data also suggested that there is a limit to how much happiness money can buy" (Zolfagharifard and Gillman 200). For instance, Germans, who are generally well off, rated their lives only a few percentage points higher than people in Malaysia, where incomes are not as high. Also, other evidence suggests that income is not the only factor that influences one's happiness. For example, the same survey showed that women are usually happier than men and that married people are happier than single people (Zolfagharifard and Gillman 200). At the end of the article, Nguyen Thi Mai, a retired teacher from Vietnam, is quoted as questioning the link between money and happiness: "There are people who don't have any money but they lead a happy life because family members love and respect each other. But there are rich families where husbands and wives often quarrel and children are addicted to drugs" (Zolfagharifard and Gillman 200). Nguyen is correct: money cannot guarantee a happy family or a healthy lifestyle.

Moreover, evidence from other studies suggests that having money does not make a person happy. John Grohol, PhD in psychology, reports on studies that show money can make people happy *only if* they give their money away or use that money to buy an experience, such as a vacation, rather than buying a product. This makes sense. When I think of the things that have made me the happiest in my life, I think about experiences I have had, such as traveling to Hawaii with my family. We hiked the rugged Na Pali coast trail; we snorkeled in blue waters and saw amazing colored fish; we laughed and played on the beach. In contrast, I cannot remember any possession I bought as giving me such fond memories or making me feel connected to the people I love or to the natural world around me.

Perhaps there are people who truly enjoy having money and being rich. Tony Wong, a businessman from Malaysia, seems to be one of these, as he says, "Money can buy lots of happiness for me because I am very materialistic" (qtd. in Zolfagharifard and Gillman 200). Mr. Wong claims that money is at the top of his list of things that make him happy, followed by "health, family, dogs, and friends" (qtd. in Zolfagharifard and Gillman 200). But maybe Mr. Wong has his priorities mixed up. After all, he puts his dogs before his friends. For those of us who are not "very materialistic"—who care more about people than possessions—having money may not be as important as having people we love and friends we can depend on. The idea that friends and family are a greater source of happiness than money is confirmed in part by research in *The Wall Street Journal*. In the article, a San Francisco State University professor, Ryan Howell, explains that while people may *think* material possessions will give them lasting happiness, in fact his studies show people are happier when they buy experiences, like vacations or concert tickets, than when they buy products (Blackman). In the same article, Thomas Gilovich, a psychology professor at Cornell University, confirms Howell's research and explains that when experiences are "shared with other people [they] giv[e] us a greater sense of connection" (Blackman). In other words, human relationships and experiences are more important than possessions for true happiness.

So for people who are very materialistic, like Tony Wong, perhaps money can make them happy. But for people who want to be happy and have a more enriching life, then how to use money is more important than having money itself. Money can't buy happiness or health; give it away or enjoy it with your family and friends instead!

Works Cited

Blackman, Andrew. "Can Money Buy You Happiness?" *The Wall Street Journal*, 10 Nov. 2014, www.wsj.com/articles/can-money-buy-happiness -heres-what-science-has-to-say-1415569538.

Grohol, John. "Can Money Really Buy Happiness?" *Writing to Read, Reading to Write*, edited by Alison Kuehner, McGraw-Hill Education, 2020, pp. 207–08.

Zolfagharifard, Ellie, and Ollie Gillman. "More Money *Does* Make You Happier." *Writing to Read, Reading to Write*, edited by Alison Kuehner, McGraw-Hill Education, 2020, pp. 199–208.

Read to Write Activity 7.11

Analyze Drafts

Review Figure 7.4 ("Draft of a Response Essay") and Figure 7.5 ("Revised Response Essay"). Then answer the following questions using complete sentences.

1. What improvements have been made in the revised response essay in Figure 7.5? That is, in what ways is the writing more effective than in the draft in Figure 7.4? Note at least three positive changes, and explain how they improve the essay. In particular, consider paragraph order and development.

2. Use the checklist "Strategies for Writing a Response" to evaluate the revised response essay in Figure 7.5. Does the revised draft fulfill the items in the checklist?

Answers

1. Possible Answer:
(a) Quotes are more effectively introduced and integrated. (b) Body paragraphs contain more details and support. (c) Sentences are more effectively written.

2. The revised response essay fulfills all the items in the checklist.

Pair and Share

Exchange your essay draft with another student. Use the checklist in "Strategies for Writing a Response" to evaluate each other's essays.

CHAPTER REVIEW

Key Terms

climactic order Organization that begins with the weakest point and works up to the strongest point.

example A specific case (from personal experience, observation, reading, or research) that supports or illustrates an idea.

expert testimony The words or ideas of an *expert*—a person or organization with experience, knowledge, skill, and/or training in a particular subject or content area.

explanation The expression of reasons why an idea is true through the use of critical thinking or logical reasoning.

fact A statement that can be proved true or false.

factual evidence Grounds for belief based on the use of facts (statements that can be proved true or false) and/or statistics (facts expressed in terms of numbers).

narrative essay An essay that tells a story.

qualify To modify, limit, or restrict a statement, such as by making exceptions.

response essay An essay that gives personal reflections to and demonstrates critical thinking about a text.

simple-to-complex order Organization that begins with a point that should be easy for readers to grasp and then proceeds to more difficult points.

statistic A fact that is expressed in terms of numbers.

time order (chronological order) Organization according to time, such as oldest to newest or newest to oldest.

Chapter Summary

1. When you are reading to respond to a text, you must read critically to identify the main ideas, examine the support the author uses to convince readers of the main ideas, and consider to what extent you agree or disagree with the main ideas.

2. Writers use a variety of evidence—specifically factual evidence, expert testimony, explanations, and examples—to support ideas.

3. A common organizational pattern for writing a response is SOS (summary–opinion–support), which involves <u>s</u>ummarizing a main idea or support from the reading, stating your <u>o</u>pinion as to whether you agree with the idea or the support, and giving <u>s</u>upport for your response.

4. You can use the SOS organizational pattern to draft a paragraph or an essay in response to a reading.

5. You should take care to determine the most logical order for the body paragraphs in a response essay and develop the paragraphs in depth, with sufficient detail.

6. Read a bar graph by looking at the title, studying the x axis and y axis, and understanding the labels or key.

7. To understand a word or phrase, you may sometimes find it necessary to consult an encyclopedia for background knowledge about the word.

Apply What You Learned

Refer to the reading selections in this chapter to do the following.

1. Imagine that you have been asked to participate in a debate at your school about happiness. Your audience is your fellow students. The debate topic is "Money Can Buy Happiness." Would you agree with this proposition? Why or why not? Write a three-paragraph speech to your fellow students presenting your ideas, along with support. Take whatever position you want, and defend it.

2. If you completed the first Apply What You Learned activity, consider how you could respond to the position you took and defended in question 1. Write a three-paragraph speech explaining why you disagree with the position you took in your speech and give support for your response.

Class Activity

Assign student groups to argue for or against "money can buy happiness"; have other students judge the debate based on quality and quantity of support.

Work Cited

Smith, Emily Esfahani. "Meaning Is Healthier Than Happiness." *The Atlantic*, 1 Aug. 2013, www.theatlantic.com/health/archive/2013/08/meaning-is-healthier-than-happiness/278250/.

Credits

pp. 199–200: Zolfagharifard, Ellie, and Ollie Gillman, "More Money DOES Make You Happier: Britain and Other Rich Nations Among Most Contented Countries . . . but French and Japanese Are Determined to Be Miserable," *MailOnline*, 31 Oct. 2014. All rights reserved. Used with permission of Solo Syndication; **p. 203:** From Stevenson, Betsey, and Justin Wolfers, "Subjective Well-Being and Income: Is There Any Evidence of Statiation?" University of Michigan; **pp. 206–07:** Grohol, John, "Can Money Really Buy Happiness?" www.pbs.org/thisemotionallife/blogs/can-money-really-buy-happiness. Used by permsision of Psych Central.

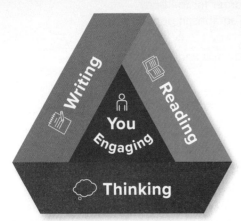

8 Reading and Writing Arguments

After reading this chapter, you will be able to

- Identify the parts of an argument.
- Organize arguments in paragraphs and essays.
- Respond to others' arguments with counterarguments.
- Evaluate to revise an argument.
- Compare denotation and connotation.
- Read and write about political cartoons.

Look for these icons throughout the chapter. They signal key strategies to use in Read to Write Activities.

Connect

Assign the LearnSmart Achieve topic "Using Evidence and Reasoning to Support a Thesis or Claim" for adaptive learning to accompany this chapter.

Class Activity

Before students read the chapter, provide them with the minimum wage map and the three questions for small-group discussion.

Theme: Should the Minimum Wage Be Raised?

What do you know about the minimum wage? For instance, consider the following:

- What does the term *minimum wage* mean?
- Do you know the current minimum wage in your state?
- Do you know the current federal (national) minimum wage?

Review the map in Figure 8.1 if you are not sure about the answers to these three questions. For example, locate your state on the map. Then determine if your state's minimum wage is above, at, or below the federal minimum wage or whether

FIGURE 8.1 **State Minimum Wage Laws**

Source: US Department of Labor, Jan. 2017; www.sandersinstitute.com/blog/state-minimum-wage-laws.

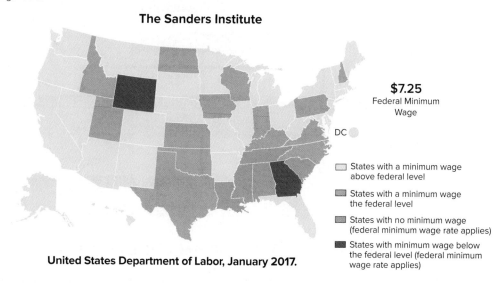

The Sanders Institute

$7.25
Federal Minimum Wage

DC

☐ States with a minimum wage above federal level

☐ States with a minimum wage the federal level

☐ States with no minimum wage (federal minimum wage rate applies)

■ States with minimum wage below the federal level (federal minimum wage rate applies)

United States Department of Labor, January 2017.

your state has no minimum wage by finding your state's color in the key at the lower right and reading the explanation for that color. Do you think the minimum wage in your state should be raised? What is the federal minimum wage, and do you believe it should be raised? What support can you provide for your opinions?

Giving your opinion on a topic, as well as support for that opinion in order to persuade someone, is the basis of an **argument**. Many essays you write in college will require you to present an argument, even if the assignment does not specifically say "argument." That is, rather than simply stating facts and information, you will give your opinion about the topic, as well as your ideas and evidence to support that opinion. For a sociology class, you might write an essay arguing that the United States should abolish the death penalty because it is "cruel and unusual" punishment, which is prohibited by the Eighth Amendment to the US Constitution; in an environmental science class, you might write a report arguing that human activity contributes substantially to climate change, using research available from NASA (the National Aeronautics and Space Administration).

The ability to read and write arguments is also a valuable set of skills for outside your classes. For example, you might read the pros and cons of legalizing marijuana before voting on an initiative, or you might consider arguments for or against enrolling your children in a charter school; you might petition the court to dismiss a traffic ticket, or you might write a letter urging city officials to install a speed bump on a busy street to prevent accidents. This chapter explains how to read and write arguments by considering the debate over whether to raise the federal minimum wage.

Handouts

Figure 8.2 is available as a reproducible handout in the Instructor's Resources. Also, a similar blank graphic is available to allow students to organize their own arguments.

FIGURE 8.2 Graphic Organizer for Claim, Reasons, and Evidence in an Argumentative Essay

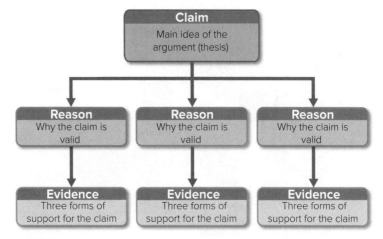

IDENTIFYING PARTS OF AN ARGUMENT

Knowing how to break down an argument into its parts is helpful. It will allow you to identify the elements of an argument in your reading and to craft an argument in your writing. Many parts of an argument should be familiar to you from previous chapters. However, argumentation introduces some new terms:

- Claim
- Reasons
- Evidence

Figure 8.2 shows how claim, reasons, and evidence form the structure for an argumentative essay.

As you read this chapter and learn about these terms, also think about developing an opinion as to whether the minimum wage should be raised. Keep the Read to Write Activity 8.1 essay topics in mind so that you can turn that opinion into an argument.

Read to Write Activity 8.1

Evaluate Essay Prompts for Reading and Writing about Raising the Minimum Wage 👥

The essay prompts that follow will help you focus your reading and plan an essay as you navigate through this chapter. Evaluate the writing topics by marking how interesting you find each one. Check "Interesting topic," "Maybe I would write on this topic," or "Can't relate to this topic" for each prompt. By the end of this chapter, as you proceed through the Read to Write activities, you will have completed a brief essay of about 250 words based on one of these topics.

1. Assume that newly hired student workers at your college earn the minimum wage. Take a position arguing that the wage of student workers on your

continued

campus should be or should not be raised. Address your argument to the college administration and others who hire student workers on campus.

- ☐ Interesting topic
- ☐ Maybe I could write on this topic
- ☐ Can't relate to this topic

2. Assume that newly hired student workers at your college earn the minimum wage. Take a position arguing that the wage of student workers on your campus should be or should not be raised. Write an essay to be published in the school newspaper, explaining your position to the student community.

- ☐ Interesting topic
- ☐ Maybe I could write on this topic
- ☐ Can't relate to this topic

3. Imagine that fast food workers in your community, who make the minimum wage, are striking and demanding higher pay. Write an essay to the owners of the local fast food chain restaurants in support of the workers' demands to earn more than minimum wage.

- ☐ Interesting topic
- ☐ Maybe I could write on this topic
- ☐ Can't relate to this topic

4. Imagine that fast food workers in your community, who make the minimum wage, are striking and demanding higher pay. Write an article to be published in the local newspaper, explaining why increasing the minimum wage for fast food workers is not a good idea for the local economy.

- ☐ Interesting topic
- ☐ Maybe I could write on this topic
- ☐ Can't relate to this topic

5. As a college student, you have been invited to testify before Congress about a bill aiming to raise the federal minimum wage. From your perspective as a student, write an argument for or against raising the minimum wage that you would present as testimony.

- ☐ Interesting topic
- ☐ Maybe I could write on this topic
- ☐ Can't relate to this topic

6. Write an essay in response either to Senator Tom Harkin, who is in favor of raising the federal minimum wage, or to David Rutigliano, who is against raising the federal minimum wage. In your essay, explain your position on the minimum wage and take a stand as to whether you agree or disagree with that person's position.

- ☐ Interesting topic
- ☐ Maybe I could write on this topic
- ☐ Can't relate to this topic

Claim

The main idea of an essay is called a thesis. If the essay is an argument, the main idea may also be called a **claim**. In an argument, the claim, or thesis, takes a *position* on the issue. An **issue** is a topic about which people disagree, such as raising the minimum wage—and therefore is *debatable*: that is, not everyone would agree with the position taken by the claim. While a thesis for another type of essay may be informative, a claim is always argumentative. Some examples will clarify how an argumentative claim is different from an informative thesis.

Teaching Tip

Help students understand the difference between an informative thesis vs. an argumentative thesis by asking them, What is the minimum wage? vs. What *should* the minimum wage be and why?

INFORMATIVE THESIS: The federal minimum wage of $7.25 per hour has not been raised since 2009, and therefore many low-wage workers and government officials are advocating for an increase to $10.10 per hour.

This informative thesis explains two facts: that the minimum wage has not been raised since 2009 and that some people want to raise the minimum wage. These facts promise an informative essay that will explain the recent history of the minimum wage and the reasons why some people are advocating for a higher minimum wage.

ARGUMENTATIVE CLAIM: The federal minimum wage, which has not been increased since 2009, should be raised from $7.25 to $10.10 per hour.

This argumentative claim, or thesis, takes a position by arguing the minimum wage should be raised. The essay will present reasons and evidence to support the claim's position.

Because an argument is a reasoned judgment, a claim cannot be based solely on the writer's personal opinion or preference. Personal opinion cannot be supported by evidence and logical reasoning. For instance, if you say you like chocolate ice cream better than vanilla or prefer dogs to cats, no one can argue for or against your statement. Your statement is simply your opinion; it is not an arguable claim. Consider these examples.

OPINION: I am happy with the minimum wage as it is.

Your feelings about the minimum wage—whether you like it or not—cannot be supported with evidence. Only you know whether you are indeed "happy" as the statement says.

ARGUABLE CLAIM: The minimum wage should remain as it is because it allows young people to get a job and gain valuable job experience.

This statement presents a claim ("The minimum wage should remain as it is") and gives reasons why this position is valid ("the minimum wage helps young people find work and gain experience").

As a reader, you can look for a claim in an argument using the same textual clues you would draw on to identify a thesis in another kind of essay. As a writer, you can use an effective strategy for determining your claim: Take a position based on what the evidence tells you about the topic. In other words, if the evidence suggests raising the minimum wage, then you can argue that increasing it is the right thing to do. Conversely, if the evidence points toward not raising the minimum wage, you can argue for that policy. Remember that an argument is a reasoned judgment, one that needs to be supported by evidence. So taking a position that can be supported by evidence makes sense.

When you are writing the claim, be specific. The first draft of your claim may be general. As you develop your reasons and evidence to support the claim, however, take care to revisit the claim to qualify it or to revise it so that it accurately reflects your argument. Look at these examples.

GENERAL CLAIM: The current minimum wage is fair.

Although the preceding claim takes a position in favor of retaining the current minimum wage, it is not specific about why the current minimum wage is fair or to whom exactly.

MORE SPECIFIC CLAIM: The current federal minimum wage is fair to teenage workers and to small-business owners.

This claim takes a position in favor of retaining the current minimum wage and specifies who would benefit. It also explains how the writer will support the claim—by looking for evidence about the effect of the minimum wage on teenage workers and small-business owners.

To sum up, a claim should state the writer's position on an issue—whether for or against. The position should be debatable; that is, others might disagree or have a different point of view. A claim must go beyond feelings and state a position on the issue based on evidence and solid reasoning.

Reasons

Because arguments are by definition debatable, people may have different opinions about the issue at the heart of an argument. So in addition to making a claim that states a position, an argument must be supported by reasons why that position is solid. A **reason** is a statement that explains or justifies. The claim expresses the debatable position on the issue, while the reasons provide the explanation as to why the claim is valid.

Let's examine a specific claim to understand how, in an argument, the claim states a position and sometimes gives reasons for that position as well.

Class Activity

Brainstorm or freewrite with students reasons the minimum wage should be raised and reasons why it should not to get students thinking about the topic and to help understand "reasons."

ARGUMENTATIVE CLAIM WITH REASONS:

The <u>federal minimum wage should be raised</u> from $7.25 to $10.10 per hour
      Claim = writer's position on the issue

to <u>benefit businesses by reducing employee turnover,</u>
              Reason 1

to <u>enable workers to earn a living wage,</u> and
            Reason 2

to <u>allow workers with families to live above the poverty line.</u>
           Reason 3

The preceding claim takes a position by arguing the minimum wage should be raised, and then it gives three reasons why raising the minimum wage would benefit employers and workers.

In an essay, sometimes reasons to support the claim are stated in the claim itself, as in the example. Other times, reasons appear elsewhere in the essay, as in the body paragraphs. For instance, the outline of an essay that states a position early on and gives reasons throughout the essay is shown here.

Sample Outline of an Argumentative Essay

Claim: The federal minimum wage should be raised from $7.25 to $10.10 per hour.

First reason: Raising the minimum wage would benefit businesses by reducing employee turnover.

Second reason: Raising the minimum wage would enable workers to earn a living wage.

Third reason: Raising the minimum wage would allow workers with families to live above the poverty line.

As a reader, you should look for the reasons supporting the claim, which are often found in the body paragraphs' topic sentences. As a writer, you should think carefully about what reasons you could give to support your position. To write a good argument, you must consider your audience and decide how you can best persuade your particular readers. Here are some examples:

- If you are trying to persuade college administrators to raise the minimum wage for student workers on campus, you might focus on how a raise will boost job stability or make the college more appealing to attend.

- If you are trying to persuade students to press for higher pay, you might present reasons such as how a raise will help them to pay for their college expenses and will make it appealing to work on campus in between classes.

Evidence

Teaching Tip

The four e's of support are explained in Chapter 7.

Evidence refers to support for a claim. The four types of support writers use, according to Professor Jennifer Hurley of Ohlone College, are these:

- Factual **E**vidence
- **E**xpert Testimony
- **E**xplanations
- **E**xamples

Like reasons, the type of evidence used often depends on what is most appropriate for the audience, purpose, and assignment. As a reader, you will want to consider the intended audience and purpose of the argument to evaluate the appropriateness of the evidence. Consider the following examples:

- A newspaper editorial on ways to reduce youth crime might include stories from your own personal experience (examples) to appeal to a general audience and persuade readers to take action.

- An article in a scholarly journal about a controversial new theory might feature statistics and researched information to appeal to professionals and change their thinking (factual evidence).

As a writer, you will want to consider the context of your argument. Consider these examples:

- If you are writing an essay for an economics class, you might include quotes from economists arguing for (or against) the minimum wage (expert testimony).
- If you are writing for a history class, you might assert that raising the minimum wage has historically been a nonpartisan issue because both Democratic and Republican presidents have supported doing so (explanation).

Reading the assignment prompt thoughtfully might provide further clues, such as references to experts or texts that should be consulted in developing your argument. If you need guidance, ask your instructor what constitutes appropriate evidence for the assignment.

You will now have a chance to put your skills to the test by reading a speech in support of raising the minimum wage. As you read, look for the parts of the argument: claim, reasons, and evidence.

READING SELECTION

"CONGRESS SHOULD INCREASE THE MINIMUM WAGE AND INDEX IT"

Complete the "Before Reading" assignment. Then read the selection while you complete the "During Reading" activities. Finally, complete the "After Reading" assignments.

 Before Reading: Recognize Prior Knowledge; Preview

Write answers to the following questions using complete sentences.

1. Have you ever had a job for which you earned the minimum wage? If so, do you feel you were adequately paid? If you have never worked for minimum wage, what do you think would be a fair minimum wage today? Why?

2. Look at the title of the article. What does it mean to increase the minimum wage? What does it mean to index the minimum wage? If you are not sure, do some research to find out.

Connect

You will find a coordinated Power of Process assignment for this reading in your Connect course.

Answers

1. Answers will vary; encourage students to explain their reasoning or to give examples to show whether they were adequately paid.

2. To raise the minimum wage means to increase the dollar amount; to index wages means to automatically increase wages as inflation increases.

3. The claim is to provide an "increase in the Federal Minimum Wage" and index it. The reasons include helping "hardworking Americans who are earning at or near the minimum wage . . . aspire to live a middle-class life"; "many low-wage families are forced to rely on safety net programs"; and doing "what is right for the economy." Support includes explanation of how the wage increases will be tied to the cost of living; facts that show the minimum wage is "worth 31 percent less than at its peak in 1968," that workers have a "third less buying power than 45 years ago," and that the minimum wage would be $10.56 if it kept up with inflation.

4. Answers will vary.

During Reading: Annotate for Claim, Reasons, and Evidence

Write responses to the following exercises using complete sentences.

3. As you read and reread, annotate the reading by marking the claim, reasons, and evidence.

4. Record your reactions to the arguments for raising the minimum wage.

Congress Should Increase the Minimum Wage and Index It

Statement by U.S. Senator Tom Harkin, 14 March 2013

Tom Harkin, Democrat from Iowa, was a member of the U.S. House of Representatives from 1974 to 1984 and a U.S. Senator from 1985 to 2015. He chaired the Senate Committee on Health, Education, Labor, and Pensions (HELP). The following remarks are part of Senator Harkin's opening statement at a hearing before the HELP Committee on the topic "Keeping Up with a Changing Economy: Indexing the Minimum Wage."

---

1   For several years now, I have held hearings in this committee focusing on the need to bolster the middle class in this country and restore the American Dream. The American Dream is supposed to be about building a better life. If you work hard and play by the rules, you should be able to support your family, join the middle class, and build a brighter future for your children.

2   But today, tens of millions of hardworking Americans who are earning at or near the minimum wage can't even aspire to live a middle-class life or achieve the American Dream. Instead, they are falling further and further behind. We need to do more to support these workers as they try to build opportunity for their families and their futures. A critical first step is to ensure that they earn a fair day's pay for a hard day's work. That is why last week I joined with Congressman George Miller [D-CA] to introduce the Fair Minimum Wage Act of 2013, which would provide a long-overdue increase in the Federal minimum wage.

3   This bill will gradually increase the minimum wage to $10.10 an hour in three annual steps, and then link future increases in the minimum wage to the cost of living, so that people who are trying to get ahead don't fall behind as our economy grows.

4   Today's hearing will focus specifically on indexing the minimum wage. This is the first hearing in this committee to look at indexing the minimum wage in more than 20 years.

5   Over the past four decades, Congress has raised the minimum wage five times. But these raises have come sporadically and after long stretches with no raise. The subsequent increases have not brought the wage up to its past levels, and so the real value of the wage has declined significantly. The minimum wage in fact is worth 31 percent less than at its peak in 1968, even as productivity has soared.

This means that as the economy has grown and corporate profits are at an all-time high, tens of millions of low-wage workers and their families have almost a third less buying power than 45 years ago. If the minimum wage had kept pace with inflation since 1968, today it would be $10.56 and a full-time worker would earn nearly $22,000. Instead, the minimum wage is $7.25, and a full-time worker earns only $15,000 a year. It is a poverty wage.

This has seriously hurt the standard of living for low-wage workers and their families. As a result, many low-wage families are forced to rely on safety net programs like food stamps and housing assistance to ensure that they can survive. And when millions of workers are barely surviving because of low wages, they cannot hope to join the middle class. This ends up hurting everyone, especially our economy.

The middle class is the backbone of our economy, and we must grow our middle class in order to have a growing economy in the long run. Businesses need customers to buy things if they want to grow and prosper. But when workers earn a poverty wage and have no purchasing power, they can't help the economy thrive. That's one reason why so many businesses, large and small—from the CEO of Costco to the record store owner we will hear from today—support a higher minimum wage, and support indexing the minimum wage to inflation so that it will no longer lose value.

We stand at a rare moment of opportunity—where we can do what is right for the economy and, at the same time, do what is simply right. A fair minimum wage that is predictable, with modest increases that keep wages steadily growing in pace with inflation, rather than falling behind, benefits everyone. Indexing will do all of these things. That is why 10 States have already implemented this policy, and we will hear from one of them today. At the federal level, this policy is long overdue.

Of course, indexing the minimum wage must be done right. We have to be sure to set an adequate minimum wage in the first place, before locking it in in real terms for the indefinite future. That is why my legislation would first increase the minimum wage to $10.10 an hour, phased in through three increases spread out over three years.

Once we make sure that the minimum wage is an adequate wage, indexing means that American workers will be able to count on fair wages in the future. No longer will low-wage workers go years without even a penny raise. When groceries get more expensive or the gas or electric bills go up, when the bus fare climbs again or the rent goes up—these workers, who typically must live paycheck to paycheck, will have the assurance that they have a raise coming to them. Indexing the minimum wage, then, not only helps working families keep up with the economy and deal with rising costs, it also gives them peace of mind.

I want to thank our witnesses for being here today, and I look forward to an informative discussion of this critically important issue.

Answers

5. The senator's claim is "A fair minimum wage that is predictable . . . benefits everyone." This statement includes the specific topic and a reason.

6. The reasons are "hardworking Americans . . . can't even aspire to live a middle-class life" and "we must grow our middle class . . . to have a growing economy." These statements explain why raising the wage is important.

7. A fact is today's minimum wage would be $10.56 if indexed to inflation; an explanation is businesses need customers to buy; an example is low-wage families rely on food stamps; the CEO of Costco could be an expert.

After Reading: Evaluate an Argument

Write responses to the following exercises using complete sentences.

5. Review your annotations and identify Harkin's claim. Select the sentence that best sums up the claim and quote it. Explain why you chose this sentence as the claim: what clues in the speech did you use? (Note: If you cannot locate a sentence in the speech, then state the claim in your own words.)

6. Review your annotations: What reasons support Harkin's claim? What clues helped you to identify the reasons? Summarize the reasons.

7. Review your annotations: What evidence supports the claim? Try to find examples of the four types of evidence: examples, expert testimony, factual evidence, and explanations. (Note: Not all arguments will include all types of evidence.) Summarize the evidence.

Read to Write Activity 8.2

Engage with the Reading

Write responses to the following exercises using complete sentences.

1. Do you find Harkin's claim and reasons to be persuasive? Why or why not? How could someone argue against them?

2. Which pieces of evidence in the reading do you find most convincing? Why? Can you think of evidence that might counter the reading's evidence?

Answers

1. Answers will vary. Students should list specific reasons in the reading and identify possible rebuttals.

2. Answers will vary. Even if students generally disagree with the claim, they should locate the *most* convincing evidence for it.

Pair and Share

- Review your responses from "After Reading": Compare your statement of Harkin's claim (from exercise 5), the support (exercise 6), and the evidence in support of the claim (exercise 7) with those identified by a partner. Create a graphic organizer, like the one in Figure 8.2, to illustrate Harkin's argument.

- Review your answers from Read to Write Activity 8.2. Compare your analyses of the claim, reasons, and evidence with those of a partner. Did you find Harkin's argument convincing? Which are the most compelling aspects of the argument? Which did you think were the weakest aspects?

Read to Write Activity 8.3

Prewrite on a Topic

Follow the instructions in each exercise.

1. Select one of the essay topics from Read to Write Activity 8.1 and do some prewriting on the topic. In your prewriting, consider both sides of the argument; that is, whether the minimum wage should be raised. For instance, you might create a pro (in favor of) and con (against) list as a way to get started.

2. Reread your prewriting and select the side you think is strongest. Write a claim stating your position.

3. Reread your prewriting and look for reasons to support your claim. Either include the reasons in your claim or list them separately.

4. Provide evidence to support your reasons. For each reason, list at least two pieces of evidence.

5. Using your ideas from exercises 1, 2, 3, and 4, create a graphic organizer, like the one shown in Figure 8.2, to illustrate your argument.

Answers

1. See Chapter 3 for examples of listing.

2. Encourage students to write an *argumentative, specific* claim by looking at the example earlier in the chapter.

3. Suggest students think about *why* they believe their claim is persuasive.

4. Challenge students to list evidence from each of the four types.

5. You can provide students with a blank organizer, or they can create their own graphic organizer.

Pair and Share

- Compare your prewriting on your topic (from exercise 1 in Read to Write Activity 8.3) with that of a partner. Try to add more reasons and evidence on both sides of the argument.

- Compare your graphic organizers (from exercise 5 in Read to Write Activity 8.3) with that of a partner. Brainstorm for ideas to add to the claim, ways to add more reasons, and suggestions for more evidence.

Vocabulary Strategy: Comparing Denotation and Connotation

Connect

Vocabulary Practice is available to be assigned as Practice in Connect.

Writers think carefully about language. They consider not only what words mean precisely but also how words or phrases convey feelings they want to evoke in readers. The literal meaning of a word—its dictionary definition—is the **denotation** of the word. The suggested or implied meaning of a word—such as the associations or feelings we might have about a word—is the **connotation** of the word. For instance, the words *nosy* and *curious* mean about the same: "inquisitive. " *Nosy,* however, has a somewhat negative connotation, while *curious* has a more positive connotation. When developing arguments, writers often choose words or phrases with strongly positive or negative connotations to persuade readers of their point of view.

continued

Answers

1. Denotation: Safety net programs are government support services, such as food stamps or housing assistance.

Connotation: Positive because they are for protection

2. Denotation: Backbone of economy means supporting the economy in a fundamental way.

Connotation: Positive

3. Denotation: Poverty wage means a wage below the government-set poverty level.

Connotation: Negative

4. Denotation: Living paycheck to paycheck means spending all your income on essentials with no savings.

Connotation: Negative

Vocabulary Practice

Consider the underlined word or phrase in each sentence below from the reading selection "Congress Should Increase the Minimum Wage and Index It." Determine the denotation of each, as well as its connotation. If you do not know the definition, use context clues or a dictionary or encyclopedia to determine the denotation. Then identify the connotation of each underlined word as "Negative," "Positive," or "Neutral." An example follows.

Example: "For several years now, I have held hearings in this committee focusing on the need to bolster the middle class in this country and restore the American Dream" (Harkin 228).

Denotation: The idea that all American citizens can be successful and prosperous if they work hard.

Connotation: Positive

1. "As a result, many low-wage families are forced to rely on safety net programs like food stamps and housing assistance to ensure that they can survive" (Harkin 229).

2. "The middle class is the backbone of our economy, and we must grow our middle class in order to have a growing economy in the long run" (Harkin 229).

3. "But when workers earn a poverty wage and have no purchasing power, they can't help the economy thrive" (Harkin 229).

4. "When groceries get more expensive or the gas or electric bills go up, when the bus fare climbs again or the rent goes up—these workers, who typically must live paycheck to paycheck, will have the assurance that they have a raise coming to them" (Harkin 229).

READING AND WRITING ABOUT POLITICAL CARTOONS

A political cartoon is an illustration or comic strip with a political or social message, usually about a current event (such as raising the minimum wage) or about a well-known person (such as the president of the United States). Political cartoons are written to make a point: they express an opinion or present an argument. To understand a political cartoon, follow these guidelines:

- **Look at the pictures.** Identify what the pictures mean—literally as well as symbolically. Cartoonists often use certain strategies to get their message across:

  ○ *Exaggeration* may be used to stress a point. For instance, a customer complaining that a $2.50 Happy Meal will cost $15 if the minimum wage is raised is an example of exaggeration because it's unlikely the cost of a hamburger would rise so drastically.

  ○ *Symbolism* is the use of an image to represent something else. For instance, a dollar sign or a dollar bill could represent money.

- **Read the text.** Remember that a political cartoon is meant to be humorous and to make a point. To achieve these effects, cartoonist often use *irony*, which means saying one thing but meaning the opposite. For instance, it would be ironic for a fat businessman dressed in a suit to say to a skinny worker in tattered clothes that his request for a raise is greedy. In this case, not only the words but also the images would convey the irony of the situation.

Consider Figures 8.3 and 8.4—two political cartoons about raising the minimum wage—and answer the following questions about each cartoon:

1. What is the claim—for instance, does the cartoon favor or oppose raising the minimum wage?

2. What reason(s) are given to support the claim? That is, *why* does the cartoon suggest the minimum wage should or should not be raised?

3. What evidence, if any, is presented to support the claim?

FIGURE 8.3
"Minimum Wage"

Source: Pat Bagley; *Salt Lake Tribune*, 2014.

FIGURE 8.4
"2 out of 3 Like a Minimum Wage Hike"

Source: Gary Varvel; *The Indianapolis Star*, 2014.

Read to Write Activity 8.4

Use Information from Visuals in an Argument

Write responses to the following exercises using complete sentences.

1. Review your claim and reasons for your position on the minimum wage (from Read to Write Activity 8.3). Do the cartoons in Figures 8.3 and 8.4 provide any new ideas or reasons to support your claim? If so, add them to your essay plan.

2. Review the visual shown in Figure 8.1. Does the map showing minimum wage laws in the states provide any new ideas, reasons, or evidence to support your claim? If so, add them to your essay plan.

ORGANIZING ARGUMENTS IN PARAGRAPHS AND ESSAYS

Class Activity

Discuss why or when a writer might use a particular organizational pattern in an argument.

Identifying the claim, reasons, and evidence in a text will help you see how arguments are organized. Determining the organizational pattern will also help you follow the author's thinking. Two common ways of organizing arguments are (1) from claim or reason to evidence and (2) from evidence to claim or reason.

Arguing from Claim or Reason to Evidence

FIGURE 8.5
Claim to Evidence

Claim or Reason
• Main idea

Evidence
• Support for claim

One strategy for organizing an argument is to begin with a claim (in an essay) or a reason (in a paragraph) and then present evidence to support that claim or reason. This pattern is typical of academic writing: to present a thesis or topic sentence and then provide proof for it.

For instance, suppose an argument begins by stating that raising the minimum wage would lead to job losses, and then provides statistics to show that past increases in the minimum wage are correlated with higher unemployment. That would be an argument that moves from claim to evidence. Figure 8.5 illustrates how a writer might begin with a claim or reason and then give supporting evidence to lead readers to a conclusion.

Arguing from Evidence to Reason or Claim

A different organizational strategy is to begin with evidence and then reach a conclusion or claim. You can think of this organizational structure as moving from evidence to reason or claim. This organizational strategy can be powerful because the writer seems to lead readers, by force of the evidence, to a logical conclusion. Often scientific writing proceeds in this way.

An argument that begins with examples of minimum-wage workers who cannot pay their bills and with statistics showing that these workers make poverty-level wages and then leads to the claim that the minimum wage should be raised is an argument that moves from evidence to claim. Figure 8.6 illustrates how a writer might begin by presenting evidence that leads readers to the claim.

You might find the organizational patterns of claim to evidence or of evidence to claim used for an entire piece of writing or on a smaller scale, such as in a paragraph or section of a reading. For instance, a paragraph that begins with a reason to support the claim in the topic sentence and then provides support for that reason in the following sentences moves from reason to evidence (see Figure 8.7). A paragraph that begins with facts, quotes, or examples and then leads to a strong concluding sentence moves from evidence to reason (see Figure 8.8).

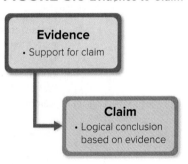

FIGURE 8.6 Evidence to Claim

FIGURE 8.7 Paragraph Organized from Reason to Evidence

The following information on the minimum wage was posted on the White House website during the administration of President Barack Obama. The information is organized from reason to evidence because it begins with a general statement of the reason that is followed by factual evidence to support that statement.

Paragraph	Annotations
Raising the wage could help workers make ends meet. For example, a $10.10 wage could, over the course of a year, help a full-time, full-year minimum-wage worker in Arizona afford either 4 months of rent, 24 weeks of groceries, 68 tanks of gas, or the equivalent of 31 months of electricity. Raising the federal minimum wage would not only benefit more than 28 million workers across the country, but 19 million workers from all types of households would see a direct increase in their wages. Today, the real value of the minimum wage has fallen by nearly one-third since its peak in 1968. And right now, a full-time minimum wage worker makes $14,500 a year, which leaves too many families struggling to make ends meet. Since President Obama called for a minimum wage increase in his 2013 State of the Union address, 13 states and Washington, D.C. have passed laws to raise their minimum wage. According to estimates from the Council of Economic Advisers, about 7 million American workers will benefit from these increases as of 2017.	*Reason: raising minimum wage helps workers have enough money* *Factual evidence: what workers can buy with increased wages* *Factual evidence: number of workers affected* *Factual evidence: numerical decline in real value of the minimum wage* *Factual evidence: current annual income of full-time minimum wage earner* *Factual evidence: number of states increasing the minimum wage*

FIGURE 8.8 Paragraph Organized from Evidence to Reason

In this paragraph, which is organized from evidence to reason, Senator George Miller, Democrat from California, argues in support of raising the minimum wage. His remarks are part of the same hearing from which both reading selections in this chapter are taken—the March 14, 2013, hearing before the Senate Health, Education, Labor, and Pensions (HELP) Committee on the topic "Keeping Up with a Changing Economy: Indexing the Minimum Wage." Notice that the evidence (statistics and examples) is presented first and leads to the statement of the reason at the conclusion.

Paragraph	Annotations
Right now, tens of millions of Americans are working hard <u>stocking shelves</u>. They're working the line at a <u>fast food restaurant</u> and <u>cleaning bathrooms in a downtown office building</u>. They work full-time. Some work two or three part-time jobs. They play by the rules. They contribute. Yet, they still live in poverty. And they are falling behind because their paychecks aren't keeping up. Today, <u>40 percent of Americans make less than what the minimum wage was worth in 1968</u>. This is immoral. And it is economically dangerous. Income inequality threatens the economic security of working families and the strength of our Nation. That's why we are here today—workers and business leaders alike—to say that it's time for $10.10.	*Evidence:* examples of people working minimum-wage jobs *Evidence:* statistic about how the minimum wage has lost value *Reason:* need to raise the minimum wage to $10.10

Structuring Body Paragraphs in an Argument

Teaching Tip

PIE Paragraphs are explained in Chapter 6.

Whether it is organized from reason to evidence or from evidence to reason, an argument needs to link the evidence clearly to the reasons and to the claim. The PIE paragraph structure—**P**oint, **I**nformation, **E**xplanation—can be useful when you write an argument text. In an argument, the point of a paragraph can be the reason or claim, the information is the evidence, and the explanation is the link between the evidence and the claim (see Figure 8.9).

As the reader of an argument text, always look for the author's explanation linking evidence to reasons for the claim. As the writer of an argument text, strive to make clear to readers how the evidence supports your position by explaining the link between evidence and claim.

Let's turn now to a second reading looking at the debate over raising the minimum wage. As you read, analyze, and annotate the author's argument, your goals will be to identify the claim, reasons, evidence, and organizational pattern.

FIGURE 8.9 Argumentative PIE Paragraph

Representing the National Restaurant Association, Melvin Sickler, owner of several Auntie Anne's Pretzels and Cinnabon stores, explains why raising the minimum wage would be a burden on businesses like his. His remarks are part of the same hearing from which both reading selections in this chapter are taken—the March 14, 2013, hearing before the Senate Health, Education, Labor, and Pensions (HELP) Committee on the topic "Keeping Up with a Changing Economy: Indexing the Minimum Wage."

Paragraph	Annotations
While, in theory, it may sound to some as a good idea to increase the starting wage, the ramifications go much further. If I increase the wage that I pay entry level employees by $2.85, then I also have to give a $2.85 raise to my employees that are making $10, $12, and even $14 an hour. Otherwise, it would not be fair to these employees who have been with me for several years and worked their way up the ladder. I would love to give all of my employees a $2.85 raise, but the reality is I simply can not afford it. In fact, if the starting wage was increased to $10.10, then, approximately, 75 percent of my employees would end up getting a $2.85 an hour pay increase. That would result in a 22 percent jump in my labor costs, which would be very difficult for my business to withstand.	*Point (reason):* raising minimum wage would affect a business and its employees *Information (evidence):* facts of salary increase if minimum wage law passed *Explanation:* why raising minimum wage would raise business expenses *Information (evidence):* facts about the rise in wages for employees *Point (reason):* raising minimum wage hard on businesses

READING SELECTION

"CONGRESS SHOULD NOT INCREASE THE MINIMUM WAGE"

Complete the "Before Reading" assignment. Then read the selection while you complete the "During Reading" activities. Finally, complete the "After Reading" assignments.

Connect

You will find a coordinated Power of Process assignment for this reading in your Connect course.

Answers

1. The author will argue that the minimum wage should not be increased.

2. The author might argue that raising the minimum wage will mean fewer jobs; he might use statistics showing that higher wages are correlated with more unemployment, or he might quote a business owner.

Answers

3. The claim is in the last sentence, that "any mandated increase to costs will damage an already fragile industry." The author gives many reasons, such as the high cost to businesses, loss of jobs, as well as how a minimum wage is a training wage. Evidence includes the 39.3% wage increase, and explanations that the minimum wage is intended as a starter wage.

4. Answers will vary.

 Before Reading: Predict

Write answers to the following questions using complete sentences.

1. Based on the title of the reading, what do you predict will be the author's claim?

2. What reasons might the author give to support the claim? What evidence might he use to support the claim?

During Reading: Annotate for Claim, Reasons, and Evidence

Write responses to the following exercises using complete sentences.

3. As you read and reread, annotate the reading by marking the claim, reasons, and evidence.

4. Record your reactions to the arguments against raising the minimum wage.

Congress Should Not Increase the Minimum Wage

Statement by Connecticut State Senator David Rutigliano, 14 March 2013

Like the previous reading selection, the following statement is from the hearing before the Senate Health, Education, Labor, and Pensions (HELP) Committee on "Keeping Up with a Changing Economy: Indexing the Minimum Wage." David Rutigliano—member of the Connecticut Restaurant Association (CRA) and partner in the SBC Restaurant Group—represents the restaurant industry in Connecticut and also serves in the Connecticut General Assembly.

I have two business partners, and we were all born and raised in Connecticut. We all got married and started families in Connecticut, and Connecticut is where we decided to start our business. We want our State and our country to succeed and prosper. However, we don't believe the Fair Minimum Wage Act of 2013 (S. 460) is the right avenue to achieve that prosperity.   1

    This proposal seeks to increase the Federal minimum wage from $7.25 per hour to $10.10 per hour. That equates to a 39.3 percent minimum wage increase. In addition, it seeks to increase the cash wage for tipped employees from $2.13 per hour to $7.07 per hour, a 232 percent increase. These numbers are, simply put, staggering. At a time when many businesses are struggling to keep their doors open and in some cases employers are foregoing their own paychecks to avoid laying off employees, mandating wage increases will only hurt those employees which this proposal seeks to help.   2

    In my home state of Connecticut, where we already have the fourth highest minimum wage at $8.25 and one of the highest tipped wages at $5.69, there is currently a proposal in the State legislature which seeks to increase the minimum   3 wage to $9.75 and the tipped wage to $6.73. That, along with the recently enacted mandatory paid sick leave law, is making an already difficult situation even worse. Add to that the Affordable Care Act, and I ask anyone here to explain how those of us in the restaurant industry, which is labor-heavy and runs on extremely low profit margins, will survive, let alone prosper, should these proposals become law.

To be specific: In Connecticut, this bill would add roughly $2,800 per year to the cost of a full-time tipped employee. In other States, it would add as much as $10,000 to the annual cost of that employee. In an industry that just earns roughly $2,600 in profit for each employee, an increase of this magnitude just isn't feasible. 4

The question of whether employers can bear the costs of increased minimum wages should be discussed on the merits, not on scare tactics or appeals to emotion. If an additional mandate means that employers like me will be forced to scale back, then employees could actually be worse off after it passes. 5

This is what the academic research suggests. Economists from the University of California–Irvine and the Federal Reserve Board published the results of a comprehensive review of all research conducted over the last 20 years on the effects increases to the minimum wage had on employment rates. They found that 85 percent of all credible studies came to the same conclusion: Increases in the minimum wage are almost always followed by a reduction in the number of jobs—particularly entry-level jobs. Simply put, increasing the cost of labor means employers are even less likely to hire—especially in a down economy. 6

We value our employees, and they're compensated well. Our servers and bartenders work hard, receive tips, and are therefore compensated well above the minimum wage, some making upwards of $20 to $25 per hour. 7

A mandated increase in server wages only limits the amount of money left over for wage increases for other employees, like those working in the kitchen. 8

The unemployment rate amongst our young people hovers around the 25 percent range. An increase in the minimum wage will only increase that number. The minimum wage is meant to be a learning wage. It is meant to give people the opportunity to gain experience and job training. When government increases the cost of labor, employers typically respond by reducing the number of entry-level, low-skilled workers they hire. I understand that not all people who work at the minimum wage are young people, but there are other alternatives—like the Earned Income Tax Credit—that can help these workers without reducing jobs.

Wage mandates are an ineffective way to reduce poverty and cause restaurant operators to make very difficult decisions, including the elimination of jobs, cutting staff hours, or increasing prices. These decisions end up hurting the very employees that wage increases are meant to help. 9

This proposal will undoubtedly have a negative effect on hundreds of small businesses and employees in Connecticut and across the country. 10

I urge you to reject this proposal. Any mandated increase to costs will damage an already fragile industry. 11

Answers

5. The claim is that "any mandated increase to costs will damage an already fragile industry," because it argues against raising the minimum wage.

6. The author gives many reasons, such as the high cost to businesses, loss of jobs, as well as how a minimum wage is a training wage.

7. Evidence includes lots of factual evidence, such as the 39.3% wage increase, and explanations that the minimum wage is intended as a starter wage.

8. The speaker begins and ends with his claim, but his claim is more specific at the end.

Answers

1. Answers will vary. Students should list specific reasons in the reading and identify possible rebuttals.

2. Answers will vary. Even if students generally disagree with the claim, they should locate the *most* convincing evidence for it.

Class Activity

Students can share their graphic organizers by writing these on poster paper, then do a "gallery walk" to look at and comment on other groups' posters.

 ## After Reading: Evaluate an Argument

Write responses to the following exercises using complete sentences.

5. Review your annotations and identify Rutigliano's claim. Select the sentence in the reading that best sums up the claim and quote it. Explain why you chose this sentence as the claim: what clues in the reading did you use? (Note: If you cannot locate a sentence in the essay, then state the claim in your own words.)

6. Review your annotations: What reasons support Rutigliano's claim? What clues helped you to identify the reasons? Summarize the reasons.

7. Review your annotations: What evidence supports the claim? Try to find examples of the four types of evidence: factual evidence, expert testimony, explanations, and examples. (Note: Not all arguments will include all types of evidence.) Summarize the evidence.

8. How does Rutigliano organize his argument—from claim to evidence or from evidence to claim? Explain.

Read to Write Activity 8.5

Engage with the Reading

Write responses to the following exercises using complete sentences.

1. Do you find Rutigliano's claim and reasons to be persuasive? Why or why not? How could someone argue against them?

2. Which pieces of evidence in the reading do you find most convincing? Why? Can you think of evidence that might counter the reading's evidence?

Pair and Share

- Review your responses from "After Reading": Compare your statement of Rutigliano's claim (from exercise 5), the support (exercise 6), and the evidence in support of the claim (exercise 7) with those identified by a partner. Create a graphic organizer, like the one in Figure 8.2, to illustrate Rutigliano's argument.

- Discuss the organizational pattern of the argument ("After Reading" exercise 8) with a partner. Find an example of a section that demonstrates an organizational structure either of reason to evidence or of evidence to reason.

Read to Write Activity 8.6

Develop an Argument

Review your responses to the previous Read to Write Activities in this chapter, and look again at the essay prompts in Read to Write Activity 8.1. Write responses to the following exercises using complete sentences.

1. Review your claim in light of the writer's argument opposed to increasing the minimum wage. Do you still hold your original position? If not, how might you revise your claim?

2. Can you think of new or different reasons to support your claim? For instance, did the reading selection or the sample paragraphs (Figures 8.7, 8.8, and 8.9) provide new ideas? List any new ideas you find.

3. Can you think of more or different evidence to support your reasons? For instance, did the reading selection or the sample paragraphs provide new evidence? List any new evidence you locate.

4. Write a body paragraph in which you support one of your reasons (from exercise 2) with evidence (from exercise 3). Organize the paragraph either by starting with a reason and giving evidence to support it, or by starting with evidence and leading to the reason. In either case, be sure to explain how the evidence supports the reason.

Vocabulary Strategy: Comparing Denotation and Connotation

Recall from the Vocabulary Strategy earlier in this chapter that authors select words carefully, taking into consideration both the denotation (literal meaning) and the connotation (associated feelings) of words and phrases.

Vocabulary Practice

Consider the underlined word or phrase in each sentence listed from the reading selection "Congress Should Not Increase the Minimum Wage." Determine the denotation of each, as well as its connotation. If you do not know the definition, use context clues or an encyclopedia or a dictionary to determine the denotation. Then identify the connotation of each underlined word as "Negative," "Positive," or "Neutral." See the Vocabulary Strategy feature earlier in this chapter for an example.

1. "The question of whether employers can bear the costs of increased minimum wages should be discussed on the merits, not on <u>scare tactics</u> or appeals to emotion" (Rutigliano 239).

2. "If an additional <u>mandate</u> means that employers like me will be forced to scale back, then employees could actually be worse off after it passes" (Rutigliano 239).

3. "We value our employees, and they're <u>compensated</u> well" (Rutigliano 239).

4. "The minimum wage is meant to be a <u>learning wage</u>" (Rutigliano 239).

Answers

1. Denotation: *Scare tactics* refer to using fear to persuade.

Connotation: Negative

2. Denotation: *Mandate* means a commandment or order to do something.

Connotation: Negative

3. Denotation: *Compensated* means to be paid for work.

Connotation: Positive

4. Denotation: *Learning wage* refers to what an employee is paid while in training.

Connotation: Positive

RESPONDING TO OTHERS' ARGUMENTS WITH COUNTERARGUMENTS

Because an argument is debatable, there will naturally be other positions on the issue at the center of the argument. A position that is opposed to a writer's (or speaker's) claim is called a **counterargument** (see Figure 8.10). Often writers anticipate and respond to likely counterarguments in a section of their writing. This strategy strengthens the argument by showing that the writer understands possible objections and has good reasons and evidence to reject those other positions. There are two main approaches to presenting a counterargument: rebuttal and concession.

Identifying Rebuttal versus Concession

Whether you chose to rebut or concede an opponent's argument depends on the extent to which you agree or disagree with the other side's position.

- A **rebuttal** is an expression of disagreement with an opponent's position. Basically, you are saying the other side is *wrong* and then giving evidence as to why that point of view is incorrect or false.

- A **concession**, in contrast, involves an admission that your opponent has a good point and is accompanied by an explanation of why your position is still better. Essentially, you are saying, "Good point, but here is why my point is better." In this case, you must explain or demonstrate why your position is better than your opponent's position.

In presenting a counterargument, writers typically use the SOS (Summary, Opinion, Support) pattern of response, as follows:

1. Writing a brief *summary* of an opposing viewpoint: the counter-argument.
2. Stating an *opinion* about the opposing viewpoint: concede or rebut.
3. Offering *support* for that opinion: why the opposing view is wrong or why your position is better.

FIGURE 8.10 Counterargument in an Argument Essay

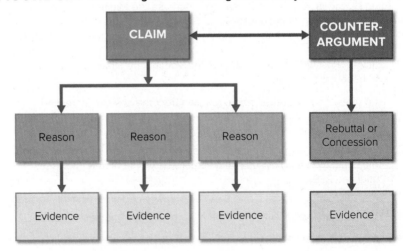

Applying Rebuttal and Concession When Reading and Writing

As a reader, look for key words and phrases, like the following, that signal that a writer is responding to opposing views:

Critics hold the view that . . .

On the other hand . . .

Opponents say . . .

Others sometimes assert that . . .

Some people might argue . . .

While it may be true that . . .

Phrases like these can be clues that a writer is summarizing the opposition's perspective. A rebuttal or concession should follow. As a writer, use rebuttal or concession to respond to arguments against your position. Through this strategy, you can strengthen your position if you deal effectively with concerns your readers may have about your position.

Imagine, for instance, a writer who is trying to counter the argument that raising the minimum wage would drive up unemployment. Here is an example of how she might begin to rebut that argument.

EXAMPLE OF A REBUTTAL: Raising the minimum wage would not create more unemployment because businesses could pass along the cost of higher wages to their customers.

This rebuttal disagrees with the idea that the minimum wage would create more unemployment and gives a reason for that disagreement.

Now consider how that same writer might instead begin to concede that argument:

EXAMPLE OF A CONCESSION: While it is true that raising the minimum wage might create some unemployment, most workers would retain their jobs and would be compensated fairly for their work.

This concession admits that the minimum wage might create more unemployment and then argues that more jobs and higher wages would be a bigger benefit to workers than some job loss.

Note that these examples are just the start of counterarguments. Each statement needs more evidence to support the stated position effectively.

To develop a counterargument, ask yourself how someone who disagrees with your claim might respond to your position or to the reasons for your position. Additionally, you can get ideas for counterarguments from your reading or from class discussion. You will want to be on the lookout for the strongest arguments against your claim. Use "Strategies for Developing Counterarguments" to get started. If you can deal successfully with compelling counterarguments, you will reinforce your own position.

Handout

"Strategies for Developing Counterarguments" is a reproducible handout in the Instructor's Resources.

Strategies for Developing Counterarguments

To begin a counterargument, you must put yourself in the position of someone who could argue against your claim. You can do this by summarizing, listing, freewriting, or brainstorming to understand other points of view. Then select the strongest argument or arguments to include as the beginning of a counterargument.

- **Summarize.** Review readings that present views on the topic that you disagree with. Summarize the claim, reasons, and evidence of an opposing view.
- **List.** Create a pro/con list of all the arguments you can think of on both sides of a topic, along with evidence to support the arguments. Decide which side you are on, and then select the strongest argument on the other side for the counterargument.
- **Freewrite.** Jot down the main reasons for the claim of your argument and the evidence for those reasons. Then imagine how someone might argue against each of your reasons or be critical of your evidence.
- **Brainstorm.** Explain your claim to a classmate, friend, or family member. Ask the person to respond to you with arguments, reasons, and evidence against your position.

EVALUATING TO REVISE AN ARGUMENT

Reading this chapter's articles on the minimum wage, taking notes on the readings, thinking about the topic, and discussing it with others are good ways to get started writing an essay that presents your own argument. Breaking your argument down into parts—claim, reasons, evidence, and counterarguments—and working systematically on each part can further help you write and refine your draft. In this section, we evaluate a student's argumentative essay on the minimum wage. This evaluation not only highlights the essay's strengths and weaknesses but also provides strategies for improving your own argument.

The checklist in "Strategies for Writing Arguments" is a good way to apply the criteria for an effective argument to your own, or anyone else's, work.

Handout

"Strategies for Writing Arguments" is a reproducible handout in the Instructor's Resources.

Strategies for Writing Arguments

_____ Does the claim take a position on a specific issue? Is the claim argumentative and specific?

_____ Are there convincing reasons to support the claim—reasons that will appeal to the audience?

_____ Is there sufficient and appropriate evidence? Is it clear how the evidence supports the reasons or the claim?

continued

_____ Does the argument address strong counterarguments? Are these counterarguments adequately summarized and dealt with through rebuttal or concession?

_____ Is the essay logically organized?

_____ Are the sentences clearly and correctly written? Are they varied and concise?

_____ Has the essay been proofread and the errors kept to a minimum?

The student essay entitled "Bachmann's Responsibility," in Figure 8.11, was written in response to the experience of Angie Bachmann, who lost all her money, including a $1 million inheritance, while gambling. Students had to respond to the following prompt: "Do you think Bachmann should be responsible for her gambling debts? Was Harrah's casino in any way responsible for her losses by encouraging her to gamble? In your essay, explain to what degree Bachmann is responsible for her gambling debts." As you read the essay, use the checklist in "Strategies for Writing Arguments" to analyze the effectiveness of the student essay. Notice, too, how counterarguments are raised and refuted throughout the essay.

Read to Write Activity 8.7

Draft an Argumentative Essay

Review the information about reading and writing arguments in this chapter, and use your work from the previous Read to Write Activities in this chapter to complete the following exercises.

1. Using your answers from Read to Write Activity 8.6, draft a complete argumentative essay, including a claim and body paragraphs with reasons and support.

2. Review your draft (from exercise 1) and think about the strongest arguments against your position. Write a paragraph to add to your draft in which you (a) summarize an argument against your position, (b) either rebut or concede that argument, and (c) provide support for your position.

3. Add the counterargument you developed (in exercise 2) to your draft. Consider placing the counterargument toward the end of the body of the essay.

Connect

Activity 8.7 is available as a writing assignment in Connect.

FIGURE 8.11 **Student Argument Essay**

Essay

Tolentino 1

Miguel Tolentino

Professor Kuehner

English 151RW

13 November 2015

Heading in MLA style

Bachmann's Responsibility

In *The Power of Habit*, author Charles Duhigg puts an emphasis on habits—their inner workings and how they can be changed. Duhigg describes how habits work through the cycle of cue (a trigger that activates a habit), routine (a habitual action), and reward (the aspect in which the brain determines if the habit is worth it). Particularly in Chapter 9 of the book, Duhigg details the descent of a woman called Angie Bachmann from being a bored housewife to losing all her money through compulsive gambling. Every time Bachmann stepped into a casino, this activated a cue within her brain, so that she automatically performed her routine of playing Blackjack thinking that she might win as a reward. Harrah's Entertainment, the casino where Bachmann played Blackjack and lost every bit of her money, sued Bachmann, "demanding that she pay her debts" (Duhigg 269). <u>Although Bachmann argued that she was acting per Harrah's manipulations, she is still responsible for her gambling debts because Harrah's actions were legal, she did not get treatment for addiction, she was fully aware of her actions, and she kept coming back to the casino even though she tried to change.</u>

Bachmann herself argued that Harrah's Entertainment should be responsible for her debts because the casino kept sending her luxurious gifts; however, <u>Harrah's Entertainment's persistent persuasion and their constant enticing of Bachmann to come back to the casino are all legal.</u> Harrah's Entertainment's gifts, such as a "free trip to Lake Tahoe with a suite, and tickets to an Eagles concert" (Duhigg 261), and its phone calls to Bachmann

Appropriate background information in introduction

Claim takes a position and includes a counterargument

Topic sentence presents a counterargument and rebuttal.

Tolentino 2

are legal because "there is no common law obligating a casino operator to refrain from attempting to entice or contact gamblers that it knows or should know are compulsive gamblers" (Duhigg 269). In short, there is no law restricting Harrah's actions even though they may seem immoral. Harrah's Entertainment is not responsible for knowing if gamblers are addicted, nor responsible for their actions. Also, it is a company's job to acquire money from customers in the first place. Moreover, the state where Bachmann played had a "voluntary exclusion program in which any person could ask for their name to be placed upon a list that required casinos to bar them from playing" (Duhigg 269). If she did place herself on the ban list, she would not have gotten Harrah's Entertainment's guilt-inducing phone calls or their free gifts. If she really wanted to change, she would have found out about this program by asking for prevention for gambling addictions. Yet she did not place herself in the voluntary exclusion program; it was her responsibility to do so.

In his article titled "How the Brain Gets Addicted to Gambling," author Feris Jabr cites the APA (American Psychiatric Association), which classifies "pathological gambling as an impulse-control disorder" or a true addiction. With gambling considered an addiction, like drug addiction, treatment is more effective and more accessible. Bachmann should have got treatment once she realized that she was addicted to gambling. People argue that gamblers "have different brain circuitry than normal people; their brain over-develops dopamine" (Jabr). According to Jabr, dopamine is a reward hormone the brain produces when people participate in activities that make them happy. Hence, the satisfaction people feel when dopamine gets produced influences them to engage in the activity over and over again. As a result, as gamblers continue to gamble, they develop higher tolerance to dopamine, and they need to "pursue even riskier ventures" to feel satisfied (Jabr). However, there are several treatments available to address this issue such as "Opioid antagonists (naltrexone), [a medication] which inhibits the brain from producing dopamine, therefore preventing cravings . . .

Evidence: factual information to support argument

Evidence: explanation to support argument

Evidence: factual information to support argument

Topic sentence presents a reason to support the claim

Counterargument

Evidence: expert testimony to support counterargument

Rebuttal, with factual information for support

Tolentino 3

cognitive-behavior therapy, which teaches people to resist unwanted thoughts and habits" (Jabr). In other words, there are no excuses to not get treatment. Prevention of gambling addiction is possible with the advancement in medications, even though only 20% of gamblers take treatment; those who do, "up to 75% return to gambling" (Jabr). It would be easy to believe that even if Bachmann got treated, she would return to gambling, but there is still a 25% chance for a successful treatment. The percentage shows that it is very possible, albeit with a small chance, to get successful treatment and prevent gambling addiction. Bachmann is ultimately responsible for seeking help or treatment for her addiction.

Evidence: factual information to support argument

Anticipates counterargument

Rebuttal, with explanation for support

Not seeking treatment is only one of Bachmann's irresponsible actions; she also kept playing knowing that she was losing more than winning, and she kept coming back to the casino. Some people argue that Bachmann did try to change by "moving to Tennessee, [changing] her phone numbers, and . . . not [telling] the casino her new address," but she still went to the casino (Duhigg 260). In short, when she moved, it was her responsibility to not go to a casino since she will fall back to her bad habits. Moreover, she argued that Harrah's Entertainment called her often to come back, but that is because she revealed to the manager her parents' passing—it was through Bachmann the manager found out she had inherited a large amount of money (Duhigg 260). It is Bachmann's fault for revealing sensitive information that Harrah's Entertainment legitimately took advantage of. Furthermore, Bachmann continued to gamble, even though she already lost about $900,000 and even after signing promissory notes "six times for a total of $125,000" (Duhigg 266–67). In short, it was definitely her choice to keep playing because she was not satisfied with one promissory note, but six. A normal person might stop at one, but Bachmann still went further signing six notes knowing that she might lose a very large amount.

Topic sentence presents a reason to support the claim

Counterargument

Rebuttal, with factual support

Counterargument

Rebuttal, with explanation for support

Evidence: factual support

Evidence: explanation for support

Bachmann was fully aware of her gambling habits the whole time, yet she still did not manage to change herself for the better. According to Duhigg, "[If a person] knows a habit exists, [he or she] has the responsibility

Evidence: quote from expert for support

Tolentino 4

to change it," and Bachmann is no exception (Duhigg 271). It is often thought that it will be hard for Bachmann to change her habit because she was acting automatically. However, as Duhigg stated, "every habit, no matter its complexity, is malleable" (Duhigg 270). Duhigg further states that to change a habit, one must "identify" cues and rewards that "drive" the routine and find "alternatives" (Duhigg 270). In other words, Bachmann needed only to identify her cues and rewards to why she would gamble in the first place, and find alternative activities to change her habit.

Evidence: quote from expert for support

Topic sentence gives reason to support claim

In conclusion, Bachmann is responsible for the extent of all her gambling losses. She had the responsibility to change her negative gambling habit, but she did not try hard enough to change. Harrah's Entertainment's actions were justified and legal; Bachmann, alone, is at fault for her actions. Nowadays, with pathological gambling being more common and considered a serious addiction, treatments are more accessible than before.

Conclusion sums up main points of argument

Tolentino 5

Works Cited

Duhigg, Charles. *The Power of Habit: Why We Do What We Do in Life and Business.*
    Random House, 2012.

Jabr, Ferris. "How the Brain Gets Addicted to Gambling." *Scientific American*, 15 Oct. 2013,
    www.scientificamerican.com/article/how-the-brain-gets-addicted-to-gambling/.

Works Cited page in MLA Style

Read to Write Activity 8.8

Evaluate an Argumentative Essay

Review the information about reading and writing arguments in this chapter, and use your work from the previous Read to Write Activities in this chapter to do the following: Apply the checklist in "Strategies for Writing an Argument" to your essay draft (from Read to Write Activity 8.7). Evaluate your draft and revise it in areas where it is weak.

Connect

Activity 8.8 is available as a writing assignment in Connect.

Pair and Share

Exchange essay drafts from Read to Write Activity 8.8 with a partner. Use the checklist in "Strategies for Writing an Argument" to identify strengths and weaknesses.

CHAPTER REVIEW

Key Terms

argument An attempt to persuade someone by giving reasons or evidence (support) for accepting a particular position.

claim The main idea of an argument; a claim takes a position on an issue.

concession An admission that an opponent in an argument has made a good point, accompanied by an explanation of why one's own position is better.

connotation The suggested or implied meaning of a word.

counterargument A position opposed to a writer's or speaker's claim.

denotation The literal, or dictionary, definition of a word.

evidence Support for a claim.

issue A topic about which people disagree.

reason A statement that explains or justifies an opinion, event, or action.

rebuttal An expression of disagreement with an opponent's position, supported by evidence that the opposing argument is incorrect or false.

Chapter Summary

1. An argument is not just a disagreement or a statement based on a personal opinion; it is a reasoned judgment supported by reasons or evidence for accepting a particular position.

2. Being able to identify the various parts of an argument—claim, reasons, evidence, and counterarguments—is the first step in understanding or writing an argument.

3. Recognizing the organizational pattern of an argument in paragraphs and in essays will help you follow the author's reasoning.

4. Including a counterargument strengthens your argument by showing that you understand possible objections and have good reasons and evidence to reject those other positions.

5. The same criteria that apply to arguments that you read also apply to the arguments you write. Using a checklist is a good way to review those criteria.

6. Read a political cartoon by looking at the picture and reading the text, knowing that illustrators use symbolism, exaggeration, and irony to make their point.

7. Writers, especially writers of arguments, think carefully about the denotations and connotations of words.

Apply What You Learned

1. Have you ever worked for minimum wage—or do you know people who have? What was your (or their) experience? How has your reading in this chapter affected the way you think about your minimum-wage experience?

2. Do more research on the topic of raising the minimum wage, looking for facts about and examples of minimum-wage workers. Who are most minimum-wage workers; that is, what is the average age, gender, and ethnicity of such workers? What struggles, if any, do minimum-wage workers face because of their wages?

Answers

1. Answers will vary. Students may draw on their own experiences or those of people they know.

2. Answers will vary. Students should be able to give sources for their information.

Credits

p. 228–229: Harkin, Tom, opening statement before the HELP Committee, "Keeping Up with a Changing Economy: Indexing the Minimum Wage." US Senate Committee on Health Education, Labor and Pensions, 14 Mar. 2013; **p. 233:** © Pat Bagley. Used with permission; **p. 233:** © Gary Varvel. Used by permission of Creators Syndicate; **p. 236:** Miller, George, statement before the HELP Committee, "Keeping Up with a Changing Economy: Indexing the Minimum Wage." US Senate Committee on Health Education, Labor and Pensions, 14 Mar. 2013; **p. 237:** Sickler, Melvin, statement before the HELP Committee, "Keeping Up with a Changing Economy: Indexing the Minimum Wage." US Senate Committee on Health Education, Labor and Pensions, 14 Mar. 2013; **p. 238–239:** Ritigliano, David, statement before the HELP Committee, "Keeping Up with a Changing Economy: Indexing the Minimum Wage." US Senate Committee on Health Education, Labor and Pensions, 14 Mar. 2013.

9 | Planning a Research Paper

After reading this chapter, you will be able to

- Write a research question.
- Locate academic sources that are relevant to your research question.
- Prepare to research your question with background reading.
- Define key terms.
- Read and write about diagrams.
- Evaluate researched sources.

Look for these icons throughout the chapter. They signal key strategies to use in Read to Write Activities.

Theme: Researching Antibiotic Resistance: How Can We Stay Healthy Using Antibiotics?

Connect

Assign the LearnSmart Achieve topic "Developing and Implementing a Research Plan" for adaptive learning to accompany this chapter.

Class Activity

To pique interest in the topic, use the question that opens the chapter for a brainstorming or freewriting session. As an alternative, give students a list of possible worldwide problems: ask them to rank them in order and discuss their priorities.

What would you say is the world's most urgent problem? Poverty, malnutrition, AIDS, the Ebola virus, climate change, and the growing human population might all be reasonable answers. In 2014, citizens of Great Britain answered this question by voting to award a £10 million prize (about $16.5 million) to something else: solving the problem of antibiotic resistance ("Longitude Prize").

According to the World Health Organization, antibiotic resistance is a serious worldwide threat to public health. To understand what antibiotic resistance is and how it affects people, study the diagram in Figure 9.1. The blue arrows in the top part show step by step how drug treatments (with antibiotics) are used to fight bacteria that cause infection and illness. The bottom part illustrates how bacteria that are either not resistant (panel 2) or resistant (panel 3) to drugs respond to treatment. Think about it:

- What is the effect of antibiotics on non–drug-resistant bacteria?
- What is the effect of antibiotics on drug-resistant bacteria?

FIGURE 9.1 **How Bacteria Respond to Antibiotics**

Source: "What Is Drug Resistance"; National Institute of Allergy and infectious Diseases; National Institute of Health; www.niaid.nih.gov.

Teaching Tip

Search online for videos, such as TED Talks or science videos, that explain antibiotic resistance to help students gain background knowledge.

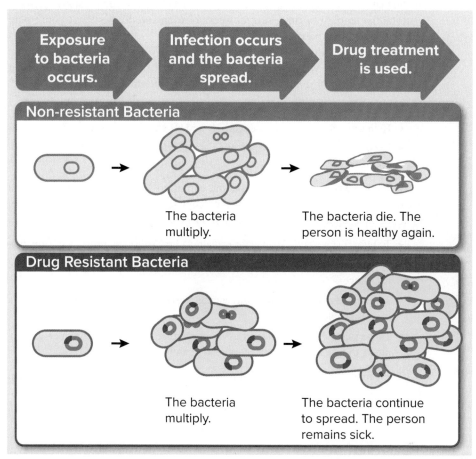

As you read the article in this chapter, you will learn about how antibiotic resistance arises, why it is a serious problem, and what we might do to solve it. At the same time, you will develop strategies for locating outside sources that will help you research and read further about this topic. After using the tools in this chapter to research this topic, you will have the opportunity in the next chapter to use the information you have gathered to write a research paper. Take care to save the work you generate as you complete this chapter for further use.

WRITING A RESEARCH QUESTION

At some point in your academic career, you will most likely write a research paper. A **research paper** is typically similar to other college essays that require you to synthesize information, such as an essay about readings or an argumentative essay.

Teaching Tip

Direct students to Chapter 6, "Writing about Reading," and Chapter 8, "Reading and Writing Arguments," for more on these topics.

The primary difference is that a research paper requires you to find information about a topic from outside sources. Moreover, because you must locate, read, and evaluate sources (the focus of this chapter), as well as take notes, plan, draft, revise, and format a research paper (the focus of the next chapter), you must give yourself a substantial amount of time, several weeks or even several months, to both plan and write a research paper.

Depending on the research paper assignment, you may be given a specific prompt to address, or you may be free to explore a topic of your choice. Either way, it is helpful to begin with a *research question*, because a question can do the following:

- Point you to appropriate sources.

- Help you read your sources effectively and efficiently.

- Encourage you to keep an open mind and develop a well-informed point of view on the topic.

If you are writing from a prompt, you can often use the prompt to develop a research question. First, annotate the prompt to determine its PAS—<u>P</u>urpose, <u>A</u>udience, and <u>S</u>ubject. The most common purposes for a research paper are these:

- To inform (for example, an essay explaining how antibiotic resistance happens).

- To instruct (for example, an essay describing a method for reducing antibiotic resistance).

- To argue (for example, an essay giving reasons why antibiotic resistance is a serious problem).

- To persuade (for example, an essay presenting evidence to convince governments to take action to halt the spread of antibiotic resistance).

Then focus on the subject of the prompt. Turn the subject into a question. Here is an example of an annotated prompt.

Teaching Tip

Direct students to Chapter 5, "Reading and Writing Essays," for more on the PAS method.

Teaching Tip

Explain that an argument essay may present reasons on both sides of an issue without aiming to convince readers to adopt a specific position.

Sample Annotated Prompt

Paper Prompt	Annotations
Using the following prompt, write a research paper from which your classmates and instructor can learn more about antibiotic resistance.	*Audience:* fellow students and instructor
Compare and contrast the challenges faced by poor or developing countries versus more affluent or technologically advanced countries in preventing antibiotic resistance. For instance, consider what different governments, doctors or health care systems, and patients can do to help prevent antibiotic resistance and what obstacles they face to implementing preventative measures.	*Purpose:* to compare and contrast obstacles and solutions; informative
	Subject: how poor and wealthy countries can prevent antibiotic resistance

To create a research question from the annotated prompt, focus on the key words in the prompt related to the subject and purpose. Then, using words such as *how*, *why*, and *what*, create one (or more questions) related to the subject. Here's an example of a research question based on the annotated prompt:

RESEARCH QUESTION: <u>How</u> can poor and wealthy countries prevent antibiotic resistance, and <u>what</u> obstacles do they face in doing so?

Take a few moments now to read the prompts in Read to Write Activity 9.1, from which the preceding Sample Annotated Prompt is taken. Evaluate the prompts. Which ones appeal to you? About which topics do you think you might have something to say?

Read to Write Activity 9.1

Choose a Prompt for a Research Paper on Antibiotic Resistance

Select one of the numbered prompts below for a research paper. The prompt will help you focus your reading and plan your paper as you navigate through this chapter. Plan to write a paper that will help your fellow students and instructor learn more about antibiotic resistance. Notice that some prompts call for an informative paper, while others suggest an argumentative or persuasive approach.

1. Compare and contrast the challenges faced by poor or developing countries versus more affluent or technologically advanced countries in preventing antibiotic resistance. For instance, consider what different governments, doctors or health care systems, and patients can do to help prevent antibiotic resistance and what obstacles they face to implementing preventative measures.

2. Research the problem of antibiotic-resistant bacteria and propose a solution or solutions. In particular, discuss the main reasons why bacteria are becoming antibiotic resistant and what interventions can solve these problems.

3. Explain how antibiotic resistance arose in bacteria, through both natural and human-made causes. In your explanation, also discuss why antibiotic medicines are losing their effectiveness and what the implications are for humans if bacteria are antibiotic resistant and antibiotic medicines lose their effectiveness.

4. Some people argue that preventing disease is the best solution to defeating antibiotic resistance in bacteria, others insist that not overusing antibiotics will be instrumental in the fight against antibiotic resistance, and still others believe that new antibiotics or new ways of fighting bacteria must be developed to prevent antibiotic resistance. Take a position as to which is the most promising strategy for ensuring that bacterial diseases can still be successfully treated in the future.

5. What can individuals—as opposed to governments or health care professionals—do to stay healthy while avoiding contributing to the problem of antibiotic resistance? Recommend practical solutions that can be employed in people's everyday lives to combat antibiotic resistance and explain why it is important to implement these solutions.

Read to Write Activity 9.2

Create a Research Question

Complete the following exercises.

1. Review Read to Write Activity 9.1. Which paper prompt did you select, and why? Write your answer using complete sentences.

2. Annotate the prompt you selected to identify its PAS—purpose, audience, and subject.

3. Create a research question based on your annotations of the prompt.

LOCATING ACADEMIC SOURCES

To research a topic, you will want to locate sources that are appropriate for the assigned prompt and for the specific class. For instance, in a history class, you may be required to use original sources from a particular period in history, such as speeches by Martin Luther King, Jr., and newspaper accounts written at the time of the Civil Rights March in Washington, DC. In a nursing class, you might be required to locate scholarly articles written by health care professionals describing the most effective procedures for drawing blood. Understanding different types of sources can help you to select the most appropriate ones. Figure 9.2 lists and describes common sources used in academic research.

Find Information in the College Library

With a specific research question in mind, you can begin to search for information. Your college library should be the first place you go. A college library's *home page*, the first page viewers see when going to a Web site, is designed to help students get started searching for quality information for academic purposes (see Figure 9.3, for example).

Moreover, you can be confident that most of the print materials in the college library are appropriate for academic use because the reading materials have been selected by college librarians, usually in consultation with faculty and others who are knowledgeable in subject fields. This guarantee of credibility is true, too, for online materials you find through the college's Web site because the library staff also screens electronic books and electronic journal articles. In fact, most college libraries have electronic **databases** (see Figure 9.4, for example), collections of information that can be searched by a computer. These databases contain links to books and e-books, as well as references to newspaper, magazine, and journal articles, in both print and downloadable formats. Consult a librarian or ask your instructor for advice about which databases would be most advantageous to search given your research question.

FIGURE 9.2 Types of Sources

Type of Source	General Description	Examples
Nonscholarly sources	Newspapers, general-interest magazines, and popular books	• *The New York Times* newspaper • *The Atlantic* magazine • *Omnivore's Dilemma: A Natural History of Four Meals* by Michael Pollan
Scholarly sources	Academic journals, university-affiliated databases, and books from academic presses	• *JAMA* (*Journal of the American Medical Association*) • *Project Muse* • *Superbugs: An Arms Race against Bacteria* by William Hall, Anthony McDonnell, Jim O'Neill (Harvard University Press)
Government publications	Reports, fact sheets, Web sites, data, and statistics collected and published by government agencies	• National Climate Assessment report • Bureau of Labor Statistics • NIH (National Institute of Health) Web site
Nontext sources or original material	Speeches, conferences, art exhibits, music, theater performances, interviews, and so on	• "The Gettysburg Address" by Abraham Lincoln • Interview with Maya Angelou on *The Oprah Winfrey Show* • TEDxTalk: *The Danger of a Single Story* by Chimamanda Ngozi Adichie

FIGURE 9.3 University of Chicago Library Home Page

Source: University of Chicago Library

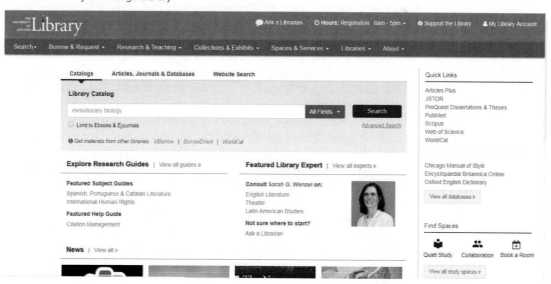

FIGURE 9.4 Library Databases on the Ohlone College Web Site

Source: Ohlone college

Search the Internet

According to the Pew Research Center, almost 98% of adults in the United States aged 18 to 49 use the Internet. Thus it is not surprising that many students first look on the Internet for information for their papers ("Internet/Broadband Fact Sheet"). Using a **search engine**—a computer program that locates documents on the Web—such as *Google*, *Bing*, or *Yahoo*—to find information online is easy, quick, familiar, and convenient. If you find what you are looking for, you can often read it online or download it to your own computer.

However, what you find when you use a search engine to locate information online is not necessarily academic in nature. In other words, there is no guarantee that the information has been checked by recognized experts or by an editor to ensure quality control. In fact, some professors (and colleges) forbid students from using Internet search engines to locate sources. They believe that students do not think critically when they use search engines to find topics and do not sufficiently practice evaluative skills in order to select quality information.

A better alternative to a general search engine, such as *Google* or *Bing*, is a search engine designed to locate academic materials online, such as *Google Scholar* or *Microsoft Academic Search*. These search programs are specifically devised to find reliable scholarly information, such as that in books and journal articles. Some college libraries include links to *Google Scholar* on their home page.

If you do a *Google* search for a topic, chances are a *Wikipedia* entry on that subject will appear in the top 10 results. Despite its popularity, *Wikipedia*, the self-described "free online encyclopedia that anyone can edit" ("Welcome to *Wikipedia*"), is a controversial information source. The articles are written collaboratively by anonymous volunteers, and just about anyone can write and post information to a *Wikipedia* entry. *Wikipedia* articles vary in length, quality, and accuracy. Even *Wikipedia*'s founder, Jimmy Wales, has said that students should not use *Wikipedia* for college work: "You're in college; don't cite the encyclopedia" (qtd. in Young).

Rather than being a main source, an encyclopedia such as *Wikipedia* might be a starting point for research—a resource for an overview of a topic. Moreover, at the bottom of most *Wikipedia* pages, you can find a list of references cited, such as newspaper or magazine articles, journal articles, books, and interviews. These sources might be worth looking up and reading or using in an academic paper. Remember, though, that whatever information you find or read on *Wikipedia* itself should be evaluated with a critical eye and documented in a second, academic source before you use it in your paper.

An alternative to *Wikipedia* might be a specialized online encyclopedia, such as a medical encyclopedia, or a government Web site that publishes information for citizens. For instance, *PubMed Health*, run by the National Institutes of Health, is dedicated to providing health information and research to the public (see Figure 9.5). This site is a good resource when you are researching a topic such as antibiotic resistance because the information is hosted on a government-supported Web site and therefore is likely to be accurate and up to date.

Teaching Tip

Demonstrate a search on a topic of students' choosing using *Google* vs. *Google Scholar* or *Bing* vs. *Microsoft Academic Search* to showcase the different results

Teaching Tip

Show students the list of sources at the end of a *Wikipedia* page—on a topic of students' choosing. Then demonstrate how to find the original source.

FIGURE 9.5 *PubMed Health* **Home Page**

Source: PubMed Health/U.S. National Library of Medicine

Read to Write Activity 9.3

Locate Sources

Use the information from this chapter to determine a strategy for searching for information about antibiotic resistance for an academic paper. Writing in complete sentences, explain which are the best places to find sources and how you would go about locating sources.

Pair and Share

Compare your results from Read to Write Activity 9.3 with a classmate's results. Try to come to a consensus about the best places to find sources and how to go about locating sources.

Use Keywords in an Online Search

Whether you are looking for information on the Web or through the college's electronic databases, a **keyword search** is the most common method to use. A **keyword** is a word, often a noun, that identifies the topic. For instance, if you are searching for information about antibiotics, *antibiotics* is a keyword. You may need to narrow or restrict your search by using more than one keyword to find sources on your particular topic. For example, if you want to find out about preventing antibiotic resistance, using the keywords *antibiotic* and *resistance* might yield more relevant results than simply using the keyword *antibiotics.* You could focus your search even more precisely by using the keywords *antibiotics* and *resistance* and *prevention.*

Notice that a keyword search does not consist of a phrase or sentence, such as "How can we prevent antibiotic resistance?" but rather of single words. Searches that respond to phrases and sentences, including questions, are called **natural language searches**.

Read to Write Activity 9.4

Search for Sources Using Keywords

Follow the instructions in each exercise.

1. Review the topic you selected in Read to Write Activity 9.1 and the research question for Read to Write Activity 9.2. Make a list of keywords that you can use to search for sources on your topic.

2. Use the strategy you identified in Read to Write Activity 9.3 and your list of keywords to locate two sources that could help answer your research question. Explain how you searched for sources by including the places searched and the keywords, and submit a copy of the sources to your instructor.

PREPARING WITH BACKGROUND READING

When you are doing research for a paper, background reading can be helpful. Background reading means reading to get an overview of a topic: to understand the topic, to learn its history, to familiarize yourself with key terminology and important concepts, and to become aware of issues or controversies surrounding the topic. Researchers and scholars traditionally have consulted encyclopedias to gain an overview. Written by experts in a field, encyclopedia entries give readers general knowledge about a specific subject. Other useful sources of information include government and research Web sites that provide information to a general audience. For instance, the government often funds research for the public good. Then it becomes the government's job to keep citizens informed of the research findings.

To gain basic information about antibiotic resistance, you will do some background reading in the following reading selection. Read to discover more about what antibiotic resistance is, how it develops, and what can be done to prevent bacteria from becoming antibiotic resistant.

READING SELECTION

"ANTIBIOTIC RESISTANCE QUESTIONS AND ANSWERS"

This reading selection is a *question and answer page* (or *Q and A page*). A Q and A page is designed to provide a clear, concise summary of important information on a topic. It includes typical *questions* that might be asked on a topic with *answers* to those questions. The purpose is to present important concepts in an informal style.

Reading about an unfamiliar or technical topic can be challenging. Writers who explain technical topics for general readers know this and therefore take pains to provide support for readers. For instance, a Q and A page may use bullet points to highlight items. It may use headings to help readers grasp main ideas. Specialized vocabulary is typically defined in the text. Drawings, diagrams, or illustrations may be used to describe concepts. As you read, notice how this fact sheet employs these strategies to help readers understand antibiotic resistance.

Complete the "Before Reading" assignment. Then read the selection while you complete the "During Reading" activities. Finally, complete the "After Reading" assignments.

Connect

You will find a coordinated Power of Process assignment for this reading in your Connect course.

Before Reading: Recognize Prior Knowledge; Preview

Write answers to these questions using complete sentences.

1. What do you already know about antibiotics? For instance, why would a person take antibiotics?

2. Skim the questions in the reading (in bold print). What are some of the topics that the questions address?

During Reading: Annotate

Read the selection twice. Write answers to these questions using complete sentences.

3. On your first reading, read for comprehension of the topic and mark the main ideas and supporting information.

4. On your second reading, look for information related to your paper topic.

Antibiotic Resistance Questions and Answers

Centers for Disease Control and Prevention

Last Updated 7 December 2017

The following Question and Answer page about antibiotic resistance was located by using the keywords antibiotic resistance prevention *to search the Centers for Disease Control and Prevention Web site. This Web site provides information to nonprofessionals and to medical professionals about the latest research on and treatment of diseases.*

QUESTIONS ABOUT BACTERIA, VIRUSES, AND ANTIBIOTICS

Q: What are bacteria and viruses?   1

A: Bacteria are single-celled organisms found all over the inside and outside of our bodies. Many bacteria are not harmful. In fact, some are actually helpful, including the majority of bacteria that live in our intestines (guts). However, disease-causing bacteria can cause illnesses such as strep throat. Viruses, on the other hand, are microbes that are even smaller than bacteria that cannot survive outside the body's cells. They cause illness by invading healthy cells.

Q: What is an antibiotic?   2

A: Antibiotics, also known as antimicrobial drugs, are drugs that fight infections caused by bacteria in both humans and animals. Antibiotics fight these infections either by killing the bacteria or making it difficult for the bacteria to grow and multiply. Antibiotics do not have any effect on viruses.

The term "antibiotic" originally referred to a natural compound that kills bacteria, such as certain types of mold or chemicals produced by living organisms. Technically, the term "antimicrobial" refers to both natural and synthetic (man-made) compounds; however, many people use the word "antibiotic" to refer to both.

Q: Which infections are caused by viruses and should not be treated with antibiotics?

3

A: Viral infections should not be treated with antibiotics. Common infections caused by viruses include the following:

- Colds
- Flu
- Most sore throats
- Most coughs and bronchitis ("chest colds")
- Many sinus infections
- Many ear infections

QUESTIONS ABOUT ANTIBIOTIC RESISTANCE

Q: What is antibiotic resistance?

4

A: Antibiotic resistance is the ability of bacteria to resist the effects of an antibiotic. Antibiotic resistance occurs when bacteria change in a way that reduces the effectiveness of drugs, chemicals, or other agents designed to cure or prevent infections. The bacteria survive and continue to multiply, causing more harm.

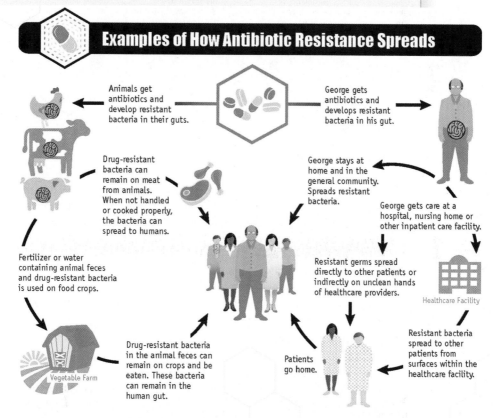

Examples of How Antibiotic Resistance Spreads

Animals get antibiotics and develop resistant bacteria in their guts.

George gets antibiotics and develops resistant bacteria in his gut.

Drug-resistant bacteria can remain on meat from animals. When not handled or cooked properly, the bacteria can spread to humans.

George stays at home and in the general community. Spreads resistant bacteria.

George gets care at a hospital, nursing home or other inpatient care facility.

Fertilizer or water containing animal feces and drug-resistant bacteria is used on food crops.

Resistant germs spread directly to other patients or indirectly on unclean hands of healthcare providers.

Healthcare Facility

Vegetable Farm

Drug-resistant bacteria in the animal feces can remain on crops and be eaten. These bacteria can remain in the human gut.

Patients go home.

Resistant bacteria spread to other patients from surfaces within the healthcare facility.

Simply using antibiotics creates resistance. These drugs should only be used to treat infections.

Antibiotic Resistance Questions and Answers Centers for Disease Control and Prevention.
https://www.cdc.gov/antibiotic-use/community/about/antibiotic-resistance-faqs.html

Q: Why should I care about antibiotic resistance?

A: Antibiotic resistance has been called one of the world's most pressing public health problems. Antibiotic resistance can cause illnesses that were once easily treatable with antibiotics to become dangerous infections, prolonging suffering for children and adults. Antibiotic-resistant bacteria can spread to family members, schoolmates, and co-workers, and may threaten your community. Antibiotic-resistant bacteria are often more difficult to kill and more expensive to treat. In some cases, the antibiotic-resistant infections can lead to serious disability or even death.

5

Although some people think a person becomes resistant to specific drugs, it is the bacteria, not the person, that become resistant to the drugs.

6

How Antibiotic Resistance Happens

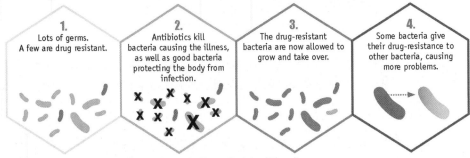

1.
Lots of germs. A few are drug resistant.

2.
Antibiotics kill bacteria causing the illness, as well as good bacteria protecting the body from infection.

3.
The drug-resistant bacteria are now allowed to grow and take over.

4.
Some bacteria give their drug-resistance to other bacteria, causing more problems.

Antibiotic Resistance Questions and Answers Centers for Disease Control and Prevention.
https://www.cdc.gov/antibiotic-use/community/about/antibiotic-resistance-faqs.html

Q: Why are bacteria becoming resistant to antibiotics?

A: Overuse and misuse of antibiotics can promote the development of antibiotic-resistant bacteria. Every time a person takes antibiotics, sensitive bacteria (bacteria that antibiotics can still attack) are killed, but resistant bacteria are left to grow and multiply. This is how repeated use of antibiotics can increase the number of drug-resistant bacteria.

7

Antibiotics are not effective against viral infections like the common cold, flu, most sore throats, bronchitis, and many sinus and ear infections. Widespread use of antibiotics for these illnesses is an example of how overuse of antibiotics can promote the spread of antibiotic resistance. Smart use of antibiotics is key to controlling the spread of resistance.

8

Q: How do bacteria become resistant to antibiotics?

A: Bacteria can become resistant to antibiotics through several ways. Some bacteria can "neutralize" an antibiotic by changing it in a way that makes it harmless. Others have learned how to pump an antibiotic back outside of the bacteria before it can do any harm. Some bacteria can change their outer structure so the antibiotic has no way to attach to the bacteria it is designed to kill.

9

After being exposed to antibiotics, sometimes one of the bacteria can survive because it found a way to resist the antibiotic. If even one bacterium becomes

10

resistant to antibiotics, it can then multiply and replace all the bacteria that were killed off. That means that exposure to antibiotics provides selective pressure making the surviving bacteria more likely to be resistant. Bacteria can also become resistant through mutation of their genetic material.

The Food and Drug Administration's (FDA's) Center for Veterinary Medicine (CVM) produced a nine-minute animation explaining how antimicrobial resistance both emerges and increases among bacteria.

Q: How should I use antibiotics to protect myself and my community from antibiotic resistance?

A: Here is what you can do to help prevent antibiotic resistance:

- Tell your healthcare professional you are concerned about antibiotic resistance.
- Ask your healthcare professional if there are steps you can take to feel better and get symptomatic relief without using antibiotics.
- Take the prescribed antibiotic exactly as your healthcare professional tells you.
- Discard any leftover medication.
- Ask your healthcare professional about vaccines recommended for you and your family to prevent infections that may require an antibiotic.
- Never skip doses.
- Never take an antibiotic for a viral infection like a cold or the flu.
- Never pressure your healthcare professional to prescribe an antibiotic.
- Never save antibiotics for the next time you get sick.
- Never take antibiotics prescribed for someone else.

Q: How can healthcare professionals help prevent the spread of antibiotic resistance?

A: Healthcare professionals can prevent the spread of antibiotic resistance by

- Prescribing an antibiotic only when it is likely to benefit the patient.
- Prescribing an antibiotic that targets the bacteria that is most likely causing their patient's illness when an antibiotic is likely to provide benefit.
- Encouraging patients to use the antibiotic as instructed.
- Collaborating with each other, office staff, and patients to promote appropriate antibiotic use.
- Continue reviewing and following the latest clinical practice guidelines for common infections, such as CDC's Adult and Pediatric Academic Detailing Sheets.

QUESTIONS ABOUT ANTIMICROBIAL CLEANING AGENTS, ACNE MEDICATION, AND PROBIOTICS

Q: Is it healthier to use antimicrobial-containing products (soaps, household cleaners) than regular products?

A: To date, studies have shown that there is no added health benefit for consumers (this does not include professionals in the healthcare setting) using soaps containing antibacterial ingredients compared with using plain soap. As a result, FDA released a proposed rule in December 2013 to require manufacturers to submit data supporting the efficacy and safety of antibacterial soaps and body washes. This proposed rule does not affect hand sanitizers, wipes, or antibacterial products used in healthcare settings. For more information, please see the CDC handwashing web page.

11

12

13

14

Teaching Tip

Show this video, or a similar one, to provide more background information on antibiotic resistance from a reliable source.

Q: Can antibiotic resistance develop from using acne medication? 15

A: Yes. Antibiotic use, appropriate or not, contributes to the development of antibiotic resistance. This is true for acne medications that contain antibiotics. Short- and long-term use of antibiotics for treatment or prevention of bacterial infections should be under the direction of a healthcare professional to ensure appropriate use and detection of resistance.

Q: Do probiotics have a role in helping to reduce antibiotic resistance? 16

A: Probiotics are defined as microorganisms that when administered in sufficient quantities may improve health. There are a variety of probiotics that have been studied for various health benefits. Their role in preventing drug-resistant infections in humans has not been established. CDC is actively researching the subject. Although some studies have shown benefit, the data are not conclusive enough for CDC to issue specific recommendations at this time.

 After Reading: Summarize

When you have finished the reading selection, write responses to the following exercises using complete sentences.

5. Explain how antibiotic resistance develops in bacteria and how resistance can spread.

6. Explain how antibiotic resistance can be prevented.

7. Why is antibiotic resistance a serious problem?

Read to Write Activity 9.5

Engage with the Reading

Write responses to the following exercises using complete sentences.

1. The reading states that "antibiotics are not effective against viral infections like the common cold, flu, most sore throats, bronchitis, and many sinus and ear infections" (Centers for Disease Control and Prevention), yet people take antibiotics to cure these illnesses. Why do you think people might use medications to treat certain illnesses if those medications do not work?

2. At the end of the reading are questions about antimicrobial soaps and cleaners, acne medication, and probiotics (Centers for Disease Control and Prevention). Do you use any of these products? If not, why not? If so, will you continue to use these after reading about antibiotic resistance?

Pair and Share

Compare your answers from "After Reading" exercises 6 and 7 with a classmate's summaries. Make a list of reasons why antibiotic resistance is a serious problem and how it can be prevented.

Read to Write Activity 9.6

Use Information from a Source

Answers will vary.

Review your work from Read to Write Activity 9.2. What information in the reading selection "Antibiotic Resistance Questions and Answers" can help answer your research question? Either quote or summarize information from the reading. Write your response using complete sentences.

Pair and Share

Compare your response in Read to Write Activity 9.6 with a classmate's response. Can you find more information from the reading selection that would help to answer either research question?

Vocabulary Strategy: Defining Technical Terms

Authors may use words and terms that are specific to a particular subject or field of study. Sometimes these technical terms are defined in the writing itself; sometimes readers are expected to know the term or look it up on their own.

Vocabulary Practice

Use context clues, word analysis, the dictionary, and/or an encyclopedia to define each underlined term in the following sentences from the reading selection "Antibiotic Resistance Questions and Answers." Be sure the definition fits the meaning of the term in the context of the sentence.

1. "<u>Bacteria</u> are single-celled organisms found all over the inside and outside of our bodies" (Centers for Disease Control and Prevention).

2. "<u>Antibiotics</u>, also known as antimicrobial drugs, are drugs that fight infections caused by bacteria in both humans and animals" (Centers for Disease Control and Prevention).

3. "Technically, the term '<u>antimicrobial</u>' refers to both natural and synthetic (man-made) compounds; however, many people use the word 'antibiotic' to refer to both" (Centers for Disease Control and Prevention).

4. "<u>Antibiotic resistance</u> is the ability of bacteria to resist the effects of an antibiotic" (Centers for Disease Control and Prevention).

5. "Antibiotics are not effective against <u>viral infections</u> like the common cold, flu, most sore throats, bronchitis, and many sinus and ear infections" (Centers for Disease Control and Prevention).

Answers

1. *Bacteria* are single-celled creatures that live in or on our bodies.

2. *Antibiotics* are drugs that fight bacterial infections.

3. *Antimicrobial* refers to either man-made or natural compounds.

4. *Antibiotic resistance* refers to the ability of bacteria to fight off the effects of an antibiotic.

5. *Viral infections* are illnesses caused by viruses, such as the common cold or a sore throat.

READING AND WRITING ABOUT DIAGRAMS

A diagram is a kind of illustration used to convey information. One main function of a diagram is to show a process (steps in a procedure) or a relationship. For example, a graphic organizer is a diagram that shows how ideas in an essay connect to one another.

Diagrams usually consists of geometric shapes—such as squares, rectangles, circles, and ovals—connected by lines or arrows. The shapes contain explanatory text, and sometimes they contain illustrations. For example, the two diagrams in the reading selection "Antibiotic Resistance Questions and Answers" by the Centers for Disease Control and Prevention ("Examples of How Antibiotic Resistance Spreads" and "How Antibiotic Resistance Happens") explain two processes: how antibiotic resistance happens at the molecular level and how antibiotic resistance occurs on a human scale. For readers, diagrams can help clarify important ideas in a reading, while for writers, diagrams can be a source of information to use in a paper (with proper citation).

To read a diagram, follow these steps:

- Read the title for insight on what the diagram represents.
- Ask yourself whether the diagram represents a process, a structure, or some other idea.
- Look for clues as to what path to take when reading. Some diagrams are best read from top to bottom; others, from left to right; still others follow a circular pattern. The arrows in a diagram provide clues about reading direction.
- Consider the relationship between the diagram and the text: typically the diagram visually represents a concept discussed in the text.

Study the diagrams shown in the reading selection "Antibiotic Resistance Questions and Answers." Then select one of the diagrams that relates to your writing prompt (from Read to Write Activity 9.1), and answer these questions:

1. What is the title of the diagram? What is the diagram explaining? Is it showing a process, a structure, or some other idea?
2. Look at the images, text, colors, lines, and arrows. What is the best order in which to read the information? How do the different parts of the diagram relate to one another?
3. After studying the diagram, explain *in your own words* the main idea of the diagram.

Answers for "Examples of How Antibiotic Resistance Spreads"

1. The title is "Examples of How Antibiotic Resistance Spreads." The graphic explains how antibiotic resistance can develop in the bodies of humans or animals and then spread to other people through various kinds of contact, such as eating meat or staying in a hospital.

2. The arrows indicate the direction to read the information, starting at the top and moving right and down or left and down.

3. Both people and livestock can harbor antibiotic-resistant bacteria, which they spread through contact with other people.

Answers for "How Antibiotic Resistance Happens"

1. The title is "How Antibiotic Resistance Happens." The graphic explains how bacteria develop resistance to antibiotics.

2. The graphic should be read from left to right; the numbers are a clue.

3. Antibiotic resistance happens when a few bacteria develop resistance and are able to multiply and spread.

Read to Write Activity 9.7

Use Information from a Diagram   Answers will vary.

Review your paper topic and research question (from Read to Write Activity 9.2). What information from the diagram relates to your research question? Summarize that information and briefly explain how it could be used to answer your research question.

EVALUATING RESEARCHED SOURCES

When you search your college's electronic databases or the Internet for sources, you will need to find sources that answer your research question. Moreover, you will need to select high-quality sources. Specifically, you will want to use sources that are *relevant, reliable, accurate, timely,* and *unbiased* to ensure they are suitable for a research paper. "Strategies for Evaluating Sources" shows how to apply these five criteria by using them to create questions about the source.

Strategies for Evaluating Sources

To evaluate a source and the information it contains, ask these questions and then answer them.

- *Relevance:* Is the source's information directly related to my research question?
- *Reliability:* Is the source authored by authorities or knowledgeable people? Does it appear in a credible publication such as a **peer-reviewed journal**? (Articles in peer-reviewed journals are assessed by experts in a field of study before being published.)
- *Accuracy:* Can the information be verified or checked?
- *Timeliness:* Is the information recent or appropriate for the topic?
- *Bias* (or appropriate bias): Does the source represent a legitimate point of view on the topic?

Handout

"Strategies for Evaluating Sources" is a reproducible handout in the Instructor's Resources.

Let's use these strategies to critically evaluate the reading selection as a source. Imagine that you are writing in response to prompt 2 from Read to Write Activity 9.1, which is repeated below:

PROMPT: Research the problem of antibiotic-resistant bacteria and propose a solution or solutions. In particular, discuss the main reasons why bacteria are becoming antibiotic resistant and what interventions can solve these problems.

You have written the following research question in response to the prompt: *What solutions can prevent antibiotic resistance?* Now you can evaluate the source and its information by asking and answering five questions.

1. **Is the source's information relevant?** *Relevant* in this case means related to the topic.

    Selecting a source with information that is relevant to your research question is crucial, especially given the overwhelming amount of information available through electronic databases and online. For instance, if you search for information using the keyword *antibiotics,* you will find a very large number of articles and Web sites. A Web site explaining how to take different types of antibiotics might not be directly related to the specific question, "What are solutions to the problem of antibiotic resistance?" In contrast, "Antibiotic Resistance Questions and Answers" includes several sections devoted to preventing antibiotic resistance. Thus the reading is relevant to the research question.

2. **Is the source reliable?** *Reliable* means having credibility to speak or write on a topic or to advance one's ideas.

Most print and online newspapers, for example, are considered reliable sources because the job of a news reporter is to get the facts and write accurately about the world. Furthermore, good newspapers employ editors who check a reporter's facts. Scholarly articles, such as those published in journals, are also generally reliable because the information has been reviewed by other scholars in the field before being published.

"Antibiotic Resistance Questions and Answers" is published on a US government Web site that focuses on research. Readers can assume the information in this article is reported accurately because the government, like researchers and reporters, is considered a reliable source of information.

Be aware, however, that you must carefully check the credibility of any sources you find via a general search engine, such as *Google* or *Yahoo*. Although reliable sources such as newspapers and journals can often be identified by a Web search, a Web site (for example, a blog) created by an individual may not be a reliable source—unless you can find convincing evidence (usually on the site itself) that the individual is an expert on the research topic. However, even if the person is an expert—for example, a physics professor at a major university—remember that the information on the person's site probably has not been reviewed and verified by an outside authority.

3. **Is the information accurate?** *Accurate* means true and correct.

Accurate information usually comes from an identifiable, reliable spokes-person or organization. Accurate information often is accompanied by a citation that clarifies the source of that information. Accurate information also tends to be specific—for instance, statistics or other details that can be checked. For example, we know from "Antibiotic Resistance Questions and Answers" that the term *antibiotic* is used to refer to "both natural and synthetic (man-made) compounds" (Centers for Disease Control and Prevention) that kill bacteria. So a personal blog that says antibiotics should not be taken at all because they are not "natural," without giving reliable support for its claim, is giving inaccurate information.

Although "Antibiotic Resistance Questions and Answers" lacks citations, it does present information, such as an explanation of how bacteria become antibiotic resistant, that can be checked against other sources to ensure accuracy. So we would consider it to be an accurate source.

4. **Is the information timely?** *Timely* means recent or appropriate for the topic.

Timeliness depends a great deal on the topic itself. For instance, if you are writing about a topic that changes rapidly, such as how fast computers can process information, then an article that is even just a few years old may be out of date. However, if you are dealing with a topic that does not change as quickly, you may be able to use sources from a greater date range. In addition, if you are focusing on a historical topic like the assassination of President Abraham Lincoln, you might actively seek out older sources, such as news articles from Lincoln's time. Also, sometimes you may wish to quote from the important works in a field. For example, for a psychology paper, you could quote from Sigmund Freud, the founder of psychoanalysis, who worked and wrote early in the twentieth century.

Although antibiotics have been around for some time, the threat of antibiotic-resistant diseases is fairly recent. You will want to take this newness into account as you read various sources.

5. **What is the source's point of view or bias?** To have a *bias* means to harbor a preference or belief that might prevent impartial (fair) judgment.

Many biases—for instance, cultural and political biases—can influence a person's or an organization's judgment or affect how information is presented. In truth, the answer to whether a source is biased is usually "yes." A more appropriate question is, "What exactly is the source's bias or point of view?" For example, one possible bias relevant to the research question "What are solutions to the problem of antibiotic resistance?" might concern whether a potential source has any commercial stake in treating bacterial diseases, such as an interest in marketing drugs.

When you are thinking about bias, ask yourself whether the source has a preference or belief that might compromise neutrality on the topic. If you are unsure, ask your instructor or classmates what they think. When you are conducting research, it is good practice to include a variety of sources with different perspectives to ensure a balanced view.

The Centers for Disease Control and Prevention's "Antibiotic Resistance Questions and Answers" seems unbiased. It presents information in an objective manner. However, the information is written from a government point of view, specifically the government of the United States. Other countries or governments might see the problem of antibiotic resistance differently or propose various solutions, depending on the needs of their population or their citizens' access to health care. For example, the US government might see the overuse of antibiotics as a threat to the future health of its citizens, while the government of a country with widespread bacterial disease might see a need to increase the current use of antibiotics to protect people's immediate health regardless of any impact on the future.

To sum up, as you research a topic and read sources, you are doing several things at once. You are reading to understand the topic. You are reading to find information relevant to answering your research question. You are critically examining the source to assess its reliability and bias. And you are evaluating the information in the source to determine whether it is accurate and timely. Figure 9.6 summarizes the questions you can use to evaluate sources and gives examples of sources that may or may not be acceptable to use in a research paper exploring a specific research question.

FIGURE 9.6 Strategic Questions to Evaluate Sources

Handout

Figure 9.6 is a reproducible handout in the Instructor's Resources.

Research question: What can be done to prevent antibiotic resistance in the future?			
Questions to Evaluate Sources	**Explanation**	**Example: Not OK to Use**	**Example: OK to Use**
1. Are the source and its information *relevant*?	Related to the topic	Fact sheet explaining physical side effects of antibiotics	Fact sheet explaining how overuse of antibiotics can lead to resistance
2. Is the source *reliable*?	Having credibility to speak or write on a topic	A Web page with no author or organization cited on a *.com* Web site (a commercial Web site); a Web page created by an individual and not associated with, or verified by, a reputable organization	An article by a scientist about antibiotic resistance on an *.edu* Web site (a college or university Web site); an article on antibiotic resistance in a peer-reviewed journal
3. Is the information *accurate*?	True and precise	General statement that there is lots of antibiotic resistance worldwide	Documented information that 700,000 people worldwide died in 2017 from antibiotic resistant infections.
4. Is the information *timely*?	Recent for the topic	An article written in 1990 about antibiotic use	An article written within the last three years about antibiotic use
5. What is the source's *bias*?	Belief that might prevent fair judgment	Research on a drug that is paid for by the drug's manufacturer	Research on a drug by a university or national laboratory

Class Activity

As a fun way to reinforce acceptable vs. not acceptable sources, have students—or student groups—locate a "good" and a "bad" source to share with the class in a brief presentation. Students should use the strategic questions to explain why sources are acceptable or not. (See also "Apply What You Learned.")

Read to Write Activity 9.8

Evaluate Sources   Answers will vary.

Write responses to the following exercises using complete sentences.

1. Review your work from Read to Write Activity 9.4, exercise 2. Use Figure 9.5 to evaluate the two sources you located.

2. Review your answers to exercise 1 and decide whether each source is appropriate for use in an academic paper. Explain your reasons.

3. Keeping Figure 9.5 in mind, locate two additional sources related to your research question. Read and evaluate each source. Submit a list of all four sources to your instructor.

Pair and Share

With a classmate, review the sources you located (from Read to Write Activity 9.8) and evaluate each other's sources. Try to come to a consensus as to whether your sources are acceptable for use in an academic paper.

Read to Write Activity 9.9

Prepare a File of Materials for Your Research Paper

Answers will vary.

Follow the instructions in each exercise. Save your work to use in the next chapter, "Writing a Research Paper."

1. Review your work from Read to Write Activities 9.1 through 9.4. Make a list of the databases you searched and the keywords you used to find information about your research question.

2. Review your work from Read to Write Activities 9.6 and 9.8. Make a list of the sources you located and evaluated related to your research question with all the information about the source such as the author, title, publication, date, and where you located the source.

CHAPTER REVIEW

Key Terms

database A collection of information that can be searched by a computer.

keyword A word, often a noun, that identifies a topic.

keyword search A type of search that uses keywords to find documents containing those keywords.

natural language search A type of search that uses phrases or sentences to find documents.

peer-reviewed journal Journal in which articles are assessed by experts in a field of study before being published.

research paper An academic essay that synthesizes information about a topic from outside sources.

search engine A computer program that locates documents on the Web.

Chapter Summary

1. Starting a research assignment with a question can help you locate appropriate sources and read your sources with an open mind to answer that question honestly.

2. You can find high-quality sources appropriate for academic use in a college library by using keyword searches.

3. Doing background reading before researching a question can provide an overview of the topic and help you identify key terms and important concepts, as well as relevant issues or controversies.

4. Determining whether sources are academically appropriate involves evaluating their relevance, reliability, accuracy, timeliness, and bias.

Apply What You Learned

1. Imagine your friend has to research a report on antibiotic resistance for her health class. She asks you for advice on locating information sources and determining whether the sources are academically appropriate. Explain to your friend how best to find academic sources, how to determine whether the sources will be good to use, and what she should avoid in her search.

2. List at least three specific sources that would be effective to use in a research paper about antibiotic resistance. Locate at least one such source using your college library database, one source using a general search engine, and one source using an academic search engine. In your list, include the author and title of the source, the database or search engine by which you located it, and an explanation of why the source is appropriate.

3. List at least three specific sources that would *not* be useful for a research paper about antibiotic resistance. Locate at least one such source using your college library database, one source using a general search engine, and one source using an academic search engine. In your list, include the author and title of the source, the database or search engine by which you located it, and an explanation of why the source is *not* appropriate.

Works Cited

"Internet/Broadband Fact Sheet." *Pew Research Center*, 5 Feb. 2018, www.pewinternet.org/fact-sheet/internet-broadband/.

"Longitude Prize." *Nesta*, 2018, longitudeprize.org/challenge.

"Welcome to *Wikipedia*." *Wikipedia*, 2018, en.wikipedia.org/wiki/Main_Page.

Young, Jeffrey. "*Wikipedia* Founder Discourages Academic Use of His Creation." *The Chronicle of Higher Education*, 12 June 2006, www .chronicle.com/blogs/wiredcampus/wikipedia-founder-discourages- academic-use-of-his-creation/2305.

Credits

p. 253: "What Is Drug Resistance." National Institute of Allergy and infectious Diseases, National Institute of Health, www.niaid.nih.gov; **p. 262:** "Antibiotic Resistance Questions and Answers." *Centers for Disease Control and Prevention*, https://www.cdc.gov/antibiotic-use/community/ about/antibiotic-resistance-faqs.html; **p. 263:** "Antibiotic Resistance Questions and Answers." *Centers for Disease Control and Prevention*, https://www.cdc.gov/antibiotic-use/community/ about/antibiotic-resistance-faqs.html; **p. 264:** "Antibiotic Resistance Questions and Answers." *Centers for Disease Control and Prevention*, https://www.cdc.gov/antibiotic-use/community/ about/antibiotic-resistance-faqs.html.

10 | Writing a Research Paper

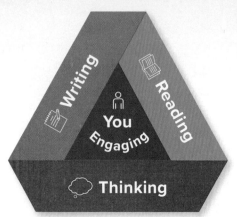

Writing · **Reading** · **You Engaging** · **Thinking**

Look for these icons throughout the chapter. They signal key strategies to use in Read to Write Activities.

After reading this chapter, you will be able to

- Review your research paper plans.
- Read and take notes on sources with your writing purpose in mind.
- Recognize and avoid plagiarism.
- Define technical terms.
- Synthesize information from sources.
- Develop an outline and a thesis.
- Document sources.
- Properly format a research paper.

Theme: Writing about Antibiotic Resistance: How Can We Stay Healthy Using Antibiotics?

Teaching Tip

As an alternative to writing about antibiotic resistance, students could be given the option to write an informative or argumentative research paper on the legalization of marijuana.

The previous chapter, "Planning a Research Paper," describes how to locate, read, and evaluate sources. This chapter focuses on taking notes from sources, organizing those notes to create a plan for the paper, and then drafting, writing, and formatting a research paper. Planning and writing a research paper typically takes time—from several weeks to several months, depending on the requirements of the assignment.

This chapter continues to focus on the theme of antibiotic resistance and what that means for the health of humans and animals. However, the chapter probes another health issue as well: the question of whether to legalize marijuana.

REVIEWING YOUR RESEARCH PAPER PLAN

To write a research paper, you must have developed a research question you want to answer. With that question in mind, you can use keywords to search for and locate relevant, reliable sources. Then you will need time to read these sources, summarizing and quoting information related to your research question. Before progressing further, check that you have a focus and question for your paper and related sources by reviewing your research paper plans.

Read to Write Activity 10.1

Review Your Research Paper Plan

Review the work you did for the previous chapter, "Planning a Research Paper." Then follow the instructions in each exercise below.

1. Restate the prompt that you chose for your paper. If you have not chosen a prompt, do so now.

2. Restate the research question that you developed from the prompt. If you have not written a research question, do so now.

3. State the paper's PAS—purpose, audience, and subject. If you have not identified the paper's PAS, do so now.

4. Retrieve the list of the sources you identified and evaluated for your paper. You should have at least four sources. If you have not researched a list of sources, do so now.

1. Answers will vary—students should recall their work from Read to Write Activity 9.1 in Chapter 9.

2. Answers will vary—students should recall their work from Read to Write Activity 9.2 in Chapter 9.

3. Answers will vary—students should recall their work from Read to Write Activity 9.1 in Chapter 9.

4. Answers will vary—students should recall their work from Read to Write Activity 9.9 in Chapter 9.

READING AND TAKING NOTES ON SOURCES

A typical college writing assignment, such as a research paper, may require you to read and synthesize information from various sources. Recall from earlier in this text that to *synthesize* means to combine different ideas into a new whole. In a history class, for example, you might be asked to draw together and explain various arguments for or against the United States' dropping of the atomic bomb on Hiroshima during World War II. In a psychology class, you might be assigned to research different treatments for depression and determine which is most effective. You might synthesize the information you read by comparing or contrasting different points of view, by highlighting important ideas from various readings, by pulling together particular information about a topic from a range of sources, and by developing your own opinion on the topic.

Importance of Taking Notes

To write an effective synthesis paper based on sources, be prepared to take notes, revise your notes, and consult them as you read and write. Annotating the reading is an excellent start on note-taking, but transferring your annotations into notes

Class Activity

Ask students if they take notes on lectures or on readings for their college classes. If so, students can share their note-taking strategies in pairs, small groups, or with the class.

will pay off with a more effective paper. Students who take extensive notes and who process the information in original ways write higher-quality papers than those who take few notes or copy directly from sources. Moreover, students report that taking notes on their reading helps them organize their thinking, see issues and complexities clearly, make connections across the readings, and document their sources properly. Think of notes as an opportunity to learn from your sources and to reflect on the information in the readings.

Taking notes means not only recording information from the readings related to your topic but also understanding *why* you are reading and what you will ultimately do with your notes. For instance, you may be asked to report objectively about the information you have read on your topic or to present an original argument. You may need to explain the various viewpoints on a topic or determine which viewpoint is most valid. To clarify your purpose, you must understand the final assignment—the end goal—before you begin reading and keep that goal in mind as you take notes.

Note-Taking Methods

There are several ways to read, take notes, and think about your sources. Knowing your options may help you understand—and better accomplish—your goal. Each of the following strategies is more or less appropriate depending on the purpose of your assignment. We will examine these strategies for use with the topic of marijuana legalization.

Teaching Tip

Direct students to Chapter 6, "Writing about Reading," for more on this topic.

Gist and List Method. The gist and list approach serves well if your purpose is to demonstrate that you have understood the content of your readings. With this method, you systematically look for main ideas (identifying the *gist*) as you read and take notes (making a *list*) on those ideas.

Let's say your instructor assigns the paper topic "Explain different views on whether marijuana should be legalized." Using the gist and list method, you would read to discover the main reasons why some people support legalizing marijuana and why others do not, and you would take notes by listing those reasons. For instance, whenever a source gives a reason or explanation why marijuana should or should not be legalized, you could create a bullet-point list by summarizing or quoting that reason and identifying the source. If more than one source gives the same or similar reasons, you could include those as one reason.

If you discovered four reasons in favor and four reasons against legalization, you would make two lists and group the in-favor reasons together and the against reasons together. Then, in your paper, you would present the arguments for and against legalization, organizing each section around the explanation of a particular viewpoint.

Teaching Tip

Direct students to Chapter 7, "Responding to Texts," for more on this topic.

TIA Method. The TIA approach is useful if your instructor assigns a response paper. TIA stands for "<u>T</u>rue, <u>I</u>mportant, I <u>A</u>gree." So, using the TIA strategy, you would concentrate on looking for ideas in the readings that seem true and important to you or ideas that you agree with. You would also identify ideas that seem untrue or trivial or that you disagree with. In your response paper, you could then present the strongest reasons in support of or in opposition to the topic.

For instance, suppose your assignment is to take a stand on whether marijuana should be legalized. You would read not only to find out why some people support legalizing marijuana and others do not, but also to evaluate each side's reasoning and evidence. You would ask yourself which reasons and evidence on each side are *true and important* and which are *untrue or trivial.* Finally, you would note whether you agree or disagree with the ideas on both sides. In your paper, you could present the arguments for and against legalization, as well as an analysis of the strengths and weaknesses of each side's position.

The Dialogue Method. The dialogue approach is useful when your goal is to develop an argument. It involves actively questioning your readings and critically evaluating them. So, as you read the sources, you might ask yourself questions such as, *What is the author's claim? What is the author's evidence? Is the evidence sufficient and convincing? Is the reasoning sound?* If sources disagree, ask yourself whose thinking and evidence are more convincing. This process might lead you to evaluate and to reject or accept certain opinions, to qualify (or limit or restrict) some arguments, and/or to propose your own ideas.

Teaching Tip

Direct students to Chapter 8, "Reading and Writing Arguments," for more on this topic.

For example, if you are reading to develop your own position on legalizing marijuana, you would read with an open mind, asking yourself questions to determine which arguments make the most sense and have the best support. You might also think about new ways to approach the topic—for instance, arguing that legalizing marijuana is valid for medical but not recreational use. Your reading and critical evaluation of the sources should lead you to develop an opinion that can be effectively supported by evidence. Figure 10.1 summarizes these three note-taking methods.

FIGURE 10.1 Note-Taking Methods

Purpose of Paper	Note-Taking Method	Example of How to Apply Method
To explain or inform	Gist and List	Summarize pro and con arguments on legalizing marijuana, and list reasons for both sides' views.
To respond	TIA (True, Important, Agree)	Record ideas that are true or important about legalizing marijuana; then explain whether you agree or disagree.
To argue	Dialogue	Examine and evaluate authors' claims and support for why marijuana should or should not be legalized to develop your own argument.

Handout

"Note-Taking Methods" is a reproducible handout in the Instructor's Resources.

TAKING EFFECTIVE NOTES

As you read more and more sources and accumulate more and more ideas, you will need a sound note-taking system to ensure that you stay organized and accurately represent the ideas from your readings in your own writing. Some researchers use note cards, some use a notebook, and still others use computer files. Whatever method you choose, "Strategies for Effective Note-Taking" will help you create useful notes.

Handout

"Strategies for Effective Note-Taking" is available as a reproducible handout in the Instructor's Manual (IM).

Strategies for Effective Note-Taking

As you take notes, make sure that you do the following:

- **Accurately reflect ideas from the reading.** Correctly restate ideas when summarizing and quote precisely when taking words directly from the reading.
- **Include summaries of ideas.** Use your own words in all your writing.
- **Include quotations.** Select quotes from authorities and particularly well-expressed ideas.
- **Keep track of sources.** Record on each note card or after each entry in a notebook or computer file the source of the information to ensure proper citation and to prevent unintentional plagiarism when you write your paper.
- **Record your own ideas and thinking.** As you read, evaluate the sources and think about making connections across readings or to the topic.

Study the following examples of notes. If you take careful notes like these, you will have all the important details to include in the body of your paper, as well as the information needed to give proper credit to your sources, such as the author and title of the article and the details of publication.

Sample Note with Summary and Quotation

Argument against legalizing marijuana
The American Medical Association has recommended against legalization, stating, "Cannabis is a dangerous drug and as such is a public health concern" (qtd. in Marcus).
"The Perils of Legalized Pot" by Ruth Marcus, The Washington Post, 2 Jan. 2014, www.washingtonpost.com/opinions/ruth-marcus-the-perils-of-legalized-pot/2014/01/02/068cee6e-73e9-11e3-8b3f-b1666705ca3b_story.html?noredirect=on&utm_term=.68ba07054c5b.

The preceding note has a heading identifying its topic. The note itself records a main idea from an article—that the American Medical Association (AMA) is opposed to legalization of marijuana—along with a quote supporting the AMA's position. At the bottom is information about the source: the article's title and author, the name of the publication, the publication date, and the URL because the article was retrieved online.

Sample Note with Summary, Quotation, and Original Ideas

Argument against legalizing marijuana
The American Medical Association has recommended against legalization, stating, "Cannabis is a dangerous drug and as such is a public health concern" (qtd. in Marcus).

COMMENT: This is an important recommendation because the AMA is a well-respected doctors' organization. If doctors believe marijuana is "dangerous" and a "public health concern," that is strong evidence against legalization.

"The Perils of Legalized Pot" by Ruth Marcus, The Washington Post.

Like the first sample note, the immediately preceding note ("Sample Note with Summary, Quotation, and Original Ideas") summarizes the AMA's position, includes a quote, and gives information about the source. Since the full information needed to cite this source was recorded previously, this note includes only the author, article title, and publication. In addition, the note comments on why this idea is important and credible. Notice how the notetaker's opinion—original idea— is set off from the note with the label "Comment" so as not to confuse the source's information with the notetaker's opinion. This note could be used as part of an argument against legalizing marijuana or even to explain the arguments on both sides of the issue.

RECOGNIZING AND AVOIDING PLAGIARISM

The word *plagiarism* comes from the Latin word *plagiarius,* which means "kidnapper." This word origin makes sense because plagiarism involves stealing another person's words or ideas. Plagiarism is a serious academic offense. Students who plagiarize may fail their assignment, fail their class, or even be expelled from college, depending on the extent of the plagiarism.

Why is plagiarism considered such a serious offense and punished with severe consequences? For one thing, getting an education is an opportunity to learn and to develop new skills. Students are expected to do their own writing and thinking and to acknowledge when they use the ideas of others. Plagiarizing suggests that a student does not care about his or her education or value learning. Faculty

Class Activity

Review your college's academic honesty policy with students and discuss why the college has such a policy—how it benefits students' learning.

question whether a student who plagiarizes is willing to put in the time and effort needed to learn. Plagiarism also cheats readers. Readers believe and trust that a writer is presenting his or her own ideas or explaining someone else's research in a paper—*not* taking credit for that research. Readers and instructors may feel angry or betrayed when students do not present their own ideas or use their own writing. Moreover, original thinking is highly valued in the academic community, and professors' careers are built on conducting original research and crediting others who have done research prior to their own contribution. In short, honesty, effort, and hard work are important components of getting an education. Plagiarism undermines all these qualities.

Plagiarism can be intentional, as when someone knowingly uses information from other sources and pretends it is his or her own ideas or words. Plagiarism can also be unintentional, as when someone inadvertently fails to credit sources properly.

Examples of *intentional plagiarism* include the following:

- Copying and pasting information from the Internet into your own paper.
- Buying a paper online and turning it in as your own work.
- Having a friend write a paper for you or submitting a friend's previously written paper as your own.
- Asking a family member to substantially rewrite or "correct" your paper to improve the writing.

Examples of *unintentional plagiarism* include the following:

- Not putting quotation marks around words or phrases copied from another source, even if the borrowed information is cited.
- Changing the wording but not the sentence structure of the source material.
- Reproducing the ideas from a source without clearly acknowledging they are someone else's ideas.

The following examples clarify what is and is not considered plagiarized writing. The original quotation is from the chapter reading selection, "Back to the Future with Antibiotic Resistance."

Class Activity

Before reading this section, present students with the original passage and with the sample sentences. Ask them to decide which are plagiarized and which are not.

ORIGINAL SOURCE: To make things worse, one species of bacteria can transfer the resistance gene to another—and often to a completely unrelated species. In this way, the commensal bacteria (the "friendly" ones we all have, and actually need, mostly in our gut) can develop resistance, and then transfer it to pathogens (the "nasty" bacteria, which cause disease) (Del Mar).

PLAGIARIZED: <u>One</u> kind <u>of bacteria can transfer the resistance</u> to another <u>unrelated species</u> of bacteria.

The plagiarized sentence uses wording (underlined) that is very similar to the wording of the original source and does not acknowledge the original source.

PLAGIARIZED: According to the article "Back to the Future with Antibiotic Resistance," <u>one</u> kind <u>of bacteria can transfer the resistance</u> to another <u>unrelated species</u> of bacteria (Del Mar 285).

Although the preceding sentence correctly cites the source, the wording of the sentence is still too similar to the wording of the original source.

NOT PLAGIARIZED: According to the article "Back to the Future with Antibiotic Resistance," one bacteria "can transfer the resistance gene to another . . . unrelated species" of bacteria (Del Mar 285).

The preceding sentence, which does not plagiarize, acknowledges the original source and uses quotation marks around the exact words from the source. Ellipses (. . .) are used to indicate where words were removed from the quotation.

NOT PLAGIARIZED: According to the article "Back to the Future with Antibiotic Resistance," bacteria can exchange resistance from one species to another, which allows resistant strains to spread (Del Mar 285).

This example of an acceptable sentence acknowledges the original source and summarizes the information using original wording and sentence structure.

One strategy to guard against plagiarism is to effectively quote or summarize information. For instance, always use quotation marks in your notes when you copy down exact words, and use your own words when you summarize. Importantly, you should also precisely record information—such as the author and title of the work, the publisher, the publication place and date, and the page number—about each source you may ultimately use in your paper. You may record that information on each note, after each entry in a notebook, or in a computer file. You will need this information to document the sources you use in your paper.

The following reading selection provides more information on the topic of antibiotic resistance and gives you practice in note-taking. As you read, keep your research question in mind and critically examine the information about antibiotic resistance.

Teaching Tip

Direct students to Chapter 6, "Writing about Reading," for more on this topic.

READING SELECTION

"BACK TO THE FUTURE WITH ANTIBIOTIC RESISTANCE"

Connect

You will find a coordinated Power of Process assignment for this reading in your Connect course.

This reading selection was published in a British newspaper, and therefore the writer uses British English. British English (English spoken and written in the United Kingdom) can be different from American English (English spoken and written in the United States). For example, British English may use different words than American English to express a similar idea. In British English, a person would *ring* a doctor, but in American English, a person would *call* or *telephone* the doctor. Words might also be spelled differently in British and American English. For instance, Americans write *mold*, but the British prefer the spelling *mould*.

Before Reading: Preview; Recognize Prior Knowledge

Answer these questions using complete sentences.

1. Read the title of the article and the information immediately preceding the reading. What do you think it means that we might be going "back to the future" because of antibiotic resistance?

2. Do you think that there are more bacteria (in terms of weight) in the world, or more people? Explain.

During Reading: Annotate

Read the selection twice. Follow the directions for each exercise.

3. On your first reading, read for comprehension of the topic and mark the main ideas and supporting information.

4. On your second reading, look for information related to your paper topic.

Back to the Future with Antibiotic Resistance

By Chris Del Mar

The Guardian, 21 July 2014

The Guardian *is a British national newspaper; the following article was published on its Web site. The author suggests the seriousness of antibiotic resistance, explains how antibiotics were first developed (both naturally and in the laboratory), and considers what we can do about antibiotic resistance in the future.*

Alarm bells have been ringing in Britain, the United States and the World Health Organization about antibiotic resistance. It seems the world is suddenly sitting up and beginning to worry about this looming catastrophe. Britain's chief medical officer, Sally Davies, has called it a threat as great as terrorism or climate change. 1

The World Health Organization estimates that 25,000 people in Europe died last year directly because of resistance. The number of deaths in the US is probably of a similar order. The toll in Australia is hard to estimate, but extrapolating from overseas numbers suggests 1,500 to 2,000 deaths a year, somewhere near the annual carnage from motor vehicle accidents. The deaths occur because the antibiotics given to people with life-threatening infections are no longer effective against the infecting organisms because they have developed resistance. 2

Before looking at exactly what resistance is, it is worth reflecting for a moment on how numerous microorganisms are. We tend to think that the world is dominated by large animals (and plants, for that matter). But most of the living things on the planet are microorganisms, with us large multicellular animals forming a thin layer 3 on the top. The amount of carbon fixed by microorganisms is roughly 60 to 100% of all plants put together; for every person on earth, there are 50 tonnes of bacteria. The infections that some microorganisms inflict on humans reflect a tiny fraction of the war constantly being waged between different microorganisms. In these wars they use chemicals on each other: the chemicals are both antibiotics and the antidotes to those antibiotics, and it is these that are the basis of resistance.

The first purposefully developed antibiotic was streptomycin. It was originally derived from *Actinomyces*, a soil-borne bacterium that secretes antibiotic to destroy a different bacterium. The defence against streptomycin produced by otherwise vulnerable species of bacteria led to the resistance now concerning us.

The mechanism of resistance can be illustrated with the example of penicillin. Secreted by a fungus—*Penicillium* mould, sometimes found as the blue-green mould that spoils fruit—penicillin acts by attacking the cell wall of many different sorts of bacteria (but not multicellular organisms like us humans—which is why it is so useful). The resistance comes in the form of a gene that makes a protein which is an enzyme, called penicillinase. This cleaves the penicillin molecule, rendering it inactive.

In other words, resistance to antibiotics didn't have to evolve anew to counteract any antibiotics we humans developed. Resistance existed—and probably for hundreds of millions of years—before vertebrates were ever thought of, let alone humans.

In any case, the numbers are against us. Remember that bacteria cells double every few hours. And we have a vast number—about a hundred million million—in our bodies. To put it another way, for every one of our own cells (there are 10 million million of them) there are 10 bacteria living in or on us. In an antibiotic environment, a few with resistance genes are selected out, and they will thrive.

These astronomical numbers mean that resistance is inevitable. Even a new synthetic antibiotic will eventually select out a resistant strain. No antibiotic has been developed without resistance appearing soon after.

To make things worse, one species of bacteria can transfer the resistance gene to another—and often to a completely unrelated species. In this way, the commensal bacteria (the "friendly" ones we all have, and actually need, mostly in our gut) can develop resistance, and then transfer it to pathogens (the "nasty" bacteria, which cause disease).

Perhaps the first scientist to express concern about resistance, as long as 60 years ago, was Alexander Fleming, who discovered penicillin before the second world war. Although the problem was mitigated somewhat in those early years by the development of new antibiotics, the pace of development has slowed in recent decades. Partly because they are not financially worthwhile for pharmaceutical companies, who prefer to develop drugs for chronic diseases because they are taken for extended periods, no new classes of antibiotics are emerging. In the race to keep ahead, we are suddenly in a position where there is often *no* alternative antibiotic to treat infections.

Adding to the pressure is our increased reliance on antibiotic "cover" for so many high-technology interventions. Antibiotics are becoming a medical tool we simply can't do without—in surgery (for example, joint replacements are undertaken under antibiotic prophylaxis), in heart interventions (inserting tubes into the heart's vessels to unblock them) and in chemotherapy for cancer (where the body's immune system is temporarily weakened). As resistance grows, so much of what we take for granted will have to stop because the intervention will become too risky.

This is the large, invisible part of an iceberg that we currently only see as deaths directly from antibiotic resistance. Deaths caused indirectly by antibiotic resistance (for example, if patients aren't able to risk chemotherapy to treat myeloid leukaemia) will vastly overshadow deaths from direct causes.   12

The question is, what can we do about it?   13

On the one hand, antibiotics can be thought of as a resource like oil: once expended they can never be used again. It is certainly true that using antibiotics causes resistance, and therefore devalues the antibiotic's future value.   14

On the other hand, however, evidence is accumulating that the process is reversible. A number of empirical studies (including some conducted here in Australia) show that during periods where no antibiotics are used the resistance goes away. Why should this be? In an environment full of antibiotics, resistance genes obviously provide a benefit in terms of selective advantage (they allow the individual bacterial cells to survive). But if that environment becomes free of antibiotics, then the extra "armour" of the gene (the protein it makes) becomes an extra weight (in metabolic terms) for the individual cell to carry around. It will compete less well against its unencumbered peers, and will tend to be selected out.   15

This means the central weapon against antibiotic resistance must be to discourage antibiotic use. Which raises a further question: when should and shouldn't they be used? This is more tricky. In general, antibiotics are most useful in treating or preventing serious illness. The less serious illnesses are generally those outside hospital care—especially those treated by general practitioners, who prescribe the greatest tonnage of antibiotics. We have known for decades now that antibiotics provide a very small benefit for acute respiratory infections, and this is even true of conditions like bacterial infections of the throat, for which, in the past, a prescription for antibiotics was almost automatic.   16

How can prescribing be reduced? In hospitals, antibiotic stewardship programs have been set up to monitor resistance and offer advice on the best antibiotic for specific common illnesses. The aim is to make sure that the treatment least likely to be resistant is used, and also that resistance is least likely to be induced. This approach is likely to be effective in the hospital hierarchy.   17

But it may not be so effective in the less-structured world of general practice and other primary care providers. This is where NPS MedicineWise, a body charged by government to improve prescribing and test-ordering in Australia, has focused its educational messages, which highlight the relative ineffectiveness of antibiotics for most respiratory infections, and aim to raise awareness of resistance. The organisation is also attempting to get doctors to share evidence with patients so they can participate in deciding whether to use antibiotics. NPS   18

MedicineWise has also run public health campaigns about antibiotics, some of which use social media. Better quantification of the various benefits and (especially) the harms associated with antibiotic use will help people more easily understand the pros and cons.

Yet the educational approach has had very modest effects in trials outside Australia (mostly in Europe and the US). The problem is the "failure of the commons"—the fact is that even a small perceived benefit to the individual is likely to outweigh a greater harm to the collective. GPs want to cover even the remote possibility of a serious infection; patients want even the small benefit that might be provided by antibiotics if they feel unwell with an acute respiratory infection.   19

If voluntary methods are not effective, we may be staring down the barrel of coercion. This could involve restricting antibiotic prescriptions in general, or restricting the options to a few. It might sound easy, but it could open up a medico-legal minefield by putting off-limits a drug that might have saved a patient's life. And it would certainly involve some responsibility passing from the clinician to a government authority. One method commonly used by the Pharmaceutical Benefits Scheme is to create a bureaucratic hurdle—such as the "authority script" arrangement, under which the doctor must first ring an authority and choose from a menu of justifications to obtain preapproval.   20

Another approach would involve input into the diagnostic process for clinicians managing acute respiratory infections. Diagnosis of the different types of acute respiratory infection is very difficult in primary care. In particular, it is difficult to know which infection is going to remain trivial, and which may become life-threatening, such as pneumonia or meningitis (both of which can start off with something that appears to be a cold). A test that can tell accurately—and quickly (at the point of care of the patient)—whether a patient has a deep-seated rather than a superficial infection has been shown in European trials to decrease antibiotic prescribing in association with the appropriate education. Establishing the infrastructure for this testing in every practice would be expensive, but the long-term gains could be very significant.   21

Other possible sources of resistance include antibiotic use in animal husbandry, because bucketloads of antibiotics are often used as food additives to increase the yield of the animals, and because antibiotics are present in imports from overseas, where resistance is much more widespread. The jury is still out on what contribution both these sources make to the problem.   22

Governments might also consider providing incentives to pharmaceutical companies to invest in new classes of antibiotics. This is likely to be expensive—and there is, in any case, no indication that new classes of antibiotics will not induce resistance within a short time like all their predecessors.   23

Antibiotic resistance is a serious threat to our way of life. Unless fixed quickly, we face a time-travel back to the 1930s and earlier, when once trivial infections will suddenly become serious threats to health and life, and modern medical treatments too dangerous to contemplate. Exactly what the "fix" will be is unclear, but serious interventions are more than likely, and soon.   24

Answers

5. The reading opens with statistics showing that 25,000 Europeans died because of antibiotic resistance, and many others in the United States and Australia.

6. Bacteria have been fighting each other with chemical weapons that are "both antibiotics and the antidotes to those antibiotics."

7. The author suggests that in the future, we no longer have access to life-saving antibiotics, thereby taking us back to a past without these drugs.

Answers

1. The author means that bacteria are so prevalent and numerous that it is difficult to develop an antibiotic to which they will not eventually become resistant.

2. The author suggests that cutting back on antibiotic use, educating people about antibiotic resistance, and putting regulations in place for antibiotic use might be possible solutions.

After Reading: Summarize; Reflect

When you have finished the reading selection, write responses to the following exercises using complete sentences.

5. What evidence does the reading give that antibiotic resistance is a serious problem?

6. What is the basis for antibiotic resistance? That is, how did antibiotic resistance develop?

7. Reflect again on the title of the reading. What does it mean that we might be going "back to the future" because of antibiotic resistance?

Read to Write Activity 10.2

Engage with the Reading

1. The author states that "the numbers [of bacteria] are against us." What does he mean?

2. The author asks, "What can we do about [antibiotic resistance]?" What are some answers?

Pair and Share

With a partner, select one of the "After Reading" exercises that you both found challenging and compare your answers. Try to come to a consensus about the answer.

Vocabulary Strategy: Defining Technical Terms

Recall that authors may use technical words and terms that are specific to their subject or field. Technical terms may be defined in a piece of writing itself, or readers may be expected to know the terms or look them up in a general or specialized reference source.

Vocabulary Practice

Use context clues, word analysis, and/or the dictionary to define each underlined term in the following sentences from the reading, "Back to the Future with Antibiotic Resistance." Be sure the definition fits the meaning of the term in the context of the sentence.

1. "But most of the living things on the planet are <u>microorganisms</u>, with us large multicellular animals forming a thin layer on the top" (Del Mar).

continued

2. "But most of the living things on the planet are microorganisms, with us large <u>multicellular</u> animals forming a thin layer on the top" (Del Mar).

3. "In this way, the <u>commensal</u> bacteria (the 'friendly' ones we all have, and actually need, mostly in our gut) can develop resistance, and then transfer it to pathogens (the 'nasty' bacteria, which cause disease)" (Del Mar).

4. "In this way, the commensal bacteria (the 'friendly' ones we all have, and actually need, mostly in our gut) can develop resistance, and then transfer it to <u>pathogens</u> (the 'nasty' bacteria, which cause disease)" (Del Mar).

Answers

1. *Microorganisms* are extremely small organisms, such as bacteria.

2. *Multicellular* means many-celled life.

3. *Commensal* means helpful.

4. *Pathogens* means harmful.

Read to Write Activity 10.3

Take Notes on Sources

Write responses to the following exercises using complete sentences.

1. Review your work from Read to Write Activity 10.1 and your notes from the previous chapter's reading selection, "Antibiotic Resistance Questions and Answers." What information in the reading selection can help answer your research question?

2. Which of the three note-taking strategies described in the text—gist and list, TIA, and dialogue—would be most appropriate for developing a paper on the topic you selected? Why?

3. Take notes on this chapter's reading selection, "Back to the Future with Antibiotic Resistance," using the note-taking strategy you identified in exercise 2.

Answers

1. If students are writing about antibiotic resistance, they can refer to Chapter 9, "Planning a Research Paper."

2. The "gist and list" method is most appropriate for an informative paper, while the TIA or dialogue method can be used for an argumentative paper.

3. Answers will vary.

Pair and Share

Compare your response to exercise 3 in Read to Write Activity 10.3 with a classmate's response. Can you find more information from the reading that would help to answer either your or your classmate's research question? If so, add to your notes.

Class Activity

To demonstrate the value of note-taking as well as how to synthesize sources, bring sample notes to class on the research topic. Allow students (in groups) to organize the notes in different ways, according to whether they might write an argument or present an informative paper; then ask them to explain their organizational strategies to the class.

SYNTHESIZING INFORMATION FROM SOURCES

Reading sources and taking notes on them are the first steps toward synthesizing your findings in a research paper. It is also important to consider the purpose of your paper and how best to organize your ideas. How you incorporate information into your paper will depend on the purpose of your paper.

Informative versus Argumentative Paper

An **informative paper** involves combining information from different sources and restating it in your own words. It is a useful way to explain what you have learned from your reading. The gist and list method of note-taking is particularly suited to writing an informative paper—a paper that educates readers. For an informative paper, you consider how best to select and arrange the diverse information from your sources around key ideas. Eventually, you develop an informative thesis to guide your paper.

In contrast, an **argumentative paper** involves combining information from different sources with the goal of presenting your own views on the content of the readings. The TIA and dialogue methods of note-taking are particularly suited to an argumentative paper. In an argumentative paper, the writer takes a position on a topic and uses the information from different sources to support a thesis. Think about having an angle or a point of view on what you have learned from your sources. You will want to craft an argumentative thesis to guide the paper.

Teaching Tip

Direct students to Chapter 8, "Reading and Writing Arguments," for an example of an argument thesis.

Organizing Notes to Create a Writing Plan

An important aspect of writing a good paper is creating an organizational plan. Rather than using your notes to write a summary of each source, you may find it useful to organize the notes around key ideas related to the paper topic. To do this, you need to identify ideas that are present in more than one source and focus your paragraphs on those important ideas.

One strategy for organizing your notes is to group related ideas and related information into categories. Suppose, for example, that you are writing an informative research paper explaining the arguments against and for legalizing marijuana. You could start to organize notes by grouping ideas from the readings into two broad categories: (1) arguments against legalization, and (2) arguments for legalization.

You could then narrow these categories into subcategories. For instance, let's say you find that the American Medical Association calls marijuana "a dangerous drug" and "a public health concern." You also discover that the federal government considers marijuana a "Schedule I substance," meaning the drug puts users at high risk for abuse. You might group these related pieces of information in a chart by specifically modifying the broad category "Arguments against legalization" to include the qualifier "Marijuana is an unsafe drug."

Similarly, you could modify the general category "Arguments for legalization" to include the qualifier "Marijuana is a safe drug." Figure 10.2 is a chart-in-progress that begins to group related information. With additional reading and note-taking, the chart would expand (see color rows at the end) to include further arguments against and for legalizing marijuana.

When grouping information, be sure each subcategory constitutes a separate and distinct classification. In this way, you can use groupings of related ideas and information to represent different issues in the readings. This strategy might be especially helpful if your goal is to restate the information from the readings or to write an informative paper.

FIGURE 10.2 Charting to Organize Notes

Paper Prompt: Explain the arguments for and against legalizing marijuana.	
Arguments Against and For	**Support from the Readings**
Argument against legalization: Marijuana is an unsafe drug	• The American Medical Association has recommended against legalization, stating, "Cannabis is a dangerous drug and as such is a public health concern" (qtd. in Marcus). • The federal government considers marijuana a Schedule I substance, meaning it puts users at high risk for abuse.
Argument for legalization: Marijuana is a safe drug	• In 2010 there were no reported drug overdose deaths for marijuana, compared with 22,134 lethal overdoses of pharmaceutical drugs (reported in the *Journal of the American Medical Association*). • According to the American Cancer Society, marijuana can help AIDS and cancer patients by relieving pain, controlling nausea, and increasing appetite.
Argument against legalization: . . .	• *Support from reading . . .*
Argument for legalization: . . .	• *Support from reading . . .*

Teaching Tip

An alternative strategy for organizing notes or information is a graphic organizer.

Read to Write Activity 10.4

Create a Chart to Organize Notes

Follow the instructions in each exercise.

1. Review the purpose you identified in Read to Write Activity 10.1. What will be your purpose for writing your research paper? For instance, will you write an informative or an argumentative paper?

2. Review your work from Read to Write Activities 10.1 and 10.3, including your notes on your research prompt and your annotated sources. Then create a chart like the one in Figure 10.2 to organize your ideas.

Answers

1. Answers will vary; students should refer to Read to Write Activity 10.1.

2. Answers will vary. Encourage students to "balance" notes when possible by aligning related arguments and counterarguments.

DEVELOPING AN OUTLINE AND A THESIS

If you have been reading sources and taking notes related to your paper topic, and if you have been using a chart to group related ideas and information, you should have a good start on your paper. In fact, your chart can form the basis of an outline from which you can develop a tentative thesis statement. This initial thesis statement (for example, "Advocates and opponents of legalizing marijuana give a number of reasons for their positions") can be refined later as you develop and clarify your understanding of the topic.

Teaching Tip

Informal outlines or essay plans are described in Chapter 5, "Reading and Writing Essays."

Once you have a tentative thesis, you can outline the rest of the paper. Alternatively, some writers prefer to outline their papers first and then compose a thesis statement based on the outline. Either option works as long as the end result includes topic sentences and a thesis statement with clearly related ideas. This plan can be reviewed, revised, and sharpened as you draft the paper itself.

Moving from Charting to Outlining Main Ideas

If you have organized your notes into categories or gathered related ideas in a chart, you can use these groupings to form the major sections of your paper. For instance, if you are writing an informative paper, you could review your chart (Figure 10.2) and decide to create one section in the paper explaining that supporters of legalization feel marijuana is a safe drug and another section explaining that opponents feel marijuana is an unsafe drug. These sections can be one paragraph each or multiple paragraphs, depending on how much supporting information you find for each viewpoint.

After determining the major sections of the paper, you can write topic sentences for each paragraph. To write effective topic sentences, use your own words to make explicit connections between the information in the sources and the purpose of the paper. If your purpose is to explain the arguments for and against legalization of marijuana, you would indicate in each topic sentence whether the focus of the paragraph is on the arguments for or against legalization and what exactly the supporting or opposing arguments are.

> **TOPIC SENTENCE IN FAVOR OF MARIJUANA LEGALIZATION:** Supporters of legalizing marijuana believe that marijuana is a drug that can be used responsibly for pleasure and for medical reasons.

Now imagine writing an argumentative paper about the legalization of marijuana based on many of the same sources. If you have collected ideas in a chart, you must decide on sections. Then, to develop a topic sentence for each paragraph in those sections, you must determine your position regarding legalization and be sure you can defend it with supporting information and logical reasoning.

> **TOPIC SENTENCE IN FAVOR OF MARIJUANA LEGALIZATION:** Legalization of marijuana to relieve the suffering of patients and for other medical reasons is justified.

To start an outline for an informative paper, you could proceed through your chart, *summing up* the arguments for or against marijuana and writing these as topic sentences. Likewise, to start an outline for an argumentative paper, you can proceed through your chart, deciding *your position* about the information from the readings and creating topic sentences. Writing topic sentences for each section of the paper forms the basis of an outline.

Now you must decide in what order to place the topic sentences that identify the sections of the paper. For guidance, you can rely on your knowledge of essay patterns. For instance, if you are explaining two points of view, you might use either a block or a point-by-point essay structure to clarify the arguments for and against legalization. The **block method** of organization describes one subject first and then switches to describing the second subject, so that the paper is divided into "blocks." The **point-by-point method** of organization moves back and forth between the two subjects and is organized around ideas, or "points," about those subjects. See Figure 10.3 for a comparison of the block and point-by-point methods of organization.

FIGURE 10.3 Block versus Point-by-Point Organization

Block Organization	Point-by-Point Organization
Arguments in favor of legalization	Point 1 about legalization: dangerous?
Reason 1: Not dangerous	Reason in favor—not dangerous
Reason 2: Tax revenues	Reason in opposition—addictive and harmful
Reason 3: Personal choice	Point 2 about legalization: economics?
Arguments opposed to legalization	Reason in favor—generates tax revenues
Reason 1: Addictive and harmful	Reason in opposition—immoral "sin" tax
Reason 2: Immoral "sin" tax	Point 3 about legalization: choice?
Reason 3: Protection from harm	Reason in favor—personal choice
	Reason in opposition—protect others from harm

Handout

"Block versus Point-by-Point Organization" is a reproducible handout in the Instructor's Resources.

In contrast, if you are writing an argumentative paper, you might organize topic sentences in several different ways (see Figure 10.4):

- Building from the weakest to the strongest reasons for your argument, including a counterargument at the end. This strategy allows you to present a strong case and then to respond to opposing views.

- Presenting reasons and then raising and refuting counterarguments for each reason. This organization can work well if for each reason there is a clear opposing viewpoint.

- Organizing the reasons for your argument in response to a counterargument. This order might be especially appropriate if you feel you are taking an unpopular position, such as arguing for marijuana's legalization.

Handout

"Organizational Patterns for an Argumentative Paper" is a reproducible handout in the Instructor's Resources.

FIGURE 10.4 Organizational Patterns for an Argumentative Paper

Weakest Reason to Strongest Reason	Argument and Counterargument	Counterargument and Argument
Reason 1: Legalization will provide tax revenues.	Reason 1: Marijuana can be used safely.	Counterargument: Marijuana is an addictive and dangerous drug.
Reason 2: Marijuana can be used safely.	Counterargument: Marijuana is an addictive drug.	Reason 1: Marijuana can be used safely.
Reason 3: Marijuana use should be a personal choice for adults.	Reason 2: Marijuana use should be a personal choice for adults.	Reason 2: Marijuana use should be a personal choice for adults.
Counterargument: Marijuana is an addictive drug.	Counterargument: The government has a duty to protect its citizens.	Reason 3: Legalization will provide tax revenues.
	Reason 3: Legalization will provide tax revenues.	
	Counterargument: It's immoral to profit from drug use.	

So, based on your writing purpose and the subject matter, you must decide how best to arrange the paragraphs in the body of the paper. Let's say you choose the point-by-point method and therefore plan to move back and forth throughout the paper to present the arguments for and against legalization of marijuana. As a way to get started organizing the ideas, you could create an informal outline (see Figure 10.5).

FIGURE 10.5 Informal Outline of Informative Paper with Topic Sentences (Point-by-Point Organization)

Section 1: Supporters point out that legalizing marijuana could provide tax revenues from the manufacturing and sale of the drug.

Section 2: Opponents believe that raising tax revenues by potentially getting people addicted to drugs is immoral.

Section 3: Supporters of legalizing marijuana believe that marijuana is a drug that can be used responsibly for pleasure and for medical reasons.

Section 4: Opponents of legalizing marijuana argue that cannabis is an addictive and dangerous drug and therefore should be illegal.

Section 5: Supporters argue that adults should have the personal choice to use marijuana, which is similar to alcohol, a legal drug.

Section 6: Opponents assert that it is the duty of the government to protect the health and welfare of its citizens, and therefore the state should not allow the production and distribution of harmful drugs.

Answers will vary.

Read to Write Activity 10.5

Create an Outline

Follow the instructions in each exercise.

1. Review your work from Read to Write Activity 10.4. What organizational pattern might you use for your paper? For instance, for an informative paper, would the point-by-point or block method be effective? For an argumentative paper, would (a) weak-to-strong reasons, (b) reasons then counterarguments, or (c) counterargument then reasons be most effective?

2. Create an informal outline by organizing your paper into sections according to the organizational pattern you chose for exercise 1. Write a topic sentence for each section.

Moving from Outlining Main Ideas to Adding Support

If you organize your paper by creating an outline with topic sentences, your next step is to incorporate support for each section. If you have taken precise notes or created a detailed chart, adding support for each section of the paper involves going back over your notes or chart and including the relevant information at the most logical point in the outline.

For instance, if you are writing an informative paper, you could review your chart (Figure 10.2) and then refer to your informal outline (Figure 10.5) to decide where to place the support from each reading. In this way, you could create a formal outline that includes the topic sentences and the supporting information for each section (see Figure 10.6). Taking this step will help you to develop your thinking and more fully organize your notes into a paper plan.

FIGURE 10.6 Sample Formal Outline for an Informative Paper, with Topic Sentences and Supporting Information

I. Introduction: Thesis

II. Supporters of legalizing marijuana believe that marijuana is a drug that can be used responsibly for pleasure and for medical reasons.

   A. In 2010 there were no reported drug overdose deaths for marijuana, compared with 22,134 lethal overdoses of pharmaceutical drugs (reported in the *Journal of the American Medical Association*).

   B. According to the American Cancer Society, marijuana can help AIDS and cancer patients by relieving pain, controlling nausea, and increasing appetite.

   C. *Forbes* magazine reports that crime drops in states with legalized marijuana.

III. Opponents of legalizing marijuana argue that cannabis is an addictive and dangerous drug and therefore should be illegal.

   A. The American Medical Association has recommended against legalization, stating "Cannabis is a dangerous drug and as such is a public health concern."

   B. The federal government considers marijuana a Schedule I substance, meaning it puts users at high risk for abuse.

   C. *Psychology Today* reports a link between marijuana use and increased violent behavior.

Continue with main ideas and support for sections 3, 4, 5, and 6 of informal outline.

Conclusion

Class Activity

Students can complete the rest of the outline by writing topic sentences for sections 3, 4, 5, and 6. If they have some knowledge of the topic or are doing research on marijuana legalization, they could also include support in each section.

Read to Write Activity 10.6

Create a Formal Outline and Add Support

Review your informal outline from Read to Write Activity 10.5. Create a formal outline for your paper by including supporting information for each topic sentence for each section of the paper.

Answers will vary.

Teaching Tip

As an alternative to a formal outline, students could be allowed to flesh out their informal outlines with support for each main idea.

Pair and Share

With a classmate, exchange formal outlines with support. Review each other's outlines and give feedback on whether the organizational pattern makes sense and whether the writer could add more support to the main ideas.

Teaching Tip

Informative versus
persuasive thesis
statements are
demonstrated in Chapter 5,
"Reading and Writing
Essays." Informative versus
argumentative claims are
described in Chapter 8,
"Reading and Writing
Arguments."

Moving from Formal Outlining to Finalizing a Thesis Statement

Once you have drafted a formal outline, you are ready to revise and finalize your thesis statement. The thesis statement should convey the purpose of your paper—whether it is, say, informative or argumentative—and state the main points the paper will cover.

A thesis statement for an informative paper should be fair, accurate, and objective, as in this example.

INFORMATIVE THESIS: Advocates for legalizing marijuana claim that marijuana is a drug that can be used responsibly for pleasure and therefore should be regulated and taxed, while opponents of legalization argue that marijuana is a dangerous drug, and therefore legalization can lead to more addiction and social problems.

A thesis statement for an argumentative paper should give the writer's opinion on the topic, as well as capture the main points of the paper. Let's say you decide that a strong argument will focus exclusively on the legalization of marijuana for medicinal use. For a thesis statement, you can use a particular format called an "although ... because" thesis statement. This format allows you to state the opposing arguments that your paper will address (in the *although* clause), as well as your position and then (after *because*) the reasons for your position.

ARGUMENTATIVE THESIS:

<u>Although</u> marijuana is a potentially addictive, dangerous drug and therefore
Opposing arguments

should not be widely available,

<u>legalizing marijuana for some medical reasons is justified</u>
Writer's point of view

<u>because</u> the drug can relieve pain and suffering for patients.
Writer's reasons

Read to Write Activity 10.7

Write a Thesis Statement

Review your formal outline with support from Read to Write Activity 10.6. Write a thesis statement that sums up the main ideas, gives your point of view, and reflects the organizational pattern of your paper. You may choose to use the "although ... because" format or another format.

Teaching Tip

Demonstrate how a thesis
statement can anticipate
the main sections of a paper
by using the two sample
thesis statements in this
chapter.

Pair and Share

Exchange thesis statements with a classmate. Read your classmate's thesis statement and tell your classmate what you think will be the main ideas of the paper, the writer's point of view, and the paper's organization.

DRAFTING, REVISING, EDITING, AND PROOFREADING YOUR RESEARCH PAPER

With a formal outline and a thesis statement in hand, you have what you need to draft your research paper. As you write, follow your outline.

- Compose an introductory paragraph that sparks the reader's interest, gives background on your topic, and states the thesis.
- Write a body paragraph for each topic sentence and include supporting information from your sources.
- Add a conclusion that wraps up the paper and brings it to a satisfying end.

After drafting your paper, set it aside for a little while. When you return to your work, revise your paper for content and organization, edit the sentences for clarity, and proofread for errors.

Read to Write Activity 10.8

Draft, Revise, Edit, and Proofread a Research Paper

Follow the instructions in each exercise.

1. Using your notes and your formal outline with support and thesis statement from Read to Write Activities 10.6 and 10.7, write an introduction for your research paper.

2. Using your notes and formal outline from Read to Write 10.6, write the body paragraphs for your research paper.

3. Write the conclusion for your research paper.

4. Revise, edit, and proofread your paper.

Pair and Share

Exchange your draft with a classmate. Read and evaluate the paper for content and organization.

Teaching Tip

Strategies for writing effective introductions and strong conclusions are covered in Chapter 5, "Reading and Writing Essays." Strategies for writing body paragraphs are covered in Chapter 4, "Reading and Writing Paragraphs." Paragraph strategies that deal with readings, such as PIE in Chapter 6, "Writing about Reading," and SOS in Chapter 7, "Responding to Texts," might be especially helpful for students constructing a research paper.

DOCUMENTING SOURCES

As you read and take notes on your sources to answer your research question, make sure to keep track of where you are getting your information by recording information about each source, such as the author and title, with each note. In your research paper, you will need to *document*, or acknowledge, all source information in two places: (1) within the body of the paper, and (2) at the end of the paper. **Documentation** of sources in the body of the paper is called *in-text citation* or *parenthetical citation*. Documentation of source information at the end of a paper may be called *Works Cited*, *References*, or *Bibliography* depending on the documentation style.

How you record source information in the body of the paper and at the end depends on the *documentation style*. The documentation style required in most English courses is MLA (Modern Language Association) style, whereas many social sciences, such as psychology, use APA (American Psychological Association) style. Always check with your instructor as to the required documentation style. The next section provides a brief overview of the basics of citing information in a research paper using MLA style. For more guidelines for both MLA and APA style, consult the Documentation Resource Guide at the end of this book; or, for more comprehensive coverage, refer to the eighth edition of the *MLA Handbook* or to the sixth edition of the *Publication Manual of the American Psychological Association*.

In-Text Citations: MLA Style

Whenever you quote, paraphrase, or summarize a source in your writing, you should include an in-text citation either immediately after the information from your source or at the end of the sentence in which that information appears.

You may worry that including many citations might suggest that you have not done much original writing. On the contrary, frequent citations are often a sign of strong writing. First, they show readers that you have read and researched the topic. Second, they demonstrate that the support for your ideas comes from reliable sources.

MLA style for in-text citation typically consists of the author's last name and a page number in parentheses after a quote, summary, or paraphrase from a source. Following are some common examples that show how to create in-text citations in MLA style depending on whether there is an author or page number for the source.

In-text citation with an author and page number. If the source has an author and a page number, include that information in the parenthetical citation. Use the author's last name, and do not separate the name and page number with a comma.

> Antibiotics are losing their effectiveness, which is leading to "a serious threat to our way of life" (Del Mar 287).

In-text citation when there is no named author. If the source does not include an author, use the first words that appear in the works cited entry, which is usually the title of the reading, in the parenthetical citation.

> Antibiotic resistance can develop naturally, through genetic mutations or when bacteria exchange genetic material with one another ("Fact Sheet" 2).

In-text citation when source is referenced in the sentence. If you use the author's name (or the title of the source when there is no author) in the sentence, include only a page number in the parenthetical citation.

> According to the US National Library of Medicine's "Fact Sheet" about the safe use of antibiotics, the overuse and incorrect use of antibiotics can make these drugs lose their ability to fight diseases (2).

In-text citations for an online source without page numbers. If you use information from a reliable Web site or other online source, that source may not have page numbers. In this case, include the first words that appear in the works cited entry (such as the author's name, article title, or Web site title); do not provide page numbers or a URL in parentheses.

> The Centers for Disease Control and Prevention explains that antibiotic resistance is "one of the world's most pressing public health problems" ("Antibiotic Resistance").

Works Cited List: MLA Style

Teaching Tip

Point out to students that this chapter includes a works cited page in MLA style.

A list of all the sources cited in the paper (*cited* means quoted or summarized) appears at the end of the paper. In other words, if there is an in-text citation for a source in the body of the paper, there should be a full citation for that source at the end of the paper. In MLA style, the list of sources has the title "Works Cited." The sources are arranged alphabetically by the author's last name (or by title of the source if there is no author), and the list begins on a new page. Here are examples of how entries for various sources should appear.

Book

Author(s). *Title of Work*. Publisher, date.

Podolsky, Scott H. *The Antibiotic Era: Reform, Resistance, and the Pursuit of a Rational Therapeutics*. Johns Hopkins UP, 2015.

Work in an anthology

Author(s). "Title of Work." *Title of Book*, edited by Editor's Name, Publisher, year of publication, page numbers.

Kurz, Sebastian G., et al. "Drug-Resistant Tuberculosis: Challenges and Progress." *Antibiotic Resistance: Challenges and Opportunities*, edited by Richard R. Watkins and Robert A. Bonomo, Elsevier, 2016, pp. 509-22. The Clinics: Internal Medicine.

Magazine article from a database

Author(s). "Article Title." *Title of Publication,* date, page range. *Database*, doi, or URL (without https://).

Reardon, Elizabeth. "Antibiotic Resistance Sweeping Developing World." *Nature,* 6 May 2014, pp. 141-42. *EBSCOHost,* doi:10.1038/509141a.

Newspaper or magazine article published online

Author(s). "Article Title." *Periodical,* date, URL (without https://). Date of access.

Del Mar, Chris. "Back to the Future with Antibiotic Resistance." *The Guardian,* 21 July 2014, www.theguardian.com/commentisfree/2014/jul/21/back-to-the-future-with-antibiotic-resistance. Accessed 1 Nov. 2018.

Web page

Author, compiler, director, or editor (if any). "Title of the page." *Title of overall Web site*, date of publication, URL (without https://). Date of access.

"What Is Antibiotic Resistance and Why Is It a Problem?" *Alliance for the Prudent Use of Antibiotics,* Tufts University, 12 Oct. 2014, emerald.tufts .edu/med/apua/about_issue/antibiotic_res.shtml. Accessed 15 Apr. 2018.

Read to Write Activity 10.9

Cite and Document Sources

Follow the instructions in each exercise.

1. Check with your instructor as to what style guide you should use to create a research paper—MLA, APA, or another guide. Then locate a resource you can use to help you cite and document your sources, such as the information in the Documentation Resource Guide in this book or an appropriate handbook.

2. Write two sentences that include in-text citations. Use the reading selections about antibiotic resistance as your sources, or draw from sources from your own research.

3. Create two entries for a list of sources based on your response to exercise 2.

Pair and Share

- Exchange your sentences using in-text citations (from Read to Write Activity 10.9, exercise 2) with a classmate. Check that you have correctly formatted the citations and that you have not unintentionally plagiarized from the sources.

- Exchange your entries for a list of sources (from Read to Write Activity 10.9, exercise 3) with a classmate. Check that you have correctly formatted the list of sources.

FORMATTING A RESEARCH PAPER

Style guides, such as those for MLA or APA style, include rules for citing sources in the body and at the end of a research paper or other type of essay. These guides also have conventions for formatting a paper. It is important to follow these guidelines carefully and correctly to fulfill your readers' expectations. For instance, the heading of the paper needs to include certain information in a particular arrangement, the title needs to be centered and placed on a certain page, and the paper itself should be double-spaced consistently throughout and typed in an approved font.

After you have finished writing your research paper and know which sources you ultimately used, you are ready to create a list of sources used in the paper. In MLA format, this list is titled "Works Cited." Like the other pages of the paper, the list of sources should be correctly formatted. Readers expect that the page will begin on a new page at the end of the paper. The title should be centered, with each word capitalized. Sources should be listed alphabetically so that they are easy to locate. Each entry should contain the information required by the style format.

Figure 10.7 shows the format for the first page of an MLA paper and the first page of a works cited list. To see how in-text citations appear in a research paper, as well as an example of how a research paper should be formatted, from the first page to the list of references, refer to the Documentation Resource Guide at the back of this text or check the appropriate style guide.

FIGURE 10.7 **Sample First Page and Works Cited List for an MLA Paper**

Your last name 1

Your name

Your instructor's name

Your class name and number

Date Month Year

Title of Your Paper

Type your entire paper double-spaced, with no extra space above or below the title. Indent each paragraph half an inch. Allow one-inch margins at the top, bottom, and sides. Number the pages in the upper right-hand corner. Start the works cited list on a new page. Start each works cited entry at the left margin, list the entries alphabetically, and indent subsequent lines of each entry by half an inch.

(continued)

Your last name 8

Works Cited

Kurz, Sebastian G., et al. "Drug-Resistant Tuberculosis: Challenges and Progress." *Antibiotic Resistance: Challenges and Opportunities*, edited by Richard R. Watkins and Robert A. Bonomo, Elsevier, 2016, pp. 509–22. The Clinics: Internal Medicine.

Podolsky, Scott H. *The Antibiotic Era: Reform, Resistance, and the Pursuit of a Rational Therapeutics.* Johns Hopkins UP, 2015.

Reardon, Elizabeth. "Antibiotic Resistance Sweeping Developing World." *Nature,* 6 May 2014, pp. 141–42. *EBSCOHost,* doi:10.1038/509141a.

Read to Write Activity 10.10

Format a Research Paper

Follow the instructions in each exercise.

1. Review your draft from Read to Write Activity 10.8. Format the first page of your research paper draft, including the page number, heading, title, and text, all properly formatted.

2. Create a works cited page for your research paper draft, properly formatted.

Pair and Share

Exchange formatted drafts (from Read to Write Activity 10.10) with a classmate. Check the in-text citations, the list of sources, and the formatting of the first page.

CHAPTER REVIEW

Key Terms

argumentative paper A paper that combines information from different sources with the goal of presenting an original view on the content of the readings.

block method An essay structure consisting of blocks of text that alternate subjects.

documentation Acknowledgment of source information in a research paper within the body of the paper and at the end of the paper.

informative paper A paper that combines information from different sources and restates the information using original language.

point-by-point method An essay structure that moves back and forth between two subjects and is organized around ideas, or points.

Chapter Summary

1. To write an effective research paper based on sources, you should take notes by recording information related to your topic while keeping your writing purpose in mind.

2. The note-taking system you develop should reflect your paper's purpose and include accurate summaries and quotations from the readings, carefully documented information on your sources, and your own ideas.

3. Plagiarism is a serious offense. Writers must understand what constitutes plagiarism and must take measures to avoid it by always properly crediting their sources.

4. Strategies for synthesizing sources include grouping related ideas and information into categories or a chart.

5. Organizing your notes can help you create an informal outline from which you can develop a formal outline and tentative thesis statement.

6. Writing a formal outline with a thesis statement, topic sentences, and information from sources will help you draft your paper.

7. When you cite sources in the body and at the end of a research paper, it is important to follow the guidelines for the required citation style, such as MLA or APA style.

8. When you format a research paper, it is important to follow the guidelines for the required formatting style, such as MLA or APA style.

Teaching Tip

Either of these activities can be modified to require students to write an informative paper, an argumentative paper, or to have their choice of either approach.

Apply What You Learned

1. Review the arguments in the examples throughout this chapter about legalizing marijuana. Then conduct your own research on the legalization of marijuana and write an argumentative research paper, taking a position on whether marijuana should be legalized.

2. Focus on issues in your community or at your college, such as improving public transportation to campus, installing bike lanes and bike racks, or making the food on campus healthier or less expensive, and conduct research on the issue. Find at least five sources that address different ideas on the topic. Then write a research paper in which you explain the various viewpoints on that topic.

Credit

p. 282: Del Mar, Chris, "Back to the Future with Antibiotic Resistance." *The Guardian*, 21 July 2014. Used with permission of the author.

SPOTLIGHT ON STUDENT WRITING

Evaluating and Analyzing Student Writing

In the preceding chapters we discussed how to summarize from a reading and give an opinion with support in response to the author. We also saw how to develop an argumentative claim with reasons and supporting evidence, including anticipating and replying to counterarguments against the claim to make the argument stronger. Finally, we examined how to use strategies for locating and evaluating sources for an essay and how to cite and document these properly to avoid plagiarism.

In this Spotlight section, you will focus on reading to

- Analyze how students develop essays using a thesis. (Is the claim clear?)

- Analyze how students use support. (Is the claim supported with reasons and evidence?)

- Analyze how students use quotations and summaries from researched information. (Are the sources used well and properly cited?)

- Evaluate how students respond to counterarguments.

ANNOTATING, EVALUATING, AND ANALYZING STUDENT ESSAYS

What follows are two sample student papers for you to read and think about. First, you will read a successfully annotated student paper. Then you will have a chance to read and annotate a second student paper.

To explore the effects of social media on relationships, particularly whether social media isolates people or brings them together, students read various articles and were given a choice of writing prompts on the theme of social media, including the following.

> **Writing Prompt:** *To what extent do social media isolate people or bring people together? Draw from the articles you have read and from your own experiences with social media to support your position.*

The essay directions include this additional requirement.

> **Requirement:** *In this essay, you will create an argument and use evidence from various sources for support. You should draw on at least two sources (articles, graphs, or videos) to support your answer. You can also use researched information or include your own or other people's experiences. You should properly cite and document the sources you use in your paper.*

Teaching Tip

For readings on the topic of social media, see the Anthology of Theme-Based Readings: Do Social Media Connect Us—or Isolate Us?

As the title suggests, Gabrielle Reyez's essay, "Enslaved by Technology," takes a pessimistic view of social media. Brittney Kiel's essay, "Less Is More," also deals with the question of the impact of social media on human relationships while considering the advantages and disadvantages of using social media. The students' papers were written about two-thirds of the way through the semester. As you read, notice how each student summarizes and responds to the readings; uses evidence, including examples, explanations, and quotes, to support her response; and cites and documents her sources.

STUDENT PAPER 1
About the Author

Gabrielle Reyez

©Alison Kuehner

After becoming a single mother when she was twenty years old, Gabrielle Reyez was away from school caring for her daughter for six years before returning to college to get her degree. The first person in her family to attend college, Reyez works full time at the college's Extended Opportunity Programs and Services Center. Her major is human development, and she plans to transfer to a four-year college to get a degree to teach middle school. Gabrielle loves school, especially reading. She recommends students read every article assigned because, she says, "If you don't read, you can't write!" Moreover, she advises taking full advantage of any tutoring offered to be successful in classes.

 Before Reading: Predict

Complete the following exercises.

1. Review the "Writing Prompt" given above. What does the writer need to do in her writing to create a successful paper?

2. Read the "Requirement" for the essay assignment. What does the writer need to do, in addition to addressing the prompt, to create a successful paper?

Annotations for
Evaluation and
Analysis

How Effective Is
the Writing? How
Can the Writing Be
Improved?

Reyez 1

Gabrielle Reyez

Professor Kuehner

English 151RW

11 March 2016

*Heading in MLA
format*

Enslaved by Technology

*Title suggests
writer's topic
and attitude.*

Call me old-fashioned, but what happened to the good old days
where a family could sit down and eat Sunday night dinner without the
constant distraction of a son or daughter pausing after each bite to post a
picture of the meatloaf mom made on *Facebook*? In a 2012 article "The
Flight from Conversation," written by psychologist Sherry Turkle, she
states, "We live in a technological universe in which we are always
communicating. And yet we have sacrificed conversation for mere
connection" (SR1). I couldn't agree more with Turkle; the more we stare
down at our phone screens the more we miss out on real life relationships
and experiences. We can send a text, e-mail, or tweet to talk to someone
now in hopes of avoiding a real face-to-face conversation with them. I am
guilty of this; I have found myself looking down at my phone time and time
again as I walk by someone just to avoid eye contact and what could be a
potentially awkward conversation.

*Opening example
gets reader's
interest*

*Effectively
introduces and
quotes a source*

*Page number is
cited after quote*

*First paragraph
is introduction*

*Thesis: Agrees
with Turkle that
phones make us
miss real
relationships*

Generations of all ages—young, middle-age and elderly—are all
affected by social media today whether it is emotionally, mentally, or
physically. In Turkle's article she quotes a 16-year-old boy saying,
"Someday, someday, but certainly not now, I'd like to learn how to have a
conversation" (SR1). Young people today fear real conversation because all
they know is digital connection. Social media are an on-going epidemic,
causing our future generation to be so oblivious to how detrimental

*Paragraph might
benefit from a
more focused
topic sentence*

Strong quote

*Topic sentence:
Focuses on the
effects of social
media*

307

Is poor writing the best example of social media effects?

technology is to us. My 12-year-old nephew recently turned in his essay for his history class, which contained the letter "U" for "You" and the word "Wat" for "What" throughout the paper. When his teacher and I asked him what happened, he stated he was so used to abbreviating words in text messages that he forgot to write them out for his paper. This however did not shock me one bit; if people are lacking communication skills, why wouldn't their literature also be affected? So much goes for the elderly as well. Turkle also goes on to give an example in her article about a research experiment she did at an eldercare facility involving a baby seal robot: "An older woman began to talk to it about the loss of her child. The robot seemed to be looking into her eyes. It seemed to be following the conversation. The woman was comforted" (SR1). Elderly are seeking out companionship and comfort in something that is not real. Whatever happened to the sit-down sessions with a counselor where they ask you "How are you feeling today"? When my grandmother was put in a retirement home, I religiously visited her and made sure she felt safe and was able to talk to me about how she was feeling so I could reassure her I was there for her comfort.

We think that *Facebook* and *Instagram* will make us less lonely, but what we don't realize is that it is these social media that are actually in fact making us lonelier. In the article "Is Facebook Making Us Lonely?" written by author Stephen Marche he describes how social media is taking a negative toll on generations as far as making us feel less happy and more alone. "We suffer from unprecedented alienation"; "We have less and less actual society. The more connected we become the lonelier we are"; "Facebook is interfering with our real friendships, distancing us from each other, making us lonelier," Marche writes in his article highlighting that *Facebook* in fact is a huge contribution to society's present isolation. A few years back I became close with a "friend" on *Facebook*; I didn't know who they were, what they looked like, or if they could even pronounce my name correctly. Nevertheless, I confided in this person and asked them for advice and

Quote is well integrated and cited.

Example effectively supports idea that human connection is important

Acknowledges source with title and author

Lots of quotes—maybe choose one?

Strong personal experience example

Support: Example of personal experience to support Turkle

Support: Example of personal experience to support Turkle

Topic sentence: Focuses on how social media negatively affects relationships

Support: Example of personal experience

looked to them for support when I felt alone. But at the time I needed them the most, when my life was falling apart, they were not there for me; my messages were unread and they were no longer "logged in." At that point was when I felt the most alone I ever felt and I had wished I went to my REAL friends for support and a shoulder to cry on.

What ever happened to speed dating? Or talking to the guy you sit by on the bus every morning who you've had a crush on since school started? Now it's online dating sites like *E-Harmony* or *Match.com* that people use to find their potential soul mate. Many people are fearful of commitment or real relationships, so they hide behind a computer monitor and create fake relationships to ease the pain they may experience from a breakup or insecurities. In Marche's article he quotes Sherry Turkle when he says, "These days, insecure in our relationships and anxious about intimacy, we look to technology for ways to be in relationships and protect ourselves from them at the same time" (qtd. in Marche). Back when I felt self-conscious about myself, I used *Facebook* Messenger to talk and get to know someone of the opposite sex on a deeper level. This took the weight of embarrassment off my shoulders because I didn't have to meet him and have a face-to-face conversation. As I was hidden behind my computer screen, I made this connection strictly through an online messenger, but yet at the end of the day I still didn't find happiness. I couldn't run to this guy and give him a big huge hug after a long day at work or hold his hand for support at the dentist. The fact that you can send a kiss face emoji through a message to replace a real passion-filled one should tell you something. We compromise real love and real relationships for fictional ones. Love is something that can be *written* instead of *felt* nowadays.

It has become clear to me after writing this that we cannot live a full and happy life without one another. At the end of the day we as humans are fundamental to one another. Instead of sending a text saying "I'm here," take the time to walk to your friend's door, knock, and let her know her chariot

Questions are engaging

Effectively names and quotes sources

Most of the support is personal experience—consider using other types?

Strong details

Support: List of online dating sites

Topic sentence: Focuses on how social media negatively affects relationships

Support: Example of personal experience

Conclusion: Sums up opinion about social media and advises readers how to use their devices wisely

awaits. It's the simple, daily, face-to-face conversations among us that we appreciate, not the 60-second careless text message. We live in a generation that is so infatuated by technological gadgets that we forget about what we should really be in love with: each other. So instead of being enslaved to your phone, put it down, take a deep breath, and look around you. Remember all the good, natural real things in life before you were captured by that thing you call a cellphone.

Nice reminder of the essay title

Works Cited starts on a new page

Works Cited

Maybe include more readings or sources in the paper?

Marche, Stephen. "Is Facebook Making Us Lonely?" *Writing to Read, Reading to Write*, edited by Alison Kuehner, McGraw-Hill Education, 2019, p. 328.

Turkle, Sherry. "The Flight from Conversation." *The New York Times*, 21 Apr. 2012, p. SR1.

List of sources alphabetized and written in MLA style

STUDENT PAPER 2

Now it is your turn to read and annotate a student paper. Read Kiel's paper twice, using the annotation strategies you have learned (summarized as follows) and the example of annotations on Reyez's paper to guide you.

- **First Reading: Annotating for Comprehension:** Note the title, underline main ideas, mark support, and write brief summaries in the margin.

- **Second Reading: Annotating for Evaluating and Analysis:** Write comments evaluating the effectiveness of the title, introduction, thesis, topic sentences, support, and conclusion. Notice, too, whether sources are used well and properly cited, and whether the paper is correctly formatted.

Before Reading: Predict

Write answers to these questions using complete sentences.

1. Review the "Writing Prompt," given earlier in this Spotlight section. Then consider the following questions: How would you respond to the question? What evidence would you use to support your response?

2. Review the "Writing Prompt." Then consider the following questions: How much of the essay should be devoted to explaining other people's ideas? How much of the essay should be the student's opinions, experiences, or observations?

 During Reading: Annotate; Analyze

3. As you read, underline the writer's thesis, main ideas, and supporting evidence. Identify the introduction, body paragraphs, topic sentences, and the conclusion. Analyze how effective the different parts of the paper are.

4. As you read, notice where the writer introduces and cites quotes or examples from the readings and how she creates a works cited page. Consider whether the citations and documentation are correct and whether the paper is properly formatted.

About the Author

Brittney Kiel

©Alison Kuehner

Brittney Kiel is attending community college to follow her dream of becoming a movie director and writer. She has been writing screenplays since she was ten years old and is obsessed with movies, so it makes sense that she is working toward a master's degree in fine arts. She identifies as African American, German, English, and Native American. Her advice to students in writing classes is to focus in class, read the material multiple times, take notes, and ask questions. Also, try your best to make every assignment interesting, because then you will have more to write about, and your paper will be interesting for your readers, too.

Answers

1. Answers will vary. Remind students they must use sources, such as articles, as well as personal experience for support.

2. An equal balance between use of sources and other people's ideas with the student's opinions and experiences would be effective.

Handout

A sample annotated essay appears in the Instructor's Manual.

Brittney Kiel

English 151RW

Professor A. Kuehner

9 March 2016

Less Is More

C. P. Snow once said that "Technology . . . is a queer thing. It brings you great gifts with one hand, and it stabs you in the back with the other hand." This means that as people we are so interested in what technology can give us that we fail to realize what it is taking from us. The excessive use of technology or, for example, social media is slowly taking us away from real relationships and taking us away from ourselves. In the article "Is Facebook Making Us Lonely?" by Stephen Marche, he states that a former *Playboy* playmate named Yvette Vickers was found dead in her home. Her body lay mummified by a heater that was still running, but the crazy thing is that her laptop was still on. Vickers had many fans on multiple social media sites, but what she was missing in life was real relationships. Marche gave us a perfect example of how social media can isolate people (328).

In a similar article called "The Flight from Conversation" by a psychologist named Sherry Turkle, she describes the negative effects of technology and how people are sacrificing conversation for a mere connection through social media. "We expect more from technology and less from one another and seem increasingly drawn to technologies that provide the illusion of companionship without the demands of relationship," says Turkle (SR1). I happen to agree. Social media isolate us from one another, and the things that we are lacking in real relationships we tend to search for online. For instance, we are so busy posting pictures of ourselves, posts of what we are doing and how we are feeling to gain the attention of others to make us feel important.

Marche also said that "we are all left thinking about who we are all the time, without ever really thinking about who we really are" (335). We are so busy pretending to be someone we are not and forgetting about who we really are. We desperately search for so many things through social media that we lack in ourselves, like acceptance, attention, happiness, and even love. No matter how many sites and apps that we download (*Facebook*, *Instagram*, *Twitter*, or *Snapchat*), we will never fill the emptiness we have inside that is making us feel lonely. If anything, it will make us feel even lonelier.

Another example of how social media isolate us is dating sites. There are dozens, if not hundreds, of dating sites and apps for people trying to find love or who are too afraid of a face-to-face relationship. On our profiles, we state all the things that are great about us, uploading our best photos, and in the description box we try to explain ourselves to be these amazing people. We even lie in the description box just to make ourselves look even more interesting in the eyes of others. Yet we don't comment on our flaws or post any natural pictures without editing. We are afraid that who we really are isn't good enough. And while we are so busy with our heads down stuck on all of these dating sites trying to find love and acceptance, we fail to see the men or women that pass us by on the streets that may very well be interested in us and could possibly be our soul mates. We decide to settle for online imaginary relationships that most of the time leave us feeling lonelier than before we created the profile. I'm speaking from personal experiences here.

I am one of the people that currently has a *Facebook*, *Instagram*, and *Twitter* account. When I first downloaded these apps, I did it because I wanted to feel more connected to my family and friends. But what I didn't realize is that the more I was on the social media, the further I strayed from face-to-face relationships. I began to become lazy, and the social media began to become my main source of communication with others and not just family or friends but strangers. Turkle writes, "I've learned that the little devices most of us carry around are so powerful that they change not only what we do, but also who we are" (SR1). At some point, I felt that I was losing myself to the social media and forgetting about who I really am by trying to make myself look as interesting as possible to those I thought cared.

There are a lot of people that feel they are not being isolated by social media. Ask yourselves this, when you wake up in the morning, do you check your social media apps? Before you go to bed, do you check your social media apps? When you are amongst company, are you always on your phone/tablet checking your social media sites? Still don't feel like you are being isolated? Ask yourselves this, when is the last time you were around company without checking your phone/tablet in your hand? When is the last time you went one whole day without checking your social media sites? How many times have you turned down going out with friends or family and found yourself at home on the social media for hours? You see, the social media does indeed isolate us and is somewhat taking over our lives. To some the social media are their life.

Now for the question "Do social media isolate or bring people together?" Though I feel they mainly isolate us, for some they do bring them together.

With all of these articles about the negative effects of the social media and what they do to us, there are some positive things that the social media can offer to people. For instance, if you have family or friends in other states or countries, social media allow you to keep in contact with them and share memories. For people that are starting their own business, the social media can help them spread the news and gain customers. For people that are trying to make it into the entertainment industry, the social media can help them make a name for themselves and help them gain fans. Social media have positive effects, but the positive effects are outweighed by the negative effects.

In my English class, we watched "Apple—Holiday, Misunderstood." It was about a family that got together for Christmas and a young boy that spent 100% of the time on his phone. The family couldn't see what he was doing on his phone; all they noticed was that his phone was glued to his hand. On Christmas morning while the family was opening their gifts, the young boy connected his phone to the television and played a video for his family. The whole time the young boy was on his phone, he was recording all the family activities and all of the things that they did together. He recorded a memory that his family will cherish forever. This is an example of one of the positive effects of technology and the social media. However, though the video showed the boy creating memories for his family, the young boy also missed out on being a part of the memory. With him spending so much time recording his family, he missed out on spending time with his family. The family will forever have this video of this specific Christmas, but what they won't have is the boy behind the camera in this special memory. My point is that we need to find a median between filming the memory and being a part of the memory!

So yes there are some positive effects that come from the social media, but they do not compare to the negative effects created. Since social media and technology were created, life has changed a lot. Instead of children going outside playing and meeting new friends, they are too busy inside on their tablets or on the computer. Instead of friends getting together and enjoying each other's company, they are too busy ignoring each other and hypnotized by the social media (I see it happen every day). When a fight breaks out, instead of people try to stop it, they are too busy getting out their phones to record it so they can post the violence online. Instead of finding love and real connections with people that are in our presence, we are too busy looking to the social media for temporary love and happiness. Social media have gotten out of control and continue to turn people into what I like to call "robots." We feel more comfortable being someone else online than being our real selves in person.

In conclusion, we will soon stray so far from ourselves that we will forget who we really are if we continue to live our lives through the social media. We need to take a few steps back and begin to find ourselves and also ask ourselves why we spend so much time on the social media. What is it that we are searching for, and how can we find it in ourselves? We as people need to work on our real relationships outside of the social media and begin to live in the moment instead of trying to film the moment. Every day we waste away on the social media is another day we forget about who we are and the closer we get to total and complete isolation. Aren't you tired of feeling lonely and trying to shape yourself into someone that you "think" others will love? As of today, I plan on spending more time finding out who I really am and less time trying to be what I think others want me to me. Today my loneliness ends.

Works Cited

"Apple—Holiday, Misunderstood." *YouTube*, uploaded by Avert.ge, 2 Jan. 2015,

www.youtube.com/watch?v=A_qOUyXCrEM.

Marche, Stephen. "Is Facebook Making Us Lonely?" *Writing to Read, Reading to*

Write, by Alison Kuehner, McGraw-Hill Education, 2019, p. 328.

Turkle, Sherry. "The Flight from Conversation." *The New York Times*, 12 Apr. 2012,

p. SR1.

Answers

5. The thesis is in the introduction: "The excessive use of technology or, for example, social media is slowly taking us away from real relationships and taking us away from ourselves."

6. The student uses three sources, which is effective; however, the student's own examples might be more specific, and she might have included more details or evidence from the readings and from the video.

7. Quotes and summaries are properly cited in the body paragraphs and on the works cited page.

8. Answers will vary, but students might point out that the student uses three different sources and develops her thesis over several paragraphs.

9. Answers will vary, but students might feel the writing is sometimes wordy or repetitive, and the examples could be more specific.

10. Answers will vary, but students might consider using a variety of sources in their papers, beginning paragraphs by referencing the sources and then responding to these.

After Reading: Evaluate the Argument

5. What is the writer's thesis? Is it clearly written?

6. Examine the body paragraphs. Are the main ideas effectively supported with evidence, such as factual evidence, quotes from experts, explanations, and examples? Do you think the student uses too much of her own experience or opinions and not enough research?

7. Examine the use of quotations and summaries from the readings. Does the writer use quotes and summaries effectively to support the main ideas? Are the sources of quotes and summaries identified and correctly cited?

8. What do you think are the most effective aspects of the student's essay? Be specific by referencing words or sentences, examples, or paragraphs that you feel are especially strong and explaining why.

9. Are there any parts of the essay you feel could be improved? If so, identify these specifically by referencing words or sentences, examples, or paragraphs and explaining how these could be stronger.

10. What aspects of this essay might you use in your own writing?

Spotlight Activity: Analyze Your Own Writing

If you completed an argument essay for your course, read and annotate your essay to understand and analyze the writing. Ask yourself these questions:

- Does the introduction establish the topic, get the reader's attention, and state the thesis?
- Do body paragraphs have topic sentences that relate to the thesis?
- Do body paragraphs contain relevant supporting information, such as quotations or summaries, from the readings?
- Is evidence used effectively to support the main ideas? Is there a logical connection between the evidence and the main idea of a paragraph?

- Are quotes integrated grammatically into sentences? Is there context for each quote? Is the source of the quotation correctly cited?
- Are summaries specific and detailed? Is the source of the summary identified and correctly cited?
- Does the conclusion explain why the information in the essay is important and bring the essay to a satisfying end?
- Does the title effectively represent the focus of the paper?

Apply What You Learned

1. Did you feel that one of the sample student papers was more convincing than the other, or were they equally effective? Explain your answer.

2. If you are currently working on a piece of writing for your English class or for any other subject, annotate and analyze the writing. Identify the main ideas and examples; then review the writing to examine the introduction, body paragraphs, use of support, conclusion, and citations. Use your annotations to help you evaluate and improve the writing.

3. What have you learned about analyzing student writing from reading this chapter, examining the annotated student paper, and annotating a student paper?

4. What have you learned about writing an effective essay using sources from studying the two student papers in this chapter?

Pair and Share

If you completed an argument essay for your course, exchange essays with a classmate. Read and annotate your classmate's essay. Then use the questions in the Spotlight Activity to provide feedback about your classmate's paper.

PART FOUR

Anthology of Theme-Based Readings

Do Social Media Connect Us—or Isolate Us?

Have you checked your *Facebook* page today? Did you take a selfie and post it on *Instagram*? Did you tweet about the latest gossip or news story? If so, you might be one of the almost 70 percent of Americans who use social media ("Social Media Fact Sheet").

If you did not answer "yes" to those questions or if you are not sure what social media are, consider the graphic image "Social Media Explained by My Donut" shown here. The icons and bold text running down the middle of the image identify various types of social media. The gray text gives humorous hints about the function of each social media application. For instance, because *YouTube* is a Web site on which users can post videos, one could "watch me eat donuts" on

What does the graphic reveal about how people relate to social media?

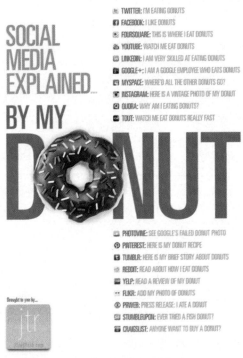

SOCIAL MEDIA EXPLAINED... BY MY DONUT

- **TWITTER:** I'M EATING DONUTS
- **FACEBOOK:** I LIKE DONUTS
- **FOURSQUARE:** THIS IS WHERE I EAT DONUTS
- **YOUTUBE:** WATCH ME EAT DONUTS
- **LINKEDIN:** I AM VERY SKILLED AT EATING DONUTS
- **GOOGLE+:** I AM A GOOGLE EMPLOYEE WHO EATS DONUTS
- **MYSPACE:** WHERE'D ALL THE OTHER DONUTS GO?
- **INSTAGRAM:** HERE IS A VINTAGE PHOTO OF MY DONUT
- **QUORA:** WHY AM I EATING DONUTS?
- **TOUT:** WATCH ME EAT DONUTS REALLY FAST

- **PHOTOVINE:** SEE GOOGLE'S FAILED DONUT PHOTO
- **PINTEREST:** HERE IS MY DONUT RECIPE
- **TUMBLR:** HERE IS MY BRIEF STORY ABOUT DONUTS
- **REDDIT:** READ ABOUT HOW I EAT DONUTS
- **YELP:** READ A REVIEW OF MY DONUT
- **FLIKR:** ADD MY PHOTO OF DONUTS
- **PRWEB:** PRESS RELEASE: I ATE A DONUT
- **STUMBLEUPON:** EVER TRIED A FISH DONUT?
- **CRAIGSLIST:** ANYONE WANT TO BUY A DONUT?

Brought to you by...
jtr

© J. Todd Rash http://jtoddrash.com/blog/
social-media-explained/

YouTube. See how many of the icons you recognize. (Because social media change constantly, some of the icons might already be out of date, or the latest social media applications may not be represented.)

Social media are designed to bring people together online to post pictures, comment to one another, rate restaurants, or create virtual hangouts. However, some people argue that the online community is not *real* or that people in fact go online to avoid interacting with people in real life. In this chapter, you will read some of the controversy over whether social media are really connecting us—or, instead, giving us the illusion of connection and making many of us feel more isolated behind our computer screens. As you read, consider the essay prompts in the following Read to Write Activity and the theme question "Do social media connect us—or isolate us?"

Read to Write Activity

Choose a Prompt for an Essay on the Effects of Social Media

Select one of the essay prompts that follow for help in focusing your reading and planning your essay as you navigate through the reading selections on this theme. Keywords before each prompt identify the type of essay.

Essay Prompts

1. Persuasive essay: The student union on your campus wants to provide space for students to socialize and interact, as members feel students too often rush from one class to the next without time to connect with one another. Union members are debating whether, on the one hand, to include computers and allow social media in that space or, on the other hand, to preserve the area as a "technology-free zone." Present a proposal to the student government explaining your view on whether the space for socializing should include access to social media.

2. Persuasive essay: Write a *perspectives* essay—that is, a short statement of personal opinion—for public radio listeners expressing your feelings about social media.

3. Response essay: Write a response to Sarah Weld explaining why you agree or disagree with her point of view.

4. Argument essay: Take a position on whether social media connect us or whether they isolate us. Draw from the articles in this section and from your own experiences with social media to develop your argument.

5. Argument essay: In the title of his essay, Stephen Marche asks, "Is Facebook Making Us Lonely?" Write an essay directed to your fellow classmates that answers this question.

6. Research paper: Conduct your own research by surveying students at your college about their use of social media. Compare your results with the data and the conclusions in the various readings in this thematic section of the

Class Activity

Search *YouTube* for videos about cell phone use or social media. Show an appropriate video in class to spark discussion on the effects of social media use before students read the selections in this chapter.

continued

anthology. Then draw a conclusion as to whether social media connect or isolate college students.

7. Research paper: In your college library, locate three articles that are academically appropriate on the effects of social media. Read the articles and compare their information and findings with the various readings in this thematic section of the anthology. Then draw a conclusion as to whether social media connect or isolate college students.

READING SELECTION

Connect

You will find a coordinated Power of Process assignment for this reading in your Connect course.

Teaching Tip

"Be Here Now" is partly a response to a 2013 Christmas holiday advertisement for the Apple iPhone titled "Misunderstood." Consider locating the ad and showing it to students before or after they read the selection. Ask students which viewpoint they most agree with and why.

Class Activity

Search online for Weld's perspective piece and play the podcast to students. Also, look for comments posted by listeners online about Weld's perspective—ask students with which comments they agree and with which they disagree.

"BE HERE NOW"

Complete the "Before Reading" assignment. Then read the selection while you complete the "During Reading" activities. Finally, complete the "After Reading" assignment.

 ### Before Reading: Recognize Prior Knowledge

Write answers to these questions using complete sentences.

1. Some people think it is important to put away cell phones to experience life fully. Others argue that using a cell phone can help us record memorable moments to share or to relive later. With which point of view do you agree more?

2. The title of the reading selection is "Be Here Now." To what do you think the title refers, and how does the title relate to cell phones?

 ### During Reading: Annotate

Complete the following exercises.

3. As you read, mark the main ideas.

4. Identify and underline any sentences that you agree or disagree with, and state why.

Answers

1. Answers will vary. Encourage students to give specific examples to support their opinion.

2. The title suggests that people should be present in the moment and not using their cell phones to record events.

Answers

3. Sarah Weld urges listeners to put away their cell phones and live in the moment rather than take a photograph.

4. Answers will vary. Encourage students to give specific examples to support their opinion.

Be Here Now

By Sarah Weld

KQED Radio, 17 January 2014

KQED is a public radio station in the San Francisco Bay Area. The radio station invites members of the public to give their "perspectives," or personal views, on any issue that might be of interest to listeners. This perspective is meant to be read aloud on the radio in two minutes. Sarah Weld's piece is one of those perspectives.

Last month, my husband taught my son to shave. They stood side by side, faces covered in white lather, chins tilted at the same angle, sliding their razors up and down. I watched them for a minute in the mirror, and considered snapping a photo and posting it on Facebook. But I thought better of it. I watched them a little longer, and then, feeling like I was intruding, I left. As I walked up the stairs, I thought about having a son old enough to shave, about everything that follows—the looming empty nest, college and beyond.   1

Apple just released an ad for its new iPhone. It chronicles several days of a family gathering for Christmas, with a teenage boy perpetually in the background on his smartphone. We see him not participating in building a snowman, then retreating to his device after hanging a single ornament. Staring at his eerily glowing phone, he perches on the side of an outdoor ice rink, his skate-shod feet dangling below. But then, on Christmas morning, he turns on the TV—cue the sappy music—and the entire family watches his heartwarming video of the events he had removed himself from, spliced together expertly in a moving tribute to family togetherness. Turns out he was actually focused on the family the whole time, which in Apple's world makes it all better.   2

Okay, so I will admit the ad made me tear up a little bit. But I ask all of us: is it really better to have produced a touching video of family experiences instead of truly living the experiences? We see this boy hand a carrot to a young cousin for the snowman, never lifting his eyes from his phone. Wouldn't it be more meaningful if he put it away, and helped roll a snowball or two? Why is it better for him to film the skating than hit the ice himself?   3

Sometimes, reacting to images exploding on Instagram and Facebook, I consider taking and posting a photo. Yesterday a tall stand of red trees, their leaves aflame, stopped me. I pulled over to look. And then I drove on.   4

With a Perspective, I am Sarah Weld.   5

Sarah Weld, "Be Here Now" KQED Radio, January 17, 2014. Used with permission of Sarah Weld.

 After Reading: Summarize

Write a response to the following exercise using complete sentences.

5. Review your annotations. Then state the thesis and main ideas in your own words.

Answers

1. Weld begins with the example of her husband and son to illustrate how she chose to observe the moment and not intrude by taking a picture with her phone, which supports her main idea that people should experience the moment, not try to record it with their phones.

2. The author suggests that one should live the experiences, because time spent with family would be more meaningful if the boy in the ad participated in the family activities.

3. "Be Here Now" sums up the main idea that people should live in the moment and not try to use their phones to record events.

Teaching Tip

As a class, students can compare vocabulary words for this reading and for the other readings in this section with an eye to selecting the words they feel are most crucial for understanding the theme. Students can pick the top ten words, then write original sentences using the vocabulary words for practice.

Read to Write Activity

Engage with the Reading

Refer to the reading as you complete these activities.

1. Why does Weld begin with the example of her husband teaching her teenage son to shave? How does this example relate to the Apple iPhone ad she describes in the following paragraph? Do you think this is a good strategy for beginning the piece?

2. Weld asks, "Is it really better to have produced a touching video of family experiences instead of truly living the experiences?" (323) What is the author's answer? What is your answer?

3. Why do you think the piece is titled "Be Here Now"? How does the title reflect the main idea of the reading?

Pair and Share

With a classmate, compare your answers to question 2 in the "Engage with the Reading" Read to Write Activity. Try to think of answers that would both support and refute the author's point of view.

Vocabulary Strategy: Building Personal Vocabulary

Identify and list five words from the reading selection that you do not know or do not know well. Use context clues or word analysis to guess their meaning. Then consult a dictionary to look up each word and find a meaning that fits the context of the passage. Write down that definition.

READING SELECTION

Connect

You will find a coordinated Power of Process assignment for this reading in your Connect course.

Class Activity

Ask students to think of recent events in which cell phones have been used by ordinary people to share information, to generate discussion on the topic.

"ADAPT TO INACCURACY IN SOCIAL MEDIA"

Complete the "Before Reading" assignment. Then read the selection while you complete the "During Reading" activities. Finally, complete the "After Reading" assignment.

Before Reading: Recognize Prior Knowledge

Write answers to these questions using complete sentences.

1. In what ways can a cell phone be used in an emergency situation? Give examples.

2. The reading makes reference to the Boston Marathon bombing. What do you know about this incident? If you don't know or are not sure what the Boston Marathon bombing was, do some research and summarize the event in one or two sentences.

 # During Reading: Annotate

Complete the following exercises.

3. As you read, mark the main ideas.

4. Identify and underline any sentences that you agree or disagree with, and state why.

Adapt to Inaccuracy in Social Media

By Larisa Manescu

The Daily Texan, 24 April 2013

Manescu was a sophomore at the University of Texas at Austin when she wrote the following commentary. She is from Ploiesti, Romania, and majored in international relations and global studies.

It's a common sight at concerts nowadays: Instead of freely embracing the moment, the members of the smartphone-equipped crowd are more concerned with having their phones in the air, ready to document the experience for the social media realm. 1

But besides providing a new source of distraction, this attachment to our phones can also prove useful. In an emergency situation, an ordinary spectator has the technology to transform into a citizen journalist that documents not just concerts but also highly valuable information. 2

Chances are that you first heard about the Boston Marathon explosions through social media, whether from a Reddit post, a tweet, a Facebook status or some combination of the three. 3

While UT [University of Texas] students were sitting in class or at work or taking a nap at home, spectators at the Boston Marathon were suffering fatal wounds, rushing fellow runners to receive emergency care and desperately looking for loved ones, while simultaneously producing written and visual updates on the unfolding activity. 4

Within an hour of the attack, both traditional and alternative news sites began accumulating and organizing information about the bombing provided by those at the site of the tragedy to create a cohesive narrative. 5

Live coverage of the Boston explosions by both amateur and professional journalists served many purposes. It kept people around the world informed by capturing developments as they occurred, including heartwarming acts of heroism and empathy. It also captured the raw emotion of the atmosphere and provided valuable primary photo resources that the FBI later used to identify the suspects. 6

Answers

1. Answers will vary. Encourage students to give specific examples to support their opinion.

2. The Boston Marathon bombing refers to a 2013 incident in which two men set off bombs during the Boston Marathon, killing three people and seriously injuring several others.

Answers

3. People can use their cell phones to record newsworthy events, such as the Boston Marathon bombing. While social media reports can be informative, the public as well as journalists need to distinguish accurate news from false rumors.

4. Answers will vary. Encourage students to give specific examples to support their opinion.

UT journalism professor Robert Quigley, the former social media editor at the *Austin American-Statesman*, believes you cannot overstate the importance of new technology as a platform for journalists.

"You're out there, you're scraping, you're breaking things as they go and you're using Twitter," Quigley says. "If you're not comfortable in that world, this is a difficult profession for you right now."

However, as journalists increasingly use social media to reach the public, the repercussions of mistakes become more severe. It's not that there are more errors; it's that those errors stick. The mass of information shared after the Boston explosions caused mistakes in professional reporting and media coverage which were then carried rapidly across social media, triggering a vicious cycle of regurgitated misinformation. It was overwhelming, frustrating and sobering to see how an injured witness evolved into a Saudi suspect in the news, or how a Brown University student who has been missing since March became a target of suspicion on Reddit, resulting in the online harassment of his already-grieving family. That piece of misinformation was also picked up by major news organizations such as Politico, Buzzfeed and *Newsweek*, which then spread it across the web.

Scrutiny, however, can be a difficult skill for journalists to maintain when they are wrapped up in the adrenaline of sharing the latest update.

Andy Carvin, the senior product manager for online communications for National Public Radio, gave a talk about social media and the Boston explosions at the International Symposium for Online Journalism in Austin last weekend.

Carvin highlighted mistakes made by the press in coverage of the April 15 attack under the pressure to keep social media consistently updated.

"It's never been easier to spread rumors," Carvin said.

However, instead of criticizing social media for distorting the ethics of journalism, as some journalism professionals do, Carvin urged the media to think progressively about their relationship to the public. Instead of merely informing the public by telling it what the media thinks it should know, Carvin made the distinction that the media should create a more informed public, or "better consumers and producers of information."

Instead of merely slapping "breaking news" on the latest tweets, examples of engagement included organizations being more transparent about what they know by actively addressing rumors on social media platforms instead of pretending they don't exist and talking to the public about where they came from, even if this means a major news organization admitting its own factual error.

"We should help them to understand what it means to confirm something. Confirming is not just sharing something you heard on Facebook from a friend or brother-in-law," Carvin said. "Reporting is no longer enough."

The public needs this wake-up call in order to become skeptical, active consumers instead of passive re-tweeters. Just yesterday, I saw not only friends but fellow journalists re-tweet breaking news from the Associated Press that the White House had been bombed and President Barack Obama was injured. The tweet was false; the AP Twitter account had been hacked. They may be forgiven for trusting the AP as the credible source it normally is, but the fact remains that they didn't hesitate to verify the information, even in light of recent bomb-related misinformation. We must acknowledge the journalistic problems of social media before we can move forward.

My suggestion: Don't hate the game, train the players. Social media isn't just one aspect of the news process; it is intrinsically wrapped up within the news cycle and it's not going away. Surely, the platform will change, but the effects of information dissemination persists. It is a force that cannot be ignored or detested. Instead, its relationship to journalism should be analyzed and better understood.

18

Larisa Manescu, "Adapt to inaccuracy in social media" *The Daily Texan*, April 24, 2013. Used by permission of the University of Texas at Austin, Texas Student Media.

 ## After Reading: Summarize

Write an answer using complete sentences.

5. Review your annotations. Then state the thesis and main ideas in your own words.

Read to Write Activity

Engage with the Reading

Refer to the reading selection as you complete these exercises.

1. In what ways can cell phones or social media enable journalists to accurately report the news?

2. In what ways can cell phones or social media be used, intentionally or not, to spread disinformation?

3. What does Manescu mean when she writes, "Don't hate the game, train the players"? For instance, how does this concept relate to journalists using social media?

Pair and Share

With a classmate, compare your responses to exercises 1 and 2 in "Engage with the Reading." Make a list of ways that cell phones and social media can be used to accurately report information or to spread false information. Include examples from the reading selection, as well as your own experiences, to illustrate.

Vocabulary Strategy: Building Personal Vocabulary

Identify and list five words from the reading selection that you do not know or do not know well. Use context clues or word analysis to guess their meaning. Then consult a dictionary to look up each word and find a meaning that fits the context of the passage. Write down that definition.

Answers

5. Cell phones can be used frivolously or in emergencies, such as they were during the Boston Marathon bombing to contact loved ones. However, cell phones can also spread false reports and rumors. Professional journalists under pressure to report stories quickly are not immune to making mistakes and need to verify social media posts, even from credible-looking sources.

Answers

1. Eyewitness videos can provide immediate information about events.

2. If information is not checked before it is passed along, false information can rapidly spread.

3. The author means that rather than abandon social media as a tool for journalists, journalists need to learn how to use social media responsibly to accurately report news.

READING SELECTION

Connect

You will find a coordinated Power of Process assignment for this reading in your Connect course.

Answers

1. Answers will vary. Encourage students to give specific examples of how they use *Facebook* or specific reasons why they do not.

2. Answers will vary. Students might think that if someone does not have friends on *Facebook* or if friends don't reply to posts, then a person might feel lonely.

Answers

3. Section 1: Yvette Vickers's lonesome death represents how people are connected online but not in real life. Section 2: How one uses social media—for instance, to write "composed communication" or to simply "like" a post—will influence one's feelings of connectedness. Section 3: One's loneliness depends on social networks and friends outside of social media. Section 4: Social media doesn't make people lonely, but it makes it easier for people to retreat from real interactions.

4. Answers will vary. Encourage students to provide specific examples and details to support why they agree or disagree.

"IS FACEBOOK MAKING US LONELY?"

Complete the "Before Reading" assignment. Then read the selection while you complete the "During Reading" activities. Finally, complete the "After Reading" assignment.

 ### Before Reading: Recognize Prior Knowledge

Write answers to these questions using complete sentences.

1. Do you use *Facebook*? If so, why do you use it? If not, why not?

2. The title of the reading selection is "Is Facebook Making Us Lonely?" Why do you think some people may feel that a social media tool, such as *Facebook*, would make people feel lonely?

 ### During Reading: Annotate

Complete the following exercises.

3. The words in all capital letters divide the reading into four sections. As you read, mark the main ideas in each section. Then state the main idea of each section in your own words.

4. Identify and underline any sentences that you agree or disagree with, and state why.

Is Facebook Making Us Lonely?

By Stephen Marche

The Atlantic, May 2012

Stephen Marche is a Canadian writer who has authored several books and who writes frequently for magazines, such as The Atlantic.

YVETTE VICKERS, a former Playboy playmate and B-movie star, best known for her role in *Attack of the 50 Foot Woman*, would have been 83 last August, but nobody knows exactly how old she was when she died. According to the Los Angeles coroner's report, she lay dead for the better part of a year before a neighbor and fellow actress, a woman named Susan Savage, noticed cobwebs and yellowing letters in her mailbox, reached through a broken window to unlock the door, and pushed her way through the piles of junk mail and mounds of clothing that barricaded the house. Upstairs, she found Vickers's body, mummified, near a heater that was still running. Her computer was on too, its glow permeating the empty space.

1

The *Los Angeles Times* posted a story headlined "Mummified Body of Former Playboy Playmate Yvette Vickers Found in Her Benedict Canyon Home," which quickly went viral. Within two weeks, by Technorati's count, Vickers's lonesome

2

death was already the subject of 16,057 Facebook posts and 881 tweets. She had long been a horror-movie icon, a symbol of Hollywood's capacity to exploit our most basic fears in the silliest ways; now she was an icon of a new and different kind of horror: our growing fear of loneliness. Certainly she received much more attention in death than she did in the final years of her life. With no children, no religious group, and no immediate social circle of any kind, she had begun, as an elderly woman, to look elsewhere for companionship. Savage later told *Los Angeles* magazine that she had searched Vickers's phone bills for clues about the life that led to such an end. In the months before her grotesque death, Vickers had made calls not to friends or family but to distant fans who had found her through fan conventions and Internet sites.

Vickers's web of connections had grown broader but shallower, as has happened for many of us. We are living in an isolation that would have been unimaginable to our ancestors, and yet we have never been more accessible. Over the past three decades, technology has delivered to us a world in which we need not be out of contact for a fraction of a moment. In 2010, at a cost of $300 million, 800 miles of fiber-optic cable was laid between the Chicago Mercantile Exchange and the New York Stock Exchange to shave three milliseconds off trading times. Yet within this world of instant and absolute communication, unbounded by limits of time or space, we suffer from unprecedented alienation. We have never been more detached from one another, or lonelier. In a world consumed by ever more novel modes of socializing, we have less and less actual society. We live in an accelerating contradiction: the more connected we become, the lonelier we are. We were promised a global village; instead we inhabit the drab cul-de-sacs and endless freeways of a vast suburb of information. 3

At the forefront of all this unexpectedly lonely interactivity is Facebook, with 845 million users and $3.7 billion in revenue last year. The company hopes to raise $5 billion in an initial public offering [IPO] later this spring, which will make it by far the largest Internet IPO in history. Some recent estimates put the company's potential value at $100 billion, which would make it larger than the global coffee industry—one addiction preparing to surpass the other. Facebook's scale and reach are hard to comprehend: last summer, Facebook became, by some counts, the first Web site to receive 1 trillion page views in a month. In the last three months of 2011, users generated an average of 2.7 billion "likes" and comments every day. On whatever scale you care to judge Facebook—as a company, as a culture, as a country—it is vast beyond imagination. 4

Despite its immense popularity, or more likely because of it, Facebook has, from the beginning, been under something of a cloud of suspicion. The depiction of Mark Zuckerberg, in *The Social Network*, as a bastard with symptoms of Asperger's syndrome, was nonsense. But it felt true. It felt true to Facebook, if not to Zuckerberg. The film's most indelible scene, the one that may well have earned it an Oscar, was the final, silent shot of an anomic Zuckerberg sending out a friend request to his ex-girlfriend, then waiting and clicking and waiting and clicking—a moment of superconnected loneliness preserved in amber. We have all been in that scene: transfixed by the glare of a screen, hungering for response. 5

When you sign up for Google+ and set up your Friends circle, the program specifies that you should include only "your real friends, the ones you feel 6 comfortable sharing private details with." That one little phrase, Your real friends—so quaint, so charmingly mothering—perfectly encapsulates the anxieties that social media have produced: the fears that Facebook is interfering with our real friendships, distancing us from each other, making us lonelier; and that social networking might be spreading the very isolation it seemed designed to conquer. . . .

WELL BEFORE FACEBOOK, digital technology was enabling our tendency for isolation, to an unprecedented degree. Back in the 1990s, scholars started calling the contradiction between an increased opportunity to connect and a lack of human contact the "Internet paradox." A prominent 1998 article on the phenomenon by a team of researchers at Carnegie Mellon showed that increased Internet usage was already coinciding with increased loneliness. Critics of the study pointed out that the two groups that participated in the study—high-school journalism students who were heading to university and socially active members of community-development boards—were statistically likely to become lonelier over time. Which brings us to a more fundamental question: Does the Internet make people lonely, or are lonely people more attracted to the Internet? 7

The question has intensified in the Facebook era. A recent study out of Australia (where close to half the population is active on Facebook), titled "Who Uses Facebook?," found a complex and sometimes confounding relationship between loneliness and social networking. Facebook users had slightly lower levels of "social loneliness"—the sense of not feeling bonded with friends—but "significantly higher levels of family loneliness"—the sense of not feeling bonded with family. It may be that Facebook encourages more contact with people outside of our household, at the expense of our family relationships—or it may be that people who have unhappy family relationships in the first place seek companionship through other means, including Facebook. The researchers also found that lonely people are inclined to spend more time on Facebook: "One of the most noteworthy findings," they wrote, "was the tendency for neurotic and lonely individuals to spend greater amounts of time on Facebook per day than non-lonely individuals." And they found that neurotics are more likely to prefer to use the wall, while extroverts tend to use chat features in addition to the wall. 8

Moira Burke, until recently a graduate student at the Human-Computer Institute at Carnegie Mellon, used to run a longitudinal study of 1,200 Facebook users. That study, which is ongoing, is one of the first to step outside the realm of self-selected college students and examine the effects of Facebook on a broader population, over time. She concludes that the effect of Facebook depends on what you bring to it. Just as your mother said: you get out only what you put in. If you use Facebook to communicate directly with other individuals—by using the "like" button, commenting on friends' posts, and so on—it can increase your social capital. Personalized messages, or what Burke calls "composed communication," are more satisfying than "one-click communication"—the lazy click of a like. "People who received composed communication became less lonely, while people who received one-click communication experienced no change in loneliness," Burke tells me. So, you should inform your friend in writing how charming her son looks with Harry Potter cake smeared all over his face, and how interesting her sepia-toned photograph of that tree-framed bit of skyline is, and how cool it is that she's at whatever concert 9 she happens to be at. That's what we all want to hear. Even better than sending a private Facebook message is the semi-public conversation, the kind of back-and-forth in which you half ignore the other people who may be listening in. "People whose friends write to them semi-publicly on Facebook experience decreases in loneliness," Burke says.

On the other hand, non-personalized use of Facebook—scanning your friends' status updates and updating the world on your own activities via your wall, or what Burke calls "passive consumption" and "broadcasting"—correlates to feelings of disconnectedness. It's a lonely business, wandering the labyrinths of our friends' and pseudo-friends' projected identities, trying to figure out what part of ourselves we ought to project, who will listen, and what they will hear. According to Burke, passive consumption of Facebook also correlates to a marginal increase in depression. "If two women each talk to their friends the same amount of time, but one of them spends more time reading about friends on Facebook as well, the one reading tends to grow slightly more depressed," Burke says. Her conclusion suggests that my sometimes unhappy reactions to Facebook may be more universal than I had realized. When I scroll through page after page of my friends' descriptions of how accidentally eloquent their kids are, and how their husbands are endearingly bumbling, and how they're all about to eat a home-cooked meal prepared with fresh local organic produce bought at the farmers' market and then go for a jog and maybe check in at the office because they're so busy getting ready to hop on a plane for a week of luxury dogsledding in Lapland, I do grow slightly more miserable. A lot of other people doing the same thing feel a little bit worse, too.

Still, Burke's research does not support the assertion that Facebook creates loneliness. The people who experience loneliness on Facebook are lonely away from Facebook, too, she points out; on Facebook, as everywhere else, correlation is not causation. The popular kids are popular, and the lonely skulkers skulk alone. Perhaps it says something about me that I think Facebook is primarily a platform for lonely skulking. I mention to Burke the widely reported study, conducted by a Stanford graduate student, that showed how believing that others have strong social networks can lead to feelings of depression. What does Facebook communicate, if not the impression of social bounty? Everybody else looks so happy on Facebook, with so many friends, that our own social networks feel emptier than ever in comparison. Doesn't that make people feel lonely? "If people are reading about lives that are much better than theirs, two things can happen," Burke tells me. "They can feel worse about themselves, or they can feel motivated."

Burke will start working at Facebook as a data scientist this year.

JOHN CACIOPPO, THE director of the Center for Cognitive and Social Neuroscience at the University of Chicago, is the world's leading expert on loneliness. In his landmark book, *Loneliness*, released in 2008, he revealed just how profoundly the epidemic of loneliness is affecting the basic functions of human physiology. He found higher levels of epinephrine, the stress hormone, in the morning urine of lonely people. Loneliness burrows deep: "When we drew blood from our older adults and analyzed their white cells," he writes, "we found that loneliness somehow penetrated the deepest recesses of the cell to alter the way

10

11

12

13

genes were being expressed." Loneliness affects not only the brain, then, but the basic process of DNA transcription. When you are lonely, your whole body is lonely.

To Cacioppo, Internet communication allows only ersatz intimacy. "Forming connections with pets or online friends or even God is a noble attempt by an obligatorily gregarious creature to satisfy a compelling need," he writes. "But surrogates can never make up completely for the absence of the real thing." The "real thing" being actual people, in the flesh. When I speak to Cacioppo, he is refreshingly clear on what he sees as Facebook's effect on society. Yes, he allows, some research has suggested that the greater the number of Facebook friends a person has, the less lonely she is. But he argues that the impression this creates can be misleading. "For the most part," he says, "people are bringing their old friends, and feelings of loneliness or connectedness, to Facebook." The idea that a Web site could deliver a more friendly, interconnected world is bogus. The depth of one's social network outside Facebook is what determines the depth of one's social network within Facebook, not the other way around. Using social media doesn't create new social networks; it just transfers established networks from one platform to another. For the most part, Facebook doesn't destroy friendships—but it doesn't create them, either. 14

In one experiment, Cacioppo looked for a connection between the loneliness of subjects and the relative frequency of their interactions via Facebook, chat rooms, online games, dating sites, and face-to-face contact. The results were unequivocal. "The greater the proportion of face-to-face interactions, the less lonely you are," he says. "The greater the proportion of online interactions, the lonelier you are." Surely, I suggest to Cacioppo, this means that Facebook and the like inevitably make people lonelier. He disagrees. Facebook is merely a tool, he says, and like any tool, its effectiveness will depend on its user. "If you use Facebook to increase face-to-face contact," he says, "it increases social capital." So if social media let you organize a game of football among your friends, that's healthy. If you turn to social media instead of playing football, however, that's unhealthy. 15

"Facebook can be terrific, if we use it properly," Cacioppo continues. "It's like a car. You can drive it to pick up your friends. Or you can drive alone." But hasn't the car increased loneliness? If cars created the suburbs, surely they also created isolation. "That's because of how we use cars," Cacioppo replies. "How we use these technologies can lead to more integration, rather than more isolation." 16

The problem, then, is that we invite loneliness, even though it makes us miserable. The history of our use of technology is a history of isolation desired and achieved. When the Great Atlantic and Pacific Tea Company opened its A&P stores, giving Americans self-service access to groceries, customers stopped having relationships with their grocers. When the telephone arrived, people stopped knocking on their neighbors' doors. Social media bring this process to a much wider set of relationships. Researchers at the HP Social Computing Lab who studied the nature of people's connections on Twitter came to a depressing, if not surprising, conclusion: "Most of the links declared within Twitter were meaningless from an interaction point of view." I have to wonder: What other point of view is meaningful? 17

LONELINESS IS CERTAINLY not something that Facebook or Twitter or any of the lesser forms of social media is doing to us. We are doing it to ourselves. Casting technology as some vague, impersonal spirit of history forcing our actions is a weak 18 excuse. We make decisions about how we use our machines, not the other way around. Every time I shop at my local grocery store, I am faced with a choice. I can buy my groceries from a human being or from a machine. I always, without exception, choose the machine. It's faster and more efficient, I tell myself, but the truth is that I prefer not having to wait with the other customers who are lined up alongside the conveyor belt: the hipster mom who disapproves of my high-carbon-footprint pineapple; the lady who tenses to the point of tears while she waits to see if the gods of the credit-card machine will accept or decline; the old man whose clumsy feebleness requires a patience that I don't possess. Much better to bypass the whole circus and just ring up the groceries myself.

19 Our omnipresent new technologies lure us toward increasingly superficial connections at exactly the same moment that they make avoiding the mess of human interaction easy. The beauty of Facebook, the source of its power, is that it enables us to be social while sparing us the embarrassing reality of society—the accidental revelations we make at parties, the awkward pauses, the farting and the spilled drinks and the general gaucherie of face-to-face contact. Instead, we have the lovely smoothness of a seemingly social machine. Everything's so simple: status updates, pictures, your wall.

20 But the price of this smooth sociability is a constant compulsion to assert one's own happiness, one's own fulfillment. Not only must we contend with the social bounty of others; we must foster the appearance of our own social bounty. Being happy all the time, pretending to be happy, actually attempting to be happy—it's exhausting. Last year a team of researchers led by Iris Mauss at the University of Denver published a study looking into "the paradoxical effects of valuing happiness." Most goals in life show a direct correlation between valuation and achievement. Studies have found, for example, that students who value good grades tend to have higher grades than those who don't value them. Happiness is an exception. The study came to a disturbing conclusion:

21 Valuing happiness is not necessarily linked to greater happiness. In fact, under certain conditions, the opposite is true. Under conditions of low (but not high) life stress, the more people valued happiness, the lower were their hedonic balance, psychological well-being, and life satisfaction, and the higher their depression symptoms.

22 The more you try to be happy, the less happy you are. Sophocles made roughly the same point.

23 Facebook, of course, puts the pursuit of happiness front and center in our digital life. Its capacity to redefine our very concepts of identity and personal fulfillment is much more worrisome than the data-mining and privacy practices that have aroused anxieties about the company. Two of the most compelling critics of Facebook—neither of them a Luddite—concentrate on exactly this point. Jaron Lanier, the author of *You Are Not a Gadget*, was one of the inventors of virtual-reality technology. His view of where social media are taking us reads like dystopian science fiction: "I fear that we are beginning to design ourselves to suit digital models of us, and I worry about a leaching of empathy and humanity in that process." Lanier argues that Facebook imprisons us in the business of self-presenting, and this, to his mind, is the site's crucial and fatally unacceptable downside.

Sherry Turkle, a professor of computer culture at MIT who in 1995 published the   24
digital-positive analysis *Life on the Screen*, is much more skeptical about the effects
of online society in her 2011 book, *Alone Together*: "These days, insecure in our
relationships and anxious about intimacy, we look to technology for ways to be in
relationships and protect ourselves from them at the same time." The problem with
digital intimacy is that it is ultimately incomplete: "The ties we form through the
Internet are not, in the end, the ties that bind. But they are the ties that preoccupy,"
she writes. "We don't want to intrude on each other, so instead we constantly
intrude on each other, but not in 'real time.'"

A A Lanier and Turkle are right, at least in their diagnoses. Self-presentation on   25
Facebook is continuous, intensely mediated, and possessed of a phony
nonchalance that eliminates even the potential for spontaneity. ("Look how casually
I threw up these three photos from the party at which I took 300 photos!") Curating
the exhibition of the self has become a 24/7 occupation. Perhaps not surprisingly,
then, the Australian study "Who Uses Facebook?" found a significant correlation
between Facebook use and narcissism: "Facebook users have higher levels of total
narcissism, exhibitionism, and leadership than Facebook nonusers," the study's
authors wrote. "In fact, it could be argued that Facebook specifically gratifies the
narcissistic individual's need to engage in self-promoting and superficial behavior."

Rising narcissism isn't so much a trend as the trend behind all other trends. In   26
preparation for the 2013 edition of its diagnostic manual, the psychiatric profession is
currently struggling to update its definition of narcissistic personality disorder. Still,
generally speaking, practitioners agree that narcissism manifests in patterns of fantastic
grandiosity, craving for attention, and lack of empathy. In a 2008 survey, 35,000 American
respondents were asked if they had ever had certain symptoms of narcissistic personality
disorder. Among people older than 65, 3 percent reported symptoms. Among people in
their 20s, the proportion was nearly 10 percent. Across all age groups, one in 16
Americans has experienced some symptoms of NPD. And loneliness and narcissism are
intimately connected: a longitudinal study of Swedish women demonstrated a strong link
between levels of narcissism in youth and levels of loneliness in old age. The connection
is fundamental. Narcissism is the flip side of loneliness, and either condition is a fighting
retreat from the messy reality of other people.

A considerable part of Facebook's appeal stems from its miraculous fusion of   27
distance with intimacy, or the illusion of distance with the illusion of intimacy. Our
online communities become engines of self-image, and self-image becomes the
engine of community. The real danger with Facebook is not that it allows us to
isolate ourselves, but that by mixing our appetite for isolation with our vanity, it
threatens to alter the very nature of solitude. The new isolation is not of the kind
that Americans once idealized, the lonesomeness of the proudly nonconformist,
independent-minded, solitary stoic, or that of the astronaut who blasts into new
worlds. Facebook's isolation is a grind. What's truly staggering about Facebook
usage is not its volume—750 million photographs uploaded over a single
weekend—but the constancy of the performance it demands. More than half its
users—and one of every 13 people on Earth is a Facebook user—log on every day.
Among 18-to-34-year-olds, nearly half check Facebook minutes after waking up, and
28 percent do so before getting out of bed. The relentlessness is what is so new, so
potentially transformative. Facebook never takes a break. We never take a break.
Human beings have always created elaborate acts of self-presentation. But not all

the time, not every morning, before we even pour a cup of coffee. Yvette Vickers's computer was on when she died.

Nostalgia for the good old days of disconnection would not just be pointless, it would be hypocritical and ungrateful. But the very magic of the new machines, the efficiency and elegance with which they serve us, obscures what isn't being served: everything that matters. What Facebook has revealed about human nature—and this is not a minor revelation—is that a connection is not the same thing as a bond, and that instant and total connection is no salvation, no ticket to a happier, better world or a more liberated version of humanity. Solitude used to be good for self-reflection and self-reinvention. But now we are left thinking about who we are all the time, without ever really thinking about who we are. Facebook denies us a pleasure whose profundity we had underestimated: the chance to forget about ourselves for a while, the chance to disconnect.

28

 ## After Reading: Reflect on the Text

Write your response using complete sentences.

5. What ideas in the text are new to you? What ideas in the text conflict with what you already knew before you started reading?

Answers

5. Answers will vary. Encourage students to look back at their annotations to find ideas that are new or not.

Read to Write Activity

Engage with the Reading

Refer to the reading selection as you complete these exercises.

1. Why does Marche begin with the example of Yvette Vickers? How does her death relate to the question of whether *Facebook* makes people lonely? Do you feel this is an effective way to begin the reading?

2. In what ways can social media be used to connect people or bring them together?

3. In what ways can social media be used to make people feel lonely or disconnected?

Answers

1. The example of Vickers illustrates vividly how someone can be connected via social media but not have any meaningful relationships in real life. The example is an effective way to get readers interested in the topic.

2. If social media are used in active ways, such as to write messages to family or to organize meetups in the real world, then they can connect people, according to Burke and Cacioppo.

3. If social media are used in passive ways, such as to "like" someone or to scan updates, then they can contribute to feelings of loneliness.

Pair and Share

With a classmate, compare your answers to exercises 2 and 3 in "Engage with the Reading." Make a list of ways that social media can be used to bring people together or to make them feel disconnected. Include examples from the reading selection, as well as your own experiences, to illustrate both sides.

Vocabulary Strategy: Building Personal Vocabulary

Identify and list five words from the reading selection that you do not know or do not know well. Use context clues or word analysis to guess their meaning. Then consult a dictionary to look up each word and find a meaning that fits the context of the passage. Write down that definition.

Theme Activity: Write in Response to a Chosen Prompt 📖 ✍️

1. Review the prompt you chose for your essay. What is your purpose, and who is your audience?

2. Review your notes on the reading selections for this theme. Prewrite about your topic to generate additional ideas. Do additional research if necessary or required by your instructor.

3. Create an informal outline, graphic organizer, or essay plan that organizes your notes and includes a topic sentence for each paragraph.

4. Write a thesis statement that sums up the main ideas, gives your point of view, and reflects the organizational pattern of your paper.

5. Draft the introduction, body paragraphs, and conclusion for your essay using your thesis statement and your outline, graphic organizer, or essay plan.

6. Revise your essay for coherence and unity. Edit and proofread for errors in grammar and typing.

7. Document your sources and format your essay according to your instructor's directions.

THEME | What Makes Us Healthy?

Eating too much fat will make you fat. When working out, "No pain, no gain." Are these popular claims about diet and exercise true? Will doing these things make you healthy or unhealthy?

For experts' strategies on how to eat to be healthy and fit, check out the MyPlate graphic shown here. The graphic illustrates the five food groups needed to make up a balanced diet. First, look at the dinner plate in the center:

- What do the colors in the plate identify?
- What do the sizes of the colored segments suggest?

Then consider the cup or bowl in the upper right:

- What does this cup or bowl represent?
- Why do you think the cup or bowl is set off from the plate?
- According to this graphic, which foods contribute to healthy eating? How much of those foods should you eat?

Class Activity

Use these slogans as a starting point to discuss diet and exercise myths. Have students create lists of familiar sayings, then debate whether these are true or false. As a follow-up, students can research to determine the accuracy of the sayings they identified and report their findings to the class.

Explore the interactive features of this graphic at www.choosemyplate.gov. How useful would you find the graphic for planning meals?

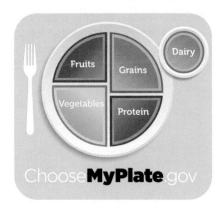

In this thematic section of the anthology, you will read examples of three common types of college texts: a news article, information on a Web page, and a journal article. The topic of each is healthy personal habits—specifically, facts about eating, exercising, and factors associated with a healthy body weight.

Read to Write Activity

Choose a Prompt for an Essay on Healthy Habits

Select one of the prompts that follows for help in focusing your reading and planning your writing as you navigate through this section of the chapter. Keywords before each prompt identify the type of writing.

Essay Prompts

1. Informative research paper: In your nursing class, you have been asked to research a national health problem and present the information from your research to your classmates. To fulfill this assignment, use the readings in this section of the chapter along with your own research to identify and explain a health problem and describe solutions to that problem.

2. Informative research paper: In your nutrition class, students must explain some popular misconceptions about healthy exercise or eating habits. To fulfill this assignment, use the readings in this section of the chapter along with your own research to explain why some popular misconceptions about healthy exercise or eating habits are wrong and present more accurate information instead.

3. Persuasive essay: Your college newspaper is preparing an edition focused on student health. Write an article for the paper that provides students with accurate information about healthy ways to eat and exercise.

4. Response essay: Select the reading from this chapter that you find most interesting or informative. Write a response to the reading, explaining what you learned and how you will apply that information to your own life.

READING SELECTION

"WHY WE'RE SO FAT: WHAT'S BEHIND THE LATEST OBESITY RATES"

Complete the "Before Reading" assignment. Then read the selection while you complete the "During Reading" activity. Finally, complete the "After Reading" assignment.

Before Reading: Preview; Recognize Prior Knowledge

Write answers to the following questions using complete sentences.

1. Consider the title. What do you think could be the answer to the question "Why are we so fat?" Also, who do you think "we" refers to?

2. What do you know about obesity? For instance, what is the definition of obesity, and how does obesity affect people?

During Reading: Annotate; Summarize

Complete the following exercise.

3. Chunk the reading into sections. Write a one- or two-sentence summary of each section of the reading.

Why We're So Fat: What's Behind the Latest Obesity Rates

By Rachel Pomerance Berl

U.S. News & World Report, 16 August 2012

The article examines why so many Americans are overweight and concludes that there are no easy explanations. It was published online in U.S. News & World Report, *a magazine that reports on national and international news. The article draws on information from the Centers for Disease Control and Prevention (CDC), a US government organization that collects data and provides information about health.*

It used to be that rich and fat were terms associated with people, not dessert. A portly shape, in fact, signaled the good life. If you ever saw the musical *Oliver!*, you may recall the number, "Food, Glorious Food," in which a stage full of scrawny orphans pine for the gluttony that money can buy: "Rich gentlemen have it boys, In-di-gestion!" Today, however, we often see the reverse scenario: the leaner your wallet, the fatter you are.

"You have this coexistence of obesity and food insecurity in America," says Susan Blumenthal, former U.S. assistant surgeon general, clinical professor at

1

2

Connect

You will find a coordinated Power of Process assignment for this reading in your Connect course.

Answers

1. The "we" in the title most likely refers to Americans, and why Americans are overweight could be because they eat too much fast food, drink sodas, and don't get enough exercise.

2. Obesity means to be extremely overweight. Obesity affects people's health. For instance, obese people are at greater risk for diabetes or heart attacks.

Answers

3. The reading begins with statistics showing that the poorest states in America suffer from the highest rates of obesity; however, other factors play a role in obesity rates, and more than 30% of Americans are obese. Obesity rates have been rising; obesity creates health risks and has financial impacts. It will take time and community effort to lower obesity rates.

Georgetown and Tufts University medical schools, and director of the Health and Medicine Program at the Center for the Study of the Presidency and Congress. Finding, and affording, healthy food along with safe places to exercise, are among the challenges that low-income populations face.

So perhaps it's not surprising that the statistics released . . . by the Centers for Disease Control and Prevention (CDC) showed that Mississippi, the poorest state in America, has the nation's highest obesity rate, at 34.9 percent. States in the South and Midwest, which, in some cases, represent the poorest parts of the country, showed the highest incidences of obesity. While financial health has a bearing on physical health, the correlation is a complicated one. Culture, gender, education, biology, and even politics, play a role. America's so-called "red" states tend to have higher rates of obesity, experts note. Plus, the prevalence of cheap, processed foods, the layout of our neighborhoods, and access to parks and public transportation also factor into one's risk for obesity and, consequently, disease. And while poor Americans may find it especially challenging to access the ingredients of a healthy lifestyle, obesity is clearly not limited to the province of the poor. More than one-third of the nation is obese, according to some data sets, and that cuts across all income levels.

"There is no single, simple answer to explain the obesity patterns" in America, says Walter Willett, who chairs the department of nutrition at the Harvard School of Public Health. "Part of this is due to lower incomes and education, which result in purchases of cheap foods that are high in refined starch and sugar. More deeply, this also reflects lower public investment in education, public transportation, and recreational facilities," he says. The bottom line: cheap, unhealthy foods mixed with a sedentary lifestyle has made obesity the new normal in America. And that makes it even harder to change, Willett says.

In 1990, not one U.S. state had an obesity rate greater than 14 percent, according to the CDC. Ten years later, 23 states reported an obesity rate between 20 to 24 percent. And in 2010, 36 states had an obesity rate of at least 25 percent, with 12 states reporting an obesity rate beyond 30 percent. (The CDC notes that it used a new methodology for its 2011 survey, rendering comparisons with past years rather rough.)

"We now see that life expectancy is for the first time decreasing in many parts of the South and Southeast," says Willett.

Obesity puts people at risk for heart disease, stroke, diabetes, and cancer. These illnesses, of course, exact a financial toll too. In 2008, this country spent approximately $147 billion on medical costs, the CDC says. If every American were to lose an average of 10 pounds, the United States would save roughly $29 billion a year within five years, says Jeffrey Levi, executive director of the Trust for America's Health, a nonprofit organization promoting national health. "If you really want to bend the cost curves, it isn't doing things at the margins" that counts, he says, but "taking on the fundamental challenge of preventing and reversing chronic disease."

But the CDC's state-by-state picture of America's obesity epidemic may not be the best way to understand, let alone tackle, the issue.

Obesity is tied not to states, per se, but to certain populations who reside in those states, says Barbara Ormond, senior research associate at the Health Policy

Center of the Urban Institute, a Washington, D.C.–based think tank. Each of these populations grapples with specific problems, she explains. Take, for example, comfort food, she says, which varies by culture and nutritional quality.

According to the CDC, non-Hispanic blacks have the highest rates of obesity, followed by Mexican Americans, all Hispanics, and non-Hispanic whites. When it comes to socioeconomic status, the data differ by gender. For example, college-educated women and women who earn higher incomes are less likely to be obese than women who didn't graduate high school or earn lower salaries. However, such correlations don't exist among men, for whom obesity is roughly the same across income levels. In fact, higher incomes were associated with increased obesity rates among non-Hispanic black and Mexican-American men, the CDC reports.   10

Such complexities explain Ormond's caveat against labeling obesity a poverty problem. It's a "shorthand way of looking at it" that reduces it almost to something that's hard to do anything about, she says. "You can't make everybody not poor, but you could give them good schools, or you could make sure the school lunch you're serving is nutritious."   11

Fixing this problem is going to take a proverbial village, public health experts say.   12

"We need to mobilize all sectors of society," Blumenthal says, calling for policies that will create more places to walk and exercise, as well as physical and health education in schools and healthier choices in vending machines, for example. But communities can begin the intervention, she says, noting the Affordable Care Act's Prevention and Public Health Fund, which can seed local efforts. Neighborhoods might come together to organize a health fair, coordinate a race to motivate community weight loss, or plant community gardens, she advises.   13

And beyond that, those working to fight obesity in this country ought to be patient and persistent, Ormond says. "It took us many, many years to get as fat as we are as a nation, and it's going to take us a similar number of years, or certainly a lot of effort to reverse that trend."   14

 ## After Reading: Reflect on the Text

Refer to the reading selection as you complete this exercise.

4. Refer to your annotations from exercise 3 in "During Reading." What did you learn about obesity from the reading selection?

Answers

4. Students might have learned that obesity is tied to poverty (Mississippi, the poorest state, has the highest obesity rates); that obesity decreases life expectancy; that blacks are most at risk for obesity; and that there is no single explanation to obesity patterns.

Read to Write Activity

Engage with the Reading

Refer to the reading selection as you complete these exercises.

1. Based on the information in the reading selection, would you change anything about your eating or exercise habits while in college? Why or why not?

2. Susan Blumenthal, former US assistant surgeon general, suggests creating policies to encourage healthy eating and exercise, such as physical education in schools or healthy foods in vending machines (Berl 341). Can you think of other policies or actions that could be implemented at your college or in your community to promote healthy eating and exercise?

Pair and Share

- With a partner, compare what you learned about obesity (from exercise 4 in "After Reading"). Can you add more information to your responses?

- With a partner, compare your ideas for taking action to prevent obesity (from question 2 in "Engage with the Reading"). Which strategies seem most realistic or most likely to work?

Vocabulary Strategy: Building Personal Vocabulary

Identify and list five words from the reading selection that you do not know or do not know well. Use context clues or word analysis to guess their meaning. Then consult a dictionary to look up each word and find a meaning that fits the context of the passage. Write down that definition.

READING SELECTION

"WEIGHT-LOSS AND NUTRITION MYTHS"

This reading selection is a fact sheet. A fact sheet is designed to provide a clear and concise summary of important information on a topic. It is called a *sheet* because typically the content is about one page in length; it is called a *fact* sheet because the purpose is to present key points in an informative, objective style.

Complete the "Before Reading" assignment. Then read the selection while you complete the "During Reading" activity. Finally, complete the "After Reading" assignment.

Before Reading: Preview; Predict

Write answers to the following questions using complete sentences.

1. Notice the headings in bold. Explain how these create an organizational structure for the reading.

2. Where were these "Weight-Loss and Nutrition Myths" published? Based on where these myths were published, do you think the information in this reading is fact or fiction? Explain your thinking.

During Reading: Annotate; Summarize

Complete the following exercise.

3. Chunk the reading into sections. Write a one- or two-sentence summary of each section of the reading.

Answers

1. The bold headings group related myths, such as myths related to diet or myths related to physical activity.

2. The "Weight-Loss and Nutrition Myths" are published on the National Institute of Diabetes and Digestive and Kidney Diseases website, which is a government website, and therefore readers can assume the information is factual.

Answers

3. The fact sheet begins by promising to counter diet and exercise myths with facts. For instance, fad diets are not effective for weight loss or health; grain foods are not intrinsically fattening and can be healthy; it's a myth that some people can eat whatever they want because weight is tied to calories consumed and used; low-fat or fat-free foods are not necessarily healthy choices; fast food, if chosen carefully, can be healthy; eating well does not mean spending lots of money; lifting weights will not make you bulky; physical activity can be effective in short bursts; eating meat or dairy products will not lead to weight gain; a vegetarian diet isn't always healthy.

Weight-Loss and Nutrition Myths

US Department of Health and Human Services, Updated October 2014

The following list of myths, excerpted from a brochure published by the US Department of Health and Human Services, is part of the National Institute of Diabetes and Digestive and Kidney Diseases Web site. This information appears on the Web site and as a downloadable fact sheet.

"Lose 30 pounds in 30 days!"

"Eat as much as you want and still lose weight!"

"Try the thigh buster and lose inches fast!"

Have you heard these claims before? A large number of diets and tools are available, but their quality may vary. It can be hard to know what to believe.

This fact sheet may help. Here, we discuss myths and provide facts . . . about weight loss, nutrition, and physical activity. This information may help you make healthy changes in your daily habits. You can also talk to your health care provider. She or he can help you if you have other questions or you want to lose weight. A registered dietitian may also give you advice on a healthy eating plan and safe ways to lose weight and keep it off.

Weight-Loss and Diet Myths

Myth: Fad diets will help me lose weight and keep it off.

Fact: Fad diets are not the best way to lose weight and keep it off. These diets often promise quick weight loss if you strictly reduce what you eat or avoid some types of foods. Some of these diets may help you lose weight at first. But these diets are hard to follow. Most people quickly get tired of them and regain any lost weight.

Fad diets may be unhealthy. They may not provide all of the nutrients your body needs. Also, losing more than 3 pounds a week after the first few weeks may increase your chances of developing gallstones (solid matter in the gallbladder that can cause pain). Being on a diet of fewer than 800 calories a day for a long time may lead to serious heart problems. . . .

Myth: Grain products such as bread, pasta, and rice are fattening. I should avoid them when trying to lose weight.

Fact: A grain product is any food made from wheat, rice, oats, cornmeal, barley, or another cereal grain. Grains are divided into two subgroups, whole grains and refined grains. Whole grains contain the entire grain kernel—the bran, germ, and endosperm. Examples include brown rice and whole-wheat bread, cereal, and pasta. Refined grains have been milled, a process that removes the bran and germ. This is done to give grains a finer texture and improve their shelf life, but it also removes dietary fiber, iron, and many B vitamins.

People who eat whole grains as part of a healthy diet may lower their chances of developing some chronic diseases. Government dietary guidelines advise making half your grains whole grains. For example, choose 100 percent whole-wheat bread instead of white bread, and brown rice instead of white rice. . . .

Meal Myths

Myth: Some people can eat whatever they want and still lose weight.

Fact: To lose weight, you need to burn more calories than you eat and drink. Some people may seem to get away with eating any kind of food they want and still lose weight. But those people, like everyone, must use more energy than they take in through food and drink to lose weight.

A number of factors such as your age, genes, medicines, and lifestyle habits may affect your weight. If you would like to lose weight, speak with your health care provider about factors that may affect your weight. Together, you may be able to create a plan to help you reach your weight and health goals. . . .

Myth: "Low-fat" or "fat-free" means no calories.

Fact: A serving of low-fat or fat-free food may be lower in calories than a serving of the full-fat product. But many processed low-fat or fat-free foods have just as many calories as the full-fat versions of the same foods—or even more calories. These foods may contain added flour, salt, starch, or sugar to improve flavor and texture after fat is removed. These items add calories. . . .

Myth: Fast foods are always an unhealthy choice. You should not eat them when dieting.

Fact: Many fast foods are unhealthy and may affect weight gain. However, if you do eat fast food, choose menu options with care. Both at home and away, choose healthy foods that are nutrient rich, low in calories, and small in portion size. . . .

Myth: If I skip meals, I can lose weight.

Fact: Skipping meals may make you feel hungrier and lead you to eat more than you normally would at your next meal. In particular, studies show a link between skipping breakfast and obesity. People who skip breakfast tend to be heavier than people who eat a healthy breakfast. . . .

Myth: Eating healthy food costs too much.

Fact: Eating better does not have to cost a lot of money. Many people think that fresh foods are healthier than canned or frozen ones. For example, some people think that spinach is better for you raw than frozen or canned. However, canned or frozen fruits and veggies provide as many nutrients as fresh ones, at a lower cost. Healthy options include low-salt canned veggies and fruit canned in its own juice or water-packed. Remember to rinse canned veggies to remove excess salt. Also, some canned seafood, like tuna, is easy to keep on the shelf, healthy, and low-cost. And canned, dried, or frozen beans, lentils, and peas are also healthy sources of protein that are easy on the wallet. . . .

Physical Activity Myths

Myth: Lifting weights is not a good way to lose weight because it will make me "bulk up."

Fact: Lifting weights or doing activities like push-ups and crunches on a regular basis can help you build strong muscles, which can help you burn more calories. To strengthen muscles, you can lift weights, use large rubber bands (resistance bands), do push-ups or sit-ups, or do household or yard tasks that make you lift or dig. Doing strengthening activities 2 or 3 days a week will not "bulk you up." Only intense strength training, along with certain genetics, can build large muscles. . . .

Myth: Physical activity only counts if I can do it for long periods of time.

Fact: You do not need to be active for long periods to achieve your 150 to 300 minutes of activity each week. Experts advise doing aerobic activity for periods of 10 minutes or longer at a time. You can spread these sessions out over the week. . . .

Food Myths

Myth: Eating meat is bad for my health and makes it harder to lose weight.

Fact: Eating lean meat in small amounts can be part of a healthy plan to lose weight. Chicken, fish, pork, and red meat contain some cholesterol and saturated fat. But they also contain healthy nutrients like iron, protein, and zinc. . . .

Myth: Dairy products are fattening and unhealthy.

Fact: Fat-free and low-fat cheese, milk, and yogurt are just as healthy as whole-milk dairy products, and they are lower in fat and calories. Dairy products offer protein to build muscles and help organs work well, and calcium to strengthen bones. Most milk and some yogurts have extra vitamin D added to help your body use calcium. Most Americans don't get enough calcium and vitamin D. Dairy is an easy way to get more of these nutrients. . . .

Myth: "Going vegetarian" will help me lose weight and be healthier.

Fact: Research shows that people who follow a vegetarian eating plan, on average, eat fewer calories and less fat than non-vegetarians. Some research has found that vegetarian-style eating patterns are associated with lower levels of obesity, lower blood pressure, and a reduced risk of heart disease.

Vegetarians also tend to have lower body mass index (BMI) scores than people with other eating plans. (The BMI measures body fat based on a person's height in relation to weight.) But vegetarians—like others—can make food choices that impact weight gain, like eating large amounts of foods that are high in fat or calories or low in nutrients.

The types of vegetarian diets eaten in the United States can vary widely. Vegans do not consume any animal products, while lacto-ovo vegetarians eat milk and eggs along with plant foods. Some people have eating patterns that are mainly vegetarian but may include small amounts of meat, poultry, or seafood. . . .

From The Weight-control Information Network (WIN) – National Institute of Diabetes and Digestive and Kidney Diseases (NIDDK) – National Institutes of Health (NIH).

 **After Reading: Summarize; Brainstorm**

Refer to the reading selection as you complete this exercise.

4. Select one of the myths in the fact sheet and explain why people might believe this myth is true. Then summarize the facts about that myth.

Read to Write Activity

Engage with the Reading

Refer to the reading selection as you complete these exercises.

1. What did you learn about healthy eating and exercise from the reading selection? What information from the fact sheet did you find most surprising or interesting? Explain.

2. Based on the information in this fact sheet, would you change anything about your eating or exercise habits while in college? Why or why not?

Pair and Share

With a partner, compare what you learned about healthy eating and exercise (from exercise 1 in "Engage with the Reading"). Can you add more information to your answers?

READING SELECTION

"FRESHMAN FIFTEEN: FACT OR FICTION?"

Journal articles are written by scholars or professionals who are experts in their fields. Often a journal article is a way to publish research results. Journal articles tend to follow a certain format that includes an Introduction to the topic, a Review of the Literature explaining what other experts have published on the topic, a Methodology section describing how the research was conducted, Results and Discussion analyzing the data, and Conclusions or Implications suggesting how the research findings could be applied.

Complete the "Before Reading" assignment. Then read the selection while you complete the "During Reading" activity. Finally, complete the "After Reading" assignment.

 Before Reading: Preview; Predict

Write answers to the following questions using complete sentences.

1. Notice where the reading was published and explain what this suggests about the authors of the article.

2. What might account for student weight gain during the first year of college?

 During Reading: Annotate; Summarize

Complete the following exercise.

3. Chunk the reading into sections. Write a one- or two-sentence summary of each section of the reading.

Answers

1. The article is published in the *College Student Journal*, which suggests the authors are college students.

2. Answers will vary; students might think that poor eating habits and not enough exercise are contributing factors.

Connect

You will find a coordinated Power of Process assignment for this reading in your Connect course.

Answers

3. **Introduction:** The research study is designed to test the theory that first-year college students typically gain 15 pounds. **Review of the Literature:** Examination of previously published studies shows that college freshmen do gain weight, but it's not clear how much. A vast majority of college students know about the Freshman 15 phenomenon, and researchers propose various theories as to why freshman gain weight. **Method:** 52 students, male and female, were tracked and surveyed to determine their eating habits and weight change. **Results and Discussion:** Two-thirds of the students gained an average of almost 11 pounds, but few gained 15 or more. **Implications:** Colleges should promote healthy eating habits and ensure that on-campus food service is healthy.

Freshman Fifteen: Fact or Fiction?

By Jennifer A. Carithers-Thomas, Shelley H. Bradford,
Christopher M. Keshock, and Steven F. Pugh

College Student Journal, June 2010

The following research article was published in College Student Journal, *a peer-reviewed journal that publishes research related to college students.*

Introduction
1

The present study examined the validity of the concept known as Freshman Fifteen. The sample included 52 freshman college students enrolled in a physical education class. Three issues were addressed: (a) amount (if any) of weight gain during the first year in college, (b) perceptions on the reasons for any weight gain, and (c) strategies for losing unwanted weight gain. Results indicated that nearly two-thirds (62%) of the sample reported weight gain (M = 10.8 lbs.). These findings did not find strong support for the notion of Freshman Fifteen. Implications for college administrators were noted.

The expression "Freshman Fifteen" is a term used to describe the weight gain by students during their first year of study in college (Thomas, 2006). This specific topic has been recently discussed by researchers, clinicians, and nutritionists. Brown (2008) reviewed the extant literature and found more than 140 newspaper articles about freshman weight gain, 20 peer reviewed articles, 141 university newspaper articles and 19 popular magazine articles on this issue, including eight books. A Google search of the term "Freshman Fifteen" yielded 7,630,000 links and articles specifically designed to provide advice, hints, and strategies to help college students avoid gaining the dreaded "Freshman Fifteen" (Google, 2009). With 1.5 million students entering United States colleges or universities each fall, the Freshman Fifteen could be considered an epidemic (Malinauskas et al., 2006).
2

The purpose of this study was to validate or negate the premise that freshman college students are likely to gain 15 pounds during their first year of college. Moreover, this study asked respondents to identify the causes of weight gain peculiar to the freshman year and inquired about specific methods that can be implemented to control weight gain. This type of research is necessary to determine if weight gain occurs and, more importantly, what behaviors can be modified to diminish the probability of further weight gain. Furthermore, if the assertion is true that students gain weight, regardless of the specific amount of pounds, universities have an obligation to provide programs, resources, and services to educate their students about the concept of the Freshman Fifteen.
3

Review of the Literature
4

The seminal reference to the concept of the "Freshman Fifteen" was found in 1989 [article] that chronicled a college freshman's fight against weight gain (see Brown, 2008). This 15 pounds of perceived weight gain that has been investigated, analyzed, evaluated, and debated for almost two decades . . . refers to the popular belief that students gain an average of 15 pounds during their first year of college (Hodge et al., 1993). An extensive review of the literature validates that weight gain typically and predictably occurs; yet a weight gain of 15 pounds has not been substantiated by most research endeavors. Some research shows the average weight gain to be only 8.8 pounds (Howell, 1985). A study by Hoffman and colleagues (2006) found that a mean of 7 pounds is gained during the first year. In another study, 59% of the volunteers gained weight in their freshman year (Graham & Jones, 2000); however, the amount of weight gained was calculated at 4.6 pounds (2000). A study conducted by researchers at Michigan State University revealed that of the 110 respondents, the average weight gain was 7 pounds, again substantially less than the predetermined 15 (Hodge et al., 1993). In fact, the authors concluded that the majority of the female students in the sample remained the same weight during their first six months of college. The *Journal of American College Health* reported that about 70% of students will gain a significant amount of weight between the start of college and the end of sophomore year (Jung et al., 2008). The researchers also found that the average weight gain is closer to 9 pounds as opposed to 15 pounds. Researchers studying men and women found that although both sexes gain weight, men appeared to gain more and experience a larger increase in body mass index (Mihalopoulous et al., 2008).

A recent study found that 90% of first year college students are aware of the freshman 15, yet many students chose to ignore the warning signs related to weight gain (Jung et al., 2008; Wyshak, 2007). The possible reasons for this superfluous weight gain are limitless in the college atmosphere. Many researchers suggest that this weight gain is attributed to the new-found freedom and accompanying stress associated with the shift to college life. Other researchers claim that the excess weight gain is due to an increase in caloric consumption through the intake of alcohol and unhealthy snacking (Jung et al., 2008). 5

Moreover, few personal characteristics have been found to distinguish women who gain, lose, or maintain their weight. In fact, contrary to predictions, self-esteem, body image, and locus of control were unconnected to weight change among women who gained weight (Hodge et al., 1993). Yet, those women who lost weight and evaluated their appearance, fitness, and health more positively lose less weight. This suggests that a favorable body image may mitigate against a pursuit of slimness (Hodge et al., 1993). 6

Method 7

Participants
The participants of this study were students who had completed their freshman year of college at the University of South Alabama. The sample comprised 52 female and male students who were enrolled in tennis and weight training physical education courses.

Instrumentation 8
Previous researchers who had studied the "Freshman Fifteen" concept had collected measurements such as height and weight, body mass, percentage of body fat, total fat mass, and waist and hip circumferences (Jung et al., 2006; Morrow et al., 2006). The current survey measure sought specific information about the amount of weight gain, loss, or maintenance during a student's freshman year. Another section asked students about factors that contributed to weight gain such as late night snacking, drinking, stress, and social eating. A final section asked students to identify the specific approaches they utilized to lose weight (if they

acknowledged that weight had been gained); for example, dieting, increasing one's activity, making better food choices, and decreasing one's amount of stress. These data were collected during the Spring semester of 2009.

Results and Discussion

9

Nearly two-thirds of our sample admitted to weight gain during their freshman year. Of the 32 students (62%) who reported weight gain, the average weight gain of the respondents was 10.78 pounds (range 2 lbs.–28 lbs.). Only six students reported a weight gain exceeding 15 pounds. Of the 18 females sampled who reported weight gain, the average weight gain was 10.5 pounds. Of the 14 males sampled that gained weight, the average increase in weight was measured at 11.14 pounds. Nine students (17.3%) reported that they actually lost weight during their freshman year. The average amount of weight loss was 9.44 pounds (range 2–30 lbs.). Interestingly, eleven students (21.15%) reported maintaining their weight (7 males; 4 females). Participants identified the most plausible reason or reasons for their weight gain. Table 1 presents the rank order of critical factors.

Participants noted several ways that they could lose their weight gain. Students identified increasing activity to be the best way to achieve weight loss (25.24%). Making better food choices (24.27%) and decreasing the amount of fast food consumed (19.42%) also ranked high on the list. In addition, students acknowledged the importance of decreasing snack ingestion (11.65%), dieting (10.68%), decreasing stress (3.88%), decreasing the amount of drinking (2.91%); interestingly, less than one percent of our sample stated that they would use an over-the-counter diet pill.

10

The current findings indicated that a sizeable majority of college students gain weight as freshman; however, the amount of weight gain appears to be moderate (about 10 lbs.). Moreover, it seems that young college students are aware of the factors that contribute to their weight gain and various methods that can be implemented which should lead to weight loss.

11

Also, the current findings support prior research endeavors that reported that many freshman students do not gain weight. In fact, 24% of our sample was able to maintain their weight and 17% were able to lose weight. Further, our findings corroborate the conclusions of earlier research efforts on the "Freshman Fifteen" issue (e.g., Hoffman et al., 2005; Howell et al., 1985; Mihalopoulous et al., 2008).

12

Implications for College Administrators

13

College preventative programs that accentuated the importance of good nutrition, consistent exercise, and healthy behaviors could possibly reverse the propensity to gain weight. Dieticians or nutritionists could be more involved in planning meals in the cafeteria setting to provide healthier food selections, such as salads, wraps, and vegetables. Physical education courses could be required for all freshman students to promote the importance of exercise. Colleges could engage nurses or other health care providers to offer seminars on the health benefits of exercise and consistent physical activity in the prevention of chronic diseases associated with obesity. Additionally, colleges should provide exercise equipment and gym facilities that students could use daily in designated areas of student housing. Educational endeavors for all students should consider annual physicals and health fairs that stress proper nutrition, exercise, and the maintenance of healthy behaviors.

The current study has several limitations; for example, the sample size is small and was obtained from one educational setting. Future research should focus on

14

longitudinal data regarding weight loss/gain and concomitant health behaviors that promote stable weight maintenance.

Table 1 Major Factors Identified to Account for Weight Gain

Reasons	Percentage
Late-night snacking	20.8
Cafeteria food selection	12.9
Social eating	11.9
Irregular schedule	11.9
General stress	10.9
Decreased activity	10.9
Lack of "healthy foods"	8.9
Social drinking	6.9

 ## After Reading: Summarize; Reflect

Refer to the reading as you complete this exercise.

4. Compare your answer about what you thought led to student weight gain in college (from exercise 2 in "Before Reading") to Table 1 at the end of the article (351). Were your predictions correct? Which factors, according to the reading, are most related to freshman weight gain?

Read to Write Activity

Engage with the Reading

Refer to the reading as you complete these exercises.

1. Carithers-Thomas et al. studied students at the University of South Alabama, a public four-year college. Do you think results might be different if the authors focused on students at a two-year college, or students at a private college, or students at a technical school? Explain.

2. What information from the study did you find most surprising or interesting? Explain.

3. According to Carithers-Thomas et al., even though most students in this study did not gain fifteen pounds, a majority (almost two-thirds) put on an average of more than ten pounds (Carithers-Thomas et al. 350). Is it fair to conclude that the freshmen fifteen is a myth or to be unconcerned about college students' gaining weight? Explain.

Answers

4. According to the reading, late-night snacking and cafeteria food are most related to weight gain.

Answers

1. Some results might be different if different student populations were studied. For instance, students at two-year schools may not eat at the cafeteria as often as students at a four-year college. In contrast, stress or an irregular schedule might contribute to students' weight gain.

2. Answers will vary; students might be surprised that a concept such as "the freshman 15" could be the focus of a research study.

3. Ten pounds is a significant amount of weight to gain, so being concerned about healthy eating and exercise should be important for college students.

Pair and Share

With a partner, compare what you learned about the freshman fifteen (from exercise 2 in "Engage with the Reading"). Can you add more information to your answers?

Vocabulary Strategy: Building Personal Vocabulary

Identify and list five words from the reading selection that you do not know or do not know well. Use context clues or word analysis to guess their meaning. Then consult a dictionary to look up each word and find a meaning that fits the context of the passage. Write down that definition.

Theme Activity: Write in Response to a Chosen Prompt

1. Review the prompt you chose for your essay. What is your purpose, and who is your audience?
2. Review your notes on the reading selections for this theme. Prewrite about your topic to generate additional ideas. Do additional research if necessary or required by your instructor.
3. Create an informal outline, graphic organizer, or essay plan that organizes your notes and includes a topic sentence for each paragraph.
4. Write a thesis statement that sums up the main ideas, gives your point of view, and reflects the organizational pattern of your paper.
5. Draft the introduction, body paragraphs, and conclusion for your essay using your thesis statement and your outline, graphic organizer, or essay plan.
6. Revise your essay for coherence and unity. Edit and proofread for errors in grammar and typing.
7. Document your sources and format your essay according to your instructor's directions.

Examine the graphic about concussions by Andrew Lucas and Jeff Goertzen from *The Denver Post* shown here. Take time to read its numbered descriptions and to relate them to the drawings, and also review the "Symptoms" list in the graphic. What information do you take away from the graphic? What is a concussion? How are football players and other athletes at risk of experiencing a concussion?

In this set of readings, we explore the problem of head injuries in sports. You will read three articles in which the authors provide evidence about the extent of this problem and propose various solutions.

Look over the essay prompts in the Read to Write box and identify one that could be the basis of an essay you might write. Keep this essay prompt in mind as you read and take notes on the article.

Class Activity

Search *YouTube* for documentaries about traumatic brain injury (TBI) or interviews with doctors or patients with TBI experience to show to students before reading the selections in this section. Have students summarize and discuss the information in the videos to gain background knowledge.

Is the graphic informational or persuasive—or both? Why?

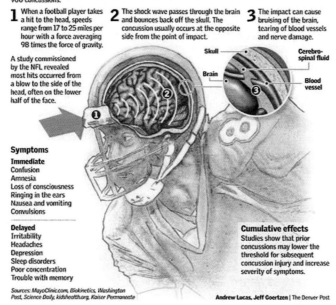

School of hard knocks

A concussion occurs when a violent blow to the head causes the brain to slam against the skull beyond the ability of the cerebrospinal fluid to cushion the impact. Between 1996 and 2001, NFL teams reported nearly 900 concussions.

1 When a football player takes a hit to the head, speeds range from 17 to 25 miles per hour with a force averaging 98 times the force of gravity.

A study commissioned by the NFL revealed most hits occurred from a blow to the side of the head, often on the lower half of the face.

2 The shock wave passes through the brain and bounces back off the skull. The concussion usually occurs at the opposite side from the point of impact.

3 The impact can cause bruising of the brain, tearing of blood vessels and nerve damage.

Skull — Cerebrospinal fluid

Brain — Blood vessel

Symptoms

Immediate
Confusion
Amnesia
Loss of consciousness
Ringing in the ears
Nausea and vomiting
Convulsions

Delayed
Irritability
Headaches
Depression
Sleep disorders
Poor concentration
Trouble with memory

Sources: MayoClinic.com, Biokinetics, Washington Post, Science Daily, kidshealth.org, Kaiser Permanente

Cumulative effects
Studies show that prior concussions may lower the threshold for subsequent concussion injury and increase severity of symptoms.

Andrew Lucas, Jeff Goertzen | The Denver Post

Andrew Lucas and Jeff Goertzen, "School of Hard Knocks" Used by permission of The Denver Post

Teaching Tip

Essay Prompts 1 and 2 could be combined into one assignment in which students first write a letter from the parent's point of view and then write a response to that letter from a coach's point of view.

Read to Write Activity

Choose a Prompt for an Essay on Head Injuries in Sports

Select one of the essay prompts that follow for help in focusing your reading and planning an essay as you navigate through this thematic section of the anthology. Keywords before each prompt identify the type of essay.

Essay Prompts

1. Argument essay: Your child plays a team sport such as football, basketball, soccer, or some other contact sport, and you are concerned about the risk of traumatic brain injury (TBI) to the players on the team. Write a letter to the coach convincing him or her that this is a serious problem.

2. Response essay: You are a coach of a youth sports team who receives a letter from a concerned parent about the risk of TBI in young players. Write a response to the parent, explaining what you know about TBI and what you will do to ensure that players are protected.

3. Persuasive essay: You are a fan of professional sports. Write an essay for publication in your local newspaper explaining your position on the risks of traumatic brain injury in professional contact sports. Address the questions of how serious the risks of TBI are and whether any action should be taken to reduce these risks.

4. Persuasive essay: You are the coach of a youth sports team. Write an essay for a youth sports magazine explaining to what extent you believe traumatic brain injury is a serious problem and what solution, if any, young players, parents, and their coaches should implement in the cause of player safety.

5. Argument essay: Imagine you are an athlete involved in a team sport. How serious do you consider the risks of experiencing traumatic brain injury while playing your sport? Are the risks worth it? Is there anything you can do as a player to prevent TBI? Write an essay to your teammates explaining your point of view.

6. Persuasive essay: Consider the problem of traumatic brain injury in a sport or other activity. Analyze the problem by examining who is most at risk for TBI or what activities are most likely to lead to TBI. Then propose a solution that addresses the cause of the problem, explain how the solution will work, and give evidence that the solution will be effective.

"FACING THE TRUTH"

Complete the "Before Reading" assignment. Then read the selection while you complete the "During Reading" activity. Finally, complete the "After Reading" assignment.

Before Reading: Recognize Prior Knowledge; Predict

Write answers to these questions using complete sentences.

1. Have you ever experienced a concussion? If so, what did it feel like? What were the physical effects? If you have not experienced a concussion, imagine what its effects would be like based on what you know.

2. Look at the title of the article. What "truth" do you think the author might want readers to face? Explain.

During Reading: Annotate

Complete the following exercise.

3. As you read, keep in mind the following question: How serious is traumatic brain injury (TBI) in athletes? Annotate and take notes, focusing on evidence that will answer that question, including evidence that shows TBI is a serious problem or that it is not serious.

Facing the Truth

By Patrick Hruby

Sports on Earth, 15 May 2014

This article reviews the research on traumatic brain injury in athletes and considers whether there is sufficient evidence to implement changes in various sports. The article originally appeared in the magazine Sports on Earth, *a joint publishing venture by the newspaper* USA Today *and Major League Baseball.*

When he first saw the data, Patrick Bellgowan figured he had made a mistake. How else to explain it? A scientist at the University of Tulsa's Laureate Institute for Brain Research, Bellgowan had been scanning the brains of college football players, comparing the results to scans of non-players. His focus was on the hippocampus, a seahorse-shaped area deep inside the brain that plays an important role in emotional control and memory formation.   1

Bellgowan knew that the hippocampus was sensitive to traumatic brain injury. That shrinkage of the region was a hallmark of Alzheimer's disease. That a similar reduction in hippocampal volume also corresponded with chronic traumatic   2

Answers

1. Students might know that concussions often make one feel dizzy or disoriented and can have lasting effects after the injury, such as making it difficult to concentrate.

2. The title suggests that some people don't want to face the truth that traumatic brain injury is a serious problem.

Answers

3. Evidence that TBI is a serious problem includes the brain scans of college football players vs. nonplayers showing that athletes had smaller hippocampi, as well as many other studies indicating that the brains of boxers, hockey players, and NFL players are physically different and damaged. Evidence that shows TBI is not a serious problem includes speculation that blows to the head may not cause the brain injury; rather, "genetic variations, environment and high levels of stress hormones" may cause it, or the brains of young athletes might be able to recover from injury.

encephalopathy (CTE), a neurodegenerative disease linked to football, boxing and other contact sports. Still, he expected to see little difference in hippocampal size between a group of 50 college players and 25 non-players, mostly because everyone in the study was relatively healthy and young.

And then Rashimi Singh, a fellow researcher at the Laureate Institute, brought a set of initial results to Bellgowan's office. 3

"Are you sure?" he said. "That can't be right." 4

The numbers were stark. A group of 25 players with no history of reported concussions had hippocampuses that were, on average, 14 percent smaller than those of a control group of 25 males of similar age and health who didn't play contact sports. 5

Moreover, the same brain region in a second group of 25 players who had suffered at least one clinically diagnosed concussion was, on average, 25 percent smaller than the control group—a larger difference in volume, Bellgowan says, than the variations scientists have observed between the brains of healthy people and patients suffering from Alzheimer's or severe depression. 6

"I can't tell you how many times we checked this over," Bellgowan says. "The effect size was really large. It was really surprising." 7

Published this week in the *Journal of the American Medical Association*, the results of Bellgowan and Singh's research may be unexpected, but they also reflect a larger scientific trend. While much of the health and safety debate over football and other contact sports focuses on the risk of developing severe, headline-grabbing neurodegenerative diseases like amyotrophic lateral sclerosis (ALS) and CTE, a growing body of evidence suggests that both concussions and subconcussive blows can alter mood, cognition and behavior while causing damage and structural changes to the brain. 8

In other words, contact sports may be worse for your cognitive health than previously assumed, even if you don't ultimately end up in a dementia ward. Consider: 9

- Bellgowan and his co-authors also found that the longer an athlete had played football, the smaller their left hippocampal region was (on average). Football players also scored lower than non-players on tests of cognitive processing speed—and again, football career length had an inverse relationship with test results. 10

- An international research team detected micro-structural brain damage in concussed male and female college hockey players—damage that can't be seen with standard hospital-based MRI scans. 11

- Purdue University researchers studying high school football players over the course of two seasons found: (a) changes in brain activity that significantly correlated to the number and distribution of hits those players took; (b) changes in regions of the brain that have been associated with CTE, results which suggest that detrimental effects of hits to the head may be cumulative and compounding. 12

- A Dartmouth University study found "small but significant" changes to the brains of college hockey and football players over the course of a season when 13 compared to non–contact sport athletes, even though none of the hockey and football players sustained a reported concussion. In addition, the contact sport athletes who performed worse than expected on cognition tests at the end of the season had greater brain changes.

- An ongoing Cleveland Clinic study of nearly 400 active and retired boxers and mixed martial arts fighters already has detected changes in the volume of specific brain regions and found that higher exposure to head trauma correlates with lower brain volume and reduced performance on cognitive testing. 14

- A study of 13 retired NFL players found major, previously unobserved abnormalities in brain activity in their frontal lobes, the area of the brain responsible for executive functions like planning ahead—a result that suggests that even players who perform relatively well on standard neuropsychological tests may have brain damage that causes them to struggle in everyday life. 15

- A study of retired NFL players published in the *Journal of Neurotrauma* linked repeated concussions and head trauma to pituitary dysfunction and reduced levels of growth hormone and testosterone, which can result in metabolic syndrome—a group of risk factors that raise the risk of heart disease and diabetes—as well as erectile dysfunction and a reduced quality of life. 16

- A National Institutes of Health–funded study found that the brains of concussion patients continue to show physical abnormalities and signs of injury months after symptoms such as dizziness, headaches and memory loss ease or resolve—which could mean that current return-to-play guidelines aren't conservative enough. 17

- Similar to the above, a National Football League Charities–funded study of college football players who were *not* diagnosed with concussions over the course of a season found that physical changes to their brains occurred after as few as 10 to 15 hard hits and that six months following the end of football season, imaging scans still "showed changes consistent with mild brain injury in about half of the players." 18

- A study published in *Pediatrics* found that in children and teenagers who have suffered a concussion, physical symptoms such as headache, nausea and fatigue tend to appear immediately, while emotional symptoms such as frustration, irritability and restlessness may take days or weeks to manifest themselves. 19

- Teenagers with a history of concussions are more than three times as likely to suffer from depression as teens who have never had a concussion, while some research indicates that children who have a history of concussion are more likely to develop attention-deficit/hyperactivity disorder (ADHD) and have difficulties controlling their moods. 20

- Teenagers who have suffered a traumatic brain injury such as a concussion have a significantly higher risk of attempting suicide, being bullied, becoming bullies themselves, using alcohol or marijuana, engaging in antisocial behavior, being prescribed anxiety and/or depression medication and seeking help for mental health issues from crisis help lines. 21

Of course, the above studies come with serious caveats: small sample sizes, a need for replication, a focus on correlation instead of causation. Much remains unknown. While scientists agree that getting hit in the head can result in both brain changes and damage, they don't always know if the former indicates the latter—and even when it does, the extent of the harm remains unclear. Likewise, researchers are still sussing out the exact mechanisms by which changes and damage affect behavior and cognition, as well as the brain's ability to compensate for injury and/or heal itself.

Take Bellgowan's study. The authors acknowledge that absorbing repeated blows to the head while playing football may not be the cause of hippocampal differences. Genetic variations, environment and high levels of stress hormones may all play a role. Bellgowan suspects that football-induced head trauma is a key factor, mostly because the difference between players and non-players is so pronounced. He also says that the inverse relationship between reaction time and hippocampal volume and years played points toward a cumulative effect—more hits producing greater damage over time.

If Bellgowan can secure funding for a follow-up study, he wants to study younger players, use more sensitive neuropsychological tests to screen for subtle cognitive impairment and test his hypothesis that the body's inflammatory markers may be crossing the blood–brain barrier and causing or influencing hippocampal changes. Looking forward, he'd like to study NFL retirees, too, the better to get a cross-sectional picture of how brain changes develop—or don't develop—over time.

In diseases like Parkinson's and Alzheimer's, hippocampal shrinkage can take place years before symptoms emerge. Do the differences observed by Bellgowan in college football players presage long-term disease? Or permanent structural harm?

Without more data, no one knows.

"The hippocampus can grow new cells," Bellgowan says. "These guys are young. So they might recover and come back once they stop playing if it's football-related. That's something we are going to try to answer. . . .

"In more severe types of TBI, you see hippocampus dysfunction and volume reduction. And with mild TBI, you've also seen that in older [football] players. What separates this study is that there are average 20-year-old males, still in the process of neurodevelopment. That is where we are driving. We think the key is to get at the developmental stage. This must be intersecting with neurodevelopment."

What does this uncertainty mean for contact sports? It means leagues such as the NFL have a choice. As do athletes and their families. And the rest of us. We can look at "League of Denial," stories of athletes whose lives have been ruined by brain damage, Bellgowan's study and others like it, a growing body of suggestive but inconclusive evidence, and conclude that, *well, we just don't know enough. Not yet. So let's not panic or do anything hasty. Make a few adjustments, but keep on keepin' on.* Alternately, we can evaluate the exact same set of incomplete facts and conclude that, *well, we just don't know enough. Not yet. So let's slow down or stop until we know what's happening. Better safe than sorry.*

So far, we've seen more of the former than the latter. Particularly from the NFL. 30 On one hand, the league has warned its players about concussions, taken steps to better identify and remove concussed players from the field, publicly acknowledged—one time, and only one time, but still—the link between football-induced brain trauma and long-term harm. On the other, commissioner Roger Goodell continues to make noise about expanded playoffs and an 18-game regular season, both of which would expose players to more hits to the head. The NFL supports a proposed concussion lawsuit settlement containing brain damage evaluation and compensation provisions that do not account for future scientific advances [or] offer relief to former players suffering from impairment that fails to rise to the level of neurodegenerative disease. It also endorses tackle football for children through a league-funded "Heads Up" program that purports to make the sport safer through altered tackling technique, never mind a lack of evidence showing that the program works.

During a London visit last year, Goodell told reporters that "the game isn't bad 31 for you—there are injuries and you need to recover from them, it's like anything"—a dubious proposition—while NFL Head, Neck and Spine Committee co-chair Richard Ellenbogen recently told an International Olympic Committee injury prevention conference that "media is not the place to debate the science on concussions." (An even more dubious proposition, given that public debate is what pressured the league to do anything beyond denying and dissembling about concussions in the first place, and that Ellenbogen likely wouldn't have his current gig without media exposés of his predecessors, Ira Casson and Elliot Pellman.)

The other week, Bellgowan says, one of his son's lacrosse teammates suffered 32 an obvious concussion. The boy had trouble balancing. Could barely walk. Concerned, Bellgowan approached the boy's father.

You really need to see a doctor, Bellgowan said. *Gotta hold him out. Go see a* 33 *specialist.*

Yeah, yeah, yeah, the father replied dismissively. 34

"I can't tell you that head hits caused the [hippocampal volume differences] 35 seen in our study," Bellgowan says. "But certainly, the correlation suggests that it may be one of the reasons. And because these guys are young and in the neurodevelopmental stage, instead of being mature adults, you should treat things conservatively. I always tell parents, 'if you miss a game but save a brain injury, that's good.'"

Is society willing to make that trade? To err on the side of caution in a way that 36 protects people more than the games they play? Without more data, no one knows. But as disturbing research keeps piling up—as the hits keep accumulating—change seems inevitable. Shrinkage, too. Just this week, the *New York Times* reported that an East Texas town scuttled its seventh-grade tackle football program in favor of flag [football]. Parents were worried about the safety of their children, and as a town lawyer told the newspaper, "there's too much evidence now." The next time a study indicates that contact sports may be worse for the brain than previously believed, nobody should be surprised.

After Reading: Reflect on the Text

Refer to the reading selection as you complete this exercise.

4. What ideas in the reading selection are new to you? What ideas in the reading conflict with what you already knew before you started reading?

Read to Write Activity

Engage with the Reading

Refer to the reading selection as you complete these exercises.

1. The author suggests people can draw different conclusions from the evidence when he writes:

> [We can look at the] growing body of suggestive but inconclusive evidence, and conclude that, *well, we just don't know enough. Not yet. So let's not panic or do anything hasty. Make a few adjustments, but keep on keepin' on.* Alternately, we can evaluate the exact same set of incomplete facts and conclude that, *well, we just don't know enough. Not yet. So let's slow down or stop until we know what's happening. Better safe than sorry. (358)*

Do you think not knowing enough about the issue means that people *should not* take action—or that they *should* take action? Explain.

2. Using your annotations, create a graphic organizer to show the evidence that traumatic brain injury is or is not a serious problem. Include evidence from the reading for both sides of the problem.

Pair and Share

- With a partner, compare your annotations and graphic organizer (from exercise 2 in the "Engage with the Reading"). Look for evidence that traumatic brain injury is a serious problem for players of contact sports and add any new information from the reading to your organizer.

- With a partner, compare your annotations and graphic organizer. Look for evidence that traumatic brain injury is *not* a serious problem for players of contact sports and add any new information from the reading to your organizer.

Vocabulary Strategy: Building Personal Vocabulary

Identify and list five words from the reading selection that you do not know or do not know well. Use context clues or word analysis to guess their meaning. Then consult a dictionary to look up each word and find a meaning that fits the context of the passage. Write down the sentence in which you found the word, underline the word, and give its definition.

"*DON'T* PUT ME IN, COACH"

Complete the "Before Reading" assignment. Then read the selection while you complete the "During Reading" activities. Finally, complete the "After Reading" assignment.

 ### Before Reading: Preview

Write answers to these questions using complete sentences.

1. Who might be speaking the words in the title of the reading? Why would the author use this sentence as a title?

2. Look at the author's credentials and notice where the article was published. Do you think the author is an expert on traumatic brain injury? Explain.

During Reading: Annotate; Analyze

Complete the following exercises.

3. As you read, mark the evidence that traumatic brain injury is or is not a serious problem for athletes.

4. As you read, consider what solution the author proposes for traumatic brain injury in athletes. How is this solution linked to her analysis of the problem?

Answers

1. A player would most likely be speaking these words to his or her coach. The sentence is catchy because usually players want the coach to put them in the game, not take them out. This also suggests that sometimes players should not be in the game.

2. Having a doctoral degree in nursing gives the author medical credentials, but she may not be an expert on traumatic brain or sports injuries.

Answers

3. Evidence that TBI is a serious problem includes data that TBI is responsible for one third of injury-related deaths, as well as the suicide of Junior Seau, a former football player.

4. The solutions the author proposes include not putting injured players back into the game and passing "return to play" laws.

Don't Put Me in, Coach

By Marie-Eileen Onieal

Clinician Reviews, 11 May 2013

The author, who has a doctoral degree in nursing, writes about seeing college basketball players get injured during their games. Note her observations about how coaches, referees, and players respond to a potentially serious brain injury.

On a recent Friday afternoon, I was watching a college basketball game on television. Seconds after the players returned to the court from a time-out, one player collided with another, knocking him backward. The opponent landed on his back, hitting his head so hard it bounced up and hit the floor again.

Lying somewhat still, he held his head as though trying to make it stop moving. Moments later, he was assisted to his feet, insisting he was fine, but the referee sent him to the bench for evaluation—despite resistance from the player and his coach.

1

2

The coach continued to pressure the referee, who firmly stood his ground. Zoom in: Player sitting on the bench, undergoing a neurologic evaluation. Even through the TV, it was evident the player was unable to hold his gaze through the visual field process. Score two points for the referee!

In another game, on a different day with different teams, a similar event occurred: A player fell, banged his head, and was obviously stunned. Yet he was allowed to return to play. His mother came out of the stands protesting, insisting her son was hurt. The referee and coach dismissed her objections, and she was ushered back to her seat by security. Technical fouls for the coach and referee!

3

While not every bump, blow, or jolt to the head will result in a traumatic brain injury (TBI), nonetheless, TBI has become a serious public health issue, contributing to one-third (30.5%) of all injury-related deaths.[1] An estimated 1.7 million TBIs occur annually; between 2001 and 2005, nearly 208,000 emergency department visits for concussions and other TBIs related to sports and recreational activities were reported per year.[1, 2]

4

Recently, we have begun to recognize that even the seemingly "benign" head injuries athletes sustain during play are not without some complications—short term as well as long term. In the past two or three years, researchers have started to focus on and explore the effects of "subconcussive" blows to the head, with unanticipated results.

5

In a 2010 study of high school football players, researchers from Purdue University identified a previously unknown category of athletes who, despite having no clinically observable signs of concussion, showed measurable impairment of neurocognitive function (primarily visual working memory) on neurocognitive tests, as well as altered activation in neurophysiologic function on MRI.[3] As a result of this and additional studies, repeated minor "bumps" are now viewed through a different lens—even the mild ones can take their toll, impeding language processing or motor skills.

6

The May 2012 suicide of Junior Seau, a former professional football player who sustained repeated blows to the head during his career, was a further wake-up call. It has become increasingly clear that the blows to the head sustained by players in a variety of sports and recreational activities require more serious attention—and we need to address it earlier in an athlete's career (amateur or professional), not once the irreparable damage is done.

7

The first law to address concussion management in youth athletics was passed in Washington State in May 2009. By 2012, 42 additional states and the District of Columbia had passed similar laws.[4] The intent of these "Return to Play" laws is to reduce the impact of youth sports and recreation-related concussions, and their tenets can extend to our college and professional athletes.

8

The long-term effects of repeated blows to the head have only begun to surface. We need to be diligent in recognizing and preventing TBI in all athletes, because doing so can prevent further brain injury or even death. Arm yourself with information; the CDC Web site is an excellent resource (www.cdc.gov/concussion/sports/index.html).

9

Finally, a message to all coaches and parents, athletes, and health care professionals: Getting your "bell rung" in a sports event should not be taken lightly. It must be recognized as the serious and potentially dangerous occurrence it is. So, don't put him in, coach—he may not be ready to play!

10

References

CDC National Center for Injury Prevention and Control, *Implementing Return to Play: Learning from the Experiences of Early Implementers.* www.cdc.gov/concussion/pdf/RTP_Implementation-a.pdf.

Faul M, Xu L, Wald MM, Coronado VG. *Traumatic Brain Injury in the United States: Emergency Department Visits, Hospitalizations, and Deaths.* Atlanta, GA: CDC, National Center for Injury Prevention and Control; 2010. www.cdc.gov/traumaticbraininjury/pdf/blue.book.pdf.

Gilchrist J, Thomas KE, Xu L, et al. Nonfatal traumatic brain injuries related to sports and recreation activities among persons aged ≤19 years—United States, 2001–2009. *MMWR Morbid Mortal Wkly Rep.* 2011;60:1337–1342.

Talavage T, Nauman E, Breedlove E, et al. Functionally detected cognitive impairment in high school football players without clinically diagnosed concussion, *J Neurotrauma.* 2010; Oct 1 [Epub ahead of print].

 ## After Reading: Reflect on the Text

Refer to the reading selection as you complete this exercise.

5. Review your annotations (from question 3 in "During Reading") and select the most compelling pieces of evidence from the reading that show TBI is a serious problem.

Read to Write Activity

Engage with the Reading

Refer to the reading selection as you complete these exercises.

1. Who is Junior Seau, and why does Onieal mention his suicide? If you do not know, look online for articles about his death.

2. What are return-to-play laws? How might they prevent traumatic brain injury? If you do not know about these laws, look them up on the Centers for Disease Control and Prevention Web site.

Pair and Share

- With a partner, compare the evidence from exercise 5 (in "After Reading") that traumatic brain injury is a serious problem for athletes. Which pieces of evidence most strongly indicate that TBI is a serious problem for athletes?

- With a partner, compare your understanding of return-to-play laws and discuss how effective you think these laws are in preventing TBI.

Answers

5. Answers will vary; some of the more compelling evidence include data, research, and facts, such as the Purdue study of high school football players showing memory problems.

Answers

1. Junior Seau was a professional football player who committed suicide. After his death, his brain showed signs of damage related to concussions.

2. Return-to-play laws may vary from state to state, but the intent is for a player to be evaluated following a head injury by a professional before he or she is allowed to participate in sports.

Vocabulary Strategy: Building Personal Vocabulary

Identify and list five words from the reading selection that you do not know or do not know well. Use context clues or word analysis to guess their meaning. Then consult a dictionary to look up each word and find a meaning that fits the context of the passage. Write down that definition.

READING SELECTION

Connect

You will find a coordinated Power of Process assignment for this reading in your Connect course.

Answers

1. Soccer players may head the ball or might be accidently hit by a ball, especially the goalie when trying to block a shot.

2. Soccer players could avoid heading the ball to avoid brain injuries.

Answers

3. Evidence of TBI in soccer players includes the testimony of Robert Cantu, a Boston University professor, government data, and the deaths of goalies during play. Evidence that TBI may not be caused by soccer include the case of Patrick Grange, who experienced concussions as a toddler.

4. The author's solution is for players to wear protective headgear.

"THIS IS WHAT HAPPENS TO YOUR BRAIN WHEN YOU GET KICKED IN THE HEAD"

Complete the "Before Reading" assignment. Then read the selection while you complete the "During Reading" activities. Finally, complete the "After Reading" assignment.

 ### Before Reading: Predict

Write answers to these questions using complete sentences.

1. The reading focuses on soccer. Predict how soccer players might be at risk for traumatic brain injury.

2. How might soccer players protect themselves from brain injuries?

 ### During Reading: Annotate

Complete the following exercises.

3. As you read, mark the evidence that traumatic brain injury is a serious problem for soccer players.

4. As you read, consider what is the author's solution to the problem of traumatic brain injury in soccer players?

This Is What Happens to Your Brain
When You Get Kicked in the Head

By Jenna McLaughlin

Mother Jones, 19 June 2014

The 2014 World Cup soccer games brought more attention than ever to soccer, as well as to concussions associated with the sport. This article argues that heading the soccer ball—driving it with one's head—is not what causes brain injuries. Rather, collisions between players or between players and the ground or goalposts are to blame. Protective headgear, especially for goalies, might be one way to prevent or lessen soccer players' head trauma.

Since February, when a *New York Times* article linked heading soccer balls to the possibility of brain injury, the media—eager for a new angle on the 2014 World Cup—has fixated on the dangers of headers. The *Boston Globe, Slate*, and Fox News have all warned that heading the ball might cause serious damage to players' brains.

Scientific studies have shown that rates of concussions and head injury in soccer are comparable to football, ice hockey, lacrosse, and rugby. But news stories that focus on the danger of heading have it all wrong. It's not the ball that soccer players should be worried about—it's everything else. Player-to-player, player-to-ground, and player-to-goalpost collisions are soccer's biggest dangers, explains Robert Cantu, a professor at Boston University who has researched the issue. An opponent's head, foot, or elbow is much more dangerous than a one-pound soccer ball. It's true that "the single most risky activity in soccer is heading the ball," Cantu says—but that's because contact with other players, the goalposts, or the ground is so much more likely when a player goes up for a header.

Government data supports the idea that contact with other players is a much bigger problem than contact with the ball. Most of the 24,184 reported cases of traumatic brain injury in soccer reported in a 2011 Consumer Products Safety Commission study resulted from player-to-player contact; just 12.6 percent resulted from contact with a ball. Head-to-head, head-to-ground, and head-to-goalpost injuries are all more common than head-to-ball injuries in U.S. youth leagues, according to the Centers for Disease Control and Prevention.

Recent speculation about the damage done by headers on the brain has centered on the case of Patrick Grange, a 29-year-old forward for the Chicago Fire's development league team who died of amyotrophic lateral sclerosis, sometimes known as Lou Gehrig's disease, in 2012. Scientists who studied Grange's brain after his death found evidence of chronic trauma encephalopathy, a disease previously found only in the brains of deceased boxers, NFL players, and military veterans. CTE, which some researchers believe is linked to repetitive head trauma, can cause memory loss, dementia, aggression, confusion, and depression. But often, symptoms don't show up for years after the initial brain trauma, and for now, doctors can only diagnose it after death.

Many studies on soccer, heading, and brain trauma don't account for dementia, mental-health issues, previous concussions, or other brain injuries or diseases.

Christopher Nowinski, the author of *Head Games: Football's Concussion Crisis from the NFL to Youth Leagues*, which focuses on head trauma in football, has linked

Grange's death to heading the ball, calling him a "prolific header." But scientists do not fully understand the link between brain injuries and concussions and the act of heading a soccer ball. Current studies of soccer, heading, and brain trauma have small sample sizes; many don't account for dementia, mental-health issues, previous concussions, or other brain injuries or diseases, such as Grange's ALS.

The *New York Times*, for example, reported that Grange's parents said he had suffered several concussions in his youth, including a fall as a toddler, as well as concussions playing soccer before advancing to the Fire's developmental team. The more concussions a person suffers, the more likely he is to sustain future, more severe brain injuries. The science suggests that headers have something to do with brain injury in some cases, but the connection is not clear yet. 7

What is clear from the science, however, is that collisions with players, goalposts, or the ground can be extremely dangerous. Take Thursday's Uruguay–England World Cup match, for example. Fighting for the ball, Uruguayan defender Álvaro Pereira took a knee to the head and was knocked out on the pitch. Still, Pereira immediately returned to play, going directly against last year's recommendations from the American Academy of Neurology: "If in doubt, sit it out." (FIFA, international soccer's main organizing body, has a similar suggestion on its website but has no hard rules regarding concussions and required time off the pitch.) (Update: On Friday, FIFPro, the world soccer players' union, accused FIFA of failing to protect Pereira by removing him from the game after he was briefly knocked unconscious.) 8

Goalkeepers, who spend their games diving into the ground and colliding with other players, are arguably the most vulnerable to brain injury. Their risk for injury to the head and cervical spine is comparable to that of skydivers and pole vaulters, according to a 2000 study Cantu coauthored. FIFA has published an article on its website warning that goalkeepers are constantly "subjected to direct trauma" resulting from contact with the ground, the goalposts, and other players. 9

In April 2010, Briana Scurry, who played goalkeeper for United States Olympic and World Cup teams, was in her second season with D.C.'s Washington Freedom when she collided head-on with a striker. Scurry began getting severe headaches and feeling depressed—symptoms she later attributed to a concussion and neck injury. "All my career, my success has been based on my mentality. It all starts with my mind," Scurry said later. "And so, for me, my brain was broken." 10

Scurry isn't alone—goalkeepers have fallen victim to traumatic brain injuries for decades. In 1933, Jon Kristbjornsson, a goalkeeper for the Icelandic soccer team Valur Reykjavik, died of brain trauma after colliding with another player. The rule in soccer forbidding players from kicking the ball once the goalkeeper has possession was the result of the death of keeper Jimmy Thorpe, who perished after being kicked in the head and chest in a game in 1936. In 2006, Petr Cech, the goalkeeper for Chelsea, needed skull decompression surgery after colliding with a midfielder in the penalty box. He now wears safety headgear when he plays. Last year, Boubacar Barry, an Ivorian keeper, hit the goalpost while making a save and fell unconscious, missing the rest of the season. In April, a keeper from Gabon died because a striker accidentally stepped on his head after he saved a shot and was lying on the ground. 11

Soccer headbands and headgear may offer a partial solution. A study published in 2003 by the National Athletic Trainers' Association in coordination with the 12

National Institutes of Health found a significant reduction in peak force of impact on soccer players' heads with three different marketed headbands, and a 2006 McGill University study that tracked 278 adolescent soccer players over a season found that using headgear was associated with cutting concussion risk in half. Players who didn't wear headgear were twice as likely to get concussions. Despite these and similar findings, FIFA does not require or recommend the use of headgear for soccer players—including goalkeepers—at any age level.

 ## After Reading: Reflect on the Text

Refer to the reading selection as you complete this exercise.

5. What ideas in the text are new to you? What ideas in the text conflict with what you already knew before you started reading?

Read to Write Activity

Engage with the Reading

Refer to the reading selection as you complete these exercises.

1. Were you convinced by McLaughlin's evidence that "collisions with players, goalposts, or the ground" (366) are the most serious risks to soccer players rather than heading the ball? Why or why not?

2. The article mentions the American Academy of Neurology's advice "If in doubt, sit it out" (qtd. in McLaughlin) but notes that FIFA does not require players with suspected injuries to stay out of the game. Should there be official rules to enforce "sit[ting] it out"? Explain.

3. McLaughlin suggests that "headbands and headgear may offer a partial solution" (367) to the problem of traumatic brain injury in soccer players. How does the author support the idea that headgear would solve the problem?

Pair and Share

- With a partner, compare your annotations from exercise 3 in "During Reading" that traumatic brain injury is a serious problem for soccer players. Which pieces of evidence most strongly indicate that TBI is a serious problem?

- With a partner, compare the author's solution from exercise 4 in "During Reading." Do you feel this is a good solution? Can you think of other possible solutions?

Answers

5. Answers will vary. Encourage students to look back at their annotations to identify new ideas and conflicting ideas.

Answers

1. The author presents a convincing argument that contact with other players is a more serious risk than heading the ball. Particularly compelling evidence includes the deaths of goalies who have collided with other players or been kicked or stepped on.

2. There could be a rule, like the return-to-play rule in football, for soccer players.

3. The author provides statistics showing that players who wear protective headgear suffer fewer concussions.

Vocabulary Strategy: Building Personal Vocabulary

Identify and list five words from the reading selection that you do not know or do not know well. Use context clues or word analysis to guess their meaning. Then consult a dictionary to look up each word and find a meaning that fits the context of the passage. Write down that definition.

Theme Activity: Write in Response to a Chosen Prompt 📖 📝

1. Review the prompt you chose for your essay. What is your purpose, and who is your audience?
2. Review your notes on the reading selections for this theme. Prewrite about your topic to generate additional ideas. Do additional research if necessary or required by your instructor.
3. Create an informal outline, graphic organizer, or essay plan that organizes your notes and includes a topic sentence for each paragraph.
4. Write a thesis statement that sums up the main ideas, gives your point of view, and reflects the organizational pattern of your paper.
5. Draft the introduction, body paragraphs, and conclusion for your essay using your thesis statement and your outline, graphic organizer, or essay plan.
6. Revise your essay for coherence and unity. Edit and proofread for errors in grammar and typing.
7. Document your sources and format your essay according to your instructor's directions.

Works Cited

Berl, Rachel Pomerance. "Why We're So Fat: What's Behind the Latest Obesity Rates." *Writing to Read, Reading to Write,* edited by Alison Kuehner, McGraw-Hill Education, 2019, pp. 339–341.

Manescu, Larisa. "Adapt to Inaccuracy in Social Media." *Writing to Read, Reading to Write,* edited by Alison Kuehner, McGraw-Hill Education, 2019, pp. 325–327.

McLaughlin, Jenna. "This Is What Happens to Your Brain When You Get Kicked in the Head." *Writing to Read, Reading to Write,* edited by Alison Kuehner, McGraw-Hill Education, 2019, pp. 365–367.

"Social Media Fact Sheet." Pew Research Center, 5 Feb. 2018, www.pewinternet.org/fact-sheet/social-media/.

Weld, Sarah. "Be Here Now." *Writing to Read, Reading to Write,* edited by Alison Kuehner, McGraw-Hill Education, 2019, pp. 323.

Grammar and
Style Handbook

GRAMMAR IN CONTEXT

Writing Strong Sentences

Choosing Words Well

Using Punctuation Effectively

In college, you will want to write clearly and correctly, especially when others will read your work, such as a homework assignment, a status report for a project, or a formal paper. Remember that your writing reflects how you think. Take the time and effort to write well so your ideas are communicated with clarity, concision, and correctness.

One strategy for developing strong writing is to pay close attention to how professional and skilled writers use words, sentences, and other elements in their writing. That is, you can read for more than one purpose: (1) to understand and respond to an author's message, and (2) to appreciate and learn from his or her **writing style.** *Writing style* refers to how an author uses words, sentences, or punctuation to express his or her ideas. Mike Rose, in his interview "Writing as a Process," explains how writers can hone their skills by reading other writers:

> When you find authors who write well in your discipline or people who just write well, a favorite novelist, read them and read them like a writer, rather than reading them like a reader. In other words, read them with an eye to figuring out what it is they do that makes their writing work so well. You read them analytically, you read them with an eye to stealing a trick or two. So I think there are a lot of things that students can do to help themselves become better writers. (75)
> Tina Arora, *"Writing as a Process: An Interview with Mike Rose" InterActions: UCLA Journal of Education and Information Studies* 6(2) 2010. Used with permission of Mike Rose.

For this reason, we will examine **grammar** (sentence structure and language rules) as it is used *in context* in the readings throughout this book. Excerpts from the text's professional reading selections and from sample student papers appear at the beginning of most sections. Highlighted examples are then taken from these excerpts to illustrate specific grammar and language elements. As you read about these grammar and language elements, you can refer to the excerpt from which the examples are taken. In that way, you can see how the authors use them in their writing and then practice how to translate these proficient moves into your own writing. However, rather than simply copying what other skilled writers do, try to analyze, understand, and then apply those principles to your own writing so you can communicate your original ideas with confidence and competence.

This Grammar and Style Handbook is not intended to be a complete or comprehensive guide to all kinds of usage in English—there are entire books devoted to grammar. Rather, think of this as a brief guide, one that will expand your sentence-writing style, improve your word choice, and help you use punctuation effectively. If you need more guidance or practice, ask your instructor for additional resources.

This handbook is divided into three sections, each focusing on different areas of writing: (1) composing sentences, (2) choosing words, and (3) using punctuation. In each section, you will find explanations and examples of different aspects of that area of writing. At the end of each section is an activity that allows you to apply what you learned to a piece of writing.

You can use this handbook as you would any handbook—that is, on a need-to-know basis. For instance, you can read specific areas about which you are interested, such as how to use transition words, or you can study parts you feel will help improve your writing, such as checking sentences for run-ons. You can also work your way systematically through the handbook, learning about different aspects of writing as you go.

Teaching Tip

The Mike Rose interview, "Writing as a Process," can be found in Chapter 3.

Teaching Tip

Connect is one resource that provides more practice with grammar and mechanics

Connect

Assign the LearnSmart Achieve topic "Coordination and Subordination" for adaptive learning to accompany this material.

WRITING STRONG SENTENCES

This section first focuses on ways to compose strong sentences—by writing clear, effective sentences and by developing sentence variety. Then the section provides strategies for correcting the most common sentence errors: sentence fragments and run-on sentences.

Composing Sentences

In her memoir *The Writing Life*, American author Annie Dillard tells of a well-known writer who was asked by a university student, "Do you think I could be a writer?" "Well," the writer replied, "I don't know. . . Do you like sentences?" (70). The point of this anecdote is that the basic currency of writing is the sentence. Readers encounter prose one sentence at a time. Writers must write one sentence at a time. Appreciating a well-written sentence is at the heart of good writing.

▌ Simple and Compound Sentences in Context

Teaching Tip

"Rethinking the Writing Process" appears in Chapter 3.

The following excerpt is from "Rethinking the Writing Process: What Best-Selling and Award-Winning Authors Have to Say" by Michael R. Sampson, Evan Ortlieb, and Cynthia B. Leung. Passages highlighted in green *are repeated below as examples of simple sentences. Passages highlighted in* pink *are repeated below as examples of compound sentences.*

The academic writers surveyed start with an outline or plan, but they also add and change ideas once they start writing. Yetta Goodman commented that with professional writing, "I do know that ideas shift and change as I am writing even when I have an outline or organizational chart that I follow." The outline or plan may be in their mind before they begin writing, as with Thomas Gunning: "I may have a general idea of the piece if it is nonfiction. Often I will plan the piece in my head for a day or more before I start writing." Some writers use different processes for writing different genres, as in this response from an anonymous writer:

> In screenplays or contemporary novels, I do an outline. But in writing historical fiction, I find I work best with a loose structure; then, as I do research, the history I unearth often suggests plotlines or characters that take the story in unexpected directions. If I find the plot turns unexpectedly, I figure the readers will, too.

Revision

Textual evolution also requires author reflection and revision. The number of revisions that writers make to their manuscripts varies from none to more than 10, with most authors making 4 to 10 revisions per piece of writing and others making more than 10. The many iterations and revisions that these highly successful authors make to their manuscripts are in stark contrast to the writing process that occurs in schools. Some writers use self-created systems for revising. Sol Stein uses a "lockstitch technique," revising and revisiting what he has written throughout the writing process. Yetta Goodman said,

continued

It is hard to specify. I rewrite segments of my text over a long period of time, so I can't count separate revisions. It goes on continually until I believe I'm ready to send articles or books to the publishers.

Simple Sentences. The most basic sentence type is a simple sentence.

- A **simple sentence** contains one main, or independent, clause.
- A **clause** is a group of words that contains a subject and a verb.
- A **subject** is the noun or pronoun that captures the action: the person, place, thing, or idea that the clause or sentence is about.
- A **verb** is the word that conveys the essential action or state of being in the clause or sentence—what the subject does or is.

Notice that a simple sentence includes a subject and verb, as in the sentences that follow from "Rethinking the Writing Process," in which the authors describe the revision process.

> **Examples of Simple Sentences**
>
> "Textual evolution also requires author reflection and revision" (372).
>   subject   verb
> "Some writers use self-created systems for revising" (372).
>   subject verb

Compound Sentences. Some sentences are formed through **coordination**, a technique for combining two simple sentences of equal importance. The resulting combined sentence is called a **compound sentence**. Writers use coordination when they want to join related ideas into one sentence.

In English, seven **coordinating conjunctions** are used to join two simple sentences (that is, independent clauses): *for, and, nor, but, or, yet, so.* You can remember these coordinating conjunctions as the FANBOYS, an acronym made up of the first letter of each conjunction.

> **Coordinators (FANBOYS)**
>
> | for | and | nor | but | or | yet | so |

Notice that a comma is used before a coordinating conjunction that joins two independent clauses, as in the following example sentences from "Rethinking the Writing Process."

> **Examples of Compound Sentences**
>
> "The academic writers surveyed start with an outline or plan, but they
> also add and change ideas once they start writing" (372).   *coordinator*

Connect

Assign the LearnSmart Achieve topic "Parts of Speech" for adaptive learning to accompany this material.

continued

> "I rewrite segments of my text over a long period of time, **so** I can't count separate revisions" (372).
>
> *coordinator*

▌ Complex and Compound-Complex Sentences in Context

Teaching Tip

"Forget A's, B's, and C's" appears in Chapter 5.

Class Activity

Students could also identify simple and compound sentences in this passage to understand how the author uses sentence variety.

The following excerpt is from "Forget A's, B's, and C's—What Students Need Is More Zzzz's" by Mary A. Carskadon. Passages highlighted in blue *are repeated below as examples of complex sentences. Passages highlighted in* orange *are repeated below as examples of compound-complex sentences.*

Some advertisers routinely entreat us to undermine our health, but rarely through overt attacks on healthy behavior. When one such unhealthful message assaulting sleep reached my university's campus this fall, I began to hear about it from offended and sympathetic colleagues. One saw it in her freshman daughter's dorm. Another saw it in a campus convenience store. The makers of the energy drink Red Bull advised students that "Nobody ever wishes they'd slept more during college."

Decades of studies about the neurological and psychiatric importance of sleep in teens and young adults indicate that this "advice" is rubbish. Unlike the drink maker's aluminum cans, it should never be recycled.

In adolescents—and younger college students, according to recent data from my lab—sleep is a neurologically important process during which the fast-growing brain becomes better organized. Many neural connections forged earlier in life during rapid growth are pruned away if they are no longer needed, and new pathways are established to the parts of the brain that are responsible for such things as planning, organizing, and abstract thinking. . . .

To be fair to the advertiser and its fun-loving sentiment, there really are a lot of opportunities for college students to have a good time. If students were getting enough sleep, they probably would miss out on some fun. But many studies, including Orzech's, have found that on average, young college students are not within shouting distance of the amount of sleep clinicians believe to be healthy. I tell my students that they should get about eight and a half hours of sleep every night, but a recent study found that students on average are getting nearly an hour less than that. I'll make that more explicit: College students should sleep more. . .

Other activities limit sleep as well, including texting, tweeting, and Facebooking in bed, which can keep students awake by producing light and causing social stimulation. (Studying late at night also involves light, although it is surely not as stimulating as is social networking.) Once teens get to college, whatever help their parents still provided to set a bedtime, or at least to encourage sleep, is no longer available. Students are left to exercise their judgment about when to sleep, and their decisions are based more on what to do while awake than when to sleep.

Complex Sentences. A subordinating conjunction joins related ideas to create a **complex sentence**—a sentence that contains at least one main clause and one subordinating clause. Like a coordinating conjunction, a **subordinating conjunction** is a word (or phrase) that links two clauses; a subordinating conjunction, however, signals that one clause is *subordinate,* or less important. Subordinating conjunctions are useful for connecting related ideas and making writing flow logically. The following table lists common subordinating conjunctions.

Subordinating Conjunctions					
after	because	if	that	when	wherever
although	before	if only	though	whenever	whether
as	even if	rather than	unless	where	which
as if	even though	since	until	whereas	while

A **subordinate** (or **dependent) clause** is a clause that is of secondary importance in the sentence. A subordinate clause can come at the beginning of a sentence, as in the first example that follows. Such a sentence usually requires a comma after the subordinate clause. A subordinate clause can also occur at the end of a sentence, as in the second example. The examples are taken from "Forget A's, B's, and C's—What Students Need Is More Zzzz's."

Examples of Complex Sentences

"<u>When</u> one such unhealthful message assaulting sleep reached my
subordinator
university's campus this fall, I began to hear about it from offended and

sympathetic colleagues" (127).

"Other activities limit sleep as well, including texting, tweeting, and

Facebooking in bed, <u>which</u> can keep students awake by producing
                          subordinator
light and causing social stimulation" (128).

Compound-Complex Sentences. As its name implies, a **compound-complex sentence** combines both a compound sentence and a complex sentence; in other words, it contains two or more independent clauses joined by a coordinator (a compound sentence) and one or more subordinate clauses (a complex sentence). While compound-complex sentences may sound technically difficult to write, you may find that writers often use these, especially in academic writing, because they help explain complicated ideas. The examples are taken from "Forget A's, B's, and C's—What Students Need Is More Zzzz's."

Examples of Compound-Complex Sentences

"Many neural connections forged earlier in life during rapid growth are
      independent clause

pruned away if they are no longer needed, **and** new pathways are
          subordinate clause   *independent clause*

established to the parts of the brain that are responsible for such things
                             subordinate clause

as planning, organizing, and abstract thinking" (127).

"I tell my students that they should get about eight and a half hours of
independent clause   *subordinate clause*

sleep every night, **but** a recent study found that students on average
               independent clause   *subordinate clause*

are getting nearly an hour less than that" (128).

▌ Parallel Structure in Context

Teaching Tip

"This Is What Happens to
Your Brain When You Get
Kicked in the Head"
appears in Part 4,
"Anthology of Theme-Based
Readings."

The following excerpt is from "This Is What Happens to Your Brain When You Get Kicked in the Head" by Jenna McLaughlin. Passages highlighted in purple *are repeated below as examples of sentences using parallel structure. Additional examples of parallelism in the excerpt are underlined.*

     Since February, when a *New York Times* article linked heading soccer balls to the possibility of brain injury, the media—eager for a new angle on the 2014 World Cup—has fixated on the dangers of headers. The *Boston Globe*, *Slate*, and Fox News have all warned that heading the ball might cause serious damage to players' brains.

     Scientific studies have shown that rates of concussions and head injury in soccer are comparable to [rates in] football, ice hockey, lacrosse, and rugby. But news stories that focus on the danger of heading have it all wrong. It's not the ball that soccer players should be worried about—it's everything else. Player-to-player, player-to-ground, and player-to-goalpost collisions are soccer's biggest dangers, explains Robert Cantu, a professor at Boston University who has researched the issue. An opponent's head, foot, or elbow is much more dangerous than a one-pound soccer ball. It's true that "the single most risky activity in soccer is heading the ball," Cantu says—but that's because contact with other players, the goalposts, or the ground is so much more likely when a player goes up for a header.

     Government data supports the idea that contact with other players is a much bigger problem than contact with the ball. Most of the 24,184 reported cases of traumatic brain injury in soccer reported in a 2011 Consumer Products Safety

continued

Commission study resulted from player-to-player contact; just 12.6 percent resulted from contact with a ball. Head-to-head, head-to-ground, and head-to-goalpost injuries are all more common than head-to-ball injuries in U.S. youth leagues, according to the Centers for Disease Control and Prevention.

Recent speculation about the damage done by headers on the brain has centered on the case of Patrick Grange, a 29-year-old forward for the Chicago Fire's development league team who died of amyotrophic lateral sclerosis, sometimes known as Lou Gehrig's disease, in 2012. Scientists who studied Grange's brain after his death found evidence of chronic trauma encephalopathy, a disease previously found only in the brains of deceased boxers, NFL players, and military veterans. CTE, which some researchers believe is linked to repetitive head trauma, can cause memory loss, dementia, aggression, confusion, and depression. But often, symptoms don't show up for years after the initial brain trauma, and for now, doctors can only diagnose it after death.

Jenna McLaughlin, "This Is What Happens to Your Brain When You Get Kicked in the Head," from *Mother Jones*, June 19, 2014. Copyright © 2014 Foundation for National Progress. All rights reserved. Used by permission and protected by the Copyright Laws of the United States. The printing, copying, redistribution, or retransmission of this content with express written permission is prohibited.

Parallel Structure. One strategy for incorporating details into a sentence is to use **parallel structure**, which means repeating the same grammatical pattern. Parallel structure, also known as *parallelism*, is an efficient way to write and to connect related ideas or details.

The grammatical pattern can vary in parallel structure. A sentence using parallel structure, for example, might repeat nouns, adjectives, phrases, clauses, or some other element. However, once a pattern has been established, the other elements should repeat that pattern. If the sentence does not repeat the same pattern, the series of elements will not be parallel, and the sentence will be ungrammatical. Moreover, the ideas or details written in parallel structure should have the same level of importance. Notice in the example sentences from "This Is What Happens to Your Brain When You Get Kicked in the Head" how the writer uses words and phrases to add details or examples to the sentences using parallelism. Following each parallel sentence is an ungrammatical version that demonstrates lack of parallel structure. In the first ungrammatical example, the series consists of two nouns and a phrase. In the second ungrammatical example, the series consists of (1) an adjective plus a noun, (2) a noun plus a phrase, and (3) a noun plus a clause.

Connect

Assign the LearnSmart Achieve topic "Parallelism" for more practice understanding parallel structure and correcting faulty parallelism.

Examples of Sentences Using Parallel Structure

Parallel: "It's true that 'the single most risky activity in soccer is heading the ball,' Cantu says—but that's because contact with other players, the goalposts, or the ground is so much more likely when a player goes up for a header" (365).

Not Parallel (Ungrammatical): It's true that "the single most risky activity in soccer is heading the ball," Cantu says—but that's because contact with other players, the goalposts, or by falling on the ground is so much more likely when a player goes up for a header.

---

continued

> **Parallel:** "Scientists who studied Grange's brain after his death found evidence of chronic trauma encephalopathy, a disease previously found only in the brains of <u>deceased boxers</u>, <u>NFL players</u>, and <u>military veterans</u>."
>
> **Not Parallel (Ungrammatical):** Scientists who studied Grange's brain after his death found evidence of chronic trauma encephalopathy, a disease previously found only in the brains of <u>deceased boxers</u>, <u>players of football</u>, and <u>people who served in the military</u>.

▌Sentence Variety in Context

Teaching Tip

"Facing the Truth" can be found in Part 4, "Anthology of Theme-Based Readings."

The following excerpt is from "Facing the Truth" by Patrick Hruby. Passages highlighted in aqua *are repeated below as examples of sentence variety.*

When he first saw the data, Patrick Bellgowan figured he had made a mistake. How else to explain it? A scientist at the University of Tulsa's Laureate Institute for Brain Research, Bellgowan had been scanning the brains of college football players, comparing the results to scans of non-players. His focus was on the hippocampus, a seahorse-shaped area deep inside the brain that plays an important role in emotional control and memory formation.

Bellgowan knew that the hippocampus was sensitive to traumatic brain injury. That shrinkage of the region was a hallmark of Alzheimer's disease. That a similar reduction in hippocampal volume also corresponded with chronic traumatic encephalopathy (CTE), a neurodegenerative disease linked to football, boxing and other contact sports. Still, he expected to see little difference in hippocampal size between a group of 50 college players and 25 non-players, mostly because everyone in the study was relatively healthy and young.

And then Rashimi Singh, a fellow researcher at the Laureate Institute, brought a set of initial results to Bellgowan's office.

"Are you sure?" he said. "That can't be right."

The numbers were stark. A group of 25 players with no history of reported concussions had hippocampuses that were, on average, 14 percent smaller than those of a control group of 25 males of similar age and health who didn't play contact sports. Moreover, the same brain region in a second group of 25 players who had suffered at least one clinically diagnosed concussion was, on average, 25 percent smaller than the control group—a larger difference in volume, Bellgowan says, than the variations scientists have observed between the brains of healthy people and patients suffering from Alzheimer's or severe depression.

"I can't tell you how many times we checked this over," Bellgowan says. "The effect size was really large. It was really surprising."

Published this week in the *Journal of the American Medical Association*, the results of Bellgowan and Singh's research may be unexpected, but they also reflect a larger scientific trend. While much of the health and safety debate over football and

continued

other contact sports focuses on the risk of developing severe, headline-grabbing neurodegenerative diseases like amyotrophic lateral sclerosis (ALS) and CTE, a growing body of evidence suggests that both concussions and subconcussive blows can alter mood, cognition and behavior while causing damage and structural changes to the brain.

In other words, contact sports may be worse for your cognitive health than previously assumed, even if you don't ultimately end up in a dementia ward.

Sentence Variety. A passage consisting of many sentences of the same length or type may seem monotonous to readers. In contrast, **sentence variety**—sentences of different lengths and types—can provide interest and emphasis. For example, long sentences work well to provide detailed information, while short sentences can highlight important points. Notice how the writer of "Facing the Truth" uses sentence variety to get the reader's attention at the beginning of the article and then again later when he introduces statistics, as the example that follows demonstrates.

Connect

Assign the LearnSmart Achieve topic "Eliminating Redundancies and Recognizing Sentence Variety" for more practice understanding and writing various types of sentences.

Example of Sentence Variety

"When he first saw the data, Patrick Bellgowan figured he had

complex sentence

made a mistake" (355).

"How else to explain it?" (355).

short question

"A scientist at the University of Tulsa's Laureate Institute for Brain

longer sentence

Research, Bellgowan had been scanning the brains of college football

players, comparing the results to scans of non-players" (355).

"His focus was on the hippocampus, a seahorse-shaped area deep

complex sentence

inside the brain that plays an important role in emotional control and

memory formation" (355).

How to Create Sentence Variety. Here are two ways to enliven your writing with sentence variety, with examples from "Facing the Truth."

1. Use long and short sentences in each paragraph. Use short sentences for emphasis.

   Example of a short sentence used for emphasis: "The numbers were stark. A group of 25 players with no history of reported concussions had hippocampuses that were, on average, 14 percent smaller than those of a control group of 25 males of similar age and health who didn't play contact sports" (356).

2. Vary sentence openings. Always beginning sentences with a noun or with words such as *the, it, this,* and *there* can seem repetitious.

   Example of starting with a phrase acknowledging the source: "Published this week in the *Journal of the American Medical Association*, the results of Bellgowan and Singh's research may be unexpected, but they also reflect a larger scientific trend" (356).

   Example of starting with a subordinate clause: "While much of the health and safety debate over football and other contact sports focuses on the risk of developing severe, headline-grabbing neurodegenerative diseases like amyotrophic lateral sclerosis (ALS) and CTE, a growing body of evidence suggests that both concussions and subconcussive blows can alter mood, cognition and behavior while causing damage and structural changes to the brain" (356).

   Example of starting with a transition: "In other words, contact sports may be worse for your cognitive health than previously assumed, even if you don't ultimately end up in a dementia ward" (356).

Checking Sentences

Connect

Assign the LearnSmart Achieve topics "Fused (Run-on) Sentences and Comma Splices" and "Phrases, Clauses, and Fragments" for adaptive learning to accompany this material.

This section demonstrates how to proofread to ensure sentences are correctly written, focusing on two types of common errors: sentence fragments and run-on sentences. You want to be sure you have written grammatically correct sentences, or else readers may think you are not a skillful writer or may be confused by your sentences.

Sentence Fragments. A simple sentence contains a subject and a verb. When a sentence does not contain either a subject or a verb, then it is an incomplete sentence, or **sentence fragment**. Study the examples of sentence fragments.

Examples of Sentence Fragments

Missing a subject: <u>Motivates</u> students to keep working at a task.
        verb

Missing a verb: <u>Students' mindsets</u> in college.
                subject

To identify sentence fragments, read a sentence carefully and ask yourself if it has both a subject and a verb. If not, then it is a fragment. Correct a fragment by adding what is missing: either a subject or verb.

Examples of Corrected Sentence Fragments

Subject added: <u>A growth mindset</u> <u>motivates</u> students to keep working
        subject   *verb*
at a task.

Verb added: <u>Students' mindsets</u> in college <u>can be changed</u>.
      subject   *verb*

Run-on Sentences. A **run-on sentence** is a type of ungrammatical sentence that contains two independent clauses that are joined together without proper punctuation. Some run-ons have no punctuation, and some have insufficient punctuation (only a comma). Study the examples of run-on sentences that follow.

Examples of Run-on Sentences

No punctuation:

<u>College students often multitask while studying</u><u>they like to listen to</u>
independent clause 1   *independent clause 2*
<u>music or check social media.</u>

Insufficient punctuation:

<u>Students think multitasking makes them more productive,</u> <u>this is</u>
independent clause 1
<u>an illusion.</u>
independent clause 2

To identify run-on sentences, read a sentence carefully and ask yourself whether it includes what could be two independent clauses, each with a subject and a verb. If so, check that the two clauses are correctly connected.

How to Correct Run-on Sentences. Use these methods to change run-ons into grammatical sentences.

1. Insert a *coordinator*, preceded by a comma, between the two clauses to logically link the ideas.
   Example: Students think multitasking makes them more productive, **but** this is an illusion.

2. Insert a *semicolon* between the two clauses, if the ideas in the clauses are closely related.
   Example: College students often multitask while studying; this is an illusion.

3. Use a *transition word* (other than a coordinator) preceded by a semicolon to logically link ideas.
   Example: Students think multitasking makes them more productive; however, this is an illusion.

4. Place a period between the two independent clauses to create two sentences.
   Example: College students often multitask while studying. They like to listen to music or check social media.

Apply What You Learned

In this section, you will have an opportunity to use the sentence composing and sentence checking skills from the previous sections to improve a piece of writing. Your goal is to review the sample draft and make changes to strengthen the sentences.

A good strategy is to read the draft several times, each time checking different aspects of the sentences. Here is a recommended step-by-step process for reading and revising:

1. Read the sample draft aloud. Listen to the flow of the sentences. Notice whether the sentences have variety. If not, try to vary the sentences using different sentence types, such as simple, compound, complex, or compound-complex. Consider different ways to begin sentences, or consider using parallelism to include details and examples. Rewrite any sentences to improve the paragraphs.

2. Read the sample draft slowly and carefully, one sentence at a time. Check that the sentences are grammatically correct. For instance, look for sentence fragments and rewrite any you find so they are complete sentences. Check for run-on sentences and revise any you find by using correct punctuation and/or transition words.

3. Read aloud your revised version of the sample draft (after completing steps 1 and 2) and check again that the sentences are effectively written and grammatically correct. Make any changes needed to improve the writing.

Sample Draft

Teaching Tip

After students revise the sample draft, they can compare their sentences to the student's final draft in Chapter 3.

Writing was never interesting to me. I always caught myself talking more than putting words down on the paper. I had energy to run around. I had none to sit down and write. I figured that writing had a lot of benefits. I was able to organize my thoughts, I could think more carefully before making a decision, I was able to express myself.

After my last year in middle school realizing I should find a better way to keep my ideas together. I started to write a lot since then. At first, it

continued

was only for fun purposes. I wrote songs about what I feel like when my crush turned his head around and looked at my direction. I wrote down my crazy dreams after I woke up, I thought that one day I could publish them; Ironically, those dreams were from a movie I saw the night before. I wrote down my mom's grocery list, and put it in her purse before she went to the store; those things on the list were my favorite treats. Going to high school. I realized I should write to improve my grades at school. I began to put more effort into turning my dream journal into a personal journal. I began to create to-do lists for myself, so I would not forget any important things I had to get done. I began to write longer songs with more meaningful lyrics, mostly about positivity because we could never get enough of it. Maintaining my writing habit throughout high school. I moved to college and started to be familiar with "assignments". When I realized I had to write no matter if I wanted to or not. I wrote more and more after purchasing a smartphone. I wrote on the bus, in the car, and flying on the airplane; whenever something came to mind, I wrote it down on my phone. I liked to highlight and mark my books with a lot of colors and margin notes. A colorful book will be more helpful to me when I need to find a piece of evidence for my paper. However, writing has its own challenges when it comes to college writing. Being unfamiliar with the topic that I was assigned was also a difficulty for me. To write about something that I have never heard before, I should do some research before analyzing the topic. It is hard to write when you look at a blank page on a computer knowing that the word count for this paper is two thousand words and you have nothing in mind. Writing is impossible without a plan or an outline. It is similar to the 80/20 rule, if you put 80% of your effort into doing the thinking process, then you would only need 20% of your effort to start writing. On the other hand, the word "deadline" always has one meaning to me: I'm ruining the paper if I wait until the due day to start writing it. We cannot hope for some last-minute miracle. As writing requires some thoughtful thinking. It also requires some time, too.

Writing is not as hard as some people think it is. Only when you have no ideas of what you are writing about, or you are not giving yourself enough time to write, that's when everything gets harder. At the end of the day, writing is not only about getting that good grade at school, but it is also a tool to sharpen our thoughts.

CHOOSING WORDS WELL

In addition to conveying meaning, well-chosen words used grammatically and strategically can engage readers and encourage them to continue reading.

Choosing Effective Words

Being a good writer requires using words well. This means selecting words that state exactly what you want to say. Like Dr. Seuss's character Horton the Elephant, you should be able to declare about your writing, "I meant what I said and I said what I meant." Moreover, in academic writing especially, you will want to choose specific words that express your ideas precisely; you will want to use vivid words to capture your reader's attention; and you will want to employ well-chosen transition words to make the flow of your thinking clear to readers.

▌Specific and Vivid Words and Transitions in Context

The following excerpt is from a student paper, "Are We Using or Abusing Social Media?" by Raven Capras. Specific and vivid words are highlighted in light green, and some passages are repeated below as examples. Transitional words, including some that are subordinators, are underlined; some also appear in examples below.

They say you should go out and smell the roses once in a while, but why do that when there are Web sites like *Facebook* and *Instagram* where you can scroll past a hundred pictures of roses in a plethora of different filters. Personally, I have spent a fair share of my time smelling the roses before social media's evolution into the worldwide phenomenon it is today. While I am thankful for the afternoons I have spent bike riding and climbing trees as a kid, I do not remember a point in time where I did not use social media. From the moment I created my very first e-mail, I was hooked. Over time it became a priority. I can vividly remember carrying around a digital camera to capture all of the shenanigans a normal middle schooler would be involved in. This would later be posted on my *Facebook* wall for all of my "friends" to see. Social media have come quite a long way; it is almost unheard of nowadays not to have some form of account on the array of social media platforms offered. Although my feelings toward social media have fluctuated throughout the years, I am still an avid user. Nowadays I will log on and I am able to stay up to date with current events, connect with new people, or just chat with others when I am bored. While social media can be a great outlet for communicating with others, it is unfortunate when people take advantage of this new wave of technology by using it as a source for gossip or to pose as people they are not. Social media can either bring people together or make people feel isolated, whether we choose to use it or abuse it.

Specific and Vivid Words. Words are the foundation of sentences. English is a rich language with many words that have similar meanings with slightly different nuances. The English language provides an abundant toolbox from which you, as a writer, can craft your sentences to say or suggest what you want.

How to Select Effective Words. What follows are some tips for choosing words that bring writing to life. The final versions in the examples below are from "Are We Using or Abusing Social Media?"

Teaching Tip

Use the reading from the Chapter 5, "Forget A's, B's, and C's—What Students Need Is More Zzzz's," to demonstrate effective word choice. For instance, students could circle specific and vivid words in the reading selection.

1. Use specific words or details rather than general words.

   Less effective: I am <u>happy</u> that I have spent time <u>playing</u> as a kid.
                   general words   *general words*
   Final version: "I am <u>thankful</u> for the afternoons I have spent <u>bike riding</u> and
              specific words   *specific details*
   <u>climbing trees</u> as a kid" (384).

2. Use vivid words rather than vague words.

   Less effective: I can vividly remember carrying around a digital camera to <u>take</u>
                                    general verb
   pictures of <u>all the things</u> a normal middle schooler would be involved in.
           vague words
   Final version: "I can vividly remember carrying around a digital camera to

   <u>capture</u> all of the <u>shenanigans</u> a normal middle schooler would be involved in" (384).
   vivid verb   *vivid word*

3. Eliminate words that do not say much, or substitute more meaningful words.

   Less effective: <u>Personally</u>, <u>I think that</u> I have <u>really</u> spent <u>a lot</u> of my time
                   words that do not say much
   smelling the roses before social media's evolution into the worldwide

   phenomenon it is today.

   Final version: "I have spent <u>a fair share</u> of my time smelling the roses before
                   unnecessary words eliminated
   social media's evolution into the worldwide phenomenon it is today" (384).

Some Words to Avoid in Your Writing

General Words	Vague Words	Words That Do Not Say Much
bad/good	got	just
big/huge	had	really
everyone	is	that
lots of/many	it	there
people/society/you	thing	very

Transition Words. Transition words (and phrases) in sentences help reveal the logic of your thinking and how ideas are related. These words can help readers understand your reasoning and move smoothly through your prose. Here we will consider transition words at the beginning of sentences. For instance, if you want

Teaching Tip

This section of the Grammar and Style Handbook can be combined with the strategies for revising paragraphs for unity and coherence, in Chapter 4, which provide more suggestions for making transitions between sentences.

to signal readers that you are including an example, you can use the phrase *for example* or *for instance* at the beginning of a sentence. If you want to let readers know you are expanding on an idea, you can write *in addition* or *also*; on the other hand, words such as *however* or *in contrast* signal to readers a change in the topic.

Following is a chart with some transition words. There are many ways to make transitions in writing; these words show some examples and their implications.

Transition Words

Agreement or Addition	Opposition or Contrast	Cause or Time Order	Conclusion or Summary	Example or Evidence
also	although	as a result	as can be seen	actually
in addition	despite	consequently	clearly	case in point
in the same way	however	finally	in short	for example
moreover	instead	next	to sum up	for instance
similarly	on the other hand	then	ultimately	in fact

In the following examples from the student paper "Are We Using or Abusing Social Media?" note that the author uses transition words to show a contrast in ideas and to indicate time.

Teaching Tip

Use the student sample papers in Spotlight on Student Writing to examine effective use of transitions. For instance, students could circle transition words in the student papers and discuss how or why these are effective.

Examples of Sentences Using Transition Words

Although my feelings toward social media have fluctuated throughout
transition word (subordinator)
the years, I am still an avid user. Nowadays I will log on and I am able to
transition word
stay up to date with current events, connect with new people, or just

chat with others when I am bored.

Checking Words

Just as sentences must be grammatically correct, your choice of words should also be grammatically correct. In English, some grammatical errors are more glaring than others, as these errors interfere with a reader's ability to understand the message. You don't want readers to notice errors; instead, you want them to focus on the ideas in your writing. Errors that seriously distract readers and detract from your writing include incorrect subject–verb agreement, verb tense errors, and unclear pronoun references.

Connect

Assign the LearnSmart Achieve topic "Subject-Verb Agreement" for more practice understanding and correcting subject–verb agreement errors.

Subject–Verb Agreement. In English, the verb of a sentence must match the sentence subject in number. This is called **subject–verb agreement**. For instance, if the subject is plural, then a plural form of the verb is needed; if the subject is singular, then a singular verb is required.

How to Write with Subject–Verb Agreement. Here are some of the more common guidelines to ensure correct usage.

1. When the subject of a sentence contains two or more nouns or pronouns connected by *and*, use a plural verb.

    Example: <u>Wealth **and** giving</u> <u>make</u> people happy.
    subject *verb*

2. When the subject of a sentence contains two or more singular nouns or pronouns connected by *or* or *nor*, use a singular verb.

    Example: <u>A vacation **or** a donation</u> <u>makes</u> people happy.
    subject *verb*

3. When a phrase comes between the subject and the verb, the verb agrees with the subject, not with a noun or pronoun in the phrase.

    Example: <u>Professor Elizabeth Dunn</u>, who conducted three experiments,
    subject
    <u>concludes</u> that spending money on others or giving it away makes people
    verb
    happy.

4. **Indefinite pronouns** do not refer to any specific, or definite, person or thing. Rather, they are general in nature. Some indefinite pronouns, such as *everyone* and *anybody*, are considered singular.

    Example: <u>Everyone</u> <u>longs</u> for happiness.
    subject *verb*

Indefinite Pronouns That Are Singular

anybody	everybody	nobody	somebody	each/one
anyone	everyone	no one	someone	either/neither
anything	everything	nothing	something	other

Other indefinite pronouns, such as *both* and *many*, are considered plural.

Example: <u>Many</u> <u>long</u> for happiness.
subject. *verb*

Indefinite Pronouns That Are Plural

both	few	many	others	several

Finally, some indefinite pronouns can be either singular or plural depending on how the pronoun is used in the sentence. Look carefully to identify the noun in the sentence to which the indefinite pronoun refers and make the verb agree with that noun.

Example: <u>Some</u> of the **donation** <u>goes</u> to help the homeless.
      subject   *verb*

Example: <u>Some</u> of the **donations** <u>go</u> to help the homeless.
      subject   *verb*

Connect

Assign the LearnSmart Achieve topic "Verbs and Verbals" for adaptive learning to accompany this material.

Indefinite Pronouns That Can Be Either Singular or Plural

all	any	most	none	some

Verb Tense. In addition to agreeing with the sentence, verbs in English must use the correct tense. **Verb tense** indicates when an action has happened: in the past, in the present, or in the future. In this section, we will not cover all the verb tenses but rather point out one particular use of verb tense that applies to academic writing. That is, when writing about an author's ideas or quoting from a writer, use the present tense.

Examples of Academic Sentences Using Present Tense

<u>The "Fact Sheet: The Safe Use of Antibiotics"</u> <u>explains</u> that overuse of
             subject   *present-tense verb*
antibiotics is making these drugs less effective.

<u>Chris Del Mar</u>, writing in *The Guardian*, <u>reports</u> that "The World Health
      subject   *present-tense verb*
Organization estimates that 25,000 people in Europe died . . . because
of [antibiotic] resistance."

Connect

Assign the LearnSmart Achieve topics "Pronouns" and "Pronoun Reference" for adaptive learning to accompany this material.

Pronoun Reference. A **pronoun** is a word that takes the place of a noun. When you use a pronoun to replace a noun, be sure readers know who or what the pronoun refers to. A pronoun may not be clear if it can refer to more than one noun or the noun to which it refers is not explicitly stated. If the pronoun reference is not clear, then change the noun or pronoun, or rewrite the sentence to make the ideas understandable.

How to Write with Clear Pronoun Reference. Follow these guidelines to avoid sentences with errors in pronoun reference.

1. Make sure that the pronoun can refer to only one noun. If a pronoun's reference is unclear, replace the pronoun with a noun. In the following example, the pronoun *they* could refer either to "David Rutigliano and other restaurant owners" or to "the economists."

Unclear: David Rutigliano and other restaurant owners point to research by economists that show a loss of jobs after the minimum wage is increased. <u>They</u> use these facts to draw the conclusion that the minimum wage should not be raised.

Clear: David Rutigliano and other restaurant owners point to research by economists that show a loss of jobs after the minimum wage is increased. <u>Rutigliano</u> uses these facts to draw the conclusion that the minimum wage should not be raised.

2. Make sure the noun or noun phrase to which the pronoun refers is explicitly stated. In the example sentence, the reader has not been told what *it* refers to. The reader wonders, What exactly has been proposed in Congress? What exactly does the president support?

   Unclear: <u>It</u> has been proposed in Congress because the president supports <u>it</u>.

   Clear: <u>Legislation raising the federal minimum wage</u> has been proposed in Congress because the president supports it.

Apply What You Learned

In this section, you will have an opportunity to use the tips for choosing and using effective words and pronouns, as well as checking subject–verb agreement and verb tense, to improve a piece of writing. Your goal is to review the sample paragraph and make changes to correct or strengthen the nouns, pronouns, transition words, and verbs. A sensible strategy is to review the paragraph several times, each time focusing on a different aspect of the word choice or checking for correctness.

Here are some suggestions about how to proceed:

1. Read the sample paragraph aloud. Look carefully at the nouns, pronouns, and verbs. Consider whether the nouns and verbs are specific and vivid. Check that pronoun reference is clear. Rewrite as needed to strengthen the word choice.

2. Read the sample paragraph and look carefully at the verbs to check subject–verb agreement and verb tense. Revise any verbs that are not correct.

3. Read aloud your revised version of the sample paragraph (after completing steps 1 and 2) and check again that the words are used effectively and correctly. Make any changes needed to improve the writing.

Sample Paragraph

In "Adapt to Inaccuracy in Social Media" by Larisa Manescu, she said that we can use our cell phones for both good and for bad purposes. We can be not paying attention at a concert, or we can be helping people in an emergency. It all depends on how we use it. She gave an example of the Boston Marathon

Teaching Tip

A revised sample paragraph is included in the Instructor's Resources.

continued

bombing. Some people used their phones to call for help but other people used it by mistake. Journalists need to know when news on apps like Twitter or Facebook are wrong or they might spread misinformation. Everyone, including journalists, need to become a critical thinker and fact checker. They should explain when they know something for sure or when they don't. Manescu also said people need "to become skeptical, active consumers instead of passive re-tweeters" (326). Some people re-tweeted a fake message that the president and the White House had been bombed. Social media can become a serious problem when false messages are shared by many people. Manescu concludes that we have to "train the players" to make journalism better (327).

USING PUNCTUATION EFFECTIVELY

Punctuation creates meaning. Consider this sentence:

Woman without her man is nothing.

One way to punctuate the sentence is this:

Woman, without her man, is nothing.

With commas around the phrase "without her man," the sentence emphasizes that a woman is nothing without a man. Some women might object to that statement!

Consider another way to punctuate the same sentence:

Woman! Without her, man is nothing.

In this version, the exclamation point sets off *woman* from the rest of the sentence and suggests a man is nothing without a woman—the exact opposite meaning of the previous version. Some men may object to that statement! The moral of this story? Punctuation provides readers with important—sometimes essential—clues about how to read sentences.

As in the section about sentence types, you will first encounter excerpts from reading selections throughout the book with punctuation highlighted, followed by an explanation and analysis of how and why the punctuation is used. The intent is for you to understand how professional writers employ punctuation so you can use similar strategies in your own writing.

▌ Commas, Semicolons, and Colons in Context

Teaching Tip

"Is Facebook Making Us Lonely?" by Stephen Marche appears in Part 4, "Anthology of Theme-Based Readings."

The following excerpt is from "Is Facebook Making Us Lonely?" by Stephen Marche. Highlighted passages are repeated as examples below as follows: blue, *comma use;* pink, *semicolon use;* green, *colon use;.*

We have never been more detached from one another, or lonelier. In a world consumed by ever more novel modes of socializing, we have less and less actual

continued

society. We live in an accelerating contradiction: the more connected we become, the lonelier we are. We were promised a global village; instead, we inhabit the drab cul-de-sacs and endless freeways of a vast suburb of information. . . .

The researchers also found that lonely people are inclined to spend more time on Facebook: "One of the most noteworthy findings," they wrote, "was the tendency for neurotic and lonely individuals to spend greater amounts of time on Facebook per day than non-lonely individuals." . . .

Still, Burke's research does not support the assertion that Facebook creates loneliness. The people who experience loneliness on Facebook are lonely away from Facebook, too, she points out; on Facebook, as everywhere else, correlation is not causation. The popular kids are popular, and the lonely skulkers skulk alone. . . .

In one experiment, Cacioppo looked for a connection between the loneliness of subjects and the relative frequency of their interactions via Facebook, chat rooms, online games, dating sites, and face-to-face contact . . .

We make decisions about how we use our machines, not the other way around. Every time I shop at my local grocery store, I am faced with a choice. I can buy my groceries from a human being or from a machine. I always, without exception, choose the machine. It's faster and more efficient, I tell myself, but the truth is that I prefer not having to wait with the other customers who are lined up alongside the conveyor belt: the hipster mom who disapproves of my high-carbon-footprint pineapple; the lady who tenses to the point of tears while she waits to see if the gods of the credit-card machine will accept or decline; the old man whose clumsy feebleness requires a patience that I don't possess. Much better to bypass the whole circus and just ring up the groceries myself.

Stephen Marche, "Is Facebook Making Us Lonely?" *The Atlantic*, April 2, 2012 © 2012 The Atlantic Media Co., as first published in The Atlantic Magazine. Used with permission. All rights reserved. Distributed by Tribune Content Agency, LLC.

Commas. The **comma (,)** is a very common type of punctuation mark that indicates a pause between parts of a sentence. For instance, commas are used to help readers see phrases and clauses, to distinguish which part of a sentence is more or less important, or to separate items within a sentence.

How to Use Commas Correctly. There are many rules for comma usage; here we review the most common. The examples are from "Is Facebook Making Us Lonely?"

1. Use a comma to set off an opening phrase or clause.

   Example: "Every time I shop at my local grocery store, I am faced with a

opening clause
   choice" (333).

2. Use commas to separate words, phrases, or clauses in a series.

   Example: "In one experiment, Cacioppo looked for a connection between the loneliness of subjects and the relative frequency of their interactions via Facebook, chat rooms, online games, dating sites, and face-to-face contact" (332).

elements in a series

Connect

Assign the LearnSmart Achieve topic "Commas" for adaptive learning to accompany this material.

3. Use a comma to form a compound sentence that uses a conjunction (FANBOYS).

   Example: "The popular kids are popular, **and** the lonely skulkers skulk alone" (331).
   conjunction

4. Use commas to mark off a phrase, a clause, or words that interrupts the sentence and are not essential to the sentence's meaning.

   Example: "I always, without exception, choose the machine" (333).
   nonessential phrase

Connect

Assign the LearnSmart Achieve topics "Colons" and "Semicolons" for more practice understanding colons and semicolons and using these correctly.

Semicolons. The **semicolon (;)** is typically used to join two independent clauses and in this way a semicolon signals to readers that ideas are closely related. A semicolon can also alert readers to a transition word between two independent clauses. In addition, a semicolon can separate items in a series, particularly when a sentence is complicated and using commas might be confusing. Semicolons tend to be used sparingly by writers.

How to Use Semicolons Correctly. **Semicolons**, used correctly, can add nuances of meaning to your writing. The following examples are from "Is Facebook Making Us Lonely?"

1. A semicolon joins two independent clauses or two sentences whose ideas are closely related.

   Example: "The people who experience loneliness on Facebook are lonely away
   sentence 1
   from Facebook, too, she points out; on Facebook, as everywhere else, correlation
   sentence 2
   is not causation" (331).

2. A semicolon is used before a transition word that is not a coordinator or subordinator and that joins two independent clauses or two sentences.

   Example: "We were promised a global village; instead, we inhabit the drab
   transition word
   cul-de-sacs and endless freeways of a vast suburb of information" (329).

3. A semicolon separates items in a series when commas are already present in the sentence or when the series items are complicated.

   Example: "It's faster and more efficient, I tell myself, but the truth is that I prefer not having to wait with the other customers who are lined up alongside the conveyor belt: the hipster mom who disapproves of my high-carbon-footprint pineapple; the lady who tenses to the point of tears while she waits to see if the gods of the credit-card machine will accept or decline; the old man whose clumsy feebleness requires a patience that I don't possess" (333).

Colons. The **colon (:)** is a punctuation mark used to precede a list of items, a quotation, or an explanation. A colon tells readers that what follows will clarify what precedes the colon. In other words, before the colon is a general idea and after the colon are specific details, examples, or explanations of that idea. Colons can also be used to introduce quotations.

One important rule for colon use is that what comes before the colon must be an independent clause (complete sentence). In other words, you could place a period where the colon is. What comes after the colon, however, can be a word, phrase, or clause. Like semicolons, colons tend to be used sparingly by writers.

How to Use Colons Correctly. "Is Facebook Making Us Lonely?" provides these examples.

1. Place a colon after an independent clause to introduce a sentence or phrase that gives an explanation, details, or examples supporting the general idea in the independent clause.

   Example: "We live in an accelerating contradiction: the more connected we

   independent clause   explanation

   become, the lonelier we are" (329).

2. Use a colon after an independent clause that introduces a quotation.

   Example: "The researchers also found that lonely people are inclined to spend

   independent clause

   more time on Facebook: 'One of the most noteworthy findings,' they wrote,

   quotation

   'was the tendency for neurotic and lonely individuals to spend greater amounts

   of time on Facebook per day than non-lonely individuals.'"

▌ Dashes, Parentheses, and Apostrophes in Context

The following excerpt is from "Back to the Future with Antibiotic Resistance" by Chris Del Mar. Highlighted passages appear as examples below as follows: aqua, *dashes;* purple, *parentheses;* green, *apostrophes.*

In other words, resistance to antibiotics didn't have to evolve anew to counteract any antibiotics we humans developed. Resistance existed—and probably for hundreds of millions of years—before vertebrates were ever thought of, let alone humans.

In any case, the numbers are against us. . . . To put it another way, for every one of our own cells (there are 10 million million of them) there are 10 bacteria living in or on us. In an antibiotic environment, a few with resistance genes are selected out, and they will thrive.

These astronomical numbers mean that resistance is inevitable. Even a new synthetic antibiotic will eventually select out a resistant strain. No antibiotic has been developed without resistance appearing soon after.

To make things worse, one species of bacteria can transfer the resistance gene to another—and often to a completely unrelated species. In this way, the commensal bacteria (the "friendly" ones we all have, and actually need, mostly in our gut) can develop resistance, and then transfer it to pathogens (the "nasty" bacteria, which cause disease). . . .

continued

Teaching Tip

Review the reading selections in the chapter Introduction to College Reading and Writing to understand how writers use colons in sentences and to introduce quotes.

Teaching Tip

"Back to the Future with Antibiotic Resistance" by Chris Del Mar appears in Chapter 10.

Adding to the pressure is our increased reliance on antibiotic "cover" for so many high-technology interventions. Antibiotics are becoming a medical tool we simply can't do without—in surgery (for example, joint replacements are undertaken under antibiotic prophylaxis), in heart interventions (inserting tubes into the heart's vessels to unblock them) and in chemotherapy for cancer (where the body's immune system is temporarily weakened). As resistance grows, so much of what we take for granted will have to stop because the intervention will become too risky.

The following excerpt is from "Antibiotic Resistance Questions and Answers" by the Centers for Disease Control and Prevention. The passages highlighted in purple *are repeated below as examples of parentheses use.*

The Food and Drug Administration's (FDA's) Center for Veterinary Medicine (CVM) produced a nine-minute animation explaining how antimicrobial resistance both emerges and increases among bacteria. . . . As a result, FDA released a proposed rule in December 2013 to require manufacturers to submit data supporting the efficacy and safety of antibacterial soaps and body washes.

Chris Del Mar, "Back to the Future with Antibiotic Resistance," *The Guardian*, July 21, 2014. Used with permission of the author.

Teaching Tip

"Antibiotic Resistance Questions and Answers" by the Centers for Disease Control and Prevention appears in Chapter 9.

Connect

Assign the LearnSmart Achieve topics "Dashes" and "Parentheses" for adaptive learning to accompany this material.

Dashes. A **dash (—)** is a punctuation mark that is used to show a break in thought or in the structure of a sentence. Like colons, dashes can create emphasis and clarity if used sparingly and properly. Dashes have two common purposes: (1) to show an interruption in thought in mid-sentence; (2) to create emphasis or clarity, especially at the end of a sentence. If dashes are used to set off ideas in the middle of a sentence, then a dash must come before and after the phrase or clause that is set off. If a dash sets off an element at the end of a sentence, then a dash comes before the element and a period comes after, at the end of the sentence.

Teaching Tip

Review the reading selections in Chapters 9 and 10 to show students more examples of how dashes are used in sentences.

How to Use Dashes Correctly. These examples are from the "Back to the Future with Antibiotic Resistance" excerpt, above.

1. Use dashes to show an interruption in thought in the middle of a sentence.

   Example showing an added idea: "Resistance existed—and probably for hundreds of millions of years—before vertebrates were ever thought of, let alone humans" (285).

   Use a dash to create emphasis at the end of a sentence.

   Example showing emphasis: "To make things worse, one species of bacteria can transfer the resistance gene to another—and often to a completely unrelated species" (285).

Parentheses. **Parentheses [( )]** are punctuation marks used to include information in a sentence. Unlike dashes, parentheses tend to deemphasize information. They may be used to add information that is interesting but not essential to the main idea of the sentence or to clarify a word or phrase in the main sentence. They may also be used to introduce an abbreviation: the complete term is spelled out in the sentence, and, in parentheses, an abbreviation is included. After that, the abbreviation may be used in the text since writers assume readers will understand the abbreviation.

A parenthesis is placed before and after the added information. To check that you have used parentheses correctly, try removing the parenthetical words or phrases from the sentence; the sentence should still make sense and be grammatically correct.

How to Use Parentheses Correctly. The first two examples are from the "Back to the Future with Antibiotic Resistance" excerpt and the third example is from the "Antibiotic Resistance Questions and Answers" excerpt.

Teaching Tip

Review the reading selections in Chapters 9 and 10 to show students more examples of how parentheses are used in sentences.

1. Use parentheses to add nonessential information.

   Example: "To put it another way, for every one of our own cells (there are 10
   nonessential information
   million million of them) there are 10 bacteria living in or on us" (285).

2. Use parentheses to clarify information.

   Example: "In this way, the commensal bacteria (the "friendly" ones we all have,
   clarifying information
   and actually need, mostly in our gut) can develop resistance, and then transfer

   it to pathogens (the "nasty" bacteria, which cause disease)" (285).
   clarifying information

3. Use parentheses to explain or introduce an abbreviation. After introducing the abbreviation the first time that the full term appears, you can use the abbreviation without explanation in the rest of the writing.

   Example: "The Food and Drug Administration's (FDA's) Center for Veterinary
   abbreviation (first use)
   Medicine (CVM) produced a nine-minute animation explaining how antimicrobial
   abbreviation (first use)
   resistance both emerges and increases among bacteria. . . . As a result, FDA
   abbreviation (subsequent use)
   released a proposed rule in December 2013 to require manufacturers to submit

   data supporting the efficacy and safety of antibacterial soaps and body

   washes" (265).

Apostrophes. As explained in the introduction to this section, punctuation creates meaning. Consider the difference in meaning between these two sentences:

Connect

Assign the LearnSmart Achieve topic "Apostrophes" for more practice understanding apostrophes and using these correctly.

Sentence 1: Those dogs are his brothers.

Sentence 2: Those dogs are his brothers'.

Now, if the sentence is intended to be exclusively about dogs, then saying "Those dogs are his brothers" makes sense (sentence 1). If, however, the sentence is about male siblings who own dogs, then writing "Those dogs are his brothers'" makes sense (sentence 2). That's because an apostrophe—the punctuation mark following *brothers* in sentence 2—is used to show possession or ownership. Writing "Those dogs are his brothers'"—meaning "Those dogs are his brothers' dogs"—signals that his brothers own the dogs.

Apostrophes also indicate where a letter is missing in a contraction, as in *it's* (which stands for *it is*) and *didn't* (which stands for *did not*). Checking that you have used contractions correctly—or that you need to use a contraction—requires knowing the rules for using apostrophes, plus careful proofreading.

How to Use Apostrophes Correctly.   Guidelines and tips for using apostrophes follow here.

1. To show possession, add an apostrophe and the letter *s* after a noun (*'s*). If the noun already ends in the letter *s,* you usually can eliminate the *s* after the apostrophe.

    Examples: the <u>heart's</u> vessels; the <u>body's</u> immune system our <u>hearts'</u> vessels; our <u>bodies'</u> immune systems

2. To indicate a missing letter in a contraction, insert an apostrophe where the letter is missing.

    Examples: resistance to antibiotics <u>didn't</u> have to evolve; a medical tool we simply <u>can't</u> do without

3. Remember that possessive pronouns (such as *his, hers, its, theirs, yours,* and *ours*) do not take an apostrophe.

    Examples: The dogs are <u>theirs</u>.

    <u>His</u> advice was good.

    Examples: <u>It's</u> difficult to know whether antibiotic resistance will ever be
    _{*it's = it is*}
    controlled.

    The hospital will try to control <u>its</u> use of antibiotics.
    its = belonging to it

NOTE: In academic writing, the use of contractions is sometimes unacceptable; writing out full words is recommended instead. Be aware of your instructor's and readers' expectations with respect to using contractions.

Apply What You Learned

In this section, you will have an opportunity to use punctuation to improve a piece of writing. Your goal is to review the sample introductions given below and add punctuation where needed. These introductions are adapted from student papers: most of the original punctuation has been removed. The sentences themselves are defined with periods or question marks, but you must decide if punctuation, such as commas, semicolons, colons, or parentheses, is needed *within* sentences. Also check whether apostrophes are needed. Remember that commas are the most common type of punctuation. You may not need to always use semicolons, colons, or parentheses.

Here are some suggestions for how to proceed:

1. Read each sample introduction aloud. Listen to where pauses occur in sentences and decide whether punctuation is needed to indicate breaks between clauses or phrases or items in a series. Determine whether commas, semicolons, or colons are most appropriate, and revise as needed.

2. Read each sample introduction and consider whether parentheses are needed to mark off nonessential or clarifying information, or if apostrophes are necessary to show possession or indicate a contraction. Revise as needed.

3. Read aloud your revised version of the sample introductions (after completing steps 1 and 2) and check that punctuation is used appropriately and correctly in sentences. Make any needed changes.

Sample Introduction: Adapted from the Student Paper "Involuntary Resignation"

> In the article "Brainology" author Carol S. Dweck states that by having a fixed mindset we have less probabilities of being successful rather than the ones with a growth mindset (13). But is this true? Can we guarantee that we will be successful by having a growth mindset? I admit I do agree with Dweck's observations of both mindsets putting in effort and challenging ourselves with new things to increase our intelligence growth mindset is indeed more beneficial for us compared to convincing our mind that intelligence is a talent that we either have or not fixed mindset. However throughout my life I have observed and known many people that started with a growth mindset and ended up converting into a fixed mindset. How is this possible? After experiencing high school in two different countries Mexico and United States I was able to notice that those who switched into a fixed mindset did not do it because they wanted to but because they realized that they had no other option and gave up. In some places, putting effort into learning and being academically successful is still not enough. In Mexico for example if students do not have enough money to attend and actually graduate from a prestigious school even if they have a growth mindset there is a very low possibility that they will achieve their dream job or any job. Having a growth mindset does not guarantee our success.

Teaching Tip

The original paper, Veronica Alvarez's "Involuntary Resignation," appears in Spotlight on Student Writing: Annotating and Evaluating Student Writing.

Teaching Tip

Have students compare the way they punctuated these introductions to the sample student papers in the Spotlight sections. Discuss which punctuation choices are the best and why.

Class Activity

Students can bring to class two versions of an introduction they have written: one with punctuation and one that takes out all the punctuation except for periods and question marks. Students can exchange the unpunctuated introductions with a partner and punctuate the writing. Finally, students can return the introductions and discuss their punctuation choices, explaining their decisions and determining the most effective choices.

Teaching Tip

The original student paper, Gabrielle Reyez's "Enslaved by Technology," appears in Spotlight on Student Writing: Evaluating and Analyzing Student Writing.

Sample Introduction: Adapted from the Student Paper "Enslaved by Technology"

Call me old-fashioned but what happened to the good old days where a family could sit down and eat Sunday night dinner without the constant distraction of a son or daughter pausing after each bite to post a picture of the meatloaf mom made on Facebook? In a 2012 article "The Flight from Conversation" written by psychologist Sherry Turkle she states "We live in a technological universe in which we are always communicating. And yet we have sacrificed conversation for mere connection" (SR1). I couldnt agree more with Turkle the more we stare down at our phone screens the more we miss out on real life relationships and experiences. We can send a text e-mail or tweet to talk to someone now in hopes of avoiding a real face-to-face conversation with them. I am guilty of this I have found myself looking down at my phone time and time again as I walk by someone just to avoid eye contact and what could be a potentially awkward conversation.

Works Cited

"Antibiotic Resistance Questions and Answers," Centers for Disease Control and Prevention. *Writing to Read, Reading to Write,* edited by Alison Kuehner, McGraw-Hill Education, 2019, pp. 262–266.

Carskadon, Mary. "Forget A's, B's, and C's—What Students Need Is More Zzzz's." *Writing to Read, Reading to Write,* edited by Alison Kuehner, McGraw-Hill Education, 2019, pp. 127–129.

Del Mar, Chris. "Back to the Future with Antibiotic Resistance." *Writing to Read, Reading to Write,* edited by Alison Kuehner, McGraw-Hill Education, 2019, pp. 284–287.

Dillard, Annie. *The Writing Life*. Harper Perennial, 2013.

Dr. Seuss. *Horton Hatches the Egg*. Random House, 1968.

Dweck, Carol. "Brainology." *Writing to Read, Reading to Write,* edited by Alison Kuehner, McGraw-Hill Education, 2019, pp. 12–18.

Hruby, Patrick. "Facing the Truth." *Writing to Read, Reading to Write,* edited by Alison Kuehner, McGraw-Hill Education, 2019, pp. 355–359.

Marche, Stephen. "Is Facebook Making Us Lonely?" *Writing to Read, Reading to Write,* edited by Alison Kuehner, McGraw-Hill Education, 2019, pp. 328–335.

McLaughlin, Jenna. "This Is What Happens to Your Brain When You Get Kicked in the Head." *Writing to Read, Reading to Write,* edited by Alison Kuehner, McGraw-Hill Education, 2019, pp. 365–367.

Rose, Mike. "Writing as a Process." *Writing to Read, Reading to Write*, edited by Alison Kuehner, McGraw-Hill Education, 2019, pp. 73–75.

Sampson, Michael R., et al. "Rethinking the Writing Process: What Best-Selling and Award-Winning Authors Have to Say." *Writing to Read, Reading to Write,* edited by Alison Kuehner, McGraw-Hill Education, 2019, pp. 61–65.

Documentation Resource Guide

DOCUMENTATION RESOURCE GUIDE

Acknowledging and Citing Sources at the Sentence Level

Documenting Sources and Formatting Papers Correctly

Much of your writing will be your own thinking and your own words. However, in college you will often engage with other people's ideas through lectures or readings or even visuals. Referring to others' ideas can be a way to support your own thinking or a starting point for responding to a topic. When you use other people's ideas or their words, you must acknowledge them. You can give credit to your sources in several ways: by mentioning the source in the sentence, by providing a citation after the sentence, and by creating a list of citations at the end of the paper. This section will demonstrate multiple ways to properly acknowledge source material.

First, you will learn strategies for acknowledging sources in sentences. Then you will review two major citation styles for college papers: MLA (Modern Language Association) and APA (American Psychological Association).

ACKNOWLEDGING AND CITING SOURCES AT THE SENTENCE LEVEL

You should acknowledge information that comes from others, such as quotes and summaries, at the moment in your writing when you include that information. In other words, in each sentence that includes information from a source, acknowledge that source. You can often do that by including key information in the sentence itself, such as the name of the author or the title of the reading. Sometimes this information will be sufficient for a citation, such as when your instructor provides an article for you to read and write about. However, always check with your instructor about how you should cite your sources.

Introductory Phrases to Acknowledge Sources

When you are writing about a reading, such as summarizing or quoting from a text, it is important to let readers know which text you are writing about. One way to provide this information is to add an *introductory phrase* that identifies the author or the title of the reading.

You can craft such an introductory phrase by writing, for example, "According to . . ." or "In the article . . ." at the beginning of the sentence and then stating the article title and/or the author's name. After your introductory phrase, place a comma. Then write the main idea (subject and verb) of the sentence. "Introductory phrase + main idea of reading" is a useful sentence pattern you can use to acknowledge the source of a quotation or summary.

Example Sentences Using Introductory Phrases That Acknowledge the Source

According to assistant professor Zheng Wang, college students enjoy
     introductory phrase acknowledging source

multitasking while studying because "it makes them feel good" (44).

In the article "Don't Multitask: Your Brain Will Thank You" by Issie Lapowsky,
     introductory phrase acknowledging source

multitasking is described as doing two things at the same time (34).

Attribution

When you summarize or quote, you should identify the source of that information and convey why that source is reputable. In such cases, you can reference the person or organization by providing *attribution*. That is, along with the quote or summary, you identify the source of the information. You may also want to state the *credentials* of the source—that is, say what makes the source qualified to address the topic.

Teaching Tip

Suggest that students look for examples of sentences that use attribution in their assigned readings.

Examples of Sentences Using Attribution

The author of ten best-selling books on personal finance, Suze Orman
attribution
explains that "writing is hard work, not magic" (Kuehner 51).

Research published in a peer-reviewed academic journal, the *Journal of*
attribution
Adolescent and Adult Literacy, shows that most professional writers
create multiple drafts (Sampson et al. 63).

Appositives

One special type of attribution is an *appositive*, which is a noun or noun phrase that gives descriptive information about a noun. The appositive usually appears immediately after the noun, although it can appear right before the noun. An appositive that comes after a noun is typically followed by a comma or enclosed within commas. An appositive can give more information about a person, an organization, a publication, or any other noun.

Teaching Tip

Suggest that students look for examples of appositives in their assigned readings.

Examples of Sentences Using Appositives

Carol Dweck, professor of psychology at Stanford University, believes that
appositive
a student's mindset can powerfully affect his or her learning and academic
achievement (12).

Education Week, a nonprofit news organization that focuses on K–12
appositive
education, surveyed teachers about the effect of a growth mindset on
students' learning (Flannery 24).

Signal Verbs

When summarizing, paraphrasing, or quoting, you can acknowledge the source of information, as well as reflect the tone of the source, by using a *signal verb*. Well-chosen signal verbs show an understanding of an author's purpose. For instance, using a neutral verb, such as *states*, indicates the author is writing to inform. If the author has a strong opinion, then a verb such as *argues* or *asserts* would indicate the writer is developing an argument.

Signal Verbs and Their Purposes

Neutral			
believes	observes	says	tells
explains	reports	states	thinks
Argues For			
argues	claims	emphasizes	proposes
asserts	declares	offers	reasons
Argues Against			
contradicts	disagrees	objects	rebuts
criticizes	disputes	opposes	refutes
States Indirectly			
hints	implies	insinuates	suggests
Concludes			
concludes	decides	determines	finds
Gives Support			
cites	describes	references	supports

Examples of Sentences Using Signal Verbs

A retired teacher from Vietnam, Nguyen Thi Mai, <u>believes</u> that "money
signal verb
can't secure happiness" (qtd. in Zolfagharifard and Gillman).

The Pew Research Center <u>reports</u> that women are happier than men, that
signal verb
married people are happier than singles, and that younger people are
more satisfied than older folks (qtd. in Zolfagharifard and Gillman).

Teaching Tip

Use the sample student papers in Spotlight on Student Writing: Reading and Analyzing Student Writing to demonstrate signal verbs. Students can review the student papers looking at the signal verbs and noting how effective each is.

DOCUMENTING SOURCES AND FORMATTING PAPERS CORRECTLY

Different academic disciplines have different citation styles. For instance, most English courses require students to use MLA (Modern Language Association) style, while many social sciences, such as psychology, use APA (American Psychological Association) style. Always check with your instructor as to the required documentation style. Because MLA is frequently used in English courses, this chapter presents basic guidelines for this style. To understand MLA style in depth,

Teaching Tip

Look online for videos that walk students through the process of formatting a paper using MLA or APA style to share with the class.

you should consult the most recent edition of the *MLA Handbook*. Since APA is a commonly used style in college writing, the basic guidelines for this style will be explained as well. To understand APA style in depth, consult the most recent edition of the *Publication Manual of the American Psychological Association.*

Both MLA and APA have guidelines for citing sources in the text of the paper itself, in parentheses following quoted or summarized information. These are *in-text citations* since they occur within the text of the paper. Both styles also have guidelines for creating at the end of the paper a list of sources used in the paper. This section will review the basic guidelines for in-text citations and list of sources, as well as how to format a paper according to first MLA and then APA style.

MLA Style: In-Text Citations

Whenever you use information in your essay—whether you quote, paraphrase, or summarize—you should include a citation immediately after the information from your source. An in-text citation serves the important purpose of clearly separating your ideas from the ideas or information of sources. An in-text citation should appear after *each and every* piece of information taken from a source, usually at the end of the sentence in which that information appears.

MLA style for in-text citation typically requires the author's last name and a page number to appear in parentheses after a quote, summary, or paraphrase from a source. In-text citations in MLA style are sometimes referred to as parenthetical citations because the author and page number appear in parentheses. Following is a general guide for in-text citations, followed by examples that illustrate MLA style for in-text citations for different situations.

General Guidelines for MLA In-Text Citations

1. Place the in-text citation (usually the author's last name and the page number) in parentheses at the end of the sentence.

2. Leave a space between the last word in the sentence and the parenthetical citation.

3. Place the period at the end of the sentence after the parenthetical citation.

4. Do not use a comma or *p* or *pg* before the page number. Simply leave a space between the author's last name and the page number.

Example: Because bacteria are so numerous and multiple so rapidly, "resistance is inevitable" (Del Mar 285).

The following examples illustrate MLA style for in-text citations for different situations.

Summary with in-text citation

In some developing countries, people may buy and use antibiotics without a doctor's prescription for diseases that do not respond to antibiotic treatment (Reardon 141).

Quote with in-text citation

In some developing countries, "overprescribing or unregulated use of antibiotics" is fueling antibiotic resistance (Reardon 141).

In-text citation when there is no named author If the source does not include an author, you should use the first words that appear in the works cited entry, which are usually the first words of the title of the reading, in the parenthetical citation.

Antibiotic resistance is "one of the world's most pressing public health problems" ("Antibiotic Resistance").

In-text citation when there is no page number If the source does not include a page number, as in the case of a Web page, you should not include a page number in parentheses. In this case, include the first words that appear in the works cited entry (such as the author's name, article title, or Web site title); do not provide page numbers or a URL in parentheses.

On their Web site, the Alliance for the Prudent Use of Antibiotics explains that bacteria can become resistant to antibiotics either "(1) by a genetic mutation or (2) by acquiring resistance from another bacterium" ("General Background").

In-text citation when the source is referenced in the sentence If you use the author's name (or the first words in the works cited entry when there is no author) in the sentence, it is not necessary to give the author's name (or the source title) in parentheses; include only a page number in the parenthetical citation.

Bubolts, Brown, and Soper in their research on college students' sleep habits report that most college students experience some type of sleep disturbance that negatively influences their academic performance (131).

Long quotations When a quotation runs four or more lines, you will need to create a block quote. Start the quote on a new line and indent the entire quotation one-half inch from the left margin (the same as for a new paragraph). Double-space the quotation, but do not put quotation marks around the words. Include the appropriate in-text citation following the quotation, but do not place a period after the parentheses.

In an interview, President Obama explained how the "National Action Plan for Combatting Antibiotic-Resistant Bacteria" would help prevent overprescribing of antibiotics:

> We're going to provide real-time data about antibiotic resistance to doctors and hospitals nationwide, so they can monitor the rates of drug resistance in their area. We're setting national goals for improving antibiotic use, and we're asking doctors and hospitals to help us meet them. And we're going to help health departments across the country achieve these goals. ("President Obama" 10)

MLA: Works Cited List

A list of sources should appear at the end of a paper that includes information taken from those sources. This way, readers can look up and read the sources if they choose. In MLA style, the sources list is called "Works Cited." The list includes all the sources cited in the paper, arranged alphabetically by the author's last name.

Depending on the type of source—book, newspaper or magazine article, Web site, or journal article, for example—the information, order, and arrangement of the information needed to complete each entry may be different. The *MLA Handbook* is your complete guide to citing various types of sources correctly and accurately. Below are general guidelines for each entry in a works cited list. Then what follows are examples of a few of the most common sources. Note that the examples present the *general format* showing how to create a works cited entry, followed by a *specific example* of a works cited entry.

General Guidelines for MLA Works Cited List Entries

1. Begin the entry with the author's name: last name, first name. Place a comma between the last and first name and a period after the first name.

2. Place quotation marks around the titles of articles, short stories, poems, songs, and Web pages; italicize the titles of periodicals, books, Web sites, and full-length works such as movies.

3. Write dates as *day, month, year*. Spell out *May, June,* and *July,* but abbreviate other months: *Jan., Feb., Mar., Apr., Aug., Sept., Oct., Nov., Dec.*

4. Place a period after the author's name and a period after the title of the article. Place a comma after the name of the publication and after the publication date. Introduce page numbers with *p.* or *pp.*

5. Indent the second line of the entry half an inch.

Newspaper Article

McNeil, Donald G., Jr. "Infant Deaths Fall Sharply in Africa with Routine Antibiotics." *The New York Times*, 25 Apr. 2018, p. 11.

Book

General format

Author. *Title of Book*. Publisher, date of publication.

Specific example

Slater, Lauren. *Opening Skinner's Box: Great Psychological Experiments.* W. W. Norton, 2004.

Work in an anthology

General format

> Author. "Title of Work." *Title of Book*, edited by Editor's Name, Publisher, year of publication, page range.

Specific example

> Marshall, Paule. "Poets in the Kitchen." *The Norton Anthology of Literature by Women*, edited by Sandra Gilbert and Susan Gubar, W.W. Norton, 2007, pp. 955–62.

Magazine article in print

General format

> Author. "Article Title." *Title of Magazine*, date, page range, OR if article is not on consecutive pages, starting page is followed by plus sign.

Specific example—one author

> Englender, Terry. "Should Fracking Stop? No, It's Too Valuable." *Nature*, 15 Sept. 2011, pp. 271+.

Specific example—two authors

> Howarth, Robert, and Anthony Ingraffea. "Should Fracking Stop? Yes, It's Too High Risk." *Nature*, 15 Sept. 2011, pp. 271–73.

Newspaper article in print

General format

> Author. "Article Title." *Title of Newspaper*, date, page range, OR if article is not on consecutive pages, starting page is followed by plus sign.

Specific example

> "The Rise of Antibiotic-Resistance." *The New York Times*, 11 May 2014, p. SR12.

Magazine article from a database

General format

> Author. "Article Title." *Title of Magazine*, date, page range. *Database*, doi, or URL (without *https://*).

Specific example

> Sturn, Simon. "Do Minimum Wages Lead to Job Losses? Evidence from OECD Countries on Low-Skilled and Youth Employment." *ILR Review*, May 2018, pp. 647–75. doi:10.1177/0019793917741259.

Newspaper or magazine article published online

General format

> Author(s). "Article Title." *Periodical*, date, URL (without *https://*). Date of access.

Specific example

> DePillis, Lydia. "The Case for Raising the Minimum Wage Keeps Getting Stronger." *CNN Money*, 27 Apr. 2018, money.cnn.com/2018/04/27/news/economy/minimum-wage-increase/index.html. Accessed 17 May 2018.

Web page

General format

> Author, compiler, director, or editor (if any). "Title of the page." *Title of overall Web site*, date of publication, URL. Date of access (if required by instructor).

Specific example

> "Antimicrobial Resistance." *World Health Assembly*, 15 Feb. 2018, www.who.int/en/news-room/fact-sheets/detail/antimicrobial-resistance. Accessed 10 May 2018.

MLA: First Page

Teaching Tip

Some word processing programs provide a template to create a document in MLA style.

The first page of a paper in MLA style consists of a heading on the upper left that includes information on four lines: (1) the name of the writer of the paper, (2) the instructor's name, (3) the class, and (4) the date. In the upper right of the page should be the writer's last name and the page number. The title of the paper is centered after the heading; it is not bold or underlined or quoted. The first line of the text and all paragraphs in the paper are indented half an inch. The whole paper is double-spaced.

Teaching Tip

Use the sample student papers in Spotlight on Student Writing: Reading and Analyzing Student Writing to demonstrate how to correctly format a paper in MLA style.

Example: First Page in MLA

> Tolentino 1
>
> Miguel Tolentino
>
> Professor Kuehner
>
> English 151RW
>
> 13 November 2015
>
>
> Bachmann's Responsibility
>
> In *The Power of Habit*, author Charles Duhigg puts an emphasis on habits—their inner workings and how they can be changed. Duhigg describes how habits work through the cycle of cue (trigger that activates a habit), routine (action of habit), and

Tolentino 2

reward (aspect in which the brain determines if the habit is worth it).
Particularly in Chapter 9 of the book, Duhigg details the descent of
a woman called Angie Bachmann from being a bored housewife to
losing all her money through compulsive gambling. Harrah's
Entertainment, the casino where Bachmann played Blackjack and
lost every bit of her money, sued Bachmann, "demanding that she
pay her debts" (Duhigg 269). Every time Bachmann steps in a
casino, that activates a cue within her brain so that she
automatically performs her routine of playing Blackjack, thinking
that she might win as a reward. Chapter 9 further discusses the
extent of Bachmann's responsibility for her actions since she was
fully aware of her actions and she had the responsibility to change,
which she did not. Although Bachmann argued that she was acting
per Harrah's manipulations, she is still responsible because
Harrah's actions were legal, she did not get treatment for addiction,
she was fully aware of her actions, and she kept coming back to the
casino even though she tried to change.

MLA: Works Cited List

The list of works cited begins on a new page at the end of your paper. The title of
the page, "Works Cited," is centered; it is not underlined, placed in quotation
marks, or bold. Entries for the sources cited in the paper are arranged in
alphabetical order by the author's last name or by the first words in the entry, if
there is no author. After the first line, all other lines for each entry are indented.
The entries are double-spaced.

Example: Works Cited List in MLA

Tolentino 6

Works Cited

Duhigg, Charles. *The Power of Habit: Why We Do What We
Do in Life and Business*, Random House, 2012.

Glass, Ira, host. "Harrah's Today, Gone Tomorrow." *Blackjack*,
part 2, act 2, *This American Life*, NPR, 8 June 2012,
www.thisamericanlife.org/466/blackjack.

Jabr, Ferris. "How the Brain Gets Addicted to Gambling."
Scientific American, 15 Oct. 2013, www.
scientificamerican.com/article/how-the-brain-gets-
addicted-to-gambling/. Accessed 13 Nov. 2015.

National Center for Responsible Gaming. "The Evolving
Definition of Pathological Gambling in the DSM-5." 19
May 2013, blog.ncrg.org/blog/2013/05/evolving-
definition-pathological-gambling-dsm-5. Accessed 13
Nov. 2015.

APA Style: In-Text Citations

In APA style, the in-text citation typically includes the author's last name followed by the year of publication in parentheses after a summary or paraphrase from a source. For a quotation from a source, APA style requires the author's last name, year of publication, and a page number in parentheses immediately following the quotation.

As an alternative, you can provide the author's name in front of a summary or paraphrase, followed immediately by the date in parentheses and a page number for a quotation. For a quotation, the page number in parentheses would immediately follow the quoted material.

General Guidelines for APA In-Text Citations

APA uses the author-date method of in-text citations. If the author is not named in the sentence, then in parentheses after a summary or quotation, include the author's last name and date of publication.

1. After a summary, place the author and date of publication in the parenthetical citation, separated with a comma.

   Example: According to an article in *The Guardian*, antibiotic resistance is serious threat to human health that causes tens of thousands of deaths worldwide every year (Del Mar, 2014).

2. After a quotation, place the author, date of publication, and the page number of the quotation in the parenthetical citation. The page number is preceded by *p.*

   Example: According to an article in *The Guardian*, "the central weapon against antibiotic resistance must be to discourage antibiotic use" (Del Mar, 2014, p. 286).

The following examples illustrate APA style for in-text citations for different situations.

Summary with in-text citation

In some developing countries, people may buy and use antibiotics without a doctor's prescription for diseases that do not respond to antibiotic treatment (Reardon, 2014).

Quote with in-text citation

In some developing countries, "overprescribing or unregulated use of antibiotics" is fueling antibiotic resistance (Reardon, 2014, p. 142).

In-text citation when there is no named author If the source does not include an author, you should use the title, or shortened title, of the reading in the parenthetical citation along with the date.

Antibiotic resistance can develop naturally, through genetic mutations or when bacteria exchange genetic material with one another ("Using Antibiotics Correctly," 2013).

In-text citation when the source is referenced in the sentence If you use the author's name (or the title of the source when there is no author) in the sentence, it is not necessary to give the author's name (or the source title) in parentheses; simply include the date in parentheses following the name(s) if you are summarizing information. Provide the page number as well if you are quoting information.

According to law professors Steven J. Hoffman and Kevin Outterson (2015), controlling antibiotic resistance cannot rely on individual countries, but rather requires "global collective action" (p. 66).

In-text citation for an organization as author If the author of a source is an organization or government agency, include the organization, either in parentheses or in the sentence itself, and the year.

On their Web site, the Alliance for the Prudent Use of Antibiotics (2015) explains that bacteria can become resistant to antibiotics either "(1) by a genetic mutation or (2) by acquiring resistance from another bacterium."

In this example, the page number is not available because this is a Web site. If a page number were available, it would appear in parentheses after the closing quotation mark but before the period, like this: . . . bacterium" (p. 29).

Long quotations When quoting forty or more words, you will need to create a block quote. Start the quotation on a new line one-half inch from the left margin (the same indentation as a new paragraph). Double-space the quotation, but do not put quotation marks around the words. Include the appropriate in-text citation following the quotation.

> In an interview, President Obama explained how the "National Action Plan for Combatting Antibiotic-Resistant Bacteria" would help prevent overprescribing of antibiotics:
>
>> We're going to provide real-time data about antibiotic resistance to doctors and hospitals nationwide, so they can monitor the rates of drug resistance in their area. We're setting national goals for improving antibiotic use, and we're asking doctors and hospitals to help us meet them. And we're going to help health departments across the country achieve these goals. ("President Obama," 2015)

APA: References List

A list of sources should appear at the end of a research paper so that readers can look up and read the sources if they choose. In APA style, the sources list is titled "References." Depending on the type of source—book, newspaper or magazine article, Web site, or journal article, for example—the information, order, and arrangement of the information needed to complete each entry may be different. Below are the general guidelines for reference entries, followed by examples for a few of the most common sources.

General Guidelines for APA References List Entries

1. Begin the entry with the author's last name followed by initials. Place a comma between the last name and initials and a period after the initials.

2. Include the date of publication in parentheses after the author's name.

3. Capitalize all major words in a journal title; however, when referencing books, chapters, articles, or Web pages, capitalize only the first letter of the first word of a title or subtitle.

4. Italicize titles of longer works, such as books or journals or magazines.

5. End with *Retrieved from* and the URL or DOI for the source, if available.

Newspaper Article

McNeil, D. G., Jr. (2018, April 25). Infant deaths fall sharply in Africa with routine antibiotics. *The New York Times*, p. 11.

Book

General format

> Author. (Year of publication). *Title of book.* Edition. City and state of publication: Name of publisher.

Specific example

> Blaser, M. J. (2013). *Missing microbes: How the overuse of antibiotics is fueling modern plagues.* New York, NY: Picador.

Work reprinted in an anthology (or book)

General format

> Author. (Year of publication). Title of work. In Editor (Ed.), *Title of book* (page numbers). City and state of publication: Name of publisher.

Specific example

Note: If there is no editor, omit "(Ed.)" as in the example below.

> Del Mar, C. (2014). Back to the future with antibiotic resistance. In A. Kuehner, *Writing to Read, Reading to Write* (pp. 284–287). New York, NY: McGraw-Hill.

Newspaper or magazine article in print

General format

> Author. (Year of Publication, Month Day). Article title. *Title of Publication.* Page number. Note: *p.* (for single page) or *pp.* (for multiple pages) precedes page numbers for a newspaper reference in APA style.

Specific example

> Tavernise, S. (2013, September 17). Antibiotic-resistant infections lead to 23,000 deaths a year, C.D.C. finds. *The New York Times*, p. A13.

Newspaper or magazine article published online

General format

> Author(s). (Year of publication, Month Day). Article title. *Title of Periodical.* Retrieved from URL

Specific example

> Tavernise, S. (2015, September 1). U.S. aims to curb antibiotic resistance. *The New York Times.* Retrieved from http://www.nytimes.com/2014/09/19/health/us-lays-out-strategy-to-combat-crisis-of-antibiotic-resistance.html

Journal article

General format

> Author(s). (Year). Article title. *Title of Journal, Volume* (Issue): Pages.

Note: If a Digital Object Identifier (DOI) number has been assigned to the article, include this number after the page numbers for the article. If no DOI has been assigned and you are accessing the periodical online, use the URL of the Web site from which you retrieved the periodical.

Specific example

> Nathan, C., & Cars, O. (2015, May). Antibiotic resistance—Problems, progress, and prospects. *New England Journal of Medicine, 371,* 1761-1763. doi:10.1056/NEJMp1408040

Magazine article from a database

General format

> Author. (Year). Article title. *Title of Publication, volume,* Page range. Retrieved from Database name or URL

Specific example

> Maron, D. F. (2015, September). Antibiotic overkill. *Scientific American, 310,* 32. Retrieved from https://www.ebscohost.com

Web page

General format

> Author. (Date of Publication). Title of document. [format description]. Retrieved from URL

Specific example

> Alliance for the Prudent Use of Antibiotics. (2014, October 12). What is antibiotic resistance and why is it a problem? Retrieved from http://www.tufts.edu/med/ apua/about_issue/antibiotic_res.shtml

APA: Title Page

Teaching Tip

Some word processing programs provide a template to create a document in APA style.

The first page of a paper in APA style is the title page. At the top of the page are the running head on the left, which is typically a shortened version of the title, and the page number in the upper right. Centered on the page are the title of the paper, the author's name, and the institution, all double-spaced.

Example: APA Title Page

Running Head: BACHMANN'S RESPONSIBILITY   1

Bachmann's Responsibility:

Determining Legal Blame for Gambling Losses

Miguel Tolentino

Ohlone College

APA: Abstract

The second page of a paper in APA style is the abstract page. At the top left is the running head; in the upper right is the page number. The title "Abstract" is centered on the page, and below it is a summary of the main points of the paper double-spaced

Example: APA Abstract Page

BACHMANN'S RESPONSIBILITY   2

Abstract

This paper argues that Angie Bachmann, as profiled in Charles

Duhigg's book *The Power of Habit*, bears full responsibility for her

gambling losses. Even though Bachmann fits the definition of a

pathological gambler, Harrah's casino's actions were justified and

legal. Moreover, Bachmann should have recognized her addiction

and could have taken steps to prevent herself from excessive

gambling and losses.

APA: Body of Paper

The body of a paper in APA style begins on the third page. The running head appears in the upper left and the page number in the upper right. The title of the paper is centered; it is not underlined, or quoted, or bolded. The first line is indented and the paper is double-spaced.

Example: APA Body of Paper

BACHMANN'S RESPONSIBILITY   3

Bachmann's Responsibility: Determining
Legal Blame for Gambling Losses

In *The Power of Habit*, author Charles Duhigg (2012) puts an

emphasis on habits—their inner workings and how they can be

changed. Duhigg describes how habits work through the cycle of

Teaching Tip

Use reading selection 1, "Brainology," in Chapter 1, "Introduction to College Reading and Writing," to demonstrate how to correctly format the body of a paper in APA style cue (trigger that activates a habit), routine (action of habit), and reward (aspect in which the brain determines if the habit is worth it). Particularly in Chapter 9 of the book, Duhigg details the descent of a woman called Angie Bachmann from being a bored housewife to losing all her money through compulsive gambling. Harrah's Entertainment, the casino where Bachmann played Blackjack and lost every bit of her money, sued Bachmann, "demanding that she pay her debts" (Duhigg, 2012, p. 269). Every time Bachmann steps in a casino, that activates a cue within her brain so that she automatically performs her routine of playing Blackjack thinking that she might win as a reward. Chapter 9 further discusses the extent of Bachmann's responsibility for her actions since she was fully aware of her actions and she had the responsibility to change which she did not. Although Bachmann argued that she was acting per Harrah's manipulations, she is still responsible because Harrah's actions were legal, she did not get treatment for addiction, she was fully aware of her actions, and she kept coming back to the casino even though she tried to change.

APA: References List

The reference list begins on a new page at the end of the paper. It includes all the sources cited in the paper in alphabetical order by the author's last name. All lines after the first line of an entry should be indented one-half inch. Title the page "References"; do not underline, bold, or use quotation marks on the title. Double-space the list.

Example: APA References List

BACHMANN'S RESPONSIBILITY   8

References

Duhigg, C. (2012). *The power of habit: Why we do what we do in life
     and business*. New York: Random House.

Glass, I. (Host). (2012, June 8). *Blackjack* [Audio podcast]. Retrieved
     from https://www.thisamericanlife.org

Jabr, F. (2013, October 15). How the brain gets addicted
     to gambling. *Scientific American*. Retrieved from www
     .scientificamerican.com/article/how-the-brain-gets-addicted
     -to-gambling/

National Center for Responsible Gaming. (2013, May 19). The
     evolving definition of pathological gambling in the DSM-5.
     Retrieved from http://blog.ncrg.org/blog/2013/05/
     evolving-definition-pathological-gambling-dsm-5

Index

A

Abbreviations, 395
Abstracts, APA formatting, 415
Accuracy
  of note-taking, 280
  of sources, 269, 270, 272
Active reading; *see also specific*
  topics below
  annotation in, 38–42
  for comprehension, 30–31
  connecting with text in, 33
  freewriting in, 32, 33, 43
  previewing in, 31–33, 43
  as process, 29–31
  purpose identification in, 33
  reflection in, 34
  summarization in, 31, 34, 38,
    39–42, 45
  topic, thesis, and main ideas
    identification in, 36–38, 40,
    42, 43
"Adapt to Inaccuracy in
  Social Media" (Manescu),
  325–327
Alvarez, Veronica, "Involuntary
  Resignation," 88–91
American Psychological
  Association; *see* APA-style
  documentation
Analogies, 110
Analysis
  annotating for, 179, 307–310
  checklist for, 190
  of essay structure, 119–123,
    178–179
  of evidence, 178–179
  of paragraph structure,
    178–179
  for peer review, 190–191

after reading, 189
  during reading, 311, 361
  of student writing, 178–181,
    189, 190–191, 305–317
  of words, 104, 130–131
  in writing, generally, 8
Annotation
  for analysis, 179, 307–310
  of arguments, 235–236,
    246–249
  for comprehension, 82, 179,
    307–310
  of essays, 142, 143
  for evaluation, 83, 307–310
  notes transferred from,
    277–278
  of paragraphs, 98, 111
  for peer review, 92–93, 190
  of prompts, 107, 124, 126, 254
  purpose of, 52
  during reading, 12, 22, 38–42,
    61, 73, 82–94, 155, 163,
    186, 199, 228, 238, 262,
    284, 311, 322, 325, 328,
    339, 343, 347, 355,
    361, 364
  reflection on, 18
  of response essays, 212–213
  reviewing, 56
  revising using, 142, 143
  strategies for, 38–39
  of student writing, 82–92,
    121–123, 179–185,
    307–310
  summarizing in, 38, 39–42, 179
Anthologies, documenting, 299,
  407, 413
Antibiotic resistance, 252–253,
  255, 261–272, 276, 283–289,
  393–396

"Antibiotic Resistance Questions
  and Answers" (CDC),
  262–266
APA-style documentation
  abstract formatting, 415
  body of paper formatting,
    415–416
  citations, 11, 410–412
  general guidelines, 411, 412
  Publication Manual of the
    American Psychological
    Association on, 298, 404
  References, 11, 17, 208, 363,
    412–414, 416–417
  title page formatting, 414
  typical use of, 403–404
Apostrophes, 393–394, 395–396
Appositives, 402
"Are We Using or Abusing Social
  Media?" (Capras), 384–386
Argument essays
  annotating, 235–236, 246–249
  body of, 236–237
  claims in, 222, 224–225,
    234–236
  concessions in, 242–243
  counterarguments in,
    242–244, 293
  denotation and connotation of
    words in, 231–232, 241
  evaluating, 230, 240, 244–245
  evidence in, 222, 226–227,
    234–237, 242–243
  identifying parts of argument,
    222–227
  opinions in, 221, 224, 242
  organization of, 226,
    234–237, 242, 290–291,
    292, 293, 296
  PIE structure for, 236–237

419

Notes

Notes

Notes

Notes

Notes

Notes